What happened where

Also by Chris Cook

The age of alignment: electoral politics in Britain, 1922–29
Sources in British political history, 1900–51 (6 vols, with Philip Jones et al.)
Britain in the Depression (with John Stevenson)
By-elections in British politics (ed. with John Ramsden)
European political facts, 1918–90 (with John Paxton)
British historical facts, 1830–1900 (with Brendan Keith)
The Longman atlas of modern British history, 1700–1970 (with John Stevenson)
The politics of reappraisal, 1918–39 (ed. with Gillian Peele)
Crisis and controversy: essays in honour of A. J. P. Taylor (ed. with Alan Sked)
European political facts, 1848–1918 (with John Paxton)
Post-war Britain: a political history (with Alan Sked)
The Longman handbook of modern British history, 1714–1995
(with John Stevenson)
The Labour Party (ed. with Ian Taylor)
Sources in European political history (3 vols, with Geoff Pugh et al.)
The Longman handbook of modern European history, 1763–1991
(with John Stevenson)
African political facts since 1945 (with David Killingray)
The Longman handbook of world history since 1914

What happened where

A guide to places and events
in twentieth-century history

Chris Cook and Diccon Bewes

UCL
PRESS

First published in 1997 by UCL Press

UCL Press Limited
1 Gunpowder Square
London EC4A 3DE
UK

The name of University College London (UCL) is a registered
trade mark used by UCL Press with the consent of the owner.

British Library Cataloguing-in-Publication Data
A CIP catalogue record for this book is available from the British Library.

Library of Congress Cataloging-in-Publication Data are available

ISBNs: 1-85728-532-8 HB
        1-85728-533-6 PB

Typeset in Plantin and Frutiger by The Studio, Exeter.
Printed and bound by Biddles Ltd, Guildford and King's Lynn, England.

Contents

Preface

This work has attempted a rather different approach for those involved with the study and teaching of contemporary history in the twentieth century. It has aimed to assemble, within a concise volume designed as a helpful desktop companion, a wide-ranging guide to the places and events that have featured in twentieth-century world history. Hence this volume provides both teacher and student with concise and informative entries on the many hundreds of places of major historical significance. The entries are worldwide in scope ranging from Auschwitz to Pearl Harbor, from Tiananmen Square to Entebbe. There are many strands of history encompassed in this volume, from diplomatic crises (Agadir) to famous battles (Anzio, Ypres), from world conferences (Tehran) to scandals (Chappaquiddick), from massacres (Soweto) to assassinations (Sarajevo, Dallas).

The book has also attempted to provide the background information on the places behind the headlines. Thus conflicts over territory or disputed boundary claims have been at the origin of many modern wars. This volume not only provides a guide to such European disputes as the Sudetenland or the Saar, recent area conflicts in, for example, former Yugoslavia, but also worldwide areas of tension in Africa, the Middle East, Asia and Latin America. Cross-references in bold refer the reader to related entries.

An area of potential confusion for the student lies with the accelerated processes of decolonization after 1945, where the rise of African and Asian nationalism has led to the proliferation of new nation states. Old colonial names are now only half-remembered, their relationship to the new nations not always easily identifiable. Meanwhile the collapse of Communist rule in Eastern Europe and the former Soviet Union has spawned a host of new nations not familiar to the student. Not all national aspirations have yet been met. The history of the twentieth century has its quota of nations enjoying only brief independence (Biafra, for example, or the Basque home-land of Euzkadi) or indeed still fighting for independence (the Tamils or Kurds) as well as puppet states created in time of war (Manchukuo or Vichy).

In line with the growing emphasis on economic and social history, this volume includes names from the world of environment (Bhopal, Chernobyl, Three Mile Island), economic conferences (Bretton Woods) as well as names from the history of trade unionism (e.g. Taff Vale, Orgreave and Wapping in Britain). There are also cultural entries (ranging from Bloomsbury to Woodstock) and milestones in the gay and women's rights movement (the Stonewall Inn riot in New York, Tattenham Corner at Epsom). Some important religious places are also included. In chronological terms, the book covers the period from 1900 to the mid-1990s. In a few cases, entries prior to 1900 are included where their significance spills over into the twentieth century, as with Fashoda or Omdurman. Much coverage is given to contemporary events in the hope that this information will be of help to students of politics and current affairs as well as historians.

Inevitably this book has had to be selective. It has not attempted surveys of individual countries. The main exception is where a country, hitherto on the sidelines, is important for one major event (e.g. the civil war in Angola, the birth of Bangladesh, the missile crisis in Cuba). There is a brief guide to the changing nations of the century in Appendix 1, while Appendix 2 gives a summary of the major conflicts of the period.

Acknowledgements

Very many people have helped in the preparation of this volume. I must particularly thank Andrew Rathmell for help on the Middle East, Harry Harmer for wide-ranging practical assistance and James Robinson for constant good advice. Ted Cater provided many suggestions for additional coverage of Latin America. I am also very indebted to John Stevenson for permission to use material in his copyright. For her secretarial help I am again indebted to Linda Hollingworth. At UCL Press my warmest thanks are due to Steven Gerrard. My very grateful thanks are due to my co-author, Diccon Bewes, for producing his part of the manuscript to an exacting deadline with unfailing good humour. Finally, I must thank Anne Mable for her long labours on the copy-editing of this manuscript.

Chris Cook

Abbreviations and acronyms

ANC	African National Congress
ANZAC	Australia and New Zealand Army Corps
BEF	British Expeditionary Force
BJP	Bharatiya Janata Party
BUF	British Union of Fascists
CENTO	Central Treaty Organization
CGT	*Confédération Générale du Travail* (General Confederation of Labour)
CIA	Central Intelligence Agency
CIS	Commonwealth of Independent States
CND	Campaign for Nuclear Disarmament
CNT–FAI	*Confederación Nacional del Trabajo–Federación Anarquista Iberia* (National Confederation of Labour–Iberian Anarchist Federation)
CSCE	Conference on Security and Co-operation in Europe
EEC	European Economic Community
ELAS	*Ethnikos Laikos Apeleutherotikos Stratos* (Hellenic People's Army of Liberation)
EOKA	*Ethniki Organósis Kypriakóu Agónos* (National Organization of Cypriot Struggle)
EU	European Union
EURATOM	European Atomic Energy Community
FLEC	Front for the Liberation of the Enclave of Cabinda
FLN	*Front de Libération Nationale* (National Liberation Front)
FLOSY	Front for the Liberation of Occupied South Yemen
FRELIMO	*Frente de Libertação de Moçambique* (Mozambique Liberation Front)
FRETILIN	*Frente Revolucionaria de Timor Leste* (Revolutionary Front of East Timor)
FROLINAT	*Front de Libération Nationale Tchadienne* (Chad National Liberation Front)
GATT	General Agreement on Tariffs and Trade
GCC	Gulf Co-operation Council
GLC	Greater London Council
HMAS	His (or Her) Majesty's Australian Ship
HMS	His (or Her) Majesty's Ship
IMF	International Monetary Fund
IPKF	Indian Peace-Keeping Force

IRA	Irish Republican Army
IWW	Industrial Workers of the World
KGB	*Komitet Gosudarstvennoi Bezopasnosti* (Committee of State Security)
LCC	London County Council
MNR (1)	*Movimiento Nacionalista Revolucionario* (National Revolutionary Movement)
MNR (2)	Mozambique National Resistance
MPLA	*Movimento Popular de Libertação de Angola* (Popular Movement for the Liberation of Angola)
NATO	North Atlantic Treaty Organization
NLF	National Liberation Front
NORAD	North American Air Defense Command
OAS (1)	*Organisation de l'Armée Secrète* (Secret Army Organization)
OAS (2)	Organization of American States
OAU	Organization of African Unity
PAC	Pan-Africanist Congress
PAIGC	*Partido Africano da Indepêndencia da Guine e Cabo Verde* (African Party for the Independence of Guinea and Cape Verde
PFLO	Popular Front for the Liberation of Oman
PLA	People's Liberation Army
PLO	Palestine Liberation Organization
POLISARIO	*Frente Popular de Saguia el Hamra y Rio de Oro* (Popular Front for the Liberation of Saguia el Hamra and Rio de Oro)
POUM	*Partido Obrero de Unificación Marxista* (Workers' Marxist Union Party)
POW	Prisoner of War
RAF	Royal Air Force
RUC	Royal Ulster Constabulary
SA	*Sturmabteilung* (Storm Troops)
SDLP	Social Democratic and Labour Party
SDP	Social Democratic Party
SNP	Scottish National Party
SOE	Special Operations Executive
SPD	*Sozialdemokratische Partie Deutschlands* (Social Democratic Party of Germany)
SS	*Schutzstaffel* (Nazi squads)
SWAPO	South West Africa People's Organization
TGWU	Transport and General Workers' Union
THORP	Thermal Oxide Reprocessing Plant
TUC	Trades Union Congress
UAR	United Arab Republic
UN	United Nations
UNITA	*União Nacional para a Independência Total de Angola* (National Union for the Total Independence of Angola)
US	United States
ZANLA	Zimbabwe African National Liberation Army
ZIPRA	Zimbabwe People's Revolutionary Army

The guide to places and events

Aachen (Germany)
First German city to be taken by the advancing Allied Armies in the west in the Second World War. The city was liberated on 21 October 1944.

Abadan (Iran)
Oil centre. In 1951 the Iranian government under Prime Minister Mossadeq nationalized the Anglo-Iranian Oil Company and expelled Western personnel from the Abadan refineries. Falling production, however, thwarted the government's hopes of generating higher revenues. Popular unrest enabled British and American intelligence to mount a coup in which Mossadeq was ousted and the oil company was taken over by an international consortium in August 1954.

Abbey Road (England)
The EMI studios at 3 Abbey Road in northwest London were used by The Beatles to record most of their records. Their first recording session (4–11 September 1962) led to the release of their first single "Love Me Do". In August 1969 The Beatles were together for the last time in a studio to record the "Abbey Road" album. The zebra crossing on the road outside the studio provided the cover picture for the album.

Aberfan (Wales)
Mining village in which over 140 people, the majority of them children in a school, were killed when a coal tip collapsed on 21 October 1966.

Abkhazia
Region near the Black Sea which began pressing for independence from **Georgia** (an independent state since the break-up of the Soviet Union). In January 1992 Georgian

tanks were sent to repress the demands. Bombing and guerrilla warfare around the Abkhazian capital of Sukhumi caused thousands of refugees to flee. Georgia accused Russian troop units deployed in the area of being pro-Abkhazian and called for a UN peacekeeping force. Meanwhile, there were clashes in nearby South Ossetia when Georgia abolished that area's autonomy.

Abucay (Philippines)

Settlement on Manila Bay. In the Second World War, the Abucay Line was the US General MacArthur's first line of defence on the **Bataan peninsula**. It was attacked by the Japanese in January 1942.

Abu Musa

Island in the Gulf whose sovereignty has long been disputed between Iran and the Arab Gulf sheikhdoms. In 1992 Iran forcibly took over the island, leading to a heightening of tensions between Tehran and the United Arab Emirates. The states in the GCC regarded the move as a sign of Iran's aggressive intent and threatened to take the matter to the International Court of Justice.

Abyssinia (now Ethiopia)

East African country which Italy unsuccessfully attempted to occupy between 1894 and 1896 to link its colonies of **Eritrea** and **Somalia**, the Italian forces being decisively defeated at **Adowa**. A further Italian attack took place on 3 October 1935 and, despite Abyssinian resistance, the country was held by Italy from 1936 to 1941. In 1941 British troops forced Italy from Abyssinia, Eritrea and Somalia in a four-month campaign.

Aceh (Indonesia)

Islamic sultanate in northern Sumatra. As the Dutch expanded their empire in the **Netherlands East Indies** (now Indonesia), Aceh resisted fiercely. The fall of the Aceh capital Kotaraja in 1873 failed to subdue resistance. Bitter fighting between 1896 and 1902 finally resulted in a Dutch conquest.

Acheh (Indonesia)

See **Aceh**.

Achin (Indonesia)

See **Aceh**.

Ådalen (Sweden)

Site of the Ådalen Incident, the killing of five union demonstrators at a strike at Ådalen in 1931. The incident occurred at the height of the depression in Sweden when wage cuts were becoming common. An enquiry punished those responsible. The incident has been called the "Peterloo" of Sweden (a reference to the break-up of a peaceful demonstration in St Peter's Fields, Manchester, in 1819 in which 11 people were killed).

Adolf Hitler Line (Italy)

German defensive line in the Second World War. It was the second line of defence after the **Gustav Line**. It was eventually forced by Canadian forces on 23 May 1944. It was also known as the Dora Line or Stenger Line.

Adowa (Eritrea)

Location, 80 miles south of Asmara, of the most calamitous defeat in the history of Italian colonial expansion in 1896. The humiliation of this defeat was a major factor in Italian foreign and colonial policy in the Fascist period under Mussolini. Italy had secured a protectorate over **Abyssinia** by a treaty of 1889. This treaty was overturned by Emperor Menelik II in 1895. Italy duly despatched 20,000 troops under General Baratieri from its Red Sea colony of **Eritrea** to northern Ethiopia in March 1895. After minor setbacks, Baratieri was ordered to secure a major victory. On 1 March 1896 the Italian Army was wiped out by Menelik's forces. The independence of Ethiopia was secured (until Mussolini's Fascist forces took revenge in 1935).

Aduwa (Eritrea)

See **Adowa**.

Afghanistan

State in south central Asia, an area of tension fuelled by conflicting imperialist ambitions between Britain and Russia in the late nineteenth and early twentieth centuries. Britain acknowledged the state's independence by the Treaty of **Rawalpindi** in 1919 following an Afghan attack on India. Afghanistan was proclaimed a parliamentary democracy in 1964, a one-party state in 1977, and a revolutionary Democratic Republic in 1978. In December 1979 Soviet troops occupied the country supporting the left-wing Armed Forces Revolutionary Council against Muslim Mujaheddin insurgents. Unable to subdue protracted guerrilla resistance during which over three million refugees fled the country, the Soviet Union withdrew in February 1989. Afghanistan was then riven by persistent war between competing factions. In September 1996 the capital, Kabul, was overrun by the Taliban, a fundamentalist Islamic student movement, and an Islamic state was proclaimed.

Agadir (Morocco)

Port in southwest Morocco which became the scene of a Franco-German crisis in 1911 which almost led to hostilities when Germany sent a gunboat to Agadir on the pretext of protecting German civilians. The move was aimed at thwarting French colonial expansion but it aroused British suspicions that Germany was seeking to establish a naval base on the African coast. The tension was defused when Germany acquiesced in French control of Morocco in return for territory in the French Congo.

Aisne (France)

River in northern France, scene of:
1) the First Battle of the Aisne from 14 to 28 September 1914 which ended in the stalemate of trench warfare;
2) Second Battle from 16 April to 9 May 1917 in which some French units mutinied following enormous losses against strong German defences;
3) Third Battle from 27 May to 6 June 1918 when a German drive to break the French armies swept to the River Marne in four days but was successfully halted.

Alam al-Halfa (Egypt)

Second World War battle for this ridge in the desert southwest of **el-Alamein**. In an attempt to outflank the Allied Forces at **el-Alamein** Rommel launched a sweeping attack from the south on 30 August 1942. The Germans failed to break through the Allied lines along Alam al-Halfa ridge, and on 2 September Rommel pulled his troops back to the Qattara Depression.

Alamein el- (Egypt)

The battle of el-Alamein in October–November 1942 was one of the turning points of the Second World War since it marked the end of German domination of North Africa. In June 1942 the British 8th Army was deployed defensively in Egypt with one flank on the Mediterranean coast at el-Alamein. General Montgomery, the army's newly-appointed commander, launched an offensive in October in which 1,200 British tanks advanced against some 500 German tanks belonging to General Rommel's Afrika Korps. The Germans withdrew to **Libya** and thereafter the battle for North Africa swung towards Britain.

(Åland) Aaland Islands (Finland)

Strategically placed islands in the northern Baltic which all powers in the area attempted to prevent being fortified. The islands (whose population is Swedish-speaking) have belonged to Finland, Russia (from 1809), Sweden (1918) and Germany (1918). In 1921 they were granted autonomy under Finnish sovereignty. A Finnish–Swedish agreement in 1938 that they should be fortified was opposed by the Soviet Union.

Albania

Country in southeastern Europe, part of the **Ottoman Empire** from the fifteenth century until it gained independence in 1912 following the Balkan Wars. Albania was a republic until becoming a monarchy under King Zog in 1928, and was then occupied by Italy from 1939. Under the post-war Communist regime of Enver Hoxha, Albania denounced Soviet revisionism in 1958 and followed Maoism until Mao's death in 1976, leaving the **Warsaw** Pact in 1968, and becoming the poorest and most impenetrable state in Europe. Albania abandoned Marxism-Leninism and became a parliamentary democracy in 1991. See also **Balkans**.

Aldermaston (England)

Town in Berkshire, site of the Atomic Weapons Research Centre. From 1958 to 1964 CND mounted an annual march protesting against nuclear weapons from Aldermaston to Trafalgar Square in London.

Alençon (France)

First town to be liberated by French forces in the Second World War. German forces were driven from the town on 12 August 1944 by French troops under General Leclerc.

Aleutian Islands (USA)

North Pacific island chain, part of the state of Alaska. During the Second World War Japanese forces captured the islands of Attu and Kiska. In May 1943 Attu was recaptured by US troops in the only ground combat of the war on North American soil.

Alexandretta (Turkey)

Province located on the northwestern border of Syria, it was Turkish until 1918 when it was annexed by Syria after the collapse of the **Ottoman Empire** in 1918. Turkish claims continued since a large majority of the population were of Turkish origin. In an effort to win Turkish support in the looming war, France, the mandatory power in Syria, ceded control of the province to Turkey in June 1939. It was subsequently fully incorporated into Turkey but remains a bone of contention between Syria and Turkey. Known as Hatay in Turkey.

Algeciras (Spain)

Location of a meeting in 1906 (known as the Algeciras Conference) between the Great Powers called at Germany's request to restrain French colonialism in Africa. Germany failed since only Austria-Hungary supported its line. Britain, Russia, Italy and the USA took the side of France and the resultant treaty regulated French and Spanish intervention in Moroccan affairs.

Algeria

Independent republic in North Africa, former French territory. After 1900 France began to extend her control over the vast desert interior which had been gradually conquered since the first French invasion of Algeria in 1830. Rising nationalism led to civil war in the 1950s. Algerian nationalists staged attacks on French military and civilian targets on 1 November 1954. In August 1956 the guerrilla groups formed the *Armée de Libération Nationale*. The French army conducted a brutal counter-insurgency campaign, which, while effective, alienated its supporters. On 13 May 1956 criticism of army methods led the commander-in-chief in Algeria, General Massu, to refuse to recognize the government of France. General de Gaulle, returned to power in France on 1 June 1958, set a course for Algerian self-determination. A mutiny by the French army in Algeria, led by Generals Challe and Salan, began on 22 April 1961, but was suppressed. Despite terrorism by French settlers of the OAS, peace talks began at **Evian-les-Bains** in May 1961, and a ceasefire was agreed on 18 March 1962. Algeria was declared independent on 3 July 1962.

Aliakmon Line (Greece)

Defensive position across northern **Greece** stretching from the Aegean Sea to the Yugoslav border. As British forces moved to occupy the line in April 1941, the Germans invaded through a gap in the western end between the British and Greek armies.

Allenby Bridge

Bridge spanning the Jordan River, the only link between the Israeli-occupied **West Bank** and **Jordan** since Israel's occupation began in 1967. It was closed to all but a trickle of Palestinian visitors and formed the symbol of the separation of the Palestinians in Jordan from their brethren in occupied Palestine. With the thawing of relations between Israel and Jordan in 1994 as part of the Middle East peace process, plans were made to modernize the small bridge to allow a greater flow of traffic.

Alma-Ata (Kazakhstan)

Now the capital city of the independent republic of Kazakhstan. In the last days of the Soviet Union, the Declaration of Alma-Ata was signed here, creating the new Commonwealth of Independent States (CIS) and effectively marking the demise of the old Soviet Union.

Alsace-Lorraine (France)

Province on the Franco-German border, control over which was long disputed by France and Germany. Under the German Empire for most of the Middle Ages, Alsace became French in 1648 and Lorraine in 1766. The population remained predominantly German in language but were loyal to France. The German Empire reconquered the region in the 1870–71 Franco-Prussian War, Germanizing its name to Elsass-Lothringen, but met with prolonged protest from the population, with the area under virtual martial law until 1911. The region was restored to France on Germany's defeat in the First World War.

Alvor (Portugal)
Location of the agreement of 15 January 1975 between Portugal and the main nationalist groups in Angola. The agreement provided for a ceasefire in Angola, established a transitional coalition government, to lead up to the agreed date of independence and also guaranteed that the **Cabinda** enclave would remain part of **Angola**. Continued fighting between the nationalist groups caused Portugal to suspend the agreement in August 1975.

Ambassador Hotel (United States)
Hotel in Los Angeles where Robert Kennedy was assassinated on 6 June 1968. He had just given a victory speech after winning the Democratic Californian primary election. The assassin, Sirhan Sirhan, was arrested at the scene.

Ambon (Indonesia)
Island in the Maluku (**Moluccas**) group. The Ambonese (one of Indonesia's few Christian communities) resisted incorporation into Indonesia in 1950. They proclaimed a Republic of the South Moluccas and perpetrated numerous terrorist acts, especially in The Netherlands. During the Second World War the Japanese captured Ambon. Many of the 800 Australian troops captured were murdered or starved to death.

Amiens (France)
Town which gave its name to the Charter of Amiens, one of the landmarks in the history of French trade unionism. In the 1906 Charter of Amiens the French CGT, the equivalent of the British TUC, advocated a general strike and factory occupations as the means by which the industrial working class could seize power.

Amritsar (India)
City in the northwest, the centre of the Sikh religion, where:
1) on 13 April 1919 Gurkha troops under Brigadier Dyer fired on an unarmed crowd of demonstrators, killing 379 and injuring 1,200, leaving a bitter legacy in Anglo-Indian relations;
2) in 1984, during a period of intense Sikh separatist agitation, armed militants occupied the Golden Temple, holding it until expelled by Indian troops on 6 June, with heavy casualties on both sides. See also **Golden Temple of Amritsar**.

Amsterdam (The Netherlands)

Capital famous for the February Strike of 25 February 1941, organized by Communists in protest against the arrest and transportation to concentration camps of 425 young Jewish men by German occupation forces on 23 February. In response the Nazis imposed a state of siege which remained in force throughout the Second World War. See also **Jordaan**.

Amur

River which marked the border between the old Soviet Union and China. As such, it was a traditional source of potential conflict between the two countries, as in 1969.

Anglo-Egyptian Sudan

The Nilotic Sudan was occupied by Egyptian forces in a series of campaigns which ended in 1821, and it was administered by Egypt until 1881. In 1898 British and Egyptian forces reoccupied the Sudan, defeating the forces of the Khalifa at **Omdurman**. An Anglo-Egyptian Condominium then administered the Sudan until independence in 1956.

Angola

Country in southwest Africa colonized by Portugal from the sixteenth century. A movement demanding independence became active in 1954. The liberation struggle began on 3 February 1961 when insurgents attempted to free political prisoners in Luanda. The risings were suppressed with great bloodshed, but a guerrilla campaign developed, and by 1974 Portugal was maintaining an army in Angola of 25,000 white and 38,000 locally enlisted troops. After the coup in Portugal on 25 April 1974, negotiations began at **Alvor**. On 15 January 1975 the Portuguese agreed to Angolan independence. As rival liberation groups fought for control of the country the independence of Angola was proclaimed on 11 November 1975, leaving the Marxist Popular Movement for the Liberation of Angola (MPLA) in power. This government was immediately challenged by the National Union for the Total Independence of Angola (UNITA) – with US and South African backing – and the country was thrown into bitter civil war. Despite a ceasefire in May 1991, fighting re-started following UNITA's dissatisfaction with the results of elections held in September 1992.

Anguilla

Caribbean island where resentment at rule by neighbouring St Kitts-Nevis came to a head in 1967. In May 1967 the Anguillans forcibly expelled the Kittitian police force. This was followed in February 1969 by a declaration of independence. The following month 300 British troops and a 50-strong police contingent invaded Anguilla to reimpose British rule. The island was then directly administered by Britain from 1971 to 1981 when it once again formally became a British Dependent Territory.

Anhwei (China)

Province north of the **Yangtze** delta, the scene of the Anhwei Incident of 1941. The Japanese had invaded the area in 1938, controlling the main communication routes, but Chinese Communist guerrillas continued to hold much of the countryside. However, in January 1941 Nationalist Chinese troops attacked the Communist New Fourth Army in Anhwei, destroying a 10,000-strong force and fuelling the growing hostility between the Nationalists and the Communists.

An Loc (Vietnam)

The siege of An Loc (April–July 1972) during the Vietnam War by North Vietnamese forces was eventually repulsed with the help of US air support.

Antwerp (Belgium)

Port on the Scheldt river estuary. Early in the First World War the fall of **Liège** and **Brussels** forced the main Belgian army of 150,000 men to retreat to Antwerp. On 27 September 1914 the Germans laid siege to the city, beginning heavy bombardment the following week. Belgian evacuation began on 6 October and by 9 October the Belgian army had retreated along the Flemish coast. Antwerp surrendered and remained under occupation for the rest of the war. Antwerp again fell to the Germans in May 1940 until being liberated by British forces on 4 September 1944.

Anual (Morocco)

Key battle in the Rif War. In 1921 the Moroccan tribal leader Abd el-Krim led a revolt against Spanish forces in North Africa, defeating them in several engagements, including a crushing victory at Anual on 21 July 1921 in which the Spanish armies lost over 12,000 men. In 1922 Abd el-Krim set up the Rif Republic. He defeated another Spanish army at Sidi Messaod in 1924. The war was a contributory factor in the assumption of power by Primo de Rivera in Spain. See also **Rif Mountains** and **Targuist**.

Anzac Cove (Turkey)

Bay on the west coast of the **Gallipoli** peninsula. Originally called Ari Birun, the cove was renamed shortly after the landings by 17,000 Australian and New Zealand troops in April 1915 as part of the ill-fated Gallipoli campaign. Anzac troops suffered heavy casualties before being withdrawn on 20 December 1915. The date of the first landings (25 April) is commemorated as Anzac Day in both Australia and New Zealand.

Anzio (Italy)

Seaborne landings were made by British and US troops at Anzio on 23 January 1944,

60 miles behind the German front line. The objective was to speed the Allied advance northwards. Although the German forces were taken by surprise, the Allies were contained in the immediate bridgehead and the strategy failed.

Aoteaoroa

The Maori name "land of the long white cloud" for New Zealand. Growing campaigns for Maori rights over land compensation, etc., have seen the use of the name become much more common since the 1970s.

Aouzou (Chad)

Strip of mineral-rich territory in northern **Chad**, subject to a tug of war between Libya and Chad for many years. Libya launched numerous incursions and sought to overthrow Chadian governments which were often backed by France.

Aqaba, Gulf of

Extension of the Red Sea bounded by Egypt, Israel, **Jordan** and Saudi Arabia. It has been of strategic significance as it represents Israel's only outlet to the Red Sea, and hence the Indian Ocean, from the port of Eilat, as well as being Jordan's only access to the sea. This strategic location has made it a focus of tension. In 1956 Israeli troops invaded the Egyptian-occupied Sinai and moved to assert control over the **Tiran Strait**, the narrow entry to the Gulf. In 1967 Egypt closed the Strait to Israeli shipping, a move which Israel regarded as a *casus belli* and contributed to its decision to launch the Six Day War. More recently, the Gulf has been a source of tension since Western navies operating there have enforced the post-Gulf War (1991) maritime blockade on Iraq by searching ships bound for Aqaba.

Aral Sea

Inland sea, formerly part of the Soviet Union, now bordered by the independent central Asian republics of Uzbekistan, Kazakhstan and Turkmenistan. Once the world's fourth largest inland sea, it has now become one of the great ecological disasters of modern times. Three-quarters of its volume has been lost through intensive irrigation projects, established in the Soviet era, aimed at boosting cotton production in Uzbekistan. The desertification of the sea (which has lost nearly half its surface area) has been accompanied by ill-health among people in the region as a result of the mass use of pesticides.

Archangel (Russia)

City on the shores of the White Sea, occupied by British and Allied troops during the Russian Civil War after 1917 as part of Western attempts to suppress the revolution.

The Allied troops were driven out in 1920. During the Second World War, Archangel was a key supply base for the convoys of British and Russian merchant ships which braved German submarines and bombers to bring vital supplies of food, weapons and fuel to the Soviet Union. The region was also home to some of the Soviet Union's most notorious gulags from the 1920s until the 1950s.

Ardeatine Caves (Italy)

Scene of worst Second World War atrocity in Italy, in which 335 civilians, including 75 Jews, were murdered outside Rome in reprisal for the killing of 33 German soldiers. Most of those initially rounded up for execution were petty thieves or vagrants, but Jews were added to bring the total for execution up to the required number (Hitler had ordered that up to ten civilians could be executed for each soldier killed by partisans, but this number was deliberately increased in the Ardeatine Caves massacre).

Ardennes (France)

Heavily forested hill region on the northeast through which German armies made a surprise attack on Allied forces on 16 December 1944. The Ardennes Campaign (or Battle of the Bulge) was intended to halt the Allied advance on Germany by capturing **Antwerp** and blocking supply lines. The initial drive broke through but the Allies held, notably at **Bastogne**, and the decisive counter-attack began on 3 January 1945.

Arica (Chile)

Province disputed by Chile and **Peru**. Occupied by Chile during the war in the Pacific (1879–83). Long diplomatic wrangle settled in 1929 when Arica awarded to Chile.

Armenia

Republic between the Black and Caspian Seas. Divided between the Russian and Ottoman Empires, Armenia suffered from genocidal pogroms against its people. An estimated 1.5 million Armenians were massacred between 1915 and 1918. Armenian independence, declared on 27 May 1918, was crushed by Soviet and Turkish forces and Armenia was incorporated into the Soviet Union in 1922. Tension over the future of **Nagorno Karabakh** led to conflict with **Azerbaijan** and the introduction of Soviet troops 1988–91. Armenian independence was re-declared on 23 September 1991 as a ceasefire with Azerbaijan came into effect. All-out war erupted in May 1992, with Armenia achieving a series of victories to give it control of ten per cent of Azerbaijan.

Armentières (France)

Town in Flanders near the Belgian border. A fierce German offensive during

September–October 1914 failed to capture the town from the British, who remained in control until the German Spring Offensive of April 1918. The town was completely destroyed during the war and rebuilt afterwards.

Arnhem (The Netherlands)

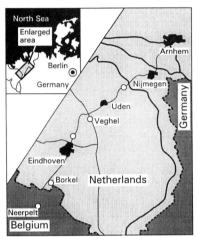

Site of a key bridge across the Rhine which US, British and Polish parachutists of 1st Allied Airborne Division attempted to capture in Operation Market Garden to open the way into Germany. 1st Airborne was to hold the bridge while the British 2nd Army advanced to link up. But the operation failed when the attackers met unexpectedly strong German opposition, suffering 7,000 casualties during heavy fighting from 17 to 26 September 1944.

Arras (France)

First World War battle around this town in northeast France. With the main Allied offensive of 1917 planned for the **Aisne** river region, a diversionary attack was launched at Arras a week earlier. On 9 April 1917 British and Canadian troops attacked German lines to the north and south of the town. Initially the Allies succeeded in advancing nearly four miles and storming **Vimy Ridge**, but German reinforcements blocked any further progress. The offensive continued until 3 May, distracting attention from other moves to the south, but at great cost: 84,000 Allied casualties and 75,000 German.

Arromanches-les-Bains (France)

Seaside town in **Normandy**, northwest of **Caen**. During the D-Day landings of 6 June 1944 it was at the centre of **Gold Beach** and captured by the British 30th Corps.

Arusha (Tanzania)

Town in the north of the country, headquarters of the East African Common Market, and the scene of President Nyerere's 1967 Arusha Declaration proposing development of the Tanzanian economy through a combination of state ownership and locally administered village planning.

Asante

See **Ashanti**.

Ashanti (Ghana)

Important state in Ghana (and adjacent areas) in the nineteenth century. The British under Sir Garnet Wolseley broke the power of Ashanti in 1873. In 1902 Ashanti was finally annexed by Britain, and the symbol of Ashanti power, the Golden Stool in Kumasi, was seized.

A Shau (Vietnam)

Fort three miles from the border with **Laos**. On 9 March 1966 3,000 North Vietnamese troops attacked the fort, which was defended by only 360 South Vietnamese soldiers and 17 US Green Berets. Deprived of air support because of bad weather, the fort fell after 39 hours of intense fighting. US helicopters managed to evacuate 200 defenders, and at least 500 North Vietnamese were killed.

Ashbourne (Ireland)

Town in County Meath, scene during the Easter Rising of an ambush by the Irish Volunteers of a 40-strong contingent of the Royal Irish Constabulary on 28 April 1916. Eight police were killed and 15 wounded, the remainder surrendering to their attackers when they ran out of ammunition.

Asiagio (Italy)

Series of First World War battles around this town in the foothills of the Dolomites. An Austrian offensive on 15 May 1916 surprised the Italians and Asiagio was captured on 31 May. Italian reinforcements arrived from the **Isonzo front**, forcing an Austrian retreat, and the lines settled. In a new offensive on 10 November 1917, Asiagio again fell to the Austrians but the Italian defensive lines held firm. The ensuing lull in the fighting was broken by an Allied offensive on 15 June 1918 which drove the Austrians back. The final Allied assault in October 1918 severed the Austrian lines, leading to a local armistice on 4 November.

Assen (The Netherlands)

Capital city of Drenthe province, twice the scene of terrorist incidents. On 23 May 1977 South Moluccan separatists (seeking independence for these islands in the

13

Indonesian archipelago) seized a train at Assen and also a school at Bovinsmilde. The siege of the school ended on 27 May. Two hostages and six terrorists were killed in an army attempt to rescue train hostages on 11 June. On 13 March 1978, the same group seized a government building killing one man and taking 71 hostages. Marines stormed the building on 14 March and captured the terrorists. Five hostages were wounded. See also **Moluccas**.

Asturias (Spain)

Mining region of northern Spain, the scene of the strike and rebellion of 4 October 1934. A socialist call for a general strike led to work stoppages in Madrid, Barcelona, the Asturias and other major cities. Two days later in the Asturias the strike developed into an insurrectionary movement as armed miners seized the major towns, including Oviedo. The army was ordered to suppress the rising and under General Ochoa marched on Oviedo and bombed Asturian strongholds. The Asturias revolt became notorious for the harshness with which it was put down. The area continued to be a strong left-wing centre and overwhelmingly supported the Republic at the outbreak of the Spanish Civil War.

Asunción (Paraguay)

Capital, where a treaty was signed in March 1991 by Argentina, Brazil, Paraguay and Uruguay setting out the conditions for the formation on the South American Southern Cone Common Market on 1 January 1995.

Aswan Dam (Egypt)

President Nasser regarded this dam on the Nile as essential to Egypt's economic development and when Britain and the USA withdrew their promise of aid on 20 July 1956, he nationalized the **Suez Canal** to raise revenues. This provoked the Anglo-French invasion and the Suez Crisis. Egypt eventually received Soviet funds for the project in 1970.

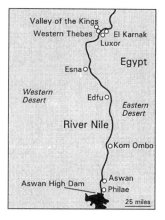

Aswan

Atjeh (Indonesia)

See **Aceh**.

Atlanta (United States)

1) As part of a campaign to deny black people the vote in Atlanta, Georgia, white mobs attacked black areas on 1 September 1906. In clashes which spread over several days, the attackers suffered heavier casualties than black people who armed to defend themselves. However, legislation to exclude black citizens from the electoral roll followed soon after.

2) Host city of the 1996 Centennial Olympic Games. A terrorist bomb on 27 July killed two and injured 111. There were suggestions that the relatively unsophisticated bomb was planted by right-wing anti-government militia.

Atlantic

The crucial naval Battle of the Atlantic, fought in the Atlantic, Caribbean and north European seas from 1940 to 1944 to protect the movement of supplies and troop reinforcements from the USA to Britain. Axis submarines, surface ships and aircraft succeeded in sinking 2,800 merchant ships, but the introduction in 1943 of more effective radar, increased air and naval support, and the capture of German U-boat bases in 1944, ensured ultimate Allied supremacy.

Atlantic Wall

Term for the German fortifications in the Second World War, built to protect against a possible Allied landing. Although not continuous, the fortifications stretched from Norway and Denmark to the French frontier with Spain.

Auckland Harbour (New Zealand)

The *Rainbow Warrior*, a ship belonging to the environmental organization Greenpeace, was blown up on 10 July 1985 in the harbour by French security agents, killing one person, following prolonged protests over French nuclear weapons testing in Polynesia. The agents were imprisoned for manslaughter and sabotage but were returned to France for medical treatment.

Audobon Ballroom (United States)

Dance hall in Harlem, New York City. On 21 February 1965 Malcolm X, Black Muslim leader and founder of the Organization of Afro-American Unity, addressed a rally at the Ballroom. He was shot at point blank range by Talmadge Hayer and died from his injuries.

Auschwitz (Poland)

Nazi concentration camp near Krakow in southern Poland. Established in March 1941 as a Jewish transit camp, it soon became a forced labour camp for nearby factories. Its central role in the "Final Solution" began in September 1941. Mass extermination of Jews and other minorities followed. Thousands of other inmates were shot at the notorious Death Wall. It is estimated that over two million were murdered in the camp before it closed in 1944. Now a museum, it is preserved as a monument to the genocide of the Jewish people by the Nazis.

Austria

Independent republic in central Europe formed following the break-up of the Austro-Hungarian Empire in 1918. After a period of destabilization from 1934, Austria was illegally annexed by Nazi Germany in the *Anschluss* of 12 March 1938. Following its liberation in 1945, Austria was divided into Soviet and Western zones but achieved full sovereignty by treaty in 1955 on condition that she renounced offensive weapons, paid reparations to the Soviet Union, did not ally herself with East or West Germany and did not attempt to restore the former Habsburg monarchy.

Austria-Hungary

Formed in 1867, it was also known as the Austro-Hungarian Empire or Dual Monarchy and covered one-eighth of Europe's population across Central and Eastern Europe. Intensive rivalry with neighbouring **Serbia** boiled over following the assassination of Archduke Franz Ferdinand, the heir to the Austrian throne, in **Sarajevo** on 28 June 1914. Throughout the First World War, Austria-Hungary was always the weaker partner to Germany and finally capitulated on 3 November 1918. The Habsburg monarchy was officially dissolved on 11 November 1918 and an Austrian republic proclaimed the next day. Under two separate treaties with the Allies (**Saint-Germain** on 10 September 1919 and **Trianon** on 4 June 1920), Austria and Hungary relinquished much of their land and population. The new states of Poland, **Czechoslovakia** and **Yugoslavia** all gained territory, as did Romania and Italy.

Ayacucho (Peru)

The Maoist-influenced guerrilla group *Sendero Luminoso* (Shining Path) began its insurgency in this Andean province. By 1989 *Sendero Luminoso* threatened Lima by isolating the capital from its hinterland.

Ayers Rock (Australia)

Huge monolith in the centre of Australia near Alice Springs. Originally named after South Australian Premier Sir Henry Ayers, it has now reverted to its Aboriginal title of Uluru. A prime tourist destination, it still holds immense magical and spiritual significance for the Aborigines. In October 1982 Lindy Chamberlain was jailed for the murder of her daughter at the Ayers Rock campsite. She persisted with her claim that a dingo had snatched the baby, and her conviction was overturned in February 1986.

Ayodhya (India)

Site in northern India of a Muslim mosque which Hindus believe covers the birthplace of their god Rama. Hindu nationalists, encouraged by the BJP, attempted to pull down the mosque to build a temple. The Indian government's refusal to countenance this provoked the BJP's withdrawal from the coalition and the fall of the administration in November 1990.

Azad Kashmir

See **Kashmir**.

Azania

Land of the Zanj, term used for the east coast of Africa from the first century. Azania is the name given to South Africa by black consciousness supporters in the country.

Azerbaijan

Predominantly Muslim area in southwest Russia, an independent state in 1918, absorbed into the Soviet Union in 1920. Azerbaijan includes the Christian enclave of **Nagorno Karabakh**, the scene of ethnic clashes in 1988–9 when neighbouring **Armenia** demanded the enclave's return. Azerbaijan became an independent republic in August 1991.

Baalbek
See **Bekaa Valley**.

Babi Yar (Ukraine)
Formerly part of the Soviet Union. A ravine outside Kiev where over 30,000 Jews, including the community's intellectual leaders, were massacred by the SS in September 1941, in one of the largest mass slaughters of the Second World War. Yevgeny Yevtushenko wrote a poem entitled "Babi Yar" after the war as a veiled criticism of Soviet anti-Semitism.

Badajoz (Spain)
Fortress town near Portuguese border. Strongly Republican in the Spanish Civil War (1936–9) it fell to the Nationalists in August 1936.

Baden-Baden (Germany)
Place where General de Gaulle and German Chancellor Konrad Adenauer signed the agreement establishing the Franco-German Axis in 1963. De Gaulle retreated to Baden-Baden in 1968 when the student revolt seemed set to overthrow his government. In December 1995, Chancellor Helmut Kohl and President Jacques Chirac met in the same hotel to reaffirm their commitment to a single currency in the EU.

Bad Godesberg (Germany)
Town outside Bonn where:
1) British Prime Minister Neville Chamberlain met German Chancellor Adolf Hitler on 22–23 September 1938 to discuss the **Sudetenland** dispute. Hitler rejected an Anglo-French proposal for Czech concessions but discussions paved the way for a further meeting at **Munich**;
2) scene of the congress of the West German SPD in 1959 at which the party dropped its nominal but nevertheless electorally unpopular Marxist position in favour of a social market economy.

Bagh (Pakistan)
Town near the Afghan border. In May 1919 the ruler of Afghanistan, Amir Amanullah, declared a holy war (*jihad*) against Britain. His forces crossed the Afghan border and occupied Bagh. In response, Jalalabad and Kabul were bombed by the RAF and a British force drove the Afghans out of Bagh, forced the **Khyber Pass** and pushed into **Afghanistan**. An armistice was signed on 31 May 1919 and the Treaty of **Rawalpindi** was signed on 8 August, ending the Third Afghan War.

Baghche (Turkey)

Town between Aleppo and Adana, and site of a Turkish internment camp. Following the British defeat at **Kut-al-Amara** on 29 April 1916 8,000 Allied troops (2,000 of them British) were taken prisoner. Conditions in the camp were so harsh and insanitary that many of the prisoners died in captivity, including over half of the British men.

Baghdad (Iraq)

Mutual defence pact (the Baghdad Pact) in February 1955 between Britain, Iran, **Iraq**, Pakistan and Turkey designed to cement the chain of containment states on the Soviet Union's borders and prevent the spread of Soviet and anti-imperialist influence in the Middle East. The Soviet Union saw it as an aggressive move and worked to undermine it by bringing Syria and Egypt into its sphere of influence. It was renamed the Central Treaty Organization (CENTO) in 1959 following the Iraq revolution and that country's subsequent withdrawal from the Pact.

Baikonur (Kazakhstan)

Town formerly in the Soviet Union. Location of the Soviet space centre, it was the launch site of manned space missions. The collapse of the Soviet Union led to negotiations between Russia and newly-independent Kazakhstan. A 20-year lease was agreed in March 1994.

Baku (Azerbaijan)

Capital on the western shore of the Caspian Sea. In early 1918 Turkish forces invaded Caucasia with support from Germany and local Bolshevik units. In order to retain control of the Caspian Sea and the Caucasian oil wells, Britain dispatched a battalion from Baghdad to reinforce local anti-Bolshevik Russian forces. By July 1918 the British, under heavy fire from the Turks and weakened by desertions of local Armenian troops, had to retreat from Baku. The city was captured by Turkish troops on 18 September 1918. Prior to 1917, Baku had been a cradle of revolutionary activity (as in the general strike of December 1904 which acted as a catalyst for the 1905 revolution).

Balaton, Lake (Hungary)

In the west near the Austrian border. On 6 March 1945 the final German offensive on the **Eastern Front**, codenamed *Frühlingserwachen*, or Spring Awakening, was launched around Lake Balaton. The offensive was quickly abandoned in the face of terrible weather, fuel shortages and strong Russian defence. Over 40,000 Germans were captured.

Balbriggan (Ireland)

Small town in northern County Dublin whose name is synonymous with the excesses of the Black and Tans in Ireland. On 20 September 1920, in reprisal for the murder of one of their men, a number of police of the Royal Irish Constabulary (RIC) terrorized and ransacked the town. They broke into and looted four public houses and went on to burn or damage 49 other houses and a hosiery factory.

Balkans

Region of southeast Europe consisting of **Albania**, **Bosnia-Hercegovina**, Bulgaria, **Croatia**, **Greece**, **Macedonia**, Romania, Slovenia, **Yugoslavia** and European Turkey. Ottoman dominance of the region was broken in the two Balkan Wars which preceded the First World War. In the First Balkan War (1912–13) Bulgaria, Greece, **Montenegro** and **Serbia** defeated Turkey, resulting in Albanian independence and Turkey retaining only a small part of Eastern Thrace. The Second Balkan War (June–July 1913) erupted as the victors fought over their spoils. Bulgaria was defeated by Serbia, Greece and Romania. Continued ethnic tension and conflict precipitated the crisis in Bosnia which led to the First World War. Political differences within Yugoslavia erupted into civil war in the early 1990s and the Yugoslav Federation collapsed.

Baltic States

Estonia, **Latvia** and **Lithuania**, which each border the Baltic Sea. They were independent states from 1919 to 1940, when the Soviet Union occupied them as part of the 1939 Nazi–Soviet Pact. With the breakdown of the Soviet Union, and the failure of the 19 August 1991 Moscow coup, the three states declared independence and were quickly recognised by the European Community and the USA.

Banaba (Kiribati)

The inhabitants of Banaba (formerly known as Ocean Island) achieved international prominence in February 1975 when they took legal action against the British Government as a result of phosphate mining on the island by the London Pacific Phosphate Company since 1900. An earlier protest in 1965 had caused the company to increase its derisory payments to the Banabans. The eventual British High Court judgment in June 1976 went against the Banaban claim on royalties but ruled that they were owed compensation.

Banat

Territory disputed between **Hungary** and former **Yugoslavia**. The territory was lost by Hungary in the peace settlement after the First World War. As part of a deal with Nazi Germany, Hungary regained Banat in 1941. In return Admiral Horthy, the regent of Hungary, sent his troops to aid the German offensive against Russia (Operation Barbarossa).

Bandung (Indonesia)

Scene of a conference from 17 to 24 April 1955 at which 29 Afro-Asian states reached agreement on the development of political non-alignment in the Cold War, on cultural and economic co-operation, and on opposition to European colonialism. Its guiding principles were the Five Principles of Peaceful Co-existence which had emerged from the settlement of the Sino-Indian conflict over **Tibet** (29 April 1954). These were:

1) mutual respect for territorial integrity and sovereignty;
2) non-aggression;
3) non-interference in each other's internal affairs;
4) equality and mutual benefit;
5) peaceful co-existence and economic co-operation.

Despite general agreement, not all countries accepted the neutralist position in world affairs advocated by China. Division and dissent marked the Second Bandung Conference in 1965.

Bangladesh

Formerly **East Pakistan**, part of Pakistan until the war of independence in 1971. The independence movement stemmed from the elections of December 1970 which resulted in a landslide victory in East Pakistan for the Awami League. On 26 March 1971 Sheikh Mujibur Rahman, the head of the League, proclaimed East Pakistan an independent republic under the name of Bangladesh. He was arrested, and West Pakistani troops and locally raised irregulars, *razakars*, put down large-scale resistance by 10 May 1971. Awami League fighters, the Mukti Bahini, began a guerrilla campaign, and clashes grew between India and Pakistan as millions of refugees fled into India. On 3 December 1971 the Pakistani air force launched surprise attacks on Indian airfields. On 4 December some 160,000 Indian troops invaded East Pakistan. Pakistani forces in East Pakistan surrendered on 16 December 1971.

Banqiao Dam (China)

On the Huai River in Henan Province. In 1975, it collapsed along with Shimantan Dam causing enormous loss of life and destruction. The Communist authorities kept news of the calamity secret. Only in the mid-1990s did it become clear that as many as 230,000 had died.

Banska Bystrica (Slovakia)

Scene in the Second World War of the Slovak national uprising against Nazi rule. Partisan activity in the Nazi-created puppet state of Slovakia increased during the latter stages of the war. By 1944 it had become widespread and the Czech government-in-exile in London instructed Lieutenant-Colonel Jan Golian to prepare a national coup (to coincide with the arrival of Soviet Red Army troops). Precipitated by German revenge for the murder of General Otto in **Martin**, the uprising was launched on

29 August 1944. A Slovak National Council was established. However, Soviet assistance was not forthcoming and Russia refused to allow the West to use Soviet air bases to aid the rebellion. On 28 October the Nazis recaptured Banska Bystrica, taking a terrible revenge in reprisals which lasted many months. An estimated 30,000 Slovaks lost their lives in the rising and the later reprisals.

Barcelona (Spain)

Capital of Catalonia, it played a central part in the radical and revolutionary movement in modern Spain. It featured most notably in the Spanish May Days, the period of bitter street fighting in Barcelona on 3–7 May 1937 between anarchists, Communists and Catalan separatists. The occasion for the fighting was the attempt by the Republican government of Prime Minister Largo Caballero, backed by Communists, and Catalan separatists, to assert control over the revolutionary forces of the anarcho-syndicalist CNT-FAI and the rival revolutionary Marxist POUM. The fighting signalled the end of the broad left popular front coalition and the subordination of the revolutionary wing of the left to the aim of winning the war under Communist control. The Communists used the events to demand the final suppression of the POUM; this Caballero refused, leading to the break-up of his coalition government and its fall from power on 17 May. Thereafter the war effort on the Republican side was dominated by the Communists.

Bardia (Libya)

Port near the border with Egypt, strategically placed near the **Halfaya Pass**. Bardia frequently changed hands during the fluctuating North African Campaign of the Second World War. The opening British offensive of early 1941 captured the town on 3 January, taking over 40,000 Italian troops prisoner. Rommel recaptured it on 12 April 1941 in his first advance across Libya, only to lose it again to the Allies during Operation Crusade in January 1942. Following the fall of **Tobruk** in June, Rommel advanced to **el-Alamein** in Egypt. The Allied victory there pushed the German Afrika Korps back and Bardia was liberated once more by the British on 11 November 1942.

Barents Sea

Second World War naval engagement near the north coast of Norway. Since August 1941 the Arctic convoys to Russia had been under constant threat from German-occupied Norway. On 30 December 1942 a British convoy en route to **Murmansk** came under attack from a German squadron of six destroyers led by the battleship *Lützow* and cruiser *Hipper*. The Germans had the tactical advantages of surprise and greater firepower, but poor leadership and organization left their attack in chaos. Two British ships were sunk but the rest survived as the Germans withdrew after losing a destroyer. Commander-in-chief of the German navy, Admiral Raeder, resigned over the débâcle and was replaced by Admiral Dönitz.

Bar-Lev Line
System of fortifications constructed by Israel along the East Bank of the **Suez Canal** after the **Sinai** was occupied in 1967. Named after General Bar Lev who constructed a sand wall along the canal and placed troops in fortified strongpoints along the wall, the Line was designed to act as a tripwire to alert mobile reinforcements in case of Egyptian attack, but the October 1973 Egyptian assault across the canal caught the Israelis by surprise and the Line was easily breached. In a daring counterstroke on 15 October 1973, Israeli forces crossed to the West Bank of the Suez Canal and encircled the Egyptian Third Army. A ceasefire became effective on 24 October 1973.

Barmen (Germany)
Location in 1934 of the Synod of Barmen in which an anti-Nazi church coalition was formed. Its most famous leaders were Pastor Martin Niemöller and Karl Barth.

Basildon (England)
Parliamentary constituency in Essex with a predominance of social group C2s which usually makes the earliest declaration in general elections. The victory of the Conservative candidate in the 1992 General Election made it clear that Labour, despite its growing hopes of winning back former supporters, had little chance of overall electoral success.

Basra (Iraq)
Scene of bitter conflict in the Iran–Iraq War which began in September 1980. After initial Iraqi successes, including the capture of **Khorramshahr**, Iran counter-attacked. On 9 January 1987 Iran launched a major offensive – codenamed Karbala-5 – with the aim of capturing Basra. The Iranians advanced some distance towards their objective, while suffering heavy casualties.

Bastogne (Belgium)
Town in the **Ardennes** near the border with Luxembourg which was a key target of the German offensive of December 1944 (known as the Battle of the Bulge). The German attack on 16 December achieved complete tactical surprise and the Allies fell back across the Ardennes Forest. By 20 December Bastogne was encircled, and the US 101 Airborne Division and 10th Armoured Division were besieged. The defences held and the town was relieved on 26 December during the Allied counter-offensive.

Bataan Peninsula (Philippines)
Second World War battle for this peninsula on the west coast of **Luzon**. Japanese troops landed on Luzon in early December 1941, advancing quickly across the island.

By January 1942 **Manila** had fallen and the US and Filipino forces under General MacArthur retreated to the Bataan Peninsula. Japanese attempts to penetrate the American defences failed and the front line stabilized. MacArthur was evacuated to Australia on 12 March 1942. A renewed Japanese offensive on 3 April achieved the vital breakthrough, and US troops in Bataan surrendered on 9 April. American resistance continued on nearby **Corregidor Island** until 6 May. Bataan was recaptured by US troops on 21 February 1945.

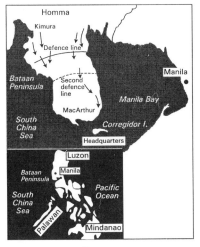

Bataan

Batak (Bulgaria)
Village in what was a province of the Ottoman Empire where over 3,000 Christians were massacred in 1876 by Turkish forces during the suppression of an uprising. The church and yard where the killings took place were preserved as a memorial to the victims.

Baton Rouge (United States)
State capital of Louisiana, the location in September 1935 of the assassination of the popular politician Huey Long by a deranged doctor. His untimely death removed the possibility of a Long candidate in the 1936 presidential elections − a candidature which could have posed a very major threat to President Roosevelt's prospects of re-election. Hundreds of thousands of mourners attended his funeral.

Bavaria (Germany)
Region in the southeast. On the night of 7–8 November 1918 King Louis III was deposed and a Bavarian republic created, led by pacifist socialist Kurt Eisner. Eisner was assassinated in **Munich** in February 1919 during increasingly violent revolutionary activity. The government fled to Bamberg and Munich was gripped by riots

and street fighting. National troops eventually restored control in May 1919, and a parliamentary republic was set up in August. Conflict with the national government continued, culminating in the Munich *putsch* of 1923. In 1945 Bavaria became part of the US occupation zone and was integrated into the new Federal Republic in 1949.

Bay of Pigs (Cuba)

Scene of an abortive invasion on 17–20 April 1961 by 1,500 anti-Castro exiles, backed by the US CIA. The invasion, planned under President Eisenhower and mounted under President Kennedy, was intended to rally internal opponents of the Castro government, but all the participants were killed or captured.

Beagle Channel

150-mile long strait at the southern tip of South America, along the coast of Tierra del Fuego. The western half of the Channel is fully part of Chile, but the eastern portion forms part of the Argentina–Chile border. These two countries have long disputed the sovereignty of Lennox, Neuva and Picton islands in the Channel. The possibility of mineral wealth beneath the islands led to renewed confrontation in the 1970s. A planned invasion by Argentina was called off after Vatican mediation in 1978–9. In a negotiated settlement, the three islands were awarded to Chile. A referendum in Argentina approved the proposals and a treaty came into force on 2 May 1985.

Beda Fomm (Libya)

This battle between the British XIII Corps under General Sir Richard O'Connor and the Italian 10th Army under Marshal Rodolpho Graziani in February 1941 resulted in the destruction of the Italian force and the capture of **Benghazi** at relatively little cost. The British forces, along with the Australian 6th Infantry, surrounded the Italians at Beda Fomm and captured 20,000 men at the cost of nine killed and 15 wounded. This battle was the culmination of a campaign by the British that annihilated the Italian Tenth Army and led to the appointment of Rommel to lead an Axis counter-offensive which soon retook all of Cyrenaica.

Beersheba

Scene of First World War battle in southern Palestine. On 31 October 1917 Allied troops attacked the 30-mile long Turkish defensive line between **Gaza** and Beersheba. A frontal assault on Beersheba was augmented by a flanking attack from Anzac cavalry units. The town was captured and the Allies advanced towards **Jerusalem**.

Beijing (China)

See **Peking**.

Beira Corridor

Strategic link between Mutare, **Zimbabwe** and the port of Beira in **Mozambique**. With a railway, a road, an oil pipeline and electricity cables, it provides vital facilities to land-locked **Zimbabwe**. During both the Zimbabwe and Mozambique civil wars, it was attacked and occupied by various factions. The last Zimbabwean troops left in April 1993.

Beirut (Lebanon)

This capital was one of the wealthiest cities in the Middle East when the French Mandate was imposed in 1920, as well as the centre of Arab nationalist thought and activity. During the French occupation, which ended in 1946, it became the capital of the newly-established Greater Lebanon and emerged as a centre for banking and economic activity. After Lebanon's independence it became a financial and tourist centre but was wracked by Christian–Muslim tensions in the civil war of 1958. During the 1975–6 civil war large tracts of the city centre were destroyed and the city divided into Christian–Muslim ghettos separated by the Green Line. There was further destruction in 1982 and 1984, by which time Christian East Beirut had become a self-governing enclave. During this period, suicide truck bomb attacks on the US marine headquarters and French paratroop barracks in Beirut killed 241 Americans and 58 French on 23 October 1983. In March 1989 the Christian General Michel Aoun launched an offensive against the Syrians and their allies, leading to intense shelling. After he rejected the **Taif** Peace Accord, fighting continued between Aoun's forces and the fellow Christian Lebanese forces. In October 1990 Syrian forces ousted Aoun and reunited Beirut. Under the Presidency of Rafiq Hariri moves are afoot to rebuild the city and revitalize its role as a commercial centre but much of the city remains in ruins.

Bekaa Valley

This Lebanese valley lies between the Lebanon and anti-Lebanon mountains and runs along the Syrian–Lebanese border. It has long been the breadbasket of Lebanon but has been separated from the central government in **Beirut** by terrain and the nature of its population which is heavily Shia Muslim. Since the late 1970s the valley has been occupied by Syrian troops and in 1982 heavy fighting took place as Israeli forces tried to reach the strategic **Damascus–Beirut** highway which crosses the valley. Since 1982 the valley's main town, Baalbek, has been a base for *Hizbollah* Muslim fundamentalist guerrillas fighting against Israel and the southern end of the valley has seen frequent clashes between *Hizbollah* and Israeli-backed troops.

Belarus

East European republic formerly known as Byelorussia or Byelarus. Part of the Russian Empire, it briefly became independent in 1918 before being split between Poland and the Soviet Union in 1919. Reunified in 1939 Belarus was devastated by the German occupation of 1941–4, with 25 per cent of the population being killed. As the Soviet Union collapsed, Belarussian independence was proclaimed on 25 August 1991 and recognized by the international community in January 1992.

Belene (Bulgaria)

Located between Nikopol and Svishtov, the site of the most notorious labour camp during the Communist era in Bulgaria. Established in 1947, it housed both political prisoners and violent criminals. Its brutality and excesses were on a par with Nazi concentration camps. Belene was closed swiftly after the fall of Communism in November 1989.

Belfast (Northern Ireland)

1) The Hillsborough Agreement, also known as the Anglo-Irish Agreement, was signed in Belfast on 15 November 1985 by the British and Irish Prime Ministers, Margaret Thatcher and Dr Garret Fitzgerald. It established an inter-governmental conference and a framework for political, security and legal consultation. Ulster Unionist parties rejected the proposals.

2) Secretariat of the Anglo-Irish Conference, established under the Anglo-Irish Agreement, is located at Maryfield, in Belfast. The secretariat operates joint consultation between Irish and British officials on Northern Ireland affairs.

Belgian Congo

Now the independent state of **Zaïre**, and known as Congo on independence in June 1960. The Berlin Conference of 1884–5 recognized King Leopold II as the sovereign head of the Congo Free State. The annexation of the state to Belgium was provided for by a treaty of 28 November 1907. The country became independent on 30 June 1960. The departure of many Belgian professionals on the day of independence left a vacuum which speedily resulted in complete chaos. Neither Joseph Kasavubu, the leader of the Abako Party, who on 24 June 1960 had been elected Head of State, nor Patrice Lumumba, leader of the Congo National Movement, who was the Prime Minister of an all-Party Coalition Government, could establish his authority. See under Zaïre for independence.

Belize

Country in Central America known as British Honduras until 1973. Independence was achieved on 21 September 1981, although it was overshadowed by the territorial claims of neighbouring Guatemala. In September 1991 Guatemala relinquished all claims to Belize, and recognized Belize's independence in November 1992. Guatemala revoked the 1991 accord in July 1993, and its territorial claim is now subject to arbitration by the International Court of Justice.

Belleau Wood (France)

First World War battle in this forest northwest of Vaux in eastern France. The German spring offensive had been successfully halted by the Americans at **Chateau-Thierry**. A counter-attack was launched on 6 June 1918, confronting the Germans in this heavily-wooded area. Stiff resistance by the four German divisions reduced the fighting to a tree-by-tree advance. Only one mile square, the wood took three weeks to be cleared by the US Marine Brigade, which sustained over 9,700 casualties. The battle ended on 1 July when the wood and nearby Vaux were captured.

Belsen (Germany)

Nazi concentration camp northwest of Celle in Prussian Hanover. Established as a POW camp and a Jewish transit centre in July 1943, it was only intended for 10,000 inmates but held 41,000 on liberation. It had no gas chambers but squalid conditions led to over 37,000 deaths, including that of Anne Frank in March 1945, from starvation and disease. Liberated by the British on 15 April 1945, it was the first concentration camp to be filmed for the outside world. The camp commandant, Josef Kramer (known as the Beast of Belsen), was tried at Nuremberg and hanged for war crimes. Also known as Bergen-Belsen.

Belzec (Poland)

Nazi concentration camp opened in March 1942, and located on the Lublin–L'vov railway. It is estimated that 600,000 perished here in the camp's six gas chambers.

Benghazi (Libya)

Port on the Gulf of Sirte. The city changed hands many times during the frequent advances and retreats of the Desert Campaign of the Second World War. On 6 February 1941 Benghazi fell to the advancing British forces, only to be retaken in Rommel's first offensive on 4 April. It was recaptured by the British on 25 December, before falling again to the Germans on 29 January 1942 and finally being liberated by the British 8th Army on 19 November 1942.

Berchtesgaden (Germany)

Town in southern Bavaria where Hitler built a retreat, the "Eagle's Nest", which Nazis planned to use as a final "national redoubt" in 1945. Hitler used the building to impress foreign visitors, including British Prime Minister Neville Chamberlain, during the **Munich** Crisis on 15 September 1938. The site was destroyed by the Allies after the war to prevent it becoming a neo-Nazi shrine.

Bergen-Belsen

See **Belsen**.

Berkeley University (United States)

On the west coast near San Francisco. In the 1960s it was the focus of student dis-content and anti-government protests, fuelled by opposition to the Vietnam War.

Berlaymont (Belgium)

Building in Brussels housing the offices of the European Commission for the admini-stration of the **European Union**. In the early 1990s the building was temporarily evacuated after lethal asbestos was found to have been used in its construction.

Berlin (Germany)

Scene of:

1) the attempted Spartacist rising of January 1919 led by Rosa Luxemburg and Karl Liebknecht;

2) 1936 Olympics, the propaganda impact of which for the Nazi regime was under-mined by the success of black American athlete Jesse Owens in winning four gold medals;

3) the Berlin Airlift from June 1948 to May 1949 when the Soviet Union, alleging the Western powers had broken post-war agreements on German status, attempted to force Britain, France and the US from the Western sector of the city by blocking road and river access. The Western powers responded with a round-the-clock airlift supplying food, fuel and mail. The crisis confirmed the division of Germany and the city into Communist and capitalist zones;

4) the construction of the Berlin Wall on 13 August 1961 intensified this division. Disparities in living standards had encouraged a stream of refugees from East to West Berlin. The German Democratic Republic attempted to stem this by blocking 68 of the 80 border crossings, erecting a concrete and wire barrier that became a symbol of the Cold War, and where many East Berliners attempting to flee were killed, until its dismantling in November 1989.

Bermuda Triangle

Area of sea bounded by Bermuda, Florida and Puerto Rico. Numerous unexplained disappearances of a variety of ships and aircraft have given rise to some fairly fanciful theories. Although no really satisfactory explanation is available, almost certainly these disappearances are to be explained by natural phenomena.

Bessarabia

Area on the former Soviet–Romanian border bounded on the north and east by the River Dniester and to the south and west by the Danube and Prut rivers. Of mixed Romanian and Ukrainian population, it was disputed between the two states but remained part of the Russian Empire until 1918, when it threw off Russian rule and proclaimed union with Romania. Romania's acquisition was confirmed at the **Paris** Peace Conference in 1919 but never recognized by the Soviet Union. A Soviet ultimatum on 28 June 1940 forced Romania to cede the territory. It was administered by Romania for much of the Second World War but became part of the Moldavian Soviet Socialist Republic in 1944. *See also* **Moldavia**.

Bhopal (India)
Capital of the central Indian state of Madhya Pradesh, the scene on 3 December 1984 of a leakage of toxic gas from the Union Carbide pesticide plant following the buildup of pressure in an underground storage tank. Over 3,000 were killed and 200,000 severely injured in the disaster.

Biafra
Name of the Ibo homeland in Nigeria which was briefly an independent state from 1967 to 1970. On 30 May 1967 the military governor of the Eastern Region of Nigeria, Colonel Ojukwu, declared the Ibo homeland an independent sovereign state under the name of the Republic of Biafra. Troops of the Nigerian federal army attacked across the northern border of Biafra on 7 July 1967. The Biafrans invaded the neighbouring Mid-West Region on 9 August 1967. The federal army recaptured Biafra on 22 September 1967, and Port Harcourt fell on 20 May 1968. Supply shortages and starvation finally led to the collapse of Biafran resistance after a four-pronged federal attack in December 1969. The Biafran army surrendered on 15 January 1970. Total civilian and military dead were estimated at 600,000. The Nigerian government received help from Britain, Russia and the USA and support from most other African countries. Biafra, however, was able to gain help from France, Portugal and the Vatican. It was also supported by a large number of charitable organizations.

Bialystok (Poland)
City in the northeast under Soviet rule after the annexation of Eastern Poland in 1939. The German lightning invasion of the Soviet Union on 22 June 1941 (Operation Barbarossa) left the Soviet 10th Army encircled in a pocket around Bialystok. The city and 290,000 Soviet troops surrendered on 3 July, remaining under German occupation until 27 July 1944.

Bias Bay (China)
Site of Japanese landing of two infantry divisions, a tank brigade and marines, on 12 October 1938 during the Sino-Japanese War. The landing at Bias Bay, just east of **Hong Kong**, was intended to close the Chinese supply of oil and other materials entering China via Canton.

Bien Hoa (Vietnam)

City 20 miles north of **Saigon**. During 1958, Communist North **Vietnam** instigated a wave of murder and terrorism directed against local government officials in non-Communist South Vietnam, marking the beginning of the second Indo-China War. The campaign was stepped up in 1959, and on 8 July the Viet Cong (Vietnamese Communists) attacked the South Vietnamese army for the first time at Bien Hoa. The rulers of North Vietnam decided that they were sufficiently secure at home to take control of the war in the South. On 20 December 1960 the National Front for the Liberation of South Vietnam (NLF) was formed as a front organization to mastermind the Communist takeover of the South.

Biggin Hill (England)

One of the most famous RAF bases in the Second World War **Battle of Britain**. Located southeast of London, it was repeatedly bombed in 1940 by the German *Luftwaffe* as it directed its attacks on the airfields of Fighter Command. Throughout the Battle of Britain the RAF continued to fly fighter aircraft from Biggin Hill.

Bikini Atoll (Marshall Islands)

Site in the central Pacific Ocean where the USA tested 23 nuclear weapons from 1946–58. The inhabitants were removed and, although the area was expected to be free from contamination by 1968, the Atoll remained uninhabitable for many years.

Bilbao (Spain)

Important port on the north coast and largest city in the Basque country. Allied to the Republicans, the Basques held key points along the north coast during the Spanish Civil War. Switching the battleground to the north, the Nationalists initiated a strong offensive on 31 March 1937. The Basques steadily retreated, surrendering **Guernica** and Durango, until reaching defensive lines around Bilbao. This "Ring of Iron" protecting the city was breached on 12 June and Bilbao was defenceless. The city was evacuated, and by 19 June was entirely in Nationalist hands.

Bilderberg Hotel (The Netherlands)

Hotel in Arnhem where the first of a series of conferences of Western politicians, industrialists and trade union leaders was held in 1954, chaired by Prince Bernhard of The Netherlands. The conferences, initiated by a Polish refugee, Joseph Retinger, were intended to encourage closer US–European understanding but were viewed with suspicion by conservative politicians.

Birkenau (Poland)

Nazi concentration camp attached to **Auschwitz** in southern Poland. The railway tracks led straight into the camp to the gas chambers, bringing a clinical efficiency to the extermination process. At its peak in August 1944 over 60,000 a day were being exterminated. The retreating Nazis attempted to destroy much of the camp, which was captured by the Red Army in January 1945. Most of the buildings were demolished after the war.

Birmingham (England)

West Midlands city where 21 were killed in the bombing of two public houses by the Provisional IRA on 21 November 1974. Anger at the attacks led to the passing of the draconian 1974 Prevention of Terrorism Act. Six Irishmen were imprisoned for life in August 1975 for allegedly planting these bombs. The six, together with many prominent supporters, continued to protest their innocence, and in February 1991 they were released following the Director of Public Prosecutions' acceptance in the Appeal Court that police and forensic evidence in the case was unsafe.

Birmingham (United States)

City in Alabama in which the Southern Christian Leadership Council and Dr Martin Luther King began non-violent campaigning for black civil rights and against racial segregation in the spring of 1963. Hundreds were arrested and many were injured in daily demonstrations until the city's leading businessmen announced their willingness to end discrimination in restaurants and job recruitment.

Birobidzhan (Russia)

Remote Jewish autonomous region in the former Soviet Union, in the far east near the Chinese frontier. The Soviet Government established it as a Jewish National District in 1928. This became an *oblast* in 1934 and by 1941 30,000 Jews were living there. In 1958 Nikita Khruschev admitted that the region had failed to attract the hoped-for 300,000.

Bisho (South Africa)

Town in the former Ciskei homeland (see **Bophuthatswana**) where troops opened fire on 70,000 ANC demonstrators on 7 September 1992, killing at least 28 and wounding 190. The ANC and the South African government accused each other of being responsible, temporarily delaying the resumption of talks on the constitutional changes which led to majority African rule.

Bishopsgate (England)

Thoroughfare in the heart of the City of London, the scene of a devastating IRA bomb attack on 24 April 1993. One person was killed and 40 injured when a truck loaded with explosives was detonated. Damage was estimated at £300 million.

Bitburg (Germany)

Town which is the site of the Kolmeshoe German military cemetery, the scene of a controversial visit by US President Reagan in May 1985. Intended as a gesture of reconciliation, the visit generated embarrassment and widespread protests when it was discovered that among the graves were those of 47 *Waffen SS* members.

Bitola (Macedonia)

See **Monastir**.

Bizerte (Tunisia)

Former base in Tunisia. After the clashes in **Sakiet**, France had agreed on 17 June 1958 to withdraw from all her military bases except Bizerte. On 5 July 1961 Tunisia made a formal claim to the Bizerte base and imposed a blockade on 17 July. France sent reinforcements, which occupied the town of Bizerte in heavy fighting on 19–22 July. An agreement for the withdrawal of French troops from the town was signed on 29 September 1961, and the French base was evacuated by 15 October 1963.

Blair House (United States)

Official guest residence of the US President, in Washington DC. It gave its name to the Blair House Accord of November 1992 on the reduction of agricultural subsidies by both the EU and the USA as part of the GATT talks. Much disagreement later arose as to the exact interpretation of the Accord.

Bleiburg (Austria)

Carinthian town near the border of Austria and Slovenia. With the collapse in 1945 of the fascist pro-German Ustasa regime in **Croatia**, the Croat army fled to Austria. The troops were disarmed by the allies and returned to the Communist partisans. Many were massacred by the partisans at Bleiburg, partly in revenge for wartime atrocities by the Croats at Glina church, the Karitska Jama Gorge and Urije village. Bleiburg, in turn, became a symbol of Croatian suffering.

Bletchley Park (England)

Country estate located near Bletchley, Buckinghamshire, that was the home of the British Government's Codes and Cyphers School. During the Second World War it became the centre for the interception and decoding of the ULTRA and ENIGMA codes.

Bloemfontein (South Africa)

Capital of Orange Free State

1) The crushing defeat at **Paardeberg** in late February 1900 left the Boers on the defensive. British forces under General Roberts crossed the Orange River and advanced towards the Boer capital. On 13 March the British launched an offensive against the city, forcing the Boers to retreat to the north. With their capital captured, Boer resistance faded and the Orange Free State was annexed by Britain on 24 May 1900.

2) The ANC, the leading black South African nationalist movement, was formed here in 1912 to promote the welfare of blacks in South Africa. Its origins date from the formation in Cape Colony in 1882 of the Native Education Association. Banned from South Africa in 1961, its leader, Nelson Mandela, the symbol of black African hopes, was convicted of sabotage in 1964 and sentenced to life imprisonment. Mandela was released in 1990 and the ANC ban was lifted.

Bloomsbury (England)
Area of central London which gave its name to the Bloomsbury Group of early twentieth century cultural figures, notably Virginia and Leonard Woolf, Lytton Strachey and Bertrand Russell. Their unifying feature was an open attitude towards sexuality and a repugnance towards what they saw as Victorian hypocrisy, combined with a cultural élitism.

Bludan (Syria)
In March 1945 a loose association of Arab states was formed in this town as the Arab League. It followed a preparatory conference in September 1944 at Alexandria, Egypt. Founder members were Egypt, Iraq, Lebanon, Saudi Arabia, Syria, Jordan and the Yemen. Other states which subsequently joined the Arab League include Libya (1951), Sudan (1956), Tunisia and Morocco (1958), Kuwait (1962), Algeria (1962), South Yemen (1968), Bahrain, Qatar, Oman and the Trucial States (1971).

Bodenstown (Ireland)
Burial place of Wolfe Tone, the Irish nationalist who led an abortive United Irishmen rising against England with the aid of French troops in 1798. The town is by the River Liffey in County Dublin and a commemorative parade is organized there every year by Sinn Fein.

Bodoland (India)
The homeland sought by the Bodo tribal hill people of Assam in northeast India. After a long struggle, an agreement of February 1993 granted the Bodos a degree of limited autonomy but Bodo anger at the continued dominance of the local Muslim Assamese led to renewed violence.

Bogota (Colombia)

1) Location of the spontaneous popular uprising, the *"Bogotazo"*, on 9 April 1948 which wrecked central Bogota after the assassination of populist Liberal leader Jorge Gaitán. Thousands of protesters looted the city, venting their anger on the social and economic system in general. The uprising was a precursor of future periods of unrest – *La Violencia* – in Colombia.

2) Town where the Ninth International Conference of American States was held in April–May 1948 which resulted in the formation of the Organization of American States (OAS).

Bogside (Northern Ireland)

Area beneath the walls of Protestant **Londonderry** where Catholics settled in the seventeenth century. An area of staunch Republican support following the Battle of Bogside when it was besieged by attacking Protestants on 13 August 1969. Further confrontation occurred in 1996 after the tension at **Drumcree**.

Bohemia (Czech Republic)

Westernmost province of the Czech Republic, including the capital Prague. Previously part of the Habsburg Empire, it joined the new Czechoslovakian state in 1918. Its location on the German border and the presence of a German minority led to the **Sudetenland** crisis of 1938. Under the **Munich** Agreement these border districts of Bohemia were given to Germany. Full German occupation followed in March 1939 and Bohemia became a protectorate within the Reich. Liberated by the Red Army, Bohemia was reintegrated into **Czechoslovakia** but ceased being an administrative district in 1949.

Boipatong (South Africa)

Township 40 miles from Johannesburg where 42 men, women and children were massacred on 17 June 1992, allegedly by Zulu Inkatha Freedom Party supporters with the tacit assistance of white-controlled South African security forces.

Boksburg (South Africa)

Mining centre east of Johannesburg. In the final years of white rule in the country, the town made headlines around the world in its attempts to return to the days of fundamentalist apartheid. In trying to turn back the clock, the white extremists only succeeded in uniting black radicals, business leaders and the South African government.

Bolimov (Poland)

First World War battle on the **Eastern Front** on 3 January 1915, constituting part of the third German assault on **Warsaw**. Gas was used tactically for the first time when the Germans fired thousands of xylyl bromide shells into the Russian lines. The cold weather prevented the liquid from being vaporised and so no gas was released. Although Russia advised the Allies of the incident, it was not acted on and the subsequent gas attack at **Ypres** surprised the British and French.

Bologna (Italy)
Scene of the worst terrorist outrage in modern Italian history. Right-wing terrorists bombed Bologna railway station on 2 August 1980 as part of the "strategy of tension" policy. There were 85 deaths in the attack.

Bophuthatswana (South Africa)
One of the ten black homelands (or bantustans) created by the South African government during the apartheid era. Six black homelands (KwaZulu, Qwaqwa, Gazankulu, Lebowa, KwaNdbele, KaNgwane) were set aside as self-governing states. Four more reached nominal independence (Transkei 1976, Bophuthatswana 1977, Venda 1979, Ciskei 1981) but only South Africa recognised them. Following the overthrow of the Bophuthatswana government by South African defence forces in March 1994, all the homelands were re-integrated into South Africa.

Bosnia-Hercegovina (formerly part of Yugoslavia)
Provinces under the **Ottoman Empire** until 1878, occupied by the Austro-Hungarian Empire and formally annexed in 1908. Friction with neighbouring **Serbia** culminated in the assassination of Austrian Archduke Franz Ferdinand in the capital **Sarajevo** on 28 June 1914, sparking the First World War (see map on p. 38). The area became part of Yugoslavia after the First World War, but was incorporated into the German puppet state of **Croatia** during the Second World War. Following the break-up of Yugoslavia, Bosnia-Hercegovina was riven by bitter inter-ethnic civil war from 1992 onwards between Serbs, Muslims and Croats. *See* **Dayton (Ohio)**.

Boston (United States)
State capital of Massachusetts. Location of the Boston police strike of 1919. On 9 September, the Boston police force came out on strike over wage levels. The governor of Massachusetts, Calvin Coolidge called out the National Guard, having proclaimed, "There is no right to strike against public safety, anywhere, any time". The strike was rapidly crushed, the leaders of the strike dismissed and a new police force created.

Bougainville (Papua New Guinea)
Mineral-rich island forming part of the state of **Papua New Guinea**. Since 1988 the

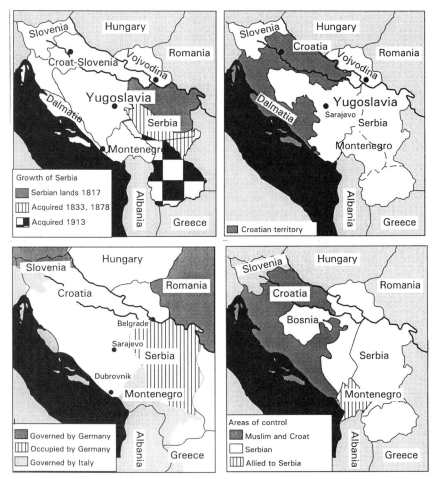

Bosnia-Hercegovina (formerly part of Yugoslavia)

Bougainville Revolutionary Army founded by Francis Ona has led a fight for independence and achieved significant early successes. The Panguna copper mine, dominating the economy of the island, was forced to close in 1989 and Papuan troops were forced to withdraw from the island in March 1990. However, no international recognition of an independent Bougainville was forthcoming and Papua re-established control over much of the island in 1992. The conflict remains.

Brasilia (Brazil)
Federal capital 600 miles northwest of Rio de Janeiro. Begun in 1956 by President Juscelino Kubitschek to honour a provision of the 1891 Constitution to build a unifying capital to ease Brazil's regional conflicts. The city, inaugurated as capital in 1960, became a symbol of Kubitschek's rapid economic developmentalism.

Braunau (Austria)
City located 31 miles north of Salzburg on the Inn River. It was the birthplace of Adolf Hitler, who was born in the Gasthaus Pommer on 20 April 1889.

Brazzaville (Congo Republic)
Formerly in French colony of Middle Congo. Town where the Brazzaville Declaration was agreed upon in January 1944 between Free French leader General de Gaulle and representatives of French colonies in West and Equatorial Africa. Although complete independence was ruled out, the territories were promised membership of a French Union with participation in French parliamentary elections, local assemblies and economic reform.

Breskens (The Netherlands)
Coastal village at the mouth of the Scheldt River. Following the liberation of **Antwerp** on 4 September 1944, the German Sixth Division was trapped in a pocket around Breskens. Canadian troops attacked on 6 October, but the strong German resistance was not finally overcome until 2 November 1944, when 12,500 Germans surrendered.

Brest-Litovsk (Poland)
Formerly part of the Russian Empire. Town in which Germany and Austria-Hungary imposed a harsh peace treaty on Bolshevik Russia on 3 March 1918 following protracted negotiations that had begun on 22 December 1917. Under this treaty the Soviet Union lost control of large sections of the former Russian empire, including **Estonia, Latvia, Lithuania** and Finland; Poland was to become independent, while the provinces of **Kars** and Batoum were lost to Turkey. The Soviet Union also agreed to recognize the independence of the **Ukraine**; in addition they agreed to pay 3,000

million gold roubles to Germany as war reparations. The harsh terms of Brest-Litovsk followed the ceasefire agreed by the Soviet Union early in December 1917. The treaty represented a huge loss of territory and population for the Soviet Union, amounting to some one million square miles.

Bretton Woods (United States)
Town in New Hampshire where a United Nations Conference on post-war trade and economic development attended by 28 nations was held in July 1944. The resulting agreement, which was intended to prevent a recurrence of the inter-war economic depression, included the creation of the IMF and the World Bank.

Brighton (England)
South coast seaside resort where five people were killed and 30 injured on 12 October 1984 by a Provisional IRA bomb at the Grand Hotel during the Conservative Party Conference. The Prime Minister, Mrs Margaret Thatcher, and a number of Cabinet ministers narrowly escaped death.

Brihuega (Spain)
Location of battle in the Spanish Civil War. In March 1937 Italian forces supporting General Franco and the Nationalists were defeated by the Republicans. The Republican victory held up Franco's advance on **Madrid**.

Britain, Battle of
The southeast and Channel coast of England was the arena for the Battle of Britain fought in the air from August to October 1940. Following the conquest of France, Germany launched an air attack with a three to one superiority on British shipping, airfields and towns as a preliminary to a planned invasion. Royal Air Force pilots shot down 1,733 German planes for the loss of 915, with the highest German losses on 15 August when 75 *Luftwaffe* aircraft were destroyed. German invasion plans were abandoned on 12 October and the night bombing of civilian targets began. See also **Biggin Hill**.

British Honduras
See **Belize**.

British North Borneo
See **Sabah**.

Brixton (England)

Suburb in south London, scene of rioting which broke out on 11 April 1981 following a week-long Operation Swamp mounted by police to reduce street crime. The local black population saw the operation as unnecessarily provocative. During three days of rioting white and black youths fought the police, burnt buildings and vehicles and looted shops. Further riots broke out in **Toxteth**, **Southall**, Handsworth, Moss Side and other inner-city areas in July. There was further rioting in Brixton on 28 September 1985, following the accidental shooting of a black woman by police, and also in December 1995.

Broadwater Farm (England)

Local authority housing estate in Tottenham, north London, where intense rioting took place on 6 October 1985 following the death of a black woman during a police raid. A police officer was killed during the clashes. Three black youths imprisoned for the killing were released in 1991 following successful appeals.

Bruges (Belgium)

Setting for Prime Minister Margaret Thatcher's virulently anti-federalist speech to the College of Europe on 20 September 1988. The town subsequently gave its name to the Bruges Group, a right-wing pressure group which supported her view of restricting European co-operation to a relationship between separate sovereign nations rather than pursuing uncompromising federal unity.

Brunei

Oil-rich sultanate on the island of Borneo. On 8 December 1962 the Brunei People's Party staged a revolt in opposition to the idea that Brunei should join the Federation of Malaysia. British and Gurkha troops were flown in from Singapore, and the rebellion was suppressed by 17 December 1962.

Brunete (Spain)

Scene of battle in Spanish Civil War. Between 6 and 25 July 1937 Republican forces launched a counter-attack against the Nationalist forces besieging **Madrid**. The Republicans achieved little and took a high number of casualties.

Brunéval (France)

Village on the Channel coast, north of Le Havre. On 27 February 1942 the British Parachute Regiment raided a German radar facility at Brunéval. The commandos landed south of the village, stormed the radar station, captured essential equipment and destroyed the facility. Three died in the action. Similar British facilities in Swanage were moved inland to Malvern to safeguard them.

Brussels (Belgium)

Capital city in which Belgium, Britain, France, Luxembourg and The Netherlands signed a treaty of 17 March 1948 giving mutual guarantees of assistance in the event of armed attack.

Bucharest (Romania)

Capital. On 10 August 1913 the Treaty of Bucharest ended the Second Balkan War. Bulgaria was forced to cede large parts of **Macedonia** and **Dobrudja** to Serbia, Greece and Romania. The second Treaty of Bucharest, signed on 7 May 1918, followed Romania's defeat by the Central Powers during the First World War. Under the harsh terms Romania lost southern Dobrudja, the Carpathian passes and control of her oilfields. The Treaty was annulled by the Armistice of 11 November 1918, and formally repealed by the Treaty of **Versailles**. After the Second World War, the Romanian People's Republic was proclaimed in Bucharest on 30 December 1947. President Ceausescu was overthrown and executed during a popular uprising on Christmas Day 1989. See also **Balkans**.

Buchenwald (Germany)

Nazi concentration camp near Weimar, opened in 1937 as a labour camp. Originally housing political prisoners, it later became a collecting point for Jews and others destined for the death camps.

Budyonnovsk (Russia)

Town 90 miles north of the breakaway republic of **Chechenia**. The town was seized in 1995 by Chechen guerrillas who held 2,000 hostages captive. The Budyonnovsk incident produced a major loss of face for the Russian government. In a string of humiliations for President Yeltsin, the armed forces reacted with crass brutality, killing some of the very hostages they were meant to rescue. The outcome was a safe return home for the rebels and much worldwide sympathy for their cause.

Buffalo (United States)

City in west New York State, on Lake Erie where President William McKinley was assassinated on 6 September 1901 by an anarchist, Leon Czolgosz.

Buganda (Uganda)

Kingdom within Uganda. In the nineteenth century a dominant power in East Africa under its ruler, the *kabaka*. The area came under British rule, but Buganda retained a large measure of self-government. Agitation for independence after 1945 led Britain to deport Kabaka Mutesa II. On independence, Uganda became a federation comprising five kingdoms, but in September 1962 President Milton Obote declared Uganda a republic. Mutesa II became president briefly before being deposed. *See* **Uganda**.

Bukovina (Ukraine)

Formerly part of the Soviet Union. Region inhabited by Ruthenes ceded to **Romania** in 1919 following the defeat of the Austro-Hungarian Empire, ceded to the Soviet Union on 28 June 1940 under the terms of the 1939 Nazi–Soviet Pact and incorporated into the Ukrainian Soviet Socialist Republic.

Bulawayo (Zimbabwe)

Capital of the Ndebele people led by their king, Lobengula (1833–94). After Lobengula granted the Rudd concession in 1888, the British South Africa Company was formed to exploit this mineral concession. White settlers moved into Mashonaland, east of Matabeleland. Lobengula sought to avoid conflict with the white settlers. In 1893, however, the British South Africa Company declared war, Bulawayo was captured and Lobengula fled.

Buraimi

Disputed group of oases on border of Abu Dhabi and **Oman**. In 1949 Saudi Arabia lodged a claim to the oases, sending an armed force in 1952. It was expelled by the British-officered Trucial Oman Scouts.

Burgenland (Austria)

Most easterly state of **Austria**. Part of **Hungary** until 1922 when it passed to Austria as part of the Treaty of **Saint Germain**. The capital, Odenburg, remained in Hungary.

Burgos (Spain)

Ancient city in which General Franco was installed as head of state and *generalissimo* on 1 October 1936.

Burma

Republic in Southeast Asia, now known as Myanmar. Formerly part of British India, it was occupied by the Japanese during the Second World War. In the year after gaining independence on 4 January 1948 the Burmese government faced armed opposition from a wide range of dissident groups: the Communists, themselves divided into the White Flag Stalinists and the Red Flag Trotskyites; a private army of wartime "old comrades" known as the People's Volunteer Organization, who made common cause with army mutineers; ethnic minorities seeking autonomy, such as the Mons and Karens; and bands of Muslim terrorists, Mujahids, in the north of Arakan. By 12 March 1949, when Mandalay fell to the Karen National Defence Organization and the Communists, most of Burma was in rebel hands. But the rebels were disunited, and Mandalay was retaken by government forces on 24 April 1949. The rebel capital, Toungoo, was captured on 19 March 1950. An offensive in November 1954 reduced the Mujahid menace, and Operation Final Victory was launched against the Karens on 21 January 1955. Outbreaks of fighting have occurred since 1955, but never on the scale of the early years of independence. The Burmese Army mounted a major offensive against the Karens in 1988–9.

Burma Road

Allied transport route during the Second World War between Lashio in northeast Burma and Kunming in China. With the Japanese controlling the Chinese coastline, this was the only route for Allied supplies to reach the Chinese Army. Its capture became a priority for the Japanese and led to the invasion of Burma on 15 January 1942. Japanese forces captured Lashio and closed the Road on 29 April. Allied supplies could now only reach China by flying over the Himalayas (the Hump). The Road was recaptured by the Allies in January 1945.

Burmi (Nigeria)

Location of colonial battle in 1903 in northern Nigeria between British troops and the Sultan of Sokoto. The Sultan, Al-Tahir, and 500 of his warriors were killed and the power of Sokoto broken. The British commander was also killed.

Burundi

Republic in Central Africa. In colonial times, along with **Rwanda**, it was part of the German Empire (the two territories were known as Ruanda-Urundi). In 1919 they were awarded to Belgium as mandates of the League of Nations. Since independence in July 1962, Burundi has been plagued by ethnic violence. On 29 April 1972 guerrillas from the majority Hutu tribe in Burundi attacked the ruling Tutsi minority, killing between 5,000 and 15,000 in an abortive coup. The Burundi armed forces, under Tutsi command, retaliated with assistance from Zaïre, and by the end of May 1972 the death toll amongst the Hutu had risen to an estimated 200,000. Refugees poured into neighbouring states. On 10 May 1973 Hutu rebels from Rwanda and Tanzania invaded Burundi. The Burundi army in response crossed into Tanzania on 29 June and killed ten people. President Mobutu of Zaïre mediated an accord between the presidents of Tanzania and Burundi on 21 July 1973. Further conflict erupted in 1986 and 1991. A coup in 1996 prompted further fears of bloodshed.

Byelarus

See **Belarus**.

Byelorussia

See **Belarus**.

Cabinda
Angolan enclave surrounded by **Congo, Zaïre** and the Atlantic Ocean. 2,800 square miles in area it is rich in resources such as oil, timber, cocoa and coffee. Although geographically separated from **Angola**, the 1975 **Alvor** Agreement guaranteed Angola sovereignty. This has since been contested by the guerrilla movement FLEC with little effect.

Cable Street (England)
Thoroughfare in the East End of London, the scene of the Battle of Cable Street in 1936. The East End of London increasingly became an arena for confrontation between Oswald Mosley's British Union of Fascists (the Blackshirts) and their left-wing opponents after the BUF adopted an increasingly anti-semitic stance. Attacks on Jews and Jewish property became commonplace. The planned march by Mosley's Blackshirts through the East End became the focus of a bitter confrontation. On Sunday 4 October 1936 the anti-Fascists forced the projected march to be cancelled. The East End streets were packed with Communists, supporters of the National Unemployed Workers Movement and Jewish organisations. After repeated police charges to clear Cable Street, and fights between Fascists and demonstrators, Mosley was requested to call off his march.

Cabora Bassa Dam (Mozambique)
Hydro-electric station on the Zambezi River. Completed in 1977, it was a regular target for the rebel Mozambique National Resistance (Renamo) during the civil war of the 1980s. Many of the power lines supplying electricity to South Africa were destroyed and the dam reduced to 1.5 per cent of its capacity.

Caen (France)
City in Normandy which was a prime objective of the Allied D-Day landings of the Second World War. German resistance was stronger than expected and the Canadian–British forces' advance was slow. The city outskirts were not reached until 13 July 1944, 38 days after D-Day. Canadian troops advanced street-by-street until most of the city was captured. By 20 July Caen had fallen and Operation Goodwood had advanced the front line more than 20 miles to the south.

Caesar Line (Italy)
German defensive position during the Second World War across the Italian peninsula. Stretching from Ostia on the coast south of Rome to Avezzano in the Appennines, it was the last major German defence before Rome. It was finally breached on 30 May 1944 by the US 5th Army.

Cairo (Egypt)

Scene of:

1) a Second World War meeting (22–26 November 1943) attended by President Roosevelt, Winston Churchill and Chiang Kai-shek to decide on post-war policy for the Far East. They demanded Japan's unconditional surrender, the return of **Manchuria** to China and Korea to its own people;

2) an attack on 22 January 1952 (known as Black Saturday) on Cairo's European quarter by members of the Muslim Brotherhood, socialists and students. The rioters were objecting to Britain's occupation of the **Suez Canal** Zone and chanted slogans such as "We want arms to fight for the Canal". Four hundred buildings were damaged and 17 Britons killed.

Calder Hall (England)

Site of Britain's first large-scale commercial nuclear power station (in Cumbria) opened on 23 October 1956. *See also* **Windscale**.

Cambodia

Independent state in Southeast Asia. France proclaimed a protectorate over the kingdom of Cambodia in 1863. In 1887 it became a constituent member of the Union of **Indo-China**. After independence, it was unable to avoid becoming involved in the **Vietnam** War. It was itself the scene of a bitter civil war. On 18 March 1970, Lieutenant General Lon Nol ousted the head of state, Prince Norodom Sihanouk, who was out of the country. Sihanouk allied himself with his former enemies, the Marxist Khmer Rouge, to form the National United Front of Cambodia. Lon Nol appealed for aid on 14 April 1970, and on 29 April US and South Vietnamese troops mounted an incursion into Cambodia to attack North Vietnamese, Viet Cong and Khmer Rouge forces. The last US troops withdrew on 29 June 1970. The Communists took control of the countryside and in 1975 cut supply routes to the capital, Phnom Penh. Lon Nol left the country on 1 April 1975 and the Khmer Rouge occupied Phnom Penh on 17 April. Following the Communist victory, Kampuchea (as Cambodia was renamed) was infamous as home of the "killing fields" of Pol Pot, where many thousands of the people were put to death in a virtual genocide of the population.

Cambrai (France)

Scene in 1917 of the first successful mass tank attack. On 20 November an attack by the British Third Army was opened by a 324-strong tank assault southwest of Cambrai, breaking a six-mile-wide gap in the German Second Army lines and advancing six miles. Ten thousand German prisoners were captured. The possibility of overall success was hampered by mechanical breakdowns and the Germans counter-attacked on 30 November, regaining the lost ground. Total British casualties were 43,000 while Germany lost 41,000.

Cameroon

West African country which became a German protectorate in 1884. During the First World War British, Belgian and Indian troops attacked from Nigeria. The long campaign lasted throughout 1915 until the remaining German forces surrendered in January 1916. A League of Nations mandate in 1919 divided the colony between France (80 per cent) and Britain (20 per cent). French Cameroon achieved full independence in 1957. A plebiscite in British Cameroon in 1961 resulted in the northern part uniting with Nigeria and the southern sector joining the Federal Republic of Cameroon. Cameroon joined the Commonwealth in 1995.

Camp David (United States)

Presidential retreat in Maryland. Following the Sadat Initiative it was the location of talks between President Sadat of Egypt and Prime Minister Begin of Israel, 5–17 September 1978, chaired by President Carter of the USA. It was agreed that a peace treaty between the two states would be signed within three months, to be followed by establishment of normal diplomatic relations within three years. Israel would withdraw from **Sinai** while UN troops were to guarantee Israel's security and access to the Red Sea. Israel agreed to stop settlement in the **Gaza Strip** and the **West Bank** and to enter negotiations with **Jordan** over the future of these areas: within five years Israeli military government was to be replaced by a government elected by the Palestinian inhabitants. But Israel was not required to give up the areas completely and no mention was made of the **Golan Heights** or East Jerusalem. The Syrians and the PLO therefore rejected the terms. Negotiations became bogged down over the ultimate future of the West Bank but on President Carter's intervention a peace treaty was finally signed in Washington on 26 March 1979.

Cam Ranh Bay (Vietnam)

Deepwater bay in central southern Vietnam. Under Japanese control during the Second World War, it was not fully developed until 1965 when the USA built a large military base covering 100 square miles at a cost of $2,000m. Transferred to South Vietnam in 1972, it was captured by Vietnamese Communist forces in April 1975. Soviet interest in developing its strategic importance led to negotiations with the Vietnamese Government in 1979. In exchange for military and diplomatic aid, Cam Ranh became a major air–naval facility as the base for the Soviet Far Eastern Fleet. Since the collapse of the Soviet Union in 1991, Russia has reduced its forces stationed there. Its continued longterm use as a Russian base is still unresolved.

Cana (Lebanon)

See **Qana**.

Canal Zone

1) Name given to the area of British military occupation of **Suez Canal** in Egypt. In

1936 Egypt agreed to permit Britain to station forces in the Suez Canal Zone and during the Second World War Britain transformed the Zone into its main military base in the Middle East. After the war Egypt agitated for the removal of British forces and frequent clashes took place. In 1954 the Egyptian Republican government negotiated a British withdrawal and Britain withdrew but sought to return during the Suez Crisis of October 1956 (see **Suez Canal**).
2) Name given to the area surrounding the 50.7 mile long **Panama Canal** in Central America.

Cancún (Mexico)

Meeting place of world leaders in October 1981 to discuss the Brandt Commission Report *North–South: A Programme for Survival 1980* which recommended fundamental changes in trade relations between the rich nations of the northern hemisphere and those of the south to confront the growing problem of unequal distribution of resources and world poverty. There was general support for the Report but few concrete results.

Cape Canaveral (United States)

NASA rocket-launching site on the east coast of Florida and home of the Kennedy Space Center. During the Apollo programme of the 1960s and 1970s it was known as Cape Kennedy.

Cape Esperance (Solomon Islands)

Scene of Second World War naval engagement off the northern tip of **Guadalcanal** in the Solomon Islands. Both Japan and the USA were attempting to land supplies and reinforcements to their troops on Guadalcanal. On the night of 11–12 October 1942 the two sides clashed near the Cape, with the USA using radar to achieve tactical surprise. The Japanese sank USS *Duncan*, but lost three ships and retreated.

Cape Kennedy

See **Cape Canaveral**.

Cape Matapan (Greece)

Second World War naval battle near the southernmost point of mainland Greece. In a major blow to Italian naval strength in the Mediterranean, the British inflicted heavy losses on the Italian fleet. While attempting to reinforce their positions in Greece, the British engaged an attacking Italian fleet on 28 March 1941. The Italians were outnumbered and outgunned, and withdrew under fire. As darkness fell, seven Italian ships were attacked and sunk by the pursuing British. Over 2,400 Italians were killed and Allied naval superiority in the Eastern Mediterranean was strengthened.

Cape St George (Papua New Guinea)

Scene of Second World War naval battle off the southern tip of New Ireland in the southwest Pacific. On 25 November 1943, five US destroyers encountered five Japanese destroyers and opened fire. Three Japanese ships were sunk as the other two withdrew.

Caporetto (Italy)

Scene of a battle fought on the River **Isonzo**, north of Trieste, between advancing Austrian and German forces and the Italian army from 24 October to 4 November 1917. The Italian army (of which 300,000 men were captured) collapsed, falling back to a new line north of Venice where it was stiffened by British and French reinforcements.

Caprivi Strip (Namibia)

Narrow corridor of land extending the border of **Namibia** (previously South West Africa) eastwards to a point where it shares a border with Botswana, Zambia and **Zimbabwe**. It was created in 1890 to give Germany, the then colonial power in Namibia, access to the Zambezi River. In the late 1970s and 1980s it was used by South Africa as a base for military raids into **Angola** and Namibia.

Carinthia (Austria)

Most southeastern province of **Austria**, Carinthia was claimed by the new state of **Yugoslavia** after the First World War. This claim was disputed by Austria and rejected in a plebiscite of 10 October 1920, when the southernmost district of Carinthia, with its overwhelming majority of Slovene speakers, voted to remain Austrian. Similar claims were made by the Yugoslav leader Tito in 1945, again unsuccessfully.

Carnaby Street (England)

Street in Soho, central London which, in 1966, came to symbolize the Swinging Sixties era in Britain when its fashion boutiques became the centre of British youth culture. It has been a tourist attraction ever since.

Carrizal (Mexico)

Town where Mexican soldiers clashed on 21 June 1916 with a US force led by General Pershing seeking guerrilla leader Pancho Villa following a raid by his men on **Columbus**, New Mexico. The Mexicans were defeated. Pershing's force advanced a further 400 miles into Mexico, breaking up Villa's army, but withdrew on 5 February 1917.

Casablanca (Morocco)

Location of a Second World War meeting, from 14 to 24 January 1943, between

Winston Churchill and President Roosevelt which reiterated the Allies' insistence on Germany's unconditional surrender. The leaders also agreed to invade Italy through **Sicily**, intensify bombing of Germany and transfer British forces to the Far East after victory in Europe. Casablanca also gave its name to the Casablanca Powers, a loose association of more radical African states consisting of Ghana, Guinea, Mali, Morocco, UAR and Algeria, set up in 1961. They combined with the Monrovia states to form the Organization of African Unity (OAU).

Caserta (Italy)
Site in northern Italy of the surrender of Axis forces on 29 April 1945, signed by General Veitinghoff. The Caserta surrender was the beginning of the end of Nazi resistance. Hitler committed suicide the next day. A further German surrender took place on **Luneberg Heath** and the war in the west ended on 8 May 1945.

Cassino (Italy)
Hill town south of Rome with a historic monastery held by German forces as part of the defensive **Gustav Line**. Allied troops mounted four attacks against Cassino from February 1944 until it was captured by Polish troops on 17 May.

Casteau (Belgium)
Near Mons, the headquarters of NATO.

Catalca (Turkey)
Fortified defensive line created by the Turks to prevent a Bulgarian attack on Constantinople (now Istanbul) on 17–18 November 1912 during the First Balkan War.

Catavi (Bolivia)
Scene of a massacre of striking Bolivian tin miners on 21 December 1941 by government troops when several hundreds were killed. The consequences of this bloody massacre were highly significant. A powerful Silver Miners' Union sprang up which in turn brought the MNR to power in December 1943. When President Estenssoro nationalized the tin mines in October 1952 Catavi was selected as the ceremonial site.

The Cavern (England)
Basement club at 8 Matthew Street, Liverpool, that was the focus of Liverpool's music scene in the 1960s. The Beatles made their debut there on 21 February 1961. See also **Abbey Road**.

Celaya (Mexico)
Scene of a decisive battle in the Mexican Civil War. Fought in 1915 between the troops of Obregón (on the side of Venustiano Carranza) and the forces of Pancho Villa. Obregón (although wounded) was victorious. Pancho Villa fled northwards and Carranza was left in effective control of Mexico.

Central African Empire
Former French colonial territory, now known as the Central African Republic. It was notorious in the 1970s for the excesses of its self-proclaimed emperor, Jean-Bedel Bokassa.

Central African Federation
Unification of the African territories of Nyasaland, Northern and Southern Rhodesia on 3 September 1953 to promote economic development and defend the interests of the white minority. Deeply unpopular with the majority African population, the federation collapsed in 1961.

Cernova (Slovakia)
Site of a demonstration on 27 October 1907 that became known as the Bloody Sunday of Hungarian rule in Slovakia. The Cernova massacre arose from a peaceful demonstration of local Slovaks, protesting against the consecration of their church by a pro-Magyar (i.e. pro-Hungarian) priest. Fifteen people were killed and scores wounded when Hungarian police fired on the crowd. The authorities laid much of the blame on the Slovak nationalist Andrej Hlinka, the Catholic pastor of Ružomberok.

Ceuta
Spanish enclave on the North African coast opposite Gibraltar. An integral part of Spain, it is administratively part of the Province of Cadiz. It was originally seized by Portugal in 1415. Melilla, another Spanish Moroccan enclave, is part of the province of Malaga.

Ceylon
See **Sri Lanka**.

Chaco (South America)
Plain between Bolivia and Paraguay, the scene of clashes between both countries since the nineteenth century. Following border incidents in the 1920s, the two states fought a bloody war from 1932 to 1935 in which over 50,000 Bolivians and 35,000 Paraguayans were killed. The region was divided, with 30,000 square miles going to Bolivia and 70,000 to Paraguay.

Chad

Republic in North Africa, formerly ruled by France. Since independence, Chad has been plagued by civil war and invasions. The civil war in Chad originated in the mid-1960s as a conflict between the French-backed government of President Tombalbaye and a number of separatist factions in the Muslim north of the country, grouped into FROLINAT and supported by Libya. By the mid-1970s FROLINAT controlled three-quarters of the country. On 6 February 1978 the head of state, General Malloum, who had overthrown President Tombalbaye in 1975, announced a ceasefire with FROLINAT. Conflict then developed between two factions in FROLINAT: one, under Hissène Habré, and the more militant group, under Goukouni Oueddei, backed by Libya. Habré's army was victorious and captured the capital, N'Djamena, on 7 June 1982. Fighting resumed in 1983. An intermittent civil war continued until the OAU negotiated a ceasefire in September 1987.

Chanak (Turkey)

Location, on the Asian side of the **Dardanelles**, of a major international crisis in autumn 1922. The crisis arose directly as a result of the resurgence of Turkish power under Kemal Atatürk. Having defeated the Greek forces in western Anatolia and captured Izmir (Smyrna) on 11 September 1922, Atatürk stood ready to carry the war to Constantinople, garrisoned by international forces, and into the area of eastern Thrace allotted to **Greece** by the unratified Treaty of **Sèvres**. Although the French and Italian forces withdrew, recognising the *fait accompli* of revived Turkish power, Prime Minister Lloyd George supported the Greek cause and ordered the British garrison at Chanak, on the Asiatic shore of the Dardanelles, to stand firm. The crisis was defused when the local British commander, General Harrington, concluded an agreement with the advancing Turkish forces at Mudania on 11 October 1922. The agreement pledged the return of eastern Thrace to Turkey, repudiating the Treaty of Sèvres and the neutralization of the Dardanelles and Bosphorus seaways. The agreement formed the basis for the Treaty of **Lausanne** signed the following year and brought a settlement to the Turkish frontiers. The crisis had important repercussions in British domestic politics.

Changi (Singapore)

Notorious location in the Second World War which housed Allied prisoners of war (and also civilians) in conditions of extreme privation. Located on Sime Road in the eastern part of the island.

Channel Islands

Small archipelago off the coast of France, the main islands being Jersey, Guernsey, Alderney, Great and Little Sark. Dependent territories of Britain, they were the only British soil occupied by the Germans during the Second World War. Captured in June 1940, they were liberated in May 1945.

Chappaquiddick (United States)
Island off Martha's Vineyard, Massachusetts, where Mary-Jo Kopechne was killed on 28 July 1969 when a car driven by Senator Edward Kennedy went off a bridge. Kennedy left the scene and did not report the accident until ten hours later. He received a two month suspended sentence and, although he remained in politics, the incident destroyed any hopes he had of becoming a presidential candidate.

Chapultepec (Mexico)
Town where an agreement was signed (the Act of Chapultepec) in 1945 between members of the Pan-American Union on military and naval co-operation for mutual defence.

Charleroi (Belgium)
First World War battle around this town on the River Sambre in southern central Belgium. The first major battle of the war (21–24 August 1914), it was initially seen as a bad defeat for the Allied Forces. The French 5th Army under General Lanzerac was encircled by the 1st, 2nd and 3rd German Armies. Both sides suffered from bad organization and a lack of equipment. The town itself changed hands three times in one day before the French were forced to retreat, exposing the British in nearby **Mons**. However, by slowing the German advance and preventing the annihilation of his forces, Lanzerac gave the French a chance to regroup and counter-attack.

Charlottetown (Canada)
Town on St Edward Island where agreement was reached on 28 August 1992 by leaders of Canada's provinces on changes to the country's constitution. The Charlottetown Accord included new powers for French-speaking **Quebec** and greater devolution in the western provinces. The Accord was rejected in a national referendum on 26 October.

Chartwell (England)
Country home near Westerham, Kent, of British politician Sir Winston Churchill from 1922 onwards. The centre in the 1930s of his campaign against appeasing Nazi Germany.

Chateau-Thierry (France)
First World War battle near this small town on the River Marne between Reims and Paris. The furthest point reached by the Germans in the Spring Offensive at the end of May 1918, when they were stopped by US and French troops. Fighting resumed in June–July with a counter-offensive by the American 2nd Division from the west and the British and French from the south. The Germans under General Ludendorff retreated and the town was recaptured by US troops on July 21.

Chechenia

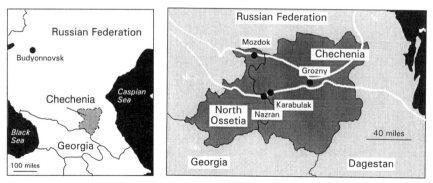

Caucasian territory, formerly part of the Soviet Union, which has attempted to secure its independence from the Russian Federation. The Chechens had fought bitterly against the expansion of Tsarist Russia in the nineteenth century, and allied themselves with the Germans in the Second World War to attempt to secure their independence. The Chechens, widely acknowledged as fierce fighters and ungovernable subjects, declared independence under their leader Dzhokhar Dudayev in 1991. Russia, faced with growing organized crime and smuggling in Chechenia, eventually launched a military assault in 1994. The subsequent diasters of the military campaign, and Chechen guerrilla raids (see **Budyonnovsk**) greatly embarrassed the Yeltsin administration. A ceasefire organized before the 1996 presidential election was soon broken. Chechen fighters subsequently seized the capital Grozny, effectively forcing the Russians to negotiate a settlement.

Checkpoint Charlie (Germany)
In the Cold War era, the most famous crossing point in the divided city of **Berlin**. It was the popular nickname for the official crossing point between West Berlin and Communist East Berlin. With the fall of Communism and the destruction of the Berlin Wall, it was no longer needed and was dismantled on 22 June 1990. It was one of the most evocative symbols of the Cold War.

Cheju (Korea)
Island off the south coast. The site of a bitter guerrilla war after 1948 which began when police arrested 2,500 people after a demonstration on 1 March 1948 against the elections on the mainland. The subsequent oppression led to the formation of a People's Army (the Immin-gun) of 3,000–4,000 strength. By June 1948 most of the island was in guerrilla hands. Casualties escalated as 20,000 homes on the island were destroyed. The final death toll was put at 15,000–30,000.

Chelmno (Poland)
Town in central Poland south of **Danzig**, and site of the first Nazi extermination

camp. Set up in 1941, it used Zyklon B gas to murder over 350,000 Jews and gypsies during the Second World War. It was closed and destroyed in 1944.

Cheltenham (England)
Location of the Government Communications Headquarters (GCHQ), an installation for collecting signals intelligence, co-ordinating a worldwide network of listening posts. The Conservative government banned GCHQ workers from union membership on 25 January 1984 following the allegedly disruptive effects of a civil service strike in 1981. Workers who refused to give up union membership were dismissed.

Chelyabinsk (Russia)
Industrial city in the Russian Federation. Formerly in the Soviet Union, it was the scene of an atomic accident in 1957.

Chenpaodao
Island between China and the former Soviet Union (also known as **Damansky**).

Cherbourg (France)
The first large French port captured by the Allies following the D-Day landings in **Normandy**. It fell on 27 June 1944.

Cheribon (Indonesia)
See **Linggadjati**.

Chernobyl (Ukraine)
Formerly part of the Soviet Union. Site of a light-water nuclear reactor where a major accident in April 1986 released a radioactive cloud which spread through Scandinavia and Europe. Thirty one people were killed in the accident, but in the aftermath over 5,000 people have died across Europe from the effects of radiation and over 350,000 contracted related illnesses.

Chiapas (Mexico)
Province whose endemic poverty and entrenched social and political problems burst into a guerrilla rising in January 1994. The threat of a further rising in December 1994 brought Mexico's economy to the point of collapse.

Chicago (United States)

City on the shores of Lake Michigan.

1) On 17 July 1919 a black teenager accidentally swam in front of a white beach on Lake Michigan. The teenager was stoned and drowned, provoking bitter race riots in Chicago. Lasting 13 days, the riots left 15 whites and 23 blacks dead and over 1,000 families homeless.

2) During the Prohibition Era (1920–33) gangland warfare over the control of illicit alcohol led to the St Valentine's Day Massacre. On 14 February 1929 members of Al Capone's gang, disguised as policemen, murdered seven unarmed men from Bugs Moran's gang.

3) The Democratic Convention of August 1968 was overshadowed by violent demonstrations against the Vietnam War. On 24 September 1969 the Chicago Eight went on trial for conspiring to cause the riot. The trial was chaotic, with one defendant, Bobby Seale, bound and gagged to keep him quiet. Seale's case was declared a mistrial, while two others were acquitted. The remaining defendants were acquitted of conspiracy but convicted of crossing State lines to riot. Their sentences were later overturned.

Chimoio (Mozambique)

Site of a refugee camp during the war of independence in neighbouring **Rhodesia**. The camp was raided by troops of the élite Rhodesian Selous Scouts as part of their counter-insurgency strategy. An estimated 1,000 Rhodesian refugees were killed during raids in November 1977.

Chittagong Hill Tracts (Bangladesh)

Heavily forested area of southeast **Bangladesh** covering a succession of hill ranges. In 1975 the Chittagong Autonomists (also known as Shati Bahini or "peace force") launched a campaign for the self-government of the native Chakma people. Violence erupted between the minority Chakmas and the Bengali majority. Thousands of Chakmas fled to India to escape the ethnic fighting. In November 1992 the violence subsided when a peace agreement providing for greater autonomy was negotiated.

Chong-jin (China)

Scene of battle in April 1904, the first land engagement of the Russo-Japanese War. After a brief struggle, and only limited casualties, the Russians under General Mischtchenko were driven back.

Chong-ju

See **Chong-jin**.

Chongqing

See **Chungking**.

Chongsanri (North Korea)

Gave its name to a policy derived from the Chongsanri agricultural co-operative in the North Korean province of South Pyongan. Under the policy, North Korean leader Kim Il Sung called on party leaders in February 1960 to base work in local planning and agricultural mechanization on the strength of the masses.

Christiania (Denmark)

Former military base in the suburbs of Copenhagen. In 1975 the site was occupied by rebellious hippie squatters. The squat went on to become Christiania, at first an "independent" hippie state but eventually a social experiment approved by the Danish Government. Cars were banned and cannabis legalized. To the radical left it was one of the great social experiments of the 1970s. It still survives.

Chumbi Valley (Tibet)

See **Lhasa**.

Chungking (China)

City on the Yangtse River in the south. During the Second World War it served as the Nationalist capital of China and was heavily damaged by Japanese air raids.

Chu Pong (Vietnam)

Mountain near the border with **Cambodia** where a battalion of the US First Cavalry Division fought the 66th North Vietnamese Regiment from 14 to 17 November 1965. The US were supported by fighter aircraft and B-52 bombers and killed at least 890 Vietnamese. The remaining 500 US troops crossed the Ia Drang River and during further clashes with the North Vietnamese suffered the highest casualties up to that point in the war, until relieved by South Vietnamese paratroops. In both battles the US lost a total of 240 and 470 were wounded. Total North Vietnamese casualties were reportedly over 2,000.

Ciénaga (Colombia)

Site of the Ciénaga Massacre of 1928, immortalized by the writer Garcia Márquez in *Cien Anos de Soledad*.

Cienfuegos (Cuba)

Town where intelligence gathered by US U-2 spy aircraft in September 1970 suggested that the Soviet Union was building a submarine base in breach of the agreement which had ended the 1962 Missile Crisis. On 27 September the Soviet Union assured the USA that this was not the case.

Ciskei (South Africa)
See **Bophuthatswana**.

Clark Field (Philippines)
US air base on the island of **Luzon**, 48 miles northwest of Manila. Established following the Spanish–American War of 1898, it was one of the primary goals of the Japanese invasion of the Philippines in December 1941. Formally leased to the USA in 1947, it became a principal strategic supply base for the US during the Vietnam War. Negotiations between the Philippines and the USA on the future of the base began in May 1990, but were disrupted by the eruption of nearby volcano Mount Pinatubo in June 1991. A settlement was finally reached and Clark Field was handed over to the Philippines in November 1991.

Cliveden (England)
Country house near Maidenhead, Berkshire, owned by Lord and Lady Astor. In the late 1930s it was a meeting place for politicians and journalists who favoured a policy of appeasement towards Nazi Germany, leading to the invention of the term Cliveden Set by Communist journalist Claud Cockburn. In the early 1960s War Minister John Profumo met Christine Keeler at Cliveden, leading to an affair which discredited Harold Macmillan's Conservative government.

Clyde (Scotland)
Major river in west Scotland. It gave its name to Red Clydeside, the period of strikes and socialist unrest in the Glasgow area from 1915 to 1919. Strikes organized by the Clyde Workers' Committee against dilution in 1915–16 led to arrests and suppression of left-wing journals by the government. Attempts to form a Workers' and Soldiers' "Soviet" in 1918 were prohibited by government. The Forty Hours' Strike in January to February 1919 led to disturbances and the placing of troops and tanks.

Colditz (Germany)
Famous as the high security camp for prisoners of war in the Second World War. Located southwest of Leipzig, the fortress housed special prisoners – those with valued connections and those who had already escaped from other prisoner-of-war camps. Despite the daringly successful escapes (130 in all) only 32 prisoners evaded recapture.

Colenso (South Africa)
Boer War battle south of **Ladysmith** in Natal. In early December 1899 the British army was deployed on three fronts, but by 11 December two of the columns had been decisively defeated by the Boers at **Stormberg** and **Magersfontein**. On 15 December

General Buller launched a third offensive to relieve besieged Ladysmith, attacking the Boers across the Tugela River at Colenso. The frontal assault failed, resulting in over 1,100 British casualties, and Buller had suffered his third defeat in a week.

Colmar (France)

Town in the Vosges region of eastern France. In November 1944, US troops captured Strasbourg and French forces captured Mulhouse, to the south. The German 17th Army became trapped in a pocket around Colmar between the Allies and the Rhine. As the Allies advanced in January 1945, many German troops managed to retreat across the Rhine, although over 36,000 casualties were left behind.

Cologne (Germany)

City on the east bank of the Rhine. An important industrial and commercial centre for the **Ruhr** region, Cologne was a prime target for Allied bombers during the Second World War. It was the first city to endure a "thousand-bomber raid" when, on 30 May 1942, 1,046 British bombers attacked. Half the city was destroyed, 500 Germans killed, and 40,000 left homeless for the loss of 40 bombers. The city was captured by the USA during their advance into Germany in March 1945.

Colombey-les-Deux-Églises (France)

Village in northeastern France to which General de Gaulle retired in 1946 following his failure to form a government of national unity. On his subsequent retirement as President of the Fifth Republic in 1969 he returned there until his death in 1970.

Colombo (Sri Lanka)

A meeting of British Commonwealth ministers in January 1950 agreed on the Colombo *Plan for Economic Development in South East Asia* under which Australia, Canada, New Zealand and Britain would provide developmental assistance. The scheme was joined by Japan and the USA who provided the bulk of funds. The title was changed in 1977 to the *Plan for Co-operative Economic and Social Development in Asia and the Pacific*.

Columbus (United States)

Town in New Mexico raided by 500 mounted bandits from the northern Mexican revolutionary regime of Pancho Villa on 8–9 March 1916. The raiders set fire to part of the town before being beaten off by 350 men of the 13th US Cavalry, with the loss of 15 lives. The US government despatched an expedition into Mexico as punishment. See also **Carrizal**.

Commonwealth of Independent States
See under **Alma Ata**.

Compiègne (France)
On 22 June 1940 the Franco-German armistice was signed here, at Rethondes in the Forest of Compiègne north of Paris. For the Germans, the setting for their triumph over the French was highly symbolical. Compiègne had been the location of the German Armistice in November 1918. In a humiliating gesture, Hitler signed the 1940 terms of surrender in the same railway carriage in which the Germans had agreed to the 1918 armistice.

Conakry (Guinea)
The country's capital, where a charter was signed between Guinea and Ghana on 1 May 1959 agreeing on union between the two countries as a preliminary to the formation of a proposed African Union of States. Although Mali joined the union on 1 July 1961 there was no further progress towards genuine unity.

Congo
See **Belgian Congo** and **Zaïre**.

Cook County (United States)
Electoral area of the state of Illinois including Chicago and its suburbs, which was historically under strong Democratic Party control, particularly under Mayor Richard Daley. Kennedy's narrow presidential election victory over Nixon in 1960 was reputedly partly won by a small number of votes acquired in a questionable way in Cook County.

Copacabana (Brazil)
Fort in Rio de Janeiro, the location of the uprising of 5–6 July 1922, an outbreak of revolt by a group of young officers and their commanders. Folk legend portrays the revolt as a heroic rebellion led by Siqueira Campos against vastly superior forces.

Coral Sea
Second World War naval battle in this southwestern part of the Pacific Ocean, bounded by New Guinea, the Solomon Islands and Australia. Japanese invasion forces, heading for Port Moresby in New Guinea and Tulagi in the Solomons, were engaged by three US Task Forces on 7–8 May 1942. This crucial battle was the first to involve no direct engagement between the opposing warships, being fought

only by aircraft. Simultaneous air strikes by both sides on 8 May left the USS *Lexington* sinking and the Japanese carrier *Shokaku* disabled. A tactical draw between the evenly-matched sides, it was a strategic victory for the USA. The invasion of Port Moresby had been halted, and the threat to Australia receded.

Corfu (Greece)
Island in the Adriatic, the scene of the Corfu Incident of 1923. The crisis was precipitated by the shooting of an Italian general and four members of his staff on Greek soil while mapping the Greek–Albanian frontier on 27 August 1923. This prompted Mussolini to lodge a claim for compensation and bombard and occupy Corfu four days later. The Greeks appealed to the League of Nations for assistance in what was a flagrant breach of the Covenant of the League. Under pressure from Britain and France, Mussolini withdrew his force from Corfu on 27 September. The dispute was referred by the League to the Council of Ambassadors, who persuaded the Greeks to apologize and pay compensation. For the 1917 Corfu Pact, see **Yugoslavia**.

Corleone (Italy)
Town in Sicily from which the Mafia Godfather Salvatore Riina controlled the world's largest criminal organization for over a decade. Riina was arrested in January 1994.

Coronel (Chile)
First World War naval battle near this coastal city in the south. During the first few months of the war a German naval squadron under Admiral von Spee harassed and raided the Allies in the west Pacific Ocean. The Germans were eventually intercepted on 1 November 1914 by a British force under Admiral Cradock. In a short but decisive battle the British were comprehensively defeated, losing two ships and 1,500 men including Cradock.

Corregidor (Philippines)
Small island off the **Bataan Peninsula**, at the entrance to Manila Bay in the Philippines. Heavily fortified by the US, it served as the headquarters of the US Forces in the Far East under General MacArthur. Following the US surrender on Bataan in April 1942, the last US troops were besieged on Corregidor. Japanese forces bombarded the island and secured a beachhead on 5 May 1942, leading to US surrender the next day. An air–sea assault by US troops on 16 February 1945 resulted in the recapture of Corregidor by 27 February.

Corsica (France)
French island in the Mediterranean. During the Second World War, some 80,000

Italian and 8,000 German troops occupied the island. Corsican resistance fighters took to the countryside, whose terrain gave birth to the term *Maquis*. It was subsequently applied to other resistance groups, as in mainland France. Italian forces surrendered in 1943 and in 1944 the island became the first *département* to be liberated by the Allies.

Corunna Road (Spain)
Scene of a battle during the Spanish Civil War from 13 December 1936 to 15 January 1937 in which the Nationalists succeeded in cutting off Republican **Madrid** from the north of the country.

Costa Rica
Republic in central America. Plagued by civil war and repeated rebel invasions in the years after 1945. Civil war broke out in March 1948 when President Teodoro Picado attempted to annul the elections. He allowed the Communists to organize a 2,000-strong militia to support the regular army. But the forces of the National Liberation Party, led by Colonel José Figueres, gradually took control of the country and entered the capital, San José, on 24 April 1948. President Picado resigned and the regular army was disbanded. On 10 December 1948 Costa Rica was invaded from Nicaragua by 1,000 armed supporters of the ex-President, Calderon Guardia. The town of La Cruz fell, but the rebels had been driven out by 17 December 1948. Further relatively minor incursions occurred in July 1954 and January 1955.

Coventry (England)
Cathedral city in the Midlands, southeast of Birmingham. One of the first cities outside London to be the target of German bombers, it was devastated in a single night, 14–15 November 1940. 449 bombers dropped over 500 tonnes of explosives and nearly 900 incendiary bombs in the 11-hour attack. Much of the city, including the cathedral, was destroyed and over 550 people killed.

Coyoacan (Mexico)
Small suburb just outside Mexico City, the scene of the assassination of Leon Trotsky. He had been granted asylum in Mexico in December 1936 and had moved to a house in Coyoacan, paid for by admirers in New York, late in 1938. On 20 August 1940 he was attacked by a Stalinist agent known as Frank Jacson (whose real name was Ramón Mercader). Trotsky was rushed to hospital but died on the evening of 21 August.

Crete (Greece)
Eastern Mediterranean island annexed by Greece in 1913. On 6 April 1941 German troops invaded the Greek mainland forcing an Allied evacuation to Crete on 28 April.

A German airborne assault on Crete began on 20 May 1941, supported by heavy aerial bombardment. By 28 May the Allies had admitted defeat and started evacuating their troops. Only 15,000 were saved, with 12,000 taken prisoner. German casualty rates were so high (7,000 killed, one third of their force), that no more major airborne operations were mounted. British troops recaptured Crete in October 1944.

Crimea (Ukraine)

Peninsula in the northern Black Sea. Russian since 1783, it became the Crimean Autonomous Republic within the Soviet Union in 1920. It was invaded by Germany in October 1941, although **Sevastopol**, the main naval base, held out until 3 July 1942. As the Soviet troops counter-attacked, the last German troops trapped in Crimea were evacuated on 9 May 1944. In 1954 Crimea became an autonomous republic within the Ukraine, with much of the Tartar population being deported. The collapse of the Soviet Union created tension between Russia and **Ukraine** over Crimea, whose population is 70 per cent Russian.

Croatia

Republic in the **Balkans**. Part of the kingdom of Hungary and the Austro-Hungarian Empire prior to the First World War. Subsequently part of the Kingdom of the Serbs, Croats and Sloves (**Yugoslavia**). Croat resentment at Serbian dominance led to the formation of the *Ustase*, a terrorist organization led by Ante Pavelic (1889–1959) which conducted terrorist activities against the Yugoslav state, including the assassination of King Alexander at Marseilles in 1934. The German conquest of Yugoslavia in 1941 led the *Ustase* to set up an independent Kingdom of Croatia, with an Italian duke as titular King of Croatia. Collaborating with the Germans and Italians, the *Ustase* fought against Tito's partisans and other opponents of the Axis occupation, committing many massacres and atrocities against Jews and rival nationalities. With the eventual collapse of post-war Yugoslavia, Croatia declared independence in spring 1991 and war ensued. See separate entries for **Krajina**, **Vukovar**, **Bosnia-Hercegovina**, etc.

Ctesiphon (Iraq)

First World War battle along the River Tigris 25 miles southeast of Baghdad. Having been routed at **Kut-al-Amara** in September 1915 the Turkish army withdrew upriver, becoming entrenched at Ctesiphon. British forces under General Townshend followed and attacked on 22 November 1915. Although outnumbered and outgunned the British took the Turkish advance trenchlines. Turkish reinforcements arrived the following day and forced the British to retreat with the loss of 4,567 men.

Cuba

Independent state in the Caribbean, the scene of the Cuban Missile Crisis of 1962 which brought the world to the brink of a nuclear confrontation. This period of extreme tension in the Cold War lasted from 22 to 28 October 1962. Intelligence agencies in Washington, aware of increased Soviet interest in Cuban affairs, discovered on 16 October evidence that Soviet ballistic missiles capable of delivering nuclear warheads on US cities were being installed in Cuba. During the previous month the Soviet government had admitted supplying arms to Cuba but denied that they were offensive in nature. On 22 October President Kennedy declared that the US Navy would blockade Cuba and requested the Soviet Union to remove its missiles. The reply on 26 October was that they would be removed if NATO missiles were removed from Turkey. President Kennedy found this offer unacceptable and the world faced a real threat of imminent nuclear war. Khrushchev, the Soviet leader, realizing perhaps that the Soviet Union had overplayed its hand, agreed on 28 October to remove the missiles. Fidel Castro, the Cuban leader, would not allow UN observers into Cuba to check that they had been dismantled, but the US Defense Department accepted by the first week in November that they had been. The blockade was ended on 20 November following Soviet promises to remove bombers and missile technicians by the end of the month.

Cuito-Cuanavale (Angola)
Southern town, the centre of the largest battle of the civil war (and the largest set battle in Africa since the Second World War). In 1987, South African and UNITA troops attempted to take the town from Angolan government forces supported by Cuban troops. Some 3,000 South African troops were killed in a successful Angolan government counter-attack, causing the South African government to re-assess its policy towards Angola.

Curragh (Ireland)
Plain near Dublin, the site of a British military base and scene of an officers' mutiny in 1914 on the question of having to go into action to force Protestants in Ulster to accept Irish Home Rule. The Ulster Volunteers had threatened armed resistance to this. The British commander, General Sir Arthur Paget, said it would be acceptable for officers with Ulster connections to resign or otherwise become unavailable, in effect countenancing their disobeying orders. The Minister of War, Colonel Seely, was forced to resign when this became public.

Curzon Line
Border between Poland and Bolshevik Russia proposed by British Foreign Secretary Lord Curzon in July 1920. Although the frontier was placed further east at Poland's insistence, the Curzon Line became the border between the Soviet and German zones in 1939 and remained so from 1945 onwards.

Cyprus

Island in the eastern Mediterranean, under British control until independence in 1960. In the 1950s many Greek Cypriots favoured *enosis* (union with Greece). Agitation for union with Greece led in April 1955 to the start of a campaign of terrorism and guerrilla warfare by EOKA, the militant wing of the *enosis* movement. A state of emergency was declared on 27 November 1955, and the Greek Cypriot leader Archbishop Makarios was deported to the Seychelles on 9 March 1956. A ceasefire came into effect on 13 March 1959, and the state of emergency was lifted on 4 December 1959. Cyprus became an independent Republic on 16 August 1960, but conflict between the two communities continued. On 15 July 1974 Archbishop Makarios was deposed as president in a coup by the National Guard, and replaced by Nikos Sampson, a former EOKA gunman. Fighting broke out between Greek and Turkish Cypriots. On 20 July 1974 Turkish forces invaded northern Cyprus. Sampson resigned on 23 July and a military standstill was agreed to on 30 July. Turkish forces renewed their advance on 14 August 1974. When a new ceasefire came into effect on 16 August the Turks controlled more than a third of the island. This became the independent republic of **North Cyprus**, recognized only by Turkey. The island remains divided and tension is high.

Czechoslovakia

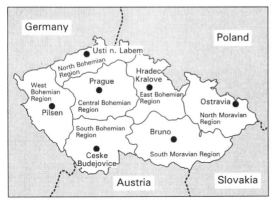

State in central Europe formed from the northern section of the Austro-Hungarian Empire following its collapse in 1918, containing a majority of Czechs in the west and Slovaks in the east, many Slovaks insisting they had separate status within a federation while the Czechs claimed to be creating one nation. Czechoslovakia also incorporated potentially destabilizing German and Hungarian minorities. Czechoslovakia made alliances with Romania and Yugoslavia (the Little Entente) in 1921, France (1924) and the Soviet Union (1935). But German minority agitation led to President Benes's acceptance of the loss of the five million population of **Sudetenland** to Nazi Germany following the **Munich** conference in 1938. Germany occupied the remainder of the country in March 1939, forming the Protectorate of Bohemia and Moravia and a

65

nominally independent **Slovakia**. President Benes returned from exile in 1945 to lead a coalition government which included the Communist Party. In 1948 the Communists under Klement Gottwald gained control with Soviet backing. A phase of liberalization ("socialism with a human face"), begun under Alexander Dubcek during the **Prague** Spring in 1968, was crushed by a Warsaw Pact invasion in August. A hardliner, Gustav Husak, became president. In December 1989 the Communist regime was ousted in the Velvet Revolution, a prominent dissident Vaclav Havel becoming president in 1990. On 1 January 1993 the country divided into separate states, the Czech Republic and Slovakia.

Czech Republic
See **Czechoslovakia**.

Dachau (Germany)

Bavarian town and site of a Nazi concentration camp. Established on 10 March 1933, it was the first concentration camp in Germany and acted as the model for all subsequent similar camps. During the Second World War it had 150 sub-camps across Bavaria and Austria under its control. It became the first and most prominent camp to use prisoners for medical and scientific experiments. An estimated 40,000 died before liberation by US forces on 29 April 1945. 260 SS officers were then imprisoned before being tried and executed for war crimes.

Dakar (Senegal)

Naval base in **French West Africa**, now capital of Senegal. Following the fall of France in June 1940 the fate of the French fleet was in doubt. The battleship *Richelieu*, stationed in Dakar, refused either to join the Allies or be disarmed. On 8 July 1940 the *Richelieu* was torpedoed and disabled by bombers from HMS *Hermes*. **Vichy** control of Dakar still posed a threat to Allied communication lines. A combined British–Free French force arrived on 23 September 1940 but after three days of exchanging fire with the Vichy defenders, the Allies withdrew. All of French West Africa switched to the Allies after the invasion of French North Africa in November 1942.

Dakota Building (United States)

Apartment block in Manhattan, New York. On 8 December 1980 Beatle John Lennon was murdered while walking home with his wife, Yoko Ono. He was shot by Mark Chapman, who was waiting for him outside Lennon's home in the Dakota Building. Lennon later died in the Roosevelt Hospital.

Dallas (United States)

City in central Texas. On 22 November 1963 President Kennedy was assassinated while driving in a motorcade through Dealey Plaza in the city centre. The Governor of Texas, John Connally, was also shot and wounded. Lyndon Johnson was sworn in as the 36th President on board the plane carrying Jacqueline Kennedy and her husband's body back to Washington. Lee Harvey Oswald, arrested for the assassination, was shot dead by Jack Ruby at the Dallas Police Headquarters on 24 November. Set up to investigate the events, the Warren Commission ruled out a conspiracy, stating that Oswald and Ruby had both acted alone. Subsequent investigations have cast doubt on this view, and many people now believe that there was more than one assassin involved.

Damansky

Disputed island (also known as Chenpaodao) in the Ussuri river on the border between China and Russia. Long-standing Sino-Soviet border disputes erupted into serious fighting on Damansky Island on 2 March 1969. Each side blamed the other for the clash, in which 31 Soviet frontier guards were killed. The fighting spread further west to the border between Sinkiang and Kazakhstan. On 11 September 1969 the Soviet leader, Alexei Kosygin, who was returning from the funeral of Ho Chi Minh in Hanoi, stopped briefly at Beijing (Peking) airport for a meeting with Chou En-lai. Talks were arranged and tension on the border subsided.

Damascus (Syria)

Former Ottoman city, captured by the British (with Arab support) in October 1918. Subsequently capital of Syria, the city gave its name to the 1991 Damascus Declaration. This declaration by Syria, Egypt and the six members of the GCC pledged Syrian and Egyptian military aid for the GCC states in return for economic assistance. It came in the wake of Iraq's ejection from **Kuwait** by UN forces in February 1991 and was meant to demonstrate Arab solidarity. The declaration has, however, not been implemented, the GCC states preferring to rely on Western military assistance.

Da Nang (Vietnam)

City and main port of central Vietnam. During the **Vietnam** War it was just south of the border dividing the North and South. On 8 March 1965, 3,500 US Marines from the 9th Brigade landed at Da Nang, marking the arrival of the first US combat troops in the Vietnam War.

Da Nang

Danzig (Poland)

Port on the Baltic Sea. In the Treaty of **Versailles** (1919) this predominantly German port was made a Free City under German administration. The **Polish Corridor** was created around it to give the new Polish state access to the sea. The Danzig Assembly elections of 1933 and 1935 gave the Nazi Party a majority of seats. In March 1939 Hitler demanded the return of Danzig to Germany, forcing Britain and France to guarantee Polish security. On 1 September Danzig's Nazi leader proclaimed the city's union with Germany as German forces crossed into Poland. Liberated by the Red Army, the city was returned to Poland in March 1945. Since the Second World War it has been known as Gdansk. In the summer of 1980 17,000 workers at the Lenin Shipyards led by Lech Walesa went on strike. As the unrest spread, 36 regional trade unions formed Solidarity, a new coalition, on 22 September 1980 and elected Walesa as chairman. Solidarity was suspended under martial law in December 1981 and then dissolved in October 1982. Walesa became President of Poland in the 1990 elections, but was defeated in the 1995 presidential contest.

Danzig

Dardanelles

The 40-mile strait between the Aegean Sea and the Sea of Marmara. By the 1841 Convention of London it was closed to all warships. In 1914, however, German warships anchored in Constantinople (now Istanbul) and in November 1914 Turkey closed the strait to all commerce, cutting Russia off from her allies, Britain and France. In January 1915 concern about Russia's position and the desire to rally Bulgaria and Greece to the Entente powers led to a plan by Lord Fisher, the First Sea Lord, and Winston Churchill, First Lord of the Admiralty, to force the Dardanelles with warships and to seize the **Gallipoli** peninsula on the southernmost European shore of the Dardanelles, with Constantinople, on the Bosphorus, as the ultimate objective. Naval bombardment of Turkish forts opened on 19 February, followed by an attempt to force the straits with a large Anglo-French fleet. When several of the vessels were disabled by mines, the naval assault was abandoned and a force of 78,000 men directed to seize the Gallipoli peninsula. The landings began on 25 April 1915, by the British at Cape Hellas on the tip of the peninsula, by a French force on the mainland of Asia Minor, and by ANZAC forces at Anzac Cove, twenty-five miles further north. The Turks were prepared for the landings and inflicted very heavy casualties on the British and ANZAC forces. Turkish command of the strategic high points prevented the attacking forces moving inland and achieving their objective. A further landing at **Suvla Bay** on 6 August failed to break the stalemate and the British commander, Sir Ian Hamilton, was relieved of his command on 15 October. The new commander, Sir Charles Monroe, recommended evacuation, confirmed by Lord Kitchener, the

Secretary of State for War, in November. Between 10 December 1915 and 9 January 1916 all troops were withdrawn after suffering 250,000 casualties. In 1918, with the collapse of the Ottoman Empire, the Straits were placed under an international commission and opened to all vessels at all times. This was modified by the 1923 Treaty of **Lausanne** which restricted passage for warships to those of under 10,000 tonnes, and only in peacetime. The 1936 **Montreux** Convention returned control to Turkey.

Darwin (Australia)

Capital of Northern Territory. A large Allied naval base during the Second World War, it was a prime target for Japan. On 19 February 1942 much of the town and base was damaged during a heavy bombing raid by 135 Japanese aircraft. Most damage was done by a direct hit on a ship loaded with explosives. The chain reaction of explosions sank a US destroyer and five other ships, ruined the port area and killed 240 people. Japanese air raids continued until the arrival of US fighter cover in March 1942. On Christmas Day 1974 the city was completely destroyed by Cyclone Tracy, killing over 50 people and leaving thousands homeless.

Daugavpils

See **Dvinsk**.

Dawson's Field (Jordan)

Desert airstrip in the north. It attracted world attention in September 1970 when Palestinian terrorists from the left-wing Popular Front for the Liberation of Palestine (PFLP) seized three planes en route to New York. The Swissair and TWA planes were flown to Dawson's Field. The Pan Am plane was flown to Beirut and then on to Cairo, where it was evacuated and blown up. A further plane, a BOAC VC10, en route from Bombay to London was hijacked on 9 September and flown to Dawson's Field. The three planes were destroyed on 12 September. The hostages were freed during the remainder of September as part of a deal for the release of Arab terrorists held in Europe. The action of the terrorists was bitterly opposed by King Hussein as well as Yasser Arafat. As a result, the incident was of major importance in Middle East history, leading as it did to the expulsion of the PLO from Jordan.

Dayton (Ohio, United States)

Location (in Wright-Patterson Air Force Base near Dayton) of the talks in November 1995 aimed at ending the war in **Bosnia-Hercegovina** (in former **Yugoslavia**). The eventual Dayton Accord envisaged the following main points: Bosnia-Hercegovina was to be preserved as a single state within its existing borders, and with international recognition; the state was to consist of the Bosnian and Croat Federation and the Bosnian Serb Republic with a "fair" distribution; **Sarajevo** was to stay united under a central government, with a national parliament, presidency and constitutional court, and the presidency and parliament would be elected democratically. In addition, a large force of US and NATO troops was to be stationed in Bosnia-Hercegovina to enforce the ceasefire. Local Bosnian Serb leaders expressed anger at the settlement.

Dayton (Tennessee, United States)

Seat of Rhea County in southern Tennessee. In May 1925 a local schoolteacher, John Scopes, was arrested for teaching Darwin's theory of evolution. The ensuing Monkey Trial (10–21 July 1925) was prosecuted by former Presidential candidate William Jennings Bryan, and defended by socialist agnostic Clarence Darrow. Although Darrow successfully discredited Bryan's interpretation of the Book of Genesis, Scopes was found guilty of violating State law and fined $100. The decision was later overturned by the Tennessee Supreme Court. Bryan died five days after the trial's conclusion.

Dazhai (China)

Commune which became the "model village" showered with praise by Mao Tse-tung. From 1964 to 1978 Dazhai (with its tiny population of 500) became the most famous village in China, visited by up to 20,000 party faithful each day (an estimated seven million in all). Of great propaganda importance to Mao, the head of the village, Chen Yonggui, was promoted to the Politburo and made a Vice Prime Minister. It is now known that the grain yields claimed for Dazhai, and its impressive buildings, were either fakes or the work of the army not the local peasants.

Deblin (Poland)

See **Ivangorod**.

Deir Yasin (Palestine)

Village site of a massacre by Zionist Irgun and Lehi guerrillas in April 1948 in which over 200 Palestinians were killed. The event is remembered by them as the spur for the mass exodus of Arabs from Palestine which followed.

Demilitarized Zone (Korea)
Zone along the **38th Parallel** dividing North and South Korea, established in 1953 following invasion of South Korea by the Communist north in 1950.

Demilitarized zone, Korea

Democracy Wall (China)
Site on Changan Avenue in Beijing (**Peking**) first prominent during the Hundred Flowers Campaign in 1957 when radical students used wall posters to protest at their courses. Students again used the wall as a focus for their calls for more democracy in 1978–9.

Demyansk (Russia)
Town between Moscow and St Petersburg. The Soviet counter-offensive of January 1942 succeeded in pushing the Germans back from their positions around Moscow. As a result over 100,000 troops from the German 16th Army became trapped in a pocket around Demyansk. In the first-ever major airlift the beleaguered troops were supplied and reinforced by air for five months until being relieved by German forces in May.

Denmark
Scandinavian country bordering with Germany. Neutral during the First World War, Denmark attempted the same in the Second World War but was invaded by Germany on 9 April 1940. Early resistance was overcome quickly and the country surrendered, giving the German *Luftwaffe* control of the airfields needed for the invasion of **Norway**. Liberation came in May 1945, King Christian X having stayed throughout the occupation. Iceland was given independence in 1945 and then Denmark abandoned its neutrality by joining NATO in 1949 and the EEC in 1973. In a crucial referendum in 1992, the Danes rejected the **Maastricht** Treaty, causing anxiety across Europe. The Treaty was approved in a second vote once certain modifications had been negotiated.

Derry (Northern Ireland)
See **Londonderry**.

Detroit (United States)

Major industrial city in Michigan, synonymous with the US automobile industry. The industrialization of Michigan began in 1903 when Henry Ford opened his car manufacturing factory in Detroit. In later years other firms, such as General Motors and Chrysler, also established automobile plants here.

Devil's Island (French Guiana)

Penal colony and place of exile for political prisoners, in use until 1937.

Dewline

Acronym for the Distant Early Warning Viewing Line, established in 1957 by NORAD. It formed a section of a comprehensive radar system built to detect the approach of nuclear missiles or enemy aircraft. It stretched across the Aleutian Islands, Alaska, North Canada, South Greenland to Iceland and its main purpose was to detect a surprise first strike by the Soviet Union against North America. The equivalent in the Soviet Union was the Tallinin Line.

Dhahran (Saudi Arabia)

Location of a key allied airbase during the 1991 Gulf War. It was later the target of a major terrorist attack by Islamic militants in June 1996, when 23 US troops were killed and over 300 other personnel injured. The explosion followed an earlier attack in November 1995 when six US troops were killed in a car bomb attack on a US training facility in Riyadh. The bombing at Khobar Towers on the King Abdul Aziz airbase was the worst outrage against American forces in the Middle East since militants blew up the marine barracks in **Beirut** in 1983, killing 241 people.

Dhofar (Oman)

Remote region, the scene of a rebellion in the 1960s against the ruling Sultan, Said bin Taimur. Civil war broke out in 1965 between the sultan's armed forces (with British, Iranian, Jordanian and Saudi Arabian support) and dissident tribesmen in the Dhofar (the PFLO), who had won control of most of the region by 1970. On 23 July 1970 Sultan Said bin Taimur was deposed by his son, Qaboos, who greatly strengthened the armed forces. With foreign assistance, including an Iranian expeditionary force of 2,000, the revolt was suppressed, and the sultan officially declared the war had ended on 11 December 1975. The PFLO denied this and occasional guerrilla activity continued. In 1976 Qaboos offered amnesty to all those who had fought in the PFLO. Many took advantage of it. Iran began to withdraw her troops in 1977 and the British also began to reduce their presence in Oman.

Diaoyutai Archipelago

See **Senkaku Islands**.

Dien Bien Phu (Vietnam)

The crucial battle which lost the French Empire in **Indo-China**. In November 1953, the French commander in Indo-China, General Navarre, fortified Dien Bien Phu, a valley 200 miles west of Hanoi, with 15,000 men to cut the supply routes of the Viet Minh guerrillas into **Laos** and to draw them into a pitched battle. But the French had underestimated the capability of General Giap, the Viet Minh commander, to concentrate men and heavy artillery on the hills overlooking Dien Bien Phu. The vital airfield was rendered unusable. On 7 May, the fifty-sixth day of the siege, the French command post was overrun, and organized resistance ceased. The French had lost 2,293, 5,134 were wounded, and 6,000 were taken prisoner. Their victory had cost the Viet Minh 23,000 casualties. On 8 May, a Peace Conference convened at **Geneva** on 26 April turned to discuss the problems of Indo-China. A ceasefire came into effect on 21 July 1954. Laos and **Cambodia** were recognized as independent and neutral countries. **Vietnam** was divided at the **17th parallel**. The north was to be controlled

Gulf of Tonkin, Saigon

by Ho Chi Minh and the Communists. The south was to be governed by Bao Dai. In this agreement lay the seeds of a further twenty years of war for Vietnam.

Dieppe (France)

Seaport on the Normandy coast. On 19 August 1942 7,000 British and Canadian troops launched an amphibious assault against the German defences (Operation Jubilee). The operation was an almost complete disaster with landing craft pinned down by heavy gunfire. Some tanks and troops established a foothold on the beach, but the order to withdraw was given. Allied casualties were high, particularly among the Canadians, with over two-thirds of their forces lost. The only redeeming factor of the débâcle was proving that a direct attack would only succeed on open beaches.

Dimona (Israel)

Site of Israel's nuclear plant in the Negev Desert. The existence of an Israeli nuclear arsenal was revealed to the world by technician Mordechai Vanunu in a *Sunday Times* report of 1986, after which he was kidnapped by *Mossad* agents in Rome and imprisoned in Israel for treason. The plant remains in operation despite international and Arab complaints that Israel is engaging in illegal nuclear proliferation.

Dixie (United States)

The name is derived from the Mason–Dixon line, the boundary between Pennsylvania and Maryland, drawn up by two English surveyors, Charles Mason and Jeremiah Dixon, between 1763 and 1767. The boundary had for some time previously been a matter of dispute. Later the line marked the boundary between the southern states which practised slavery and the northern states which did not. The Dixiecrats (the name given to those US Democrats who insisted on continuance of racial segregation and of white domination in the Southern states) attempted to block civil rights legislation by means of filibusters in the early 1960s.

Dnestr Republic

Slav-speaking region within **Moldavia**. It declared its independence of Romanian-speaking Moldavia, in August 1991, after a referendum. Bitter fighting then erupted before troops of the Russian 14th Army (which was stationed in Moldavia) intervened to end the bloodshed.

Dobrogea

See **Dobrudja**.

Dobrudja

Strategic region between the Danube and the Black Sea. Claimed by Romania and Bulgaria, control of the province was a constant goal of both countries. After the Second Balkan War, Bulgaria gained southern Dobrudja under the Treaty of **Bucharest** in 1913. During the First World War Bulgaria joined the Central Powers and occupied the region when Romanian forces capitulated. Romania, as a member of the victorious Allies, regained the province under the Treaty of **Neuilly** in 1919. Occupied again by Bulgaria in the Second World War, the **Paris** Peace Conference of 1947 resulted in the province's division, with southern Dobrudja being confirmed as Bulgarian.

Dobruja

See **Dobrudja**.

Dodecanese

Archipelago of 12 islands in the eastern Aegean. Most of the islands were seized by Italy in May 1912, with only Kastellorizon remaining in Turkish hands. In a special Article of the Treaty of **Sèvres** (1920), Turkey renounced all claims to the Dodecanese, and Italy was committed to ceding them to Greece. Italy denounced this Article in October 1922 and proceeded to extend its control. Italian became the official language and military bases were developed. British forces failed to capture the islands during the Second World War, and they were eventually occupied by German troops from 1943 to 1945. After a year of British rule, the islands were finally ceded to Greece by the Allies in 1947.

Dogger Bank

Sandbank in the North Sea about 60 miles east of the English coast. On 22 October 1904 the Russian Baltic Fleet, en route to Japan, encountered a British fishing fleet and, mistaking them for Japanese gunboats, opened fire, sinking two trawlers and their captains. Russia later paid Britain £65,000 in compensation. During the First World War Dogger Bank was the scene of the fourth naval battle of the war. A German squadron was challenged by the British Grand Fleet on 24 January 1915. Both sides sustained casualties with the German battle-cruiser *Blücher* being sunk, prompting a German retreat to **Heligoland**. The British disengaged too soon, losing the chance to capitalize on their advantage.

Dominica

Caribbean republic, the island was the scene of a civil war which broke out on 24 April 1965 between the Constitutionalists, supporting former President Bosch, and the Loyalist forces of President Reid Cabral. On 28 April 1965, 400 US marines were sent in to prevent a left-wing takeover, and during the next month a further 24,000 US troops were landed. A ceasefire was signed on 6 May and at the end of May an Inter-American Peacekeeping Force, comprising units from the USA, Honduras, Nicaragua, Costa Rica, Brazil and El Salvador, under the auspices of the OAS, was formed to keep the warring factions apart.

Donbass (Ukraine)

Heavily-industrialized region, formerly in the Soviet Union, now in the eastern part of the independent republic of the Ukraine. The name is a merger of "Don Basin". The Russian-speaking community have little sympathy for the Ukraine and there is a growing movement for union with Russia with all the implications for social unrest that this may bring.

Doornkop (South Africa)

Site where Jameson, the Imperialist associate of Cecil Rhodes, was captured after the abortive Jameson raid into the Transvaal in 1896. Jameson's force had earlier been intercepted and defeated at Krugersdorp on 1 January 1896. Jameson was handed over to the British for trial and received a short prison sentence. The humiliating failure caused the resignation of Cecil Rhodes as Prime Minister of the Cape. The whole episode constituted one more step on the road to war in South Africa.

Dora Line
See **Adolf Hitler Line**.

Dorpat (Estonia)
See **Tartu**.

Downing Street (England)
Location of the residence of the British Prime Minister (No 10). Agreement announced on 15 December 1993 between British Prime Minister John Major and Irish Prime Minister Albert Reynolds in an attempt to open the way to peace in Northern Ireland. The declaration (known as the Downing Street Declaration) offered Sinn Fein participation in multi-party talks on Ireland's future within three months of a ceasefire. Although the loyalist veto on unification remained, Britain adopted a near-neutral position on the possibility. The declaration followed meetings between Sinn Fein president Gerry Adams and SDLP leader John Hume and the revelation in November 1993 that the British government had held secret talks with Sinn Fein in February 1993. Hopes of immediate peace were disappointed but the IRA announced a ceasefire on 31 August 1994 (this was ended in early 1996).

Drancy (France)
Four miles from Paris, and originally designed as a public housing estate, Drancy assumed the role in the Second World War of an effective concentration centre for Jews to be deported to **Auschwitz**. Of 74,000 Jews sent from Drancy, including women and children, fewer than 3,000 survived. Drancy was run by the French for French Jews arrested by French police.

Dresden (Germany)
City, the capital of Saxony. Scene of one of the heaviest allied bombing raids of the Second World War. On the night of 13–14 February 1945, a massive raid began when 723 RAF Lancaster bombers and 450 Flying Fortresses of the US 8th Air Force bombed the city. The bombing was followed up on successive nights. Dresden was seen as a strategically important communications target, although it had not previously been bombed and housed an estimated 200,000 refugees. The firestorm set off by the raids tore the heart out of Dresden, whose architectural and cultural treasures had earned it the title of Florence on the Elbe. East German documents released in the early 1990s suggest some 25,000 people died. Over 30,000 buildings were destroyed, including one-third of its houses and most of its baroque and Renaissance buildings; the royal palace and the opera house were reduced to rubble. The *Frauenkirche* (Dresden's architectural symbol) collapsed two days after the raid.

Drina

First World War battle along the Drina River on the Bosnian–Serb border. On 8 September 1914 the Austrians invaded **Serbia** by crossing the Drina. Serb troops were outnumbered and outgunned across the whole front, but managed to hold the Austrians in the north. The Austrians made considerable gains in the south, but a fierce counter-offensive by the Serbs on 14 September drove them back to the river. The lines became entrenched and fighting all but ceased.

Drumcree (Northern Ireland)

Small village near Portadown in County Armagh. A Protestant group known as the Spirit of Drumcree was formed after the stand-off confrontation between Orangemen and the Royal Ulster Constabulary in summer 1995. Thousands of Orangemen gathered in Drumcree in July 1995 to enforce their demand to march their traditional route through the nationalist Garvaghy Road area of Portadown. Confrontation again took place a year later in July 1996. The mass mobilization by the Orange Order caused the RUC to allow the march, to the fury of the Catholics. These events caused a crisis in the peace talks.

Dublin (Ireland)

Capital city of the Republic, and scene of the Easter Rising (24–29 April 1916). The Irish Republican Brotherhood, supported by Sinn Fein, organized an armed insurrection beginning on Easter Monday. With 2,000 members of the Irish Citizen Army and Irish Volunteers, they seized several public buildings including the General Post Office and proclaimed an Irish republic. Fierce street fighting followed for the next five days until the British troops forced the surrender of the insurgents. Irish leaders Patrick Pearse and James Connolly were executed with 14 others, and over 2,000 more imprisoned. Although the rising had had little public support, the executions aroused anti-British sentiment and Sinn Fein won the majority vote in the 1918 election.

Dukla Pass

Traditional invasion route from Russia into Czechoslovakia. A bloody battle took place in 1944 when 80,000 Red Army troops, together with 6,500 Czechs and Slovaks, died attempting to take the valley from the defending Nazis. A huge granite memorial can be seen in memory of those who died. Nearby is Višný Komárnik, the first village to be liberated in Czechoslovakia (on 6 October 1944).

Dumbarton Oaks (United States)

Site in Washington DC of the August 1944 Conference at which delegates of the USA, Soviet Union, United Kingdom and China met to outline international post-war security. Proposals published on 7 October 1944 recommended a UN organization to preserve world peace and a Security Council on which the USA, Soviet Union, United Kingdom, France and China would play a central role with veto powers.

Dunajec (Poland)
First World War battle along this river in southern Poland. A strong Austrian–German attack in April 1915 succeeded in breaking through the Russian lines along a ten-mile front. By 11 May the Russians had been forced to retreat, losing 100,000 men as prisoners, but managed to avoid being completely routed.

Dunblane (Scotland)
Town, site of school massacre on 13 March 1996. A lone gunman, Thomas Hamilton, killed sixteen young children and a teacher in Dunblane Primary School before committing suicide. It was the worst tragedy of its type in modern British history (exceeding the high casualties at **Hungerford** in 1987). The government set up the Cullen Inquiry to report on the massacre amid calls for a major tightening of gun laws.

Dunkirk (France)
Channel port in northern France. The scene in the Second World War of the now legendary evacuation of the British Army in the face of the advancing German forces. From 27 May to 4 June 1940, almost 340,000 British and French troops, retreating from the German armoured advance as Belgian forces collapsed and French resistance wavered, were successfully ferried from the beaches across the Channel to England. Warships, other large vessels, and innumerable "little boats" from every available source carried most (but not all) the troops to the safety of England. The "Spirit of Dunkirk" refers to these events. After the war, on 4 March 1947, the Treaty of Dunkirk was signed. This was an Anglo-French agreement to provide mutual assistance against any future German aggressive threats, together with consultation over economic relations, symbolizing post-war French re-emergence as a major European power.

Durand Line
Border between Afghanistan and present-day Pakistan delineated in 1893 by Sir Mortimer Durand.

Dutch East Indies
See **Netherlands East Indies**.

Dvinsk (Latvia)
Town in southern Latvia, now called Daugavpils. Location of First World War battle.

During the first Battle of the Dvina (August 1915), German troops secured a bridgehead across the river near Dvinsk. Three successive assaults on the city were repelled by the Russians. A second battle lasted for much of 1916, until the Brusilov Offensive in **Galicia** forced both sides to redeploy troops, producing a stalemate on the Dvina.

Eastern Front
Term for the battleground between Germany and Russia in the First World War, and Germany and the Soviet Union in the Second World War.

Eastern Slavonia
Easternmost part of Croatia, bordering Serbia. It was seized by rebel Serbs during the Serbo-Croat War of 1991. Bitter fighting took place in the main towns of Osijek and **Vukovar**.

East Pakistan
Former name of **Bangladesh**, before it gained independence from Pakistan in the 1971 War of Independence. When British rule ended in the Indian sub-continent, the two nations of India and Pakistan were created. But Pakistan was geographically separated into two halves, West Pakistan to the northwest of India, and East Pakistan (essentially East Bengal). Increasingly there was resentment in East Pakistan against the domination of West Pakistan.

East Timor
Former Portuguese colony, now part of Indonesia. In June 1975 Portugal announced its intention of holding independence elections in its colony of East Timor. On 11 August 1975 the moderate Timor Democratic Union which favoured continuing links with Portugal attempted to stage a coup, but by 20 August civil war had broken out with the Communist group FRETILIN. As increasing numbers of refugees fled into Indonesian West Timor, Indonesian troops entered East Timor on 7 December 1975 to forestall a left-wing take-over. By 28 December the Indonesians were in control, and East Timor was officially integrated into Indonesia on 17 July 1976. Many thousands of FRETILIN supporters were interned. Guerrilla resistance met with ferocious Indonesian reprisals. Several massacres shocked the world (see **Santa Cruz (Indonesia)**). A limited resistance still continues against Indonesian oppression.

Eben Emael
Modern fortress on the Dutch–Belgian border at the confluence of the Maas River and Albert Canal. Built to guard strategic bridges and designed with the lessons of First World War sieges in mind, the fort was regarded as impregnable. As the German offensive in the Low Countries began on 10 May 1940, 85 German soldiers landed by glider on the fort. Pinned down by fire from nearby forts, the Germans waited for reinforcements to cross the canal by boat before capturing the fort on 11 May.

Ebola (Zaïre)
River in northern Zaïre which gave its name to the highly fatal disease, Ebola Fever, also known as Viral Haemorrhagic Fever. First diagnosed after outbreaks in 1976 in Zaïre and Sudan, it has a 60–80% mortality rate. It causes massive internal bleeding, usually resulting in death within 10 days. Further outbreaks occurred in Zaïre in 1995.

Ebro River (Spain)

Civil War battle fought along Spain's longest river. In a bid to relieve pressure on **Madrid** and Valencia, the Republicans attacked across the lower Ebro. The initial assault (24–25 July 1938) pushed the Nationalists back 25 miles before being contained in August. Over the next two months the Republicans were repeatedly bombed from the air and assaulted on land in a series of fierce counter-attacks. The International Brigades withdrew from the Republican side in late September after suffering 75 per cent casualties. A massive Nationalist offensive finally drove the Republicans back across the Ebro on 18 November. In this crucial confrontation the Republicans, with 30,000 dead and 40,000 wounded or captured, lost their last main army.

Edgewood (United States)

Site in Maryland of US Army Aberdeen Proving Ground, location of the chemical and biological testing programme.

Eelam

Name of the independent Tamil State which the Tamil Tigers in **Sri Lanka** are seeking to establish.

Eire

Name by which Southern Ireland (now Republic of Ireland) was known from 1937 to 1949 when it was part of the British Commonwealth.

Ekaterinburg (Russia)

See **Yekaterinburg**.

El Ferrol (Spain)

Port and birthplace of the Spanish dictator, General Franco, and also the largest base of the Spanish navy.

Ellis Island (United States)

Small island in Upper New York Bay off Manhattan Island. Until 1943 it served as the major immigration station for millions of Europeans arriving in the USA. It was then used as a detention centre for illegal aliens and deportees. Closed in 1954, it became part of the Statue of Liberty National Monument and was reopened to tourists in 1976.

El Mozote (El Salvador)

Abandoned village in which one of the worst massacres of the 1980s civil war was perpetrated. The Atlacatl Battalion, under the orders of Colonel Domingo Monterrosa, assassinated hundreds of defenceless peasants here in 1981. In the 1990s, forensic specialists began slowly exhuming the bodies of more than 1,000 peasants brutally killed by troops of the élite US-created Atlacatl battalion.

El Salvador
Smallest republic in Central America. The centre of a bitter civil war from the 1970s. Guerrilla activity by the left-wing Farabundo Martí National Liberation Front intensified after 1979. Conflict between the 40,000-strong Salvadoran army, backed by the USA, and 9,000 Liberation Front guerrillas reached a stalemate by the end of 1986. Following the election of Alfredo Cristiani of the right-wing Republican Nationalist Alliance as president in March 1989, talks took place with the rebels in Mexico City in September. These broke down, and a guerrilla offensive launched on 11 November 1989 brought some of the worst fighting of the decade. A UN ceasefire was negotiated on 31 December 1991. On 1 February 1992, the UN-negotiated truce went into effect, formally ending 12 years of civil war.

Elsass-Lothringen (France)
See **Alsace-Lorraine**.

Eniwetok (Marshall Islands)
Pacific atoll famous as the location of the first H-bomb test on 1 November 1952 by the USA.

Entebbe (Uganda)
Town, the scene on 3 July 1976 of one of the most spectacular operations ever mounted against terrorist hijackers. On 27 June 1976, Palestinian and Baader-Meinhof terrorists hijacked an Air France A300B Airbus en route from Tel Aviv to Paris, shortly after it left Athens. The terrorists forced the plane to fly to Entebbe in Uganda, where they demanded the release of 53 prisoners from jails in Israel, Kenya, West Germany, Switzerland and France. On 3 July, 200 Israeli commandos, transported in three C-130 Hercules aircraft, made a surprise assault on Entebbe and rescued the 106 hostages. All seven hijackers and 20 Ugandan troops were killed, together with three hostages and an Israeli officer, Lieutenant Colonel Nethanyahu. An Israeli woman, Mrs Dora Block, who had been moved to a Kampala hospital, was believed to have been murdered.

Entebbe

83

Eritrea

Former Italian colony in East Africa. It was occupied by British forces in 1941 and subsequently administered by Britain. Eritrea was integrated into the Ethiopian Empire on 14 November 1962. Separatist guerrillas succeeded in taking control of most of Eritrea except the capital, Asmara, by the end of 1977. The conclusion of the **Ogaden** war in March 1978 enabled the Ethiopian army, with Cuban and Soviet assistance, to launch a major counter-offensive in Eritrea on 15 May 1978. Warfare continued in the 1980s, and the Ethiopian government was also faced with a guerrilla campaign in Tigré Province by the Tigréan People's Liberation Army. On 18 May 1989, President Mengistu offered talks with the two separatist movements. Talks took place, but no agreement on an end to the conflict had been reached by the beginning of 1991. Guerrilla success increased in early 1991, leading to the flight of Mengistu on 21 May. Addis Ababa fell on 28 May. Eritrea subsequently proclaimed its independence, which was confirmed by referendum in 1993.

Estonia

Independent republic on the Baltic Sea. A province of the Tsarist Russian Empire, it was occupied by Germany during the First World War. Estonian independence was declared on 24 February 1918, but was not secured until 2 February 1920 after Estonian forces had defeated both German and Soviet troops. Annexed by the Soviet Union in 1940, it was again occupied by Germany 1941–4. Multi-party elections in March 1990 led to a new coalition government and a referendum on independence in March 1991. 77.8 per cent voted for independence, which was declared on 20 August 1991 and recognized by the Soviet Union on 10 September 1991.

Ethiopia

See **Abyssinia**.

Ettrick Bridge (Scotland)

Home in the Scottish borders of Liberal Party leader Sir David Steel where, on 29 May 1983, he replaced SDP leader (and Prime Minister-designate) Roy Jenkins as the main Alliance figure in the general election campaign. This followed Liberal criticisms that Jenkins, despite his political experience, was an ineffective campaigner.

Eupen-et-Malmédy (Belgium)

Territory originally part of the Austrian Netherlands, ceded to Prussia in 1815 and to Belgium in 1919 (confirmed by plebiscite in 1920). The area's significant German-speaking population prompted pre-Second World War Nazi demands for its return. A Cultural Council was established in 1972 to protect the interests of German speakers.

European Community
See **European Union**.

European Union
Political and economic union of western Europe, previously known as the European Community (EC). Created by the Treaty of **Rome** in 1957, the European Community had six original members: Belgium, France, Italy, Luxembourg, The Netherlands and West Germany. In 1973 Denmark, Ireland and the United Kingdom joined, followed by Greece in 1981 and Spain and Portugal in 1986. The **Maastricht** Treaty of December 1991 created the framework for political and economic union. The European Union was established on 1 November 1993 when Maastricht came into effect. Austria, Finland and Sweden all joined on 1 January 1995.

Euzkadi (Spain)
Basque national homeland in northeast Spain, granted autonomy in October 1936. Euzkadi was occupied by General Franco's nationalist forces in June 1937 and Basque political and cultural nationalism was repressed until his death in 1975.

Everett (United States)
Scene in the state of Washington of a massacre of members of the radical left-wing union, the IWW, who travelled to the city to support striking lumber workers in May 1916. As 250 IWW members arrived by ferry they were met with an unprovoked armed attack from a sheriff and his deputies. Five died, six were missing and 27 passengers were injured. The IWW members fired back, mortally wounding a company official. None of the assailants was charged but 74 IWW members were put on trial.

Evian-les-Bains (France)
Spa town. Site of a series of agreements in March 1962 between the government of France's General de Gaulle and Algerian nationalist leader Ben Bella. The agreements brought about a ceasefire in the eight-year-old war of Algerian independence and a guarantee of French withdrawal. They were ratified by referenda in France (April) and Algeria (July) but violently attacked by the extremist French OAS. See also **Algeria**.

Exeter (England)
Cathedral city. Target in the Second World War of the *Luftwaffe* in the so-called Baedeker Blitz. German planes attacked cities with cultural and historic treasures, allegedly selected from the popular Baedeker travel guides.

Falaise (France)

Town in Normandy, southeast of Caen. The Allied breakout from **Normandy** in August 1944 forced German troops into headlong retreat. By mid-month Canadian and British advances from the north, combined with US attacks from the west and south, had trapped 80,000 Germans in a pocket between Falaise and Argentan. Under heavy bombardment 20,000 Germans escaped through the narrow gap between the two towns before it was closed on 20 August. 50,000 troops surrendered and over 10,000 were killed.

Falkland Islands

British-ruled territory in the South Atlantic claimed by Argentina. Scene of:
1) naval battle in December 1914 in which four German cruisers (the *Scharnhorst, Gneisenau, Nurnberg* and *Leipzig*) were sunk by a British fleet with the loss of 1,800 lives. No British ships were sunk;
2) an Argentine invasion on 2 April 1982. See the Falklands War in Appendix 2.

Far Eastern Republic

Short-lived republic comprised of territories east of Lake Baikal, with its capital at Chita. It included Vladivostock and existed from 6 April 1920 until 20 November 1922 in the period of the Russian Civil War. Nominally independent, it was effectively controlled by the Bolsheviks. It served as a buffer between Japan and Soviet Russia. It was subsequently joined to the Soviet Union.

Farraka (India)

Site of a barrage on the Ganges constructed by India in 1970 to control the flow of the river's waters. Its siting less than 13 miles upstream from the border with Bangladesh provoked continuing tension between the two countries.

Fashoda (Sudan)

Location of the Fashoda Incident, a crisis in Anglo-French relations as a result of rival claims to Sudan. A French detachment under Colonel Marchand had marched to the town on the Upper Nile from **French West Africa**, reaching it in July 1898, just before the arrival of General Kitchener, fresh from his defeat of the Mahdi's forces at **Omdurman**, with a large Anglo-Egyptian army. France's claim to the area by right of prior conquest was hotly disputed by Britain who wished to retain control of the Nile Valley. A "war scare" was fanned in both countries by the popular press, but France's distraction by the Dreyfus affair and lack of support from Russia forced her to back down. Marchand withdrew from Fashoda in November 1898 and France agreed in March 1899 to renounce all claims to the Nile Valley. Now known as Kodok.

Fatima (Portugal)

Site of the alleged appearance of Our Lady of the Rosary to three shepherd girls on 13 May 1917 and on a number of occasions in later months. A chapel was built in the area and has become one of the most important places of pilgrimage for Roman Catholics. An assassination attempt was made on Pope John Paul II when he visited the shrine in 1982.

Federation of Rhodesia and Nyasaland

See **Central African Federation**.

Feldvidek

Region of Czechoslovakia between the two World Wars. Under the first Vienna Award of 2 November 1938 the region was transferred from Czechoslovakia to Hungary.

Fez (Morocco)

Town in northern Morocco.

1) Location of the protectorate treaty signed with France on 30 March 1912. This treaty (together with a convention signed between France and Spain at Madrid on 27 November 1912) divided Morocco into French and Spanish spheres of influence. France had earlier provoked international tension by occupying Fez in May 1911.

2) At the 12th Arab League Summit held in Fez in September 1982 King Fahd's proposals for a solution to the Arab–Israeli conflict were accepted by the Arab League.

Finland Station (Russia)

Major railway station in **St Petersburg** (formerly **Leningrad**, previously Petrograd) at which Lenin arrived from exile in Switzerland on 16 April 1917. Welcoming the February revolution in a speech to his waiting Bolshevik supporters, he wrongly forecast a successful German revolution as a preliminary to a world socialist revolution.

Fiume (Slovenia)

Port in the northern Adriatic and part of the Austro-Hungarian Empire until 1918. Claimed by both Italy and the emerging Yugoslav kingdom in 1919, there were proposals to make it a free city. The port was seized on 12 September 1919 by the Italian adventurer Gabriele D'Annunzio. On 12 November 1920 the Giolitti government signed an agreement at **Rapallo** settling disputes with Yugoslavia and creating an independent state of Fiume. Following clashes between Fiuman troops and Italian troops, D'Annunzio was forced out of Fiume on 5 January 1921. In January 1924 most of Fiume was incorporated into Italy, with Yugoslavia retaining the small port of Susak. Following the Second World War it was ceded to Yugoslavia. Also known as Rijeka.

Flanders

Flat region of northeastern France and southern Belgium, scene of many of the worst battles of the First World War, including **Yser, Ypres** and **Passchendaele**. The Allied advance in September–November 1918 is often referred to as the Battle of Flanders. Starting on 28 September the Allies succeeded in pushing the Germans back across Belgium, so that by Armistice Day the German frontier was in reach. The poppies that grew in the fields of Flanders after the war have since become the symbol of remembrance.

Flixborough (England)

Village in Humberside. In Britain's worst industrial accident, an explosion at the Nypro Works chemical plant near Flixborough killed 29 on 1 June 1974. The plant was destroyed by the ensuing inferno, and the village itself was reduced to rubble.

Formosa

See **Taiwan**.

Fort Breedonk (Belgium)

Fort near Antwerp. Site of the main concentration camp in Belgium during the Second World War. Used as a transit camp for deportees to eastern Europe, over 3,000 prisoners passed through the camp. 186 of them were shot or hanged by the Gestapo.

Fort Gulick (Panama Canal Zone)

Key US military training centre in Central America, it became the symbol of the "big stick" foreign policy of the USA in the region. Of the US Southern Command training schools, the School of the Americas at Fort Gulick was known throughout Latin America as the *escuela de golpes* (the school of coups).

Fourons (Belgium)

Commune which came to prominence in 1986 as the result of a language dispute when a French-speaking mayor refused to take a Flemish language test and was dismissed. The issue reflected Belgium's linguistic division – in Fourons French-speakers predominated, but the province in which it is situated (Flanders) is Flemish-speaking.

French West Africa

In 1895 French Guinea, French Sudan, Ivory Coast and Senegal were administratively united in a federation known as French West Africa. Dahomey joined in 1899, and Mauritania, Niger and Upper Volta joined as they became separate colonies.

Fulani (Nigeria)

African empire founded by Usman Dan Fodio. Its two centres were at Gwandu and Sokoto. The empire extended over much of what was to become the British Protectorate of Northern Nigeria. By 1903 the conquered Fulani empire was all under British rule but it remained a centre of Muslim religion.

Fulton (United States)

Town in Missouri, the setting in 1946 for the famous Iron Curtain speech by Winston Churchill, delivered at Westminster College. It was here that Churchill warned of the Iron Curtain that had descended over Eastern Europe, from Stettin in the Baltic to Trieste in the Adriatic.

Gaba Tepe (Turkey)

Hilly promontory on the west coast of the **Gallipoli** peninsula. Following the landings on 25 April 1915 at **Anzac Cove**, 2 miles to the north, Gaba Tepe became the southern anchor of the Allied lines. Constantly under attack, the Allied troops were finally evacuated on 20 December 1915, ending the catastrophic Gallipoli campaign.

Gabcikovo (Slovakia)

Site of the controversial hydro-electric dam on the Danube, on the border of Slovakia and Hungary. Originally planned as a joint twin-dam Hungarian–Czechoslovak project, Hungary dropped out in 1989 and planned to build its own dam at Nagymaros (125 miles downstream from Gabcikovo). The project had aroused enormous opposition, both domestic and international, on environmental and economic grounds, and soured relations between the countries involved.

Galicia

Largest province of the Austro-Hungarian Empire, now divided between Poland, Slovakia and the Ukraine. Austria-Hungary's opening offensive of the First World War was launched across the Russian–Galician border on 23 August 1914. The offensive soon collapsed as the numerically superior Russians counter-attacked, capturing **Lemberg** and **Przemysl**. Austrian losses were crippling – about two-thirds of their army. Sporadic fighting continued until the Russian assault of 1916, known as the Brusilov Offensive. Launched on 4 June, it drove deep into Galicia inflicting heavy casualties on the Austrians. German reinforcements succeeded in checking the offensive on 20 September. The campaign had forced the Central Powers to redeploy troops from the Western and Italian Fronts, saving the Allies at **Verdun** and **Asiagio**. Russia and Austria-Hungary were both so weakened that they were effectively out of the war.

Gallipolli (Turkey)

Scene of an attempt by the Allies between 25 April 1915 and 9 January 1916 to break through the **Dardanelles** to end the stalemate in the First World War, lessen the pressure on Russia and force Turkey from the war. The initial landing by Australian, British and New Zealand troops faced intense Turkish resistance. See also **Dardanelles**.

Gaza City

The British campaign in the Middle East during the First World War had several setbacks at Gaza before finally capturing this small town on the southwest coast of Palestine. In March 1917 General Murray's army attacked the Turkish defenders under the German colonel Baron von Kressenstein. The British were driven off with around 4,000 losses. In April repeated attacks resulted in no gains and over 6,400 additional losses. In November General Allenby again attacked, this time with a reinforced army and rolled up Turkish defences along the Beersheba–Gaza line. After the fall of Gaza Allenby was able to advance rapidly to **Jerusalem** which he took on 9 December.

Gazala (Libya)

Series of Second World War battles (May–June 1942) representing British armour's greatest defeat when 250 out of 300 tanks were lost to General Rommel's Afrika Korps. In a series of counter-attacks by Rommel's forces, Britain lost **Benghazi**, the inland harbour of Bir Hachem and **Tobruk**. In the so-called Gazala Gallop the remnants of the British Eighth Army fled to the Egyptian border, where General Auchinlek took charge and halted the rout. In the battles, the British lost some 45,000 men.

Gaza Strip

Small strip of land extending northeast from Egypt and bordered by Israel and the Mediterranean Sea, occupied by Israel during the 1956 crisis in the **Suez Canal** and again in the 1967 Six Day War. During the Palestinian *intifada* it saw much violence between Palestinians and Israeli troops and settlers. In the wake of the Israeli–PLO Oslo Accord of 1993 the 700,000 strong population came under PLO authority as a first step in the granting of autonomy to all the territories occupied by Israel in 1967. PLO Chairman Yasser Arafat set up his headquarters in Gaza but tension remains since Israel still controls access to the Strip and frequently denies entrance to Israel to Palestinian workers who travel into Israel. The population has been radicalized by years of hardship and is a major base for the fundamentalist Palestinian movement *Hamas* which continues to fight Israel and challenges the authority of the PLO. The worst fighting since 1967 broke out in September 1996 as a result of the crisis over the **Temple Mount**.

Gdansk

See **Danzig**.

Geneva (Switzerland)

City on the shores of Lac Léman in southwest Switzerland. Headquarters of the International Red Cross, founded here in 1864, and of the European arm of the UN. The latter replaced the League of Nations which sat here from 1919 to 1945. The original GATT agreement was signed here in 1947 and came into force on 1 January 1948. Site of many peace and disarmament conferences, the most significant of which was in April–June 1954, when a ceasefire in the Indo-China (Vietnam) War was negotiated, resulting in the division of **Vietnam** along the **17th Parallel**. Other conferences include the START talks on nuclear disarmament (1981–92), attempts to prevent the Gulf War and to agree a Bosnian Peace Plan (1992–5). The Geneva Convention, initially signed by 22 countries in 1864, covered the treatment of casualties in wartime. Revised in 1909, 1929 and 1949 it now also includes the humane treatment of prisoners of war and the protection of the civilian population. Most countries are signatories.

Georgia

Area of the Russian empire prior to 1917 between the Black and Caspian Seas, latterly a constituent republic of the Soviet Union. Following the treaty of **Brest-Litovsk**, Germany sought to stimulate national aspirations in the region and a short-lived independent Georgian Republic came into existence in 1918. With the defeat of Germany and the collapse of the southern White Russian forces in the Russian Civil War Georgia became part of the Transcaucasian Federated Republic with **Armenia** and **Azerbaijan**. Georgia became a Union Republic in 1936, but in common with the Baltic States demands for greater autonomy and even national independence emerged in the Gorbachev era. Mass demonstrations in the capital Tibilisi in early 1989 were brutally repressed, leaving several dead, amid widespread accusations of the use of poison gas by Soviet troops. The dismissal of local Communist Party bosses followed. The election of the nationalistic Zviad Gamsakhurdia as President in spring 1991 promoted virtual independence, confirmed after the failed Moscow coup in August when Georgia refused to join even the loosest association within the old Soviet Union. The leading figure in post-independence Georgia has been Edvard Shevardnadze.

German East Africa

In 1890, under the terms of the **Heligoland** Treaty, Germany abandoned, in favour of Britain, its claims to Zanzibar, the Sultanate of Witu in Kenya, and Nyasaland, in return for Heligoland, which had been governed by the British since 1807. The German East African Company relinquished its territorial rights to the German government in 1891 while retaining many of its economic privileges. The outbreak of the First World War saw a German offensive from East Africa into neighbouring British territories, surrendering to British colonial forces after the armistice of November 1918.

Ghana

See **Gold Coast**.

Gibraltar

Narrow rocky headland on the south coast of Spain. Ceded to Britain in 1713, it has remained a British Dependency despite continued Spanish claims to sovereignty. In September 1967 a referendum resulted in Gibraltar staying British (12,438 votes to 44). Spain closed the frontier in retaliation, only reopening it in January 1985.

Negotiations to settle the **Rhodesia** question were held off Gibraltar, aboard HMS *Tiger* in December 1966 and HMS *Fearless* in October 1968, but without agreement. On 6 March 1988 three IRA terrorists, allegedly planning a bombing campaign in Gibraltar, were shot dead by SAS soldiers. The incident has remained a controversial subject, fuelled by the TV programme "Death on the Rock".

Gleiwicz (Poland)

Town on the pre-Second World War German–Polish border, now Gliwice in southern Poland. On 31 August 1939 the town's German radio station was attacked by Polish troops, all of whom were killed in the raid. Hitler used this act of "Polish aggression" as a pretext for invading Poland on 1 September, precipitating the Second World War. The Polish soldiers involved in the incident were in fact German concentration camp prisoners disguised and then shot by the SS.

Gleneagles Hotel (Scotland)

Location of the agreement reached by the Commonwealth Heads of Government in 1977 banning official sporting links with South Africa as long as apartheid remained in effect.

Gliwice

See **Gleiwicz**.

Gnilla Lipa River (Russia)

Furthest point into Russia that Austrian forces advanced during the First World War. Austrian troops were forced back in fighting between 26 and 30 August 1914.

Goa (India)

Portuguese colony since 1510, Indian forces occupied Goa in 1961 incorporating it as Union Territory with Daman and Diu Island. The territory became a State of the Union in May 1987.

Golan Heights

Strategic high ground on the Syrian–Israeli border overlooking Galilee to the south and Damascus to the north. Captured by Israel in 1967 and annexed in 1981, the heights are regarded by Israelis as a vital barrier against Syrian aggression. The Syrians regard their return as a matter of national pride and see Israeli occupation as a security threat. Negotiations over the procedures for their return have been at the core of Israeli–Syrian peace talks held under the **Madrid** framework since 1991.

Israeli settlers on the Golan have, however, mounted a strong campaign to resist the handover of sovereignty to Syria.

Gold Coast

Former colonial name of the independent nation of Ghana in West Africa. The colony achieved independence from Britain as Ghana on 6 March 1957 – the first such British colony in Africa to achieve independence. The leader of Ghanaian independence was Kwame Nkrumah.

Golden Temple of Amritsar (India)

Holiest site of the Sikh religion, it was stormed by the Indian Army in 1984 because of the presence of armed Sikh militants who favoured a separate state. The attack provoked the assassination of Indian prime minister Indira Gandhi, which in turn caused communal riots in which thousands were killed.

Golden Triangle

Name given to the mountainous border areas of Thailand, Laos and Burma. Inhabited by tribal peoples, it is one of the major opium-growing areas of the world and is controlled by local Chinese and Shan warlords commanding private armies.

Gol Khana Palace (Afghanistan)

The residence of the Afghan president in Kabul.

Gondar (Ethiopia)

Town in northern **Abyssinia** (Ethiopia). In November 1941 the last remaining body of Italian troops in Abyssinia was garrisoned at Gondar. Allied forces attacked from three sides, having secured the mountain passes near the town during the summer. On 27 November 1941 the garrison of 40,000 surrendered, ending Italian resistance in Abyssinia.

Goose Green (Falkland Islands)

Settlement on the Falkland Islands which was the scene of bloody fighting between Argentina and outnumbered British troops in which 17 British and 250 Argentine lives were lost in May 1982 during the Falklands War. Over a thousand Argentines were captured and there were allegations that many had been killed by British troops after they had surrendered.

Gorizia (Italy)

First World War battle for this town on the Isonzo River, northwest of Trieste. The struggle to control this strategic town, then part of the Austro-Hungarian Empire, formed part of the battles of the **Isonzo**. The Italians triumphed in the sixth battle (6–9 August 1916) driving the Austrians out of the town. A combined Austro-German counter-attack in the autumn of 1917 recaptured it on 28 October. Gorizia changed hands once more before the war's end, and then permanently became part of Italy.

Gothic Line (Italy)

Defensive line across Italy from La Spezia over the Apennines to Pesaro in the Adriatic. Heavily fortified by the Germans, it was used as a final defence after the fall of Rome in June 1944. On 30 August the British Eighth Army broke through on the Adriatic coast, followed soon after by the US Fifth Army north of Pisa.

Gracelands (United States)

Mansion in Memphis, Tennessee. Palatial home of Elvis Presley, it has become a shrine to his memory since his death at the age of 42. He was found dead in the house on 16 August 1977.

Greece

Independent state in the Balkans, the scene of the bitter civil war from 1946 to 1949. The Greek Communist Party made the decision to renew the armed struggle on 12 February 1946, and fighting began on Mount Olympus on 30 March 1946. The Communists' wartime National Popular Liberation Army (ELAS) was renamed the Democratic Army of Greece in December 1946. The Communist guerrillas, supported by Albania, Yugoslavia and Bulgaria, were initially successful. On 29 December 1947 their leader, Markos Vafiades, proclaimed a provisional republic in the mountains of northern Greece. But large quantities of aid sent from the USA after the proclamation of the Truman Doctrine on 12 March 1947 enabled government forces to take the offensive on 19 June 1948. Yugoslavia ceased to support the partisans after its expulsion from the Comintern on 28 June 1948. The Greek Communist broadcasting station announced the end of hostilities on 16 October 1949. Greece returned to international prominence during the period of military rule (by the Greek Colonels) from 1967 to 1974. Since then, democracy has been re-established and Greece is now a member of the European Union.

Greenham Common (England)

Site near Newbury, Berkshire, of a US base at which Cruise missiles were deployed in 1983 and which became the symbol of anti-nuclear protest and feminism. Women began a vigil at the base perimeter on 12 December 1982 and a camp of demonstrators remained there until the missiles were withdrawn under the terms of agreements with the Soviet Union in 1989.

Greensboro (United States)
An anti-Ku Klux Klan rally organized in a black housing project in this North Carolina town by the Communist Workers Party (CWP) on 3 November 1979 was fired on by a nine-car convoy of Klan and Nazi Party members. Within 90 seconds five CWP members and supporters had been killed and seven wounded. Two all-white juries acquitted the attackers.

Grenada
Caribbean island whose invasion by the USA in 1983 led to the overthrow of its left-wing government. On 19 October 1983 the army took control in Grenada after a power struggle led to the murder of Prime Minister Maurice Bishop. On 21 October the Organization of Eastern Caribbean States appealed to the USA to intervene and on 25 October US marines and airborne troops invaded Grenada, together with token contingents from six Caribbean countries. Resistance from the Grenadian army and 700 Cuban construction workers with paramilitary training was overcome and order restored by 27 October 1983.

Grodno (Belarus)
City located southwest of Vilnius near the Polish border which has changed from country to country. Occupied by the German army in 1915, it was seized by Poland from Lithuania in 1920 and then annexed by the Soviet Union in 1939. Now in the independent republic of Belarus.

Groote Schuur Hospital (South Africa)
Affiliated to the University of Cape Town, and situated to the southeast of the city. Site of the world's first human heart transplant operation, performed by Christiaan Barnard on 13 December 1967.

Grosvenor Square (England)
Site of the US Embassy in London, which was the scene of violent anti-Vietnam War demonstrations, particularly in March and October 1968.

Grunwald (Poland)
See **Tannenberg**.

Guadalajara (Spain)
Civil War battle in this town, northeast of **Madrid**. Two Nationalist armies, including 30,000 Italian troops, advanced towards Guadalajara during early March 1937,

attempting to encircle and capture the city. The Republicans initially retreated but counter-attacked on 18 March, using Russian tanks to surprise the Nationalists. An Italian retreat turned into a complete rout for the Nationalists, who lost 6,500 men, one third of their force.

Guadalcanal

One of the Solomon Islands in the southwest Pacific. The battle to control Guadalcanal was a pivotal campaign of the Second World War in the Pacific. On 7 August 1942 the US First Marine Division landed on the island and captured the strategic **Henderson Field** airstrip from the Japanese. During the following months both sides sought to reinforce their positions on Guadalcanal, prompting a series of naval engagements around the Solomons, including **Savo Island, Cape Esperance** and **Santa Cruz**. Naval forces clashed off Guadalcanal itself in a major battle on 12 November 1942. Both sides suffered severe damage and high casualties in an indecisive but crucial encounter. The US Marines were finally relieved on 8 December 1942 by the US 14th Corps, and the island was taken on 9 February 1943. American casualties totalled 1,600 killed and 2,400 wounded. Japanese casualties were 14,000 killed and 1,000 captured. Victory on Guadalcanal was an immense psychological boost to the Allies.

Guam

Largest island of the Marianas group in the western Pacific. Ceded to the USA by Spain in 1898, it was invaded by Japan on 10 December 1941. US troops landed on 21 July 1943 and took three weeks to recapture the island. Over 1,700 US troops died, with Japanese losses totalling 18,250. The last remaining Japanese soldiers in the island's interior finally surrendered in 1960. Guam gained full US citizenship and self-government in 1950.

Guangdong (China)

Province of China, the scene of a dramatic increase in prosperity and consumerism, containing the three Special Economic Zones of Shenzhen, Zhuhai and Shantou. It is adjacent to **Hong Kong** and also contains Guangzhou (formerly Canton). Deng Xiaoping has urged Guangdong to be as economically strong in two decades as Asia's four newly industrializing powers – Hong Kong itself, Singapore, South Korea and Taiwan.

Guatemala

Central American republic, the scene of one of the most protracted and brutal guerrilla conflicts in the region. Guerrilla warfare began soon after the revolt against the government of President Ydigoras Fuentes on 13 November 1960 by junior army officers. The rebels were defeated, but soon launched a guerrilla campaign. In the late

1960s they allied with the Guatemalan Communist Party to form the *Fuerzas Armadas Rebeldes* (Insurgent Armed Forces), a name later changed to the Guerrilla Army of the Poor. US special forces assisted in government operations against the insurgents, who were forced to switch their attacks from the countryside to the cities. Retaliation by right-wing death squads resulted in thousands of deaths on both sides. In 1977 the USA halted military aid to Guatemala over human-rights violations, but the embargo was lifted on 17 January 1983. A state of siege was introduced on 1 July 1982. Violence subsided in 1985, but has flared intermittently since.

Guernica (Spain)
A small town in northern Spain, associated with Basque claims to independence and nationhood, Guernica became a symbol of the cruelties of the Spanish Civil War following its destruction on 26 April 1937. After being bombed repeatedly with high explosives and incendiaries, mainly by planes of the German Condor Legion, fleeing survivors from the normal population of 7,000–10,000 and refugees from the Nationalist advance were machine-gunned from the air. Although of some strategic importance as a communication centre, the manner of the attack provoked an immediate and persistently emotive polemic. Under General Franco, while attempts to establish the truth of events continued, the image of Guernica, perpetuated most strongly in the painting by Picasso, remained as a powerful symbol for the opposition of the loss of liberty, both Basque and Spanish. The return of Picasso's work to Madrid in 1981 was consequently a sign of renewed democracy.

Guildford (England)
Town in Surrey, the scene of a bombing of a public house by the Provisional IRA on 21 November 1974 during which, as part of a campaign which included Woolwich in London, eight people were killed and 59 injured. Four people were arrested, allegedly confessed to the bombings and were jailed for life in 1975. Following a long campaign in which they protested their innocence, they were released in 1989 when new evidence was presented to the Court of Appeal.

Guinea-Bissau
Former Portuguese colony in West Africa. Armed resistance to Portuguese rule was launched by PAIGC in 1963. PAIGC proclaimed the independence of the republic on 24 September 1973. Following the coup d'état in Lisbon on 25 April 1974, led by General Antonio de Spinola (who had been governor and commander-in-chief in Guinea-Bissau), the Portuguese recognized the independence of Guinea-Bissau on 10 September 1974.

Guise (France)
First World War battle (29–30 August 1914) around the town near the Belgian

border. Scene of the first French tactical victory in the early stages of the war. The retreat of the French 5th Army under General Lanzerac was temporarily halted to allow the French 6th Army time to assemble. The pursuing German 2nd Army was defeated with many casualties. In danger of being outflanked by the German 1st Army, Lanzerac could not capitalize on this victory and the French retreat resumed. Also known as the Battle of Saint-Quentin.

Gulf of Sidra
See **Sidra**.

Gulf of Tonkin
See **Tonkin**.

Gustav Line (Italy)
Axis defensive line formed in 1943 after the US 5th Army broke out from **Salerno**. It ran from the mouth of the Garigliano River, through **Cassino** to a point south of Ortona.

Habbaniya (Iraq)

Airbase, 40 miles west of Baghdad. In March 1941 the anti-British Rashid Ali ousted the pro-British ruler of Iraq, Amir Abd al-Ilah, and sought to remove the British garrison at Habbaniya. Although heavily outnumbered the British force beat off the attack and counter-attacked into Baghdad. On 30 May Rashid Ali fell and Britain restored control.

Hague, The (The Netherlands)

Host city of the Peace Conferences of 1899 and 1907. The 1899 Conference, meeting on the initiative of the Russian Foreign Minister Count Muravyov, was aimed at seeking a limitation on armaments. Little progress was achieved, although it established a Permanent Court of Arbitration. The 1907 Conference, in which US President Theodore Roosevelt had taken the lead, produced various conventions on the conduct of war. Against a background of increasing tension between European powers, the conference attempted to stem the arms race and create the machinery for resolving international disputes and proposed an International Court of Justice. War came in 1914 and the Court was not set up until 1920.

Hai Phong (Vietnam)

City in the north, the flashpoint which began the first Indo-China War. Although France had recognized the Republic of **Vietnam** as a Free State within the French Union on 6 March 1946, and the Vietnamese nationalist leader Ho Chi Minh had accepted the stationing of French troops in the north, tension rapidly escalated between the two sides. On 23 November 1946 General Valluy gave the Viet Minh a two-hour ultimatum to leave Hai Phong. When it expired, the French cruiser *Suffren* shelled the town. The Viet Minh retaliated by launching a surprise attack on French troops in Hanoi on 19 December. The Viet Minh were driven out of Hanoi and established themselves in the Viet Bac region to the north. An offensive by General Valluy into the area in 1947 failed to destroy them. The French were also unsuccessful in their attempts to establish a regime in Vietnam which would be acceptable to non-Communist nationalists. Bao Dai, the former Emperor of Annam, was made head of a new government in 1949, but he was given no real measure of independence.

Haight-Ashbury (United States)

Area of San Francisco around the intersection of Haight and Ashbury streets. In the late 1960s, it became the centre of hippie culture, typified by the "Summer of Love" in 1967.

Haiti

Republic at the eastern end of the Caribbean island of Hispaniola, occupied by the USA from 1915 to 1934. François "Papa Doc" Duvalier was elected President in 1957 and succeeded in 1971 by his son Jean-Claude "Baby Doc" Duvalier. Both leaders used the brutal *Tontons Macoutes* police force to intimidate the population. Jean-Claude Duvalier fled in 1986. A military coup in September 1991 ousted the elected President Jean Bertrand Aristide. A US-brokered agreement was reached in September 1994 allowing Aristide to return from exile. US troops were used to oversee the handover of power from the Haitian military.

Halabja (Iraq)

Kurdish town near the Iranian border in northern Iraq which was attacked by Iraq with chemical weapons on 17 March 1988. Some 6,000 of the Kurdish civilian population were killed. A day before, Kurdish forces with Iranian support had captured the town. The chemical gas onslaught was one of the most barbaric uses of chemical warfare in the modern Middle East and caused much apprehension over the future use of such weapons by President Saddam Hussein.

Halaib

Disputed border area on Red Sea claimed by both Sudan and Egypt. The area was the scene in 1995 of brief clashes between Egyptian and Sudanese troops after tension between the two countries escalated after a failed assassination attempt on President Mubarrak of Egypt in the Ethiopian capital of Addis Ababa. Egypt formally accused the Sudanese government in Khartoum of complicity in the assassination bid.

Hal Far (Malta)

Crucial airfield which served as the base for the island's defence in the Second World War. Despite almost continuous Nazi assaults, it remained operational.

Halfaya Pass (Libya)

On the Libya–Cyrenaica border, south of **Bardia**. In response to Rommel's sweeping advances into Egypt during 1941 General Wavell ordered a counter-attack (15–17 June) at the coastal town of Salum and inland at the Halfaya Pass. The British were beaten off with the loss of 1,000 men and 100 tanks, half their armoured strength. Subsequently, Wavell was replaced by General Auchinleck.

Hama (Syria)

Town, the scene of an attempted fundamentalist Muslim rising in 1985. The rising was put down by troops loyal to President Assad led by General Rifat. The revenge killings went on for several days, leaving a final death toll above 10,000.

Hamburg (Germany)

Major port and city on the Baltic. It was famous in the Second World War for the RAF "raid on Hamburg" in July 1943, where the use of intense incendiary bombing produced the first "firestorm" phenomenon, leading to uncontrollable fires and heavy loss of life. Firestorms became a feature of later bombing raids, most memorably in the bombing of **Dresden** in February 1945.

Hamilton (Scotland)

Parliamentary constituency in industrial Lanarkshire, the scene of a famous Scottish Nationalist Party (SNP) by-election victory on 2 November 1967. The seat, gained from Labour, was the first SNP victory since April 1945 at **Motherwell** and heralded a revival of Scottish Nationalist fortunes at a time of great electoral unpopularity for the Labour Government under Harold Wilson.

Hangö

Strategic peninsula at the entrance to the Gulf of Finland from the Baltic Sea. The Soviet Union acquired a 30-year lease on Hangö after the Russo-Finnish "Winter War" of 1939–40.

Hanish Islands

Two islands (Great and Little) off the coast of Yemen. The source of a brief conflict in December 1995 between Eritrea and Yemen. Located in busy shipping lanes, the surrounding seas are believed to contain oil reserves.

Hanish, Yemen

Harare (Zimbabwe)

Capital city. A Commonwealth Heads of Government conference held in Harare in 1991 issued a declaration at the prompting of British Prime Minister John Major committing Commonwealth governments to anti-corruption and pro-human rights policies.

Harem al-Sharif

See **Temple Mount**.

Harlem (United States)
Black ghetto in New York City, the scene in March 1935 of attacks on white-owned property following reports that a black youth had been killed by a shopowner. Over 200 stores were destroyed in looting. A Commission of Enquiry blamed racial discrimination and poverty for the events.

Hartlepool (England)
Seaport on the North Yorkshire coast. Along with the neighbouring ports of West Hartlepool, Whitby and Scarborough it was the target of a German attack on 16 December 1914. A battlecruiser squadron opened fire on the towns for 35 minutes, killing 137 people and wounding nearly 600. Three of the German ships sustained damage from coastal batteries.

Hatay
See **Alexandretta**.

Havana (Cuba)
Harbour of the Cuban capital, the setting for the attack on the US battleship *Maine* in 1898 and hence the outbreak of the Spanish–American War. With Spanish agreement, the *Maine* had arrived in Havana in January 1898. On the evening of 5 February 1898, it was blown up (260 of the 355 US troops on board died). No conclusive proof of responsibility has been established, although most US commentators blamed the Spaniards (the colonial power in Cuba at the time). The suspicion was enough for the administration of President McKinley to declare war on Spain.

Hebron (Israel)

A terrorist attack by an Israeli extremist on 25 February 1994 killed 48 Muslim

Palestinian worshippers at the Holy Tomb of the Patriarchs in this West Bank town. The attack sparked off widespread rioting and the introduction of an ineffective international observer force in Hebron. The Israeli Commission of Inquiry which followed provoked an outcry when it revealed that Israeli soldiers guarding the site had orders not to fire on Jews attacking Palestinians.

Hejaz (Saudi Arabia)

Red Sea coastal plain of the Arabian Peninsula. Lawrence of Arabia operated against the Turks in this area during the First World War and the Sherif of Mecca, Hussein ibn Ali, declared himself King of the Hejaz and supported the British campaign. In 1924 Abd al Aziz ibn Saud ousted Hussein and created the Kingdom of Saudi Arabia. Thousands of Muslim pilgrims come to visit the Holy City of **Mecca** in the Hejaz every year.

Hejaz Railway

Built by German engineers from Damascus to Medina between 1900 and 1908 to carry pilgrims to the holy cities. During the First World War bedouin guerrillas under Lawrence of Arabia repeatedly destroyed the line between Ma'an and Medina, preventing the movement of Turkish troops. During the 1970s the Arab States proved unable to agree on reopening the line, although Jordan now uses the section from Amman to the port of Aqaba.

Heligoland (Germany)

Small island in the North Sea 45 miles from the German coastline. Ceded by Britain in 1890, the island was fortified by Germany as part of the country's coastal defences. It became a naval and air base during the First World War but was later demilitarized under the administration of the Allied Disarmament Commission.

Heligoland Bight

Scene of First World War naval battle off the North Sea coast of Germany. On 28 August 1914 a substantial British fleet launched a surprise attack on German forces in the Bight, a stretch of water between **Heligoland** island and the mouth of the River Elbe. One German ship was sunk before the German heavy cruisers could effectively counter-attack. British reinforcements from the Grand Fleet at **Scapa Flow** arrived to regain the advantage, sinking three German heavy cruisers (the *Mainz*, *Köln* and *Ariadne*) and four other ships. The German fleet retreated having lost over 1,000 men. This first naval battle of the First World War was a striking victory for Britain, who lost no ships, and had a shattering effect on German morale.

Helsinki (Finland)

Capital of Finland. On 1 August 1975 the Helsinki Declaration (or Final Act) was adopted by 33 European countries, along with the USA and Canada. Covering security, economic, environmental and human rights issues, the agreements established the Conference on Security and Co-operation in Europe (CSCE), aimed at reducing East–West tension. The CSCE's role in Europe was expanded following the end of the Cold War, a process formalized in the Helsinki Document signed by all members on 10 July 1992.

Henderson Field

Vital airstrip on **Guadalcanal** the possession of which was essential for control of the skies around the Solomon Islands. The Guadalcanal campaign had as its primary objective control of Henderson Field.

Henzada (Burma)

Scene of revolt in August 1937 by the Karen people of this area, 100 miles northwest of Rangoon, in protest at the lack of provision for minorities in Burma in the Government of Burma Act. The revolt was suppressed by British and Indian troops stationed in Burma.

Heraklion (Crete)

Port and airfield. On 20 May 1941 German parachute landings failed to capture this objective and thus when **Crete** was abandoned by the Allies the evacuation was carried out through Heraklion.

Herrin (United States)

Town in Illinois, the scene of bitter industrial conflict in 1922 when the Southern Illinois Coal Company attempted to use strike-breakers to resume production. Two strikers were killed by company guards. In the Herrin Massacre which followed striking miners killed 19 strike-breakers.

Heysel (Belgium)

Football stadium in Brussels, the scene on 29 May 1985 of one of football's worst nights of violence. 39 people died in rioting before the start of the European Cup final between Liverpool and Juventus. A new King Baudouin Stadium was opened in 1995.

Hillsborough (England)

Football stadium in Sheffield where on 15 April 1989 95 Liverpool supporters were crushed to death in the overcrowded stands. The disaster led to the removal of pitch-side fencing and the introduction of all-seater stadiums in Britain.

Hillsborough (Northern Ireland)
Name given to agreement signed by British and Irish Prime Ministers in 1985. See **Belfast**.

Himalayas
Towering mountain range north of India, which gave its name to the border conflict between India and China in 1962, where much of the border area was ill-defined and disputed. See Sino-India War in Appendix 2.

Hindenburg Line
See **Siegfried Line**.

Hiroshima (Japan)
City on Honshu Island which was the scene of the first use of the atomic bomb on 6 August 1945. The bombing, intended to force Japan's unconditional surrender, was carried out by "Enola Gay", a US Air Force B-29. Of the 350,000 population, an estimated 80,000 were killed immediately and a further 100,000 died within a few years from the effects of radiation.

Hiroshima

Ho Chi Minh City (Vietnam)
See **Saigon**.

Ho Chi Minh Trail
Route by which North Vietnam sent men and supplies to the south in the Second **Vietnam** War. South Vietnamese Communists, trained as guerrillas in the North, began to infiltrate into South Vietnam in increasing numbers by routes through **Laos** and **Cambodia**. The so-called Ho Chi Minh Trail ran through the mountains and

jungles of eastern Laos, bypassing the heavily defended border zone between the two Vietnams. The estimated number of Viet Cong using the Trail increased from 2,000 in 1960 to 5,800 in 1962. A second supply route began at the Cambodian port of Sihanoukville. This was known as the Sihanouk Trail. The reinforcements swelled the ranks of the National Liberation Army. By 1963 its main force in the South consisted of 25,000 soldiers and its regional and village militias numbered 80,000.

Hola Camp (Kenya)

Detention centre holding suspects during the anti-British Mau Mau campaign in **Kenya** which began in 1952. Eleven detainees died in 1959 and a subsequent inquiry revealed that they had been beaten to death.

Honduras

Central American republic, known for its "soccer war" with El Salvador in 1969. Hostilities were sparked off by the harassing of a visiting Honduran soccer team in San Salvador (in retaliation for the treatment of the Salvadoran team in Honduras) and the victory of El Salvador over Honduras in a World Cup soccer match on 15 June 1969. The underlying cause was the presence of some 300,000 Salvadoran workers living, many illegally, in Honduras. Riots led to the deaths of two Salvadorans and the expulsion of 11,000 others. In response the Salvadoran army crossed the border at several points on 14 July 1969. Honduras accepted an OAS ceasefire call on 16 July but El Salvador continued fighting. El Salvador, however, began to withdraw on 30 July and this was completed by 5 August 1969.

Hong Kong

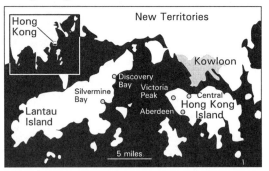

British Crown colony in the South China Sea. Hong Kong island was ceded to Britain by China under the Treaty of Nanking (1842). Japanese troops attacked on 8 December 1941 and the colony surrendered on Christmas Day. British rule was restored after the Second World War. Over one million refugees fled over the border from China in the 1950s to escape the Communist regime. Sino-British negotiations on Hong

Kong's future began in 1982, culminating in an agreement signed on 19 December 1984. Britain agreed to transfer full sovereignty of the whole colony to China on 1 July 1997. China committed itself to maintaining Hong Kong's economic and social freedoms for at least 50 years.

Hope (United States)
Town in southwest Arkansas and birthplace of US President Bill Clinton on 19 August 1946. During his election campaigns of 1992 and 1996, President Clinton used "I still believe in a place called Hope" as his catchphrase.

Hormuz, Strait of
Connects the Arabian–Persian Gulf with the Gulf of Oman and the Arabian Sea, bordered on the north by Iran and to the south by the Omani enclave of Ras Musandam. At its narrowest point the Strait is 35 miles across and the main shipping channel is on the Omani side. Much of the oil exported from the Gulf passes through the Strait although there have been efforts in recent years to construct pipelines across Arabia in order to bypass the chokepoint.

Hōsei University (Japan)
Scene of major student clashes with riot police against the visit of the US nuclear-powered aircraft-carrier USS *Enterprise*.

Houston (United States)
Members of the black 24th Infantry Regiment attacked the town of Houston, Texas, on 26 August 1917 following rumours that a black woman arrested by white police had died. The soldiers, who had suffered abuse and police violence in the city, killed 17 whites during the attack.

Huai-Hai (China)
Scene of one of the last major battles of the Chinese civil war. On this occasion, in November 1948, another crushing defeat was suffered by the Nationalist Seventh and Second Army groups deployed along the Lung-Hai railway. In the battle of Huai-Hai the Nationalists lost 600,000 men, including 327,000 prisoners. **Peking** surrendered to the Communists on 22 January 1949. On 20 April the Communists crossed the Yangtze river. **Nanking** fell on 22 April, and **Shanghai** on 27 May. On 5 August the USA cut off all further aid to Chiang Kai-shek, and the Nationalist cause was now clearly lost. On 1 October 1949 the People's Republic of China was proclaimed in Peking.

Hungary

Republic in eastern Europe. Formerly part of **Austria-Hungary**. Under communist rule after Second World War. Scene of the attempted revolution of 1956. The demonstrations of 23 October 1956 in Budapest turned into a general uprising; the Stalin statue was torn down and the radio headquarters were seized by the crowds. The insurgents fought against the troops of the State Defence Authority and the intervening Soviet troops. On 25 October, the government troops, hiding on rooftops around Kossuth Square, shot into the peaceful demonstrators, thus causing more people to join the insurgents. At dawn on 24 October, Imre Nagy became the prime minister and gradually a supporter of the revolution. On 26 October, he invited non-Communist politicians into the government; he recognized the legal status of the Workers' Councils and the local Revolutionary Committees. On 30 October, a withdrawal of the Soviet troops began. On 1 November, Imre Nagy announced that Hungary was withdrawing from the Warsaw Pact and requested that the UN recognize Hungary's neutrality. At dawn on 4 November, the second Soviet invasion was launched, with a great number of participating troops, managing to suppress the Hungarian Revolution within approximately one week.

Hungerford (England)

Town in Berkshire, the scene of mass murder on 19 August 1987. Sixteen people were killed when a lone gunman, Michael Ryan, opened fire as he walked through the town. He committed suicide before he could be arrested.

la Drang (Vietnam)
Valley near the **Vietnam–Cambodia** border where the first major battle between North Vietnamese and US forces was fought from 14 until 24 November 1965.

Ifni
Spanish-held territory in North Africa, the scene of the Ifni Incident of 1957. On 23 November 1957, some 1,200 Moroccan irregulars attacked this Spanish-held territory. The Spanish garrison was strengthened and Madrid announced that order had been restored on 8 December 1957. In the conflict, 61 Spanish were killed and 128 wounded.

Ijzer (Belgium)
See **Yser**.

Imbros (Turkey)
Island in the Aegean Sea, west of the entrance to the **Dardanelles**. Originally occupied by Greece after the First Balkan War (1912), it became a British base in the First World War. It was most extensively used during and following the evacuation of troops from the ill-fated **Gallipoli** campaign. Under the peace Treaty of **Lausanne** (1923), it became part of Turkey.

Imjin River (South Korea)
Scene of a successful defensive battle fought by UN troops from 22 to 25 April 1951 to hold back a Chinese–North Korean spring offensive.

Imphal (India)
State capital of Manipur province in northeastern India. During the Second World War, it was a primary strategic goal of the Japanese invasion of India, with the aim of securing the Naga Hills to defend Burma. By March 1944 British and Indian divisions under General Slim had created a defensive perimeter around the city and successfully resisted the attacks of the Japanese 15th Army. In the face of disrupted supply lines, Allied air supremacy and British reinforcements from **Kohima**, the Japanese retreated losing large numbers of men and equipment.

Imroz
See **Imbros**.

Inchon (Korea)
Scene of famous landing by UN troops in the Korean War. North Korean troops

invaded the south on 25 June 1950. The UN decided to intervene following an emergency session of the Security Council, which was being boycotted by the Soviet Union. The first US troops landed at **Pusan** on 1 July 1950. The whole face of the war was now changed by a dramatic counter-strike, conceived and planned by General MacArthur. At dawn on 15 September the US First Marine Division made an amphibious landing on Wolmi Island commanding Inchon Harbour, only 18 miles west of Seoul. The landings were a complete success. Inchon was captured, and the advance on Seoul began as other units of the newly-created X Corps under Major-General Edward Almond reinforced the Marines. On 18 September the 7th Division landed at Inchon and turned south. After heavy fighting, Seoul was taken on 26 September. On the same day an armoured spearhead which had broken out from the Pusan Perimeter met the 7th Division at Osan. The North Korean Army was completely broken, and 125,000 prisoners fell into the UN's hands. MacArthur had won a striking victory. The success of the Inchon landings led the UN to expand the original military and political aims of the war.

Indo-China
Name for the former French Empire in Southeast Asia. Indo-China was a federation formed in 1887 from the colony of Cochin China and the protectorates of Annam, **Cambodia** and Tonkin. To these, **Laos** was added in 1897, as a protectorate, and **Kouang-Tchéou-Wan** in 1900. Held until the Geneva Agreements of 20 July 1954 that recognized their independence as Cambodia, Laos and **Vietnam**. The name Indo-China is still used of these three countries.

Indonesia
See **Netherlands East Indies**.

Invergordon (Scotland)
Naval base in the Cromarty Firth where sailors of the Royal Navy's Atlantic Fleet mutinied on 15 November 1931 on hearing the news of pay cuts imposed by the National Government. The ratings refused to prepare their vessels for sailing, forcing the Board of Admiralty to promise that no cut would be over 10 per cent.

Irian Jaya (Indonesia)
Formerly West New Guinea, part of the Dutch East Indies. Now part of Indonesia, it has been the scene of conflict since 1962. Following a clash between Indonesian and Dutch naval forces on 15 January 1962, President Sukarno ordered military mobilization and sent armed units into West New Guinea. In a settlement negotiated through the UN, the Dutch agreed on 15 August 1962 to hand over Western New Guinea, which was incorporated into Indonesia as Irian Barat on 1 May 1963. The Free Papua

Movement, opposed to Indonesian control and seeking unification with Papua New Guinea, undertook small-scale guerrillas operations. Fighting in 1984 led to the movement of over 11,000 refugees to Papua New Guinea. Irian Jaya was known as Irian Barat from 1963 to 1976.

Iron Curtain

Symbolic division between East and West Europe following the Second World War. The term was first used by Winston Churchill in a speech in **Fulton**, Missouri. The fences and watchtowers were dismantled after the end of the Cold War and collapse of Communism in Eastern Europe between 1989 and 1991.

Iskenderun

See **Alexandretta**.

Isonzo Front (Italy)

A succession of twelve battles (May 1915–October 1917) in the First World War along the Isonzo River valley in northeastern Italy. During the first four battles repeated Italian assaults on the fortified Austrian positions on the east bank finally resulted in the capture of **Gorizia** on 9 August 1916. Intermittent fighting continued over the next year with few gains on either side. Further Italian advances in the eleventh battle prompted German reinforcements for the Austrians. In the decisive twelfth battle, also known as the Battle of Caporetto (24 October 1917), an Austrian–German offensive succeeded in crossing the Isonzo and capturing **Caporetto**. In one of the worst defeats in Italian history, the routed Italian army retreated back to the **Piave River** where they held firm with British and French reinforcements.

Israel

Independent republic in the eastern Mediterranean. After the First World War, **Palestine** became a British mandate under the League of Nations. Included in the mandate was a commitment to the establishment of a Jewish state, first given in the Balfour Declaration of 1917. In a letter to Baron Rothschild on 2 November 1917, British Foreign Secretary Arthur Balfour stated that the British Government "... viewed with favour the establishment of a national home for Jewish people..." Arab–Jewish conflict continued throughout the inter-war period, leading Britain to limit Jewish immigration after 1939 and eventually to turn to the United Nations for help. On 29 November 1947 the UN General Assembly approved a plan to create separate Arab and Jewish states in Palestine. The state of Israel was proclaimed on 14 May 1948, and the last British troops left the next day. Violence followed almost immediately (see Arab–Israeli War in Appendix 2), with Israel gaining 50 per cent more land than under the UN plan. Although Israel entered the UN in May 1949, many Arab states refused to recognize the state. Further conflict followed in 1967 and 1973 (see Appendix 2), with Israel occupying the **West Bank**, the **Golan Heights**, **Gaza** and **Sinai**. The peace process begun at **Camp David** in 1978 continued slowly despite the Israeli invasion of **Lebanon** in 1982, culminating in the **Oslo** and **Madrid** talks during 1991–4. The assassination of Prime Minister Rabin in **Tel Aviv** (November 1995), tension over the future of Jewish settlements in Palestinian areas and renewed communal violence in September 1996 have all left the success of the peace process in doubt.

Istrian Peninsula

Disputed territory at the northern end of the Adriatic. Formerly part of the Habsburg Empire, it was annexed to Italy after the First World War. Under the Italian dictator, Benito Mussolini, all Slovene and Croat identity was suppressed. In 1947 it passed to Yugoslavia and was divided between Croatia and Slovenia.

Ivangorod (Poland)

Fortress town southeast of **Warsaw**, now known as Deblin. Besieged by the German army, the town's Russian garrison launched a counter-attack in September–October 1914, breaking the siege. In July 1915 the Germans crossed the River Vistula and attacked the fortress. With Austro-Hungarian troops advancing from the south, the Russians were in danger of being encircled. On 4 August 1915 Ivangorod was abandoned by the Russians as they retreated.

Iwo Jima

Small Pacific island in the Bonin Islands group south of Japan. A primary strategic target during the Second World War for the USA, bringing the large land-based bombers in range of mainland Japan. After prolonged initial bombardment by the Fifth Fleet, the final assault began on 19 February 1945 and met fierce resistance. The first objective of Mount Suribachi fell in three days, immortalized in the famous photograph of US Marines raising the Stars and Stripes on its summit. The US push northwards was stopped by a fanatical Japanese defence strengthened by heavy fortifications and underground tunnels. Fighting continued until 16 March, producing terrible casualties on both sides. Of the 23,000 Japanese troops, only 216 survived to be taken prisoner. More than 6,500 US troops were killed with 17,400 wounded.

Jabalya
Largest Palestinian refugee camp in the **Gaza Strip** with a population of over 60,000. It was the site of riots on 9 December 1987 which marked the opening of the uprising (*intifada*).

Jaffna (Sri Lanka)
Most important city within the area controlled by the Tamil Tigers. It fell to the Tamil Tigers in 1990 but was recaptured after a massive government onslaught in December 1995.

Jajce (Bosnia)
Location of the important wartime congress (the Jajce Congress) of Tito's Yugoslav partisans, held on 29–30 November 1943. The Congress of Delegates to the Anti-Fascist National Liberation Committee set up a National Committee of Yugoslavia as a rival Communist-led government to the royalist government-in-exile in London. It resolved to create a federal Yugoslavian Republic after the war and gave the committee the powers of a provisional government with Tito as President. Tito was also awarded the title of Marshal of Yugoslavia in recognition of his military leadership of the partisans against the German-occupying forces. The resolutions of the congress paved the way for the Communist takeover of Yugoslavia at the end of the war.

Jarrow (England)
Town in the northeast synonymous with the depression of the 1930s. The most famous of all the hunger marches of the 1930s was the Jarrow Crusade of October 1936 when 200 workers from the Jarrow shipyards marched to London in protest at the closure of Palmers shipyard and the devastating levels of unemployment in the town. The Jarrow March was, however, only one of many less-publicized hunger marches. A group of Glasgow Communists and Socialists had organized a hunger march to London in October 1922. It was followed in January 1929 by a yet larger march. In October 1932, with unemployment at 2,750,000, the National Unemployed Workers' Movement staged the largest of all the hunger marches with 3,000 people converging on London from the depressed regions of Glasgow, South Wales and the north of England. After a demonstration in Hyde Park a petition of one million signatures was presented to parliament.

Java Sea
Scene of Second World War naval encounter near the north coast of Java. As the Japanese progressed through the Dutch East Indies, two invasion forces advanced towards Java. A combined American–British–Dutch–Australian fleet attempted to stop the assault by engaging the Eastern Force on 27 February 1942. The Allies suffered

severe damage with five ships sunk and HMS *Exeter* crippled. While retreating the next day, the Allies encountered the Western Force and lost HMAS *Perth*, USS *Houston* and three other ships. With this Allied fleet destroyed, the Japanese stormed ashore and captured Java.

Jenin (Palestine)
First town in the former Israeli-occupied **West Bank** to be handed over to Palestinian control. On 13 November 1995 the last Israeli military vehicles withdrew from a town in which 170 Arabs had died in the uprising (*intifada*) against Israel.

Jericho
Town in the **West Bank** region, formerly occupied by Israel, northeast of Jerusalem. Having captured Jerusalem in December 1917, the British advanced towards the Jordan River valley. Supported by two ANZAC cavalry divisions, the British took Jericho on 21 February 1918. The West Bank, including Jericho, became part of Jordan after the Arab–Israeli War of 1948, but was recaptured by Israel during the Six Day War of 1967. In 1995 Jericho was one of the West Bank towns to come under PLO rule as part of the Middle East peace process.

Jerusalem (Israel)
During the First World War Allied forces under General Allenby attacked Turkish positions around the city on 8 December 1917. Turkish defences crumbled quickly and Jerusalem was captured the next day with little damage to the Holy Places. Following the creation of the State of Israel in 1948, the city was divided between Transjordan (now Jordan) and Israel, with West Jerusalem becoming the Israeli capital in 1950. The Old City and East Jerusalem were captured from Jordan during the Six Day War of June 1967. The united city was proclaimed the capital of Israel in 1980, a fact that has never been recognized by the UN. The worst fighting since 1967 broke out in September 1996 as a result of the opening of a tunnel near the **Temple Mount**.

Jinja (Uganda)
Location of the army mutiny of 23 January 1964 which was suppressed with the help of British troops. A similar revolt took place at Lanet in Kenya the same day. Earlier in January there had been a revolution in Zanzibar and an army mutiny in Tanganyika.

Jiu Valley (Romania)
Coal-mining area whose workers have played an important role in the politics of Romania. They were transported to Bucharest to disperse anti-government demonstrations by students in 1990 and in September 1991 their protests at government economic policy forced the Prime Minister Petre Roman from office.

Jogyakarta (Indonesia)
See **Yogyakarta**.

Jonestown (Guyana)
Small agricultural commune in northwest Guyana founded in 1977 by Reverend Jim Jones. As self-proclaimed messiah of the People's Temple, an evangelical religious cult, he brought his followers here promising a new utopia. In November 1978 US Congressman Leo Ryan arrived with journalists to unofficially investigate the cult. As he prepared to leave with cult defectors, he was assassinated although others escaped. Fearing the intervention of the authorities, Jones ordered a mass suicide by drinking cyanide-laced punch, and then shot himself on 18 November. Guyanese troops arrived soon afterwards to find 913 bodies including 276 children.

Jordaan (The Netherlands)
Working-class district of Amsterdam, famous in the 1930s as a centre of labour militancy. In June 1934, at the height of the world economic crisis, the Dutch government proposed a ten per cent cut in the allowance paid to the unemployed. Working-class anger exploded and in July 1934 a protest march in the Jordaan developed into a bloody battle. Eventually military police and army units with tanks were deployed. When the riots ended on 9 July 1934 six people had died, over thirty had been injured and scores were arrested.

Jordan
Kingdom in the Middle East, bordering on Israel.
1) In 1920, following Turkey's defeat in the First World War, the League of Nations created the British mandate of **Transjordan**, which was later split into Palestine and Transjordan. The mandate ended in 1948 and the states of Jordan and Israel emerged from the Arab–Israeli War of 1948–9 to replace Transjordan and Palestine respectively. The **West Bank** was annexed by Jordan in 1950, only to be reoccupied by Israel during the Six Day War of June 1967.
2) Culmination of tensions between the Jordanian government and the radical PLO factions fighting Israel from bases in Jordan resulted in civil war (17–25 September 1970). PLO factions provoked the fighting by challenging King Hussein's authority in Amman and by hijacking foreign airliners (see under **Dawson's Field**). King Hussein declared martial law on 16 September 1970. Civil war broke out in Amman on 19 September as the army attacked the Palestinian refugee camps. Some 250 Syrian tanks entered Jordan in support of the Palestinians, but suffered losses in Jordanian air strikes and withdrew on 23 September 1970. A ceasefire was agreed to on 25 September 1970. Further heavy fighting took place early in 1971 and the PLO guerrillas withdrew from Amman on 13 April. Their expulsion from Jordan was completed by 18 July 1971.

3) The Middle East peace process, which began in October 1991, has resulted in increased co-operation between Jordan and Israel, including the opening of the first border crossing on 8 August 1994.

Juno Beach (France)

One of the **Normandy** beaches used in the D-Day landings of 6 June 1944. The central beach in the British sector, it was the target for the 3rd Canadian Infantry Division. Overcoming initial German resistance, the Canadians successfully established a beachhead and advanced seven miles inland.

Jutland

First World War naval battle off the southwest coast of Norway. On 31 May 1916 the British Grand Fleet and the German High Seas Fleet clashed in the biggest naval engagement of the First World War. The Dreadnought fleets opened fire on each other, inflicting serious damage on both sides. The British lost 14 ships, including eight destroyers and the flagship *Invincible*, and over 6,900 sailors. German losses totalled 10 ships and more than 3,000 sailors. A nominal German victory, it proved to be the last time the German fleet ventured out of its home ports. Also known as the Battle of Skaggerak.

Kabra Bassa Dam (Mozambique)
See **Cabora Bassa**.

Kagera (Tanzania)
Area which Uganda attempted to seize by force in 1978. On 27 October 1978, Ugandan armed forces, with Libyan support, invaded Tanzania and occupied some 700 square miles of Tanzanian territory known as the Kagera salient. A Tanzanian counter-offensive on 12 November 1978 ejected the Ugandans from the salient. In January 1979, Tanzanian forces, with armed Ugandan exiles, advanced into Uganda. Kampala fell on 11 April 1979 and President Amin fled the country.

Kahüta (Pakistan)
Site, near Islamabad, of the country's nuclear research project and widely suspected as the centre from which Pakistan is developing a nuclear bomb. The site, which is closed to international inspection, is within easy striking distance of those Indian airbases close to Pakistan's eastern border.

Kaifeng (China)
Civil War battle in this town in eastern central China. Having recaptured Yen-an (now **Yan'an**) in April 1948, the Communist forces advanced southeast towards the Nationalist stronghold of Kaifeng. Despite being numerically superior, the Nationalists were quickly defeated on 19 June 1948. The Communists abandoned the town a week later.

Kaliningrad (Russia)
See **Königsberg**.

Kamerun
See **Cameroon**.

Kampuchea
See **Cambodia**.

Kamsar (Iran)
Town where the 1971 "Convention on Wetlands of International Importance, Especially as Waterfowl Habitat" was signed. Although the Convention, in force since 1975, covers only three per cent of the world's wetlands it was nonetheless an important environmental step.

Karakoram Highway
Strategic and commercial land route, linking Pakistan and China. Built with Chinese help, the road passes through Azad **Kashmir** to connect Pakistan with the Chinese province of Xinjiang.

Karbala' (Iraq)
See **Kerbela**.

Karelian Isthmus (Russia)
Area of considerable strategic significance between Finland and Russia. It is the shortest land route between Leningrad and the major centres of Finnish population. The border established between the Soviet Union and Finland in October 1920 drew a line only 20 miles from Leningrad and 60 miles from the major Finnish city of Viipuri. The new border was fortified on the Finnish side by the **Mannerheim Line** from the late 1920s. Soviet demands for adjustment of the frontier in the Soviet Union's favour and for its demilitarization in 1939 were resisted by the Finns. As a result of the Russo-Finnish War of 1939–40 the Soviet Union gained the whole of the Karelian Isthmus and the Finnish second city of Viipuri. The former Finnish territories were reoccupied by the Finns in the Continuation War of 1941–4, but were returned to the Soviet Union at the conclusion of hostilities. The Isthmus remained part of the Soviet Union until its collapse in 1991 and is now part of Russia.

Karlsbad (Czech Republic)
Town in Czechoslovakia which gave its name to the Karlsbad Decrees of 24 April 1938, the last propaganda offensive of the pro-Nazi Sudeten German Party which was leading the drive by the Sudeten Germans to break away from Czechoslovakia. The Karlsbad Decrees called for complete autonomy which would have effectively rendered Czechoslovakia defenceless. Now known as Karlovy Vary. See also **Sudetenland**.

Karlshorst (Germany)
Suburb of Berlin where the final surrender of the German *Wehrmacht* to the Russian armies took place on 8 May 1945. General Keitel surrendered to the Russians led by Marshal Zhukov. German forces in the west had already surrendered the previous day.

Kars (Turkey)
Province long-disputed between Russia and Turkey. The 1921 Treaty of Kars was signed between the Armenian Socialist Republic and the Russian Soviet Government with the Turkish Government. By the Treaty the disputed area of Kars province, ceded to Russia in 1878, annexed by Turkey by the Treaty of **Brest-Litovsk**, then part

of the Republic of **Armenia**, was returned to Turkey following its conquest by the "Young Turk" armies under Karabakir Pasha.

Kashmir

Disputed territory between India and Pakistan. When India and Pakistan achieved independence, a rebellion by the Muslim majority in Kashmir led the Hindu maharajah to accede to the Indian Union, and Indian troops were flown into Kashmir on 27 October 1947. Pakistan sent aid to the Muslim Azad Kashmir irregulars, and Pakistani army units crossed into Kashmir in March 1947. An undeclared state of war between India and Pakistan continued until UN mediation brought about a ceasefire on 1 January 1949. India formally annexed Kashmir on 26 January

1957. Renewed conflicts between India and Kashmir occurred in 1965 and 1971 and since the 1980s there has been a continuous guerrilla war in the region.

Kasserine Pass

Involved in the battle for Tunisia, when US troops met German forces for the first time (14–22 February 1943) and suffered a humiliating defeat.

Kassinga (Angola)

Site of a refugee camp in Angola in which over 700 Namibians were killed in 1978. The camp, used by SWAPO guerrillas, was the target of an airborne attack on 4 May 1978 by South African troops. In addition to those killed in the attack, over 200 were abducted in the operation and detained in **Namibia**. The final group were not released until September 1984.

Kastellorizon

See **Dodecanese**.

Katanga (Zaïre)

On the granting of independence to **Zaïre** by Belgium, encouraged by Union Minière (a company with exclusive mining rights in the province), the copper- and uranium-rich area of Katanga seceded from the Belgian Congo on 11 July 1960 under its leader Moishe Tshombe. Using a white mercenary army to resist UN attempts to restore order, Katanga ended its rebellion on 14 January 1963. The province is now known as **Shaba**.

Katyn (Russia)

Forest near Smolensk in western Russia. On 13 April 1943 the German army announced the discovery of mass graves containing 4,500 Polish officers. The Soviet Union accused Germany of killing them. Germany in turn charged the Soviet Union with murdering the Poles during the occupation of western Poland in September 1939. The Polish government-in-exile in London asked the International Red Cross to investigate, prompting Soviet leader Joseph Stalin to sever relations with the Poles and set up the **Lublin** Committee. This split contributed to the establishment of the **Curzon Line** as the post-war eastern frontier of Poland. Britain and the USA accepted this frontier at Stalin's insistence during the **Tehran** Conference (November–December 1943) despite the London Poles' objections. In 1989 the Soviet government admitted responsibility for the Katyn Massacre.

Kent State University (United States)

Founded in 1910 in the city of Kent in northeastern Ohio. Not previously noted for political activism, 500 Kent students violently demonstrated against the Vietnam War in early May 1970. The authorities called in the State National Guard who used tear gas, bayonets and live ammunition to break up the demonstration. On 4 May four students were shot dead and 11 more were injured when soldiers fired into the crowds. A second peaceful protest followed in September when students set fire to their draft cards.

Kenya

Former British colony in East Africa which became independent in 1963. Prior to independence, it was the scene of the Mau Mau rebellion, one of the first conflicts to arise in post-war Africa. Violence began in 1952 and continued for another four years, mainly taking the form of attacks on the farms and homes of white settlers and Africans who did not support Mau Mau. Attacks on fellow-Africans far outnumbered those on whites, for only 32 European civilians were killed compared with 1,817 Africans. As assassinations and terrorist activities increased, the British government detained the political leaders of Mau Mau, including Jomo Kenyatta, and mounted a military campaign against Mau Mau groups in the field. African home-guard units were set up and protected villages established round the Kikuyu Reserve. British troops and the King's African Rifles backed up by the RAF drove the Mau Mau groups into the remote mountain areas of western Kenya. Over 5,000 suspects were detained and over 11,500 killed before the emergency was lifted in 1960. Over 600 British and African troops died in the operations.

Kerala (India)

State formed in 1956 from the amalgamation of the Malayalam-speaking state of Travancore-Cochin and the Malabar District of Madras. The Communist Party of India (Marxist) Democratic Front has traditional strength in this state.

Kerbela (Iraq)

One of the holy cities (along with Najaf) of the Shia Muslims. In March 1991 after the Gulf War it was the scene of one of the worst atrocities in recent Iraqi history. Under General Hussein Kamel, Saddam Hussein's trusted lieutenant and son-in-law, a rising in Kerbela was brutally suppressed, ground-to-ground missile attacks were launched on civilian areas of the city and thousands of prisoners executed after torture. The uprising in southern Iraq in 1991 had begun in Basra, rapidly engulfing the Shia areas. Hussein Kamel defected to Jordan in 1995.

Keren (Eritrea)

Town which was the scene of heavy fighting between the Italians and the advancing British troops in 1941. Well-protected by a mountain wall, it was determinedly defended by General Frusci's army. The eight-week battle, in February–March 1941, was finally won by the British, but at a cost of 563 killed and 3,229 wounded. Over 3,000 Italian troops lost their lives.

Khalistan

See **Punjab**.

Kharkov (Ukraine)

Large industrial city east of Kiev which replaced it as capital of the Ukraine in 1934. During the Second World War it was the focus of bitterly contested battles on the Eastern Front. The advancing German 6th Army easily captured the city in October 1941, but a Soviet offensive to regain it the following May failed badly with 250,000 troops taken prisoner. In February 1943 the Soviet troops managed to retake the city, only to lose control again in March. Liberation from the Germans finally occurred in August 1943 after the Soviet victory at **Kursk**.

Khartoum (Sudan)

In February 1884 General Gordon arrived in **Sudan** with instructions to evacuate the country in the face of an uprising by the Mahdi, Muhammad Ahmed. He instead decided to stand and fight and evacuated 2,500 non-combatants from Khartoum and asked London for reinforcements. On 12 March the Mahdists besieged Gordon's forces in Khartoum where he held out for ten months. On 26 January 1885 the fort was stormed and all the defenders killed, just two days before a British relief force under General Wolseley arrived.

Khe Sanh (Vietnam)

us Marine base on the Vietnam–Laos border besieged by North Vietnamese forces from January to April 1968 during the Tet Offensive. It became one of the longest, and most bloody, battles of the Vietnam War. The North Vietnamese had chosen Khe Sanh, just south of the Demilitarized Zone, to distract US forces from the cities of the south, the real targets of the Tet Offensive. The siege was a turning point in the war – the plight of the besieged US marines turning US public opinion against both the war and the policies of President Johnson. A huge US bombing operation caused 10,000 North Vietnamese casualties. Although fewer than 500 marines died, Khe Sanh was a huge psychological blow for the USA.

Khorramshahr (Iran)
Key objective of Iraqi forces in the Iran–Iraq War which began when Iraq invaded Iran on 12 September 1980. Although Khorramshahr fell to the Iraqis on 13 October 1980, Iranian resistance did not collapse. The Iranians counter-attacked and a bloody stalemate ensued.

Khota Barahu
See **Kota Bahru**.

Khyber Pass
The most important pass between Pakistan and Afghanistan. About 30 miles long, the pass reaches a height of 3,520 ft. It was of great strategic influence during the British Raj in India. Over three million refugees escaped to Pakistan by this route during the Afghan Civil War in the 1980s.

Kiaochow Peninsula (China)
In 1898 China agreed to lease it to Germany for a period of 99 years. In October 1914 it was occupied by Japan but was returned to China after the Second World War. Located in east China, it is now known as Kiaohsien.

Kibeho (Rwanda)
Refugee camp in southern **Rwanda**, the scene of one of the worst massacres of the civil war in that country. Up to 5,000 died when, in April 1995, the government acted to eradicate refugee camps on Rwandan soil. In the most savage attack by the Rwandan Patriotic Army since its victory over the Hutu regime in July 1994, troops rampaged through Kibeho, shooting and bayoneting indiscriminately in an attempt to force some 100,000 refugees to flee the area.

Kibera (Kenya)
Slum district in the capital Nairobi, the scene of the worst ethnic violence in the country in October 1995 between members of the Luo and Nubian tribes.

Kiel (Germany)

Naval base on the Baltic, the location of the Sailors' Mutinies of 1917–18. The first mutiny in summer 1917 had its roots in social discontent but was ruthlessly suppressed. The rising of October 1918 was sparked by orders of the Naval High Command of 30 October to engage the Royal Navy in battle. The sailors refused to obey the order, instead demanding the abdication of the Kaiser. Although the conciliatory attitude of the new governor of Kiel, Gustav Noske, defused the situation, the mutiny spread to such ports as Bremen and Hamburg.

Kiel Canal (Germany)

61-mile waterway linking the Baltic and North Seas. Built between 1887 and 1895, it was enlarged between 1907 and 1914 to give German naval ships easy access to the open sea. In the Treaty of **Versailles** (1919) it remained under German administration but became an international waterway. These restrictions were denounced by Hitler in 1936, but after the Second World War the treaty conditions were reinstated and the Canal became part of Schleswig-Holstein.

Kielce (Poland)

Town in central Poland, the scene in July 1946 of a post-war massacre by Poles of 42 Jews who had survived the Holocaust. The massacre, a horrific postscript to the almost total destruction of Polish Jewry in the Second World War, provoked the emigration of many of the surviving Jews. Jewish police and soldiers joined in the attack. Although nine people were later executed, under the Communist regime details of the massacre were covered up. In July 1996, the Polish prime minister apologized for the shameful incident.

Kiev (Ukraine)

Capital. Part of the Soviet Union until independence in 1991. In early September 1941 the Germans advanced on Kiev from two directions. To avoid being encircled the local Russian commanders ordered a withdrawal, but were overruled by the Soviet leader, Joseph Stalin. By 16 September the Germans had almost completed the encirclement of the city. Although 150,000 Soviet troops managed to break out, nearly 600,000 were trapped and taken prisoner.

Kimberley (South Africa)

Diamond mining town in Cape Province near the Orange Free State border. The Boer offensive to the west concentrated on **Mafeking** and Kimberley, with the latter being attacked on 14 October 1899. The British defenders were heavily outnumbered but repulsed the attack, and the siege began. Despite continuous bombardment, the garrison held out until it was relieved on 15 February 1900 by 5,000 cavalry under

General French. The Boers retreated back into the Orange Free State pursued by British troops.

King David Hotel

Prestigious Jerusalem hotel, headquarters for the British administration in Palestine during the Mandate period. Zionist guerrillas of the Irgun Zvai Leumi organization blew it up on 22 July 1946 killing 91 soldiers and civilians.

Kinmen

See Quemoy.

Kirk-Kilissa (Turkey)

Town in Thrace northwest of Constantinople (Istanbul). The outbreak of the First Balkan War in 1912 prompted Turkish offensives on two fronts. In Macedonia the Turks confronted the Serbs at **Kumanovo**, while in Thrace they clashed with Bulgarian forces at Kirk-Kilissa on 25 October. The Bulgarians won an overwhelming victory, inflicting heavy losses on the Turks.

Kiryat Shmona (Israel)

Town, the scene of one of the worst terrorist outrages of the 1970s. On 11 April 1974 three Arab guerrillas entered the town of Kiryat Shmona and killed eight people in an apartment block. The terrorists were killed when explosives they were carrying were set off.

Kishinev (Russia)

Scene of one of the worst pogroms in Tsarist Russia. In 1903 several hundred Jews were killed or injured in anti-Semitic violence. Later pogroms occurred in Odessa (1905) and **Bialystok** (1906).

Kitty Hawk (United States)

Scene in North Carolina of the first heavier-than-air powered flight. The age of air travel began on 17 December 1903 when two brothers from Ohio, Orville and Wilbur Wright, developed their first machine. On the Kitty Hawk sand dunes, Wilbur Wright flew 59 seconds in front of five witnesses and a camera.

Klaipeda

See **Memel**.

Klondike (Canada)

Scene of the famous gold rush into the Canadian North-West Territory after the discovery of gold at Rabbit (Bonanza) Creek (a tributary of the Klondike River) in 1896. The rush saw Dawson City (founded in 1897) rise to 25,000 inhabitants by 1898. The excitement faded by 1899, although Dawson's population was still 30,000 in 1900. A generation later, like the ghost towns of the American West, its population was a mere 1,000.

Knin (Croatia)

From 1991 to 1995, backed by Yugoslav army units, Knin was the self-proclaimed capital of the so-called Serb Republic of Krajina. It was the symbol of Serbian rebellion against Zagreb. Recaptured by the Croats in 1995, its pre-war population (88 per cent Serb) has been displaced.

Köbe (Japan)

City in central Japan devastated by the earthquake of January 1995. Casualties included over 4,500 dead and 23,500 missing.

Kodok

See **Fashoda**.

Kohima (India)

Town in Manipur Province, near the Burmese border. The Japanese occupation of Burma during the Second World War led to the invasion of northeast India on 7–8 March 1944. Kohima was cut off and besieged by Japanese troops on 4 April. The town's small British garrison was relieved after 12 days of intense fighting. The final Japanese withdrawal began on 31 May 1944.

Kokoda Trail (New Guinea)

Important Second World War line of Japanese advance in August 1942 from Buna to Port Moresby. The Kokoda Trail is a track across the Owen Stanley mountains. The Japanese advance was halted by Australian troops only 20 miles from Port Moresby. Fighting in some of the worst terrain in the world, the Australians then drove the Japanese back. If Port Moresby had fallen, Australia itself would have been threatened.

Kolmeshoe Cemetery

See **Bitburg**.

Kolubra
See **Rudnik Ridges**.

Kolyma (Russia)
One of the huge labour camps existing east of the Urals during the Stalinist reign of terror. Along with **Vorkuta**, these two camps symbolized the political repression and nightmare of the Gulag era. It was closed by Nikita Khrushchev, the successor to Joseph Stalin.

Königsberg
Capital of East Prussia, now Kaliningrad in Russia. A German stronghold and naval base, it was heavily fortified during the Second World War. The Soviet advance into East Prussia and Poland had isolated the city by January 1945. The German garrison held until overwhelmed by four Soviet armies on 9 April 1945. Much of the city was destroyed and over 67,000 soldiers and civilians killed. Ceded to the Soviet Union in 1945 under the **Potsdam** Agreement, it was renamed Kaliningrad in 1946.

Korneuberg (Austria)
Town which gave its name to the Korneuberg Oath, the declaration by leaders of the Austrian *Heimwehr* on 18 May 1930. The declaration provided the *Heimwehr*'s most openly Fascist ideological statement, vowing to end the Austrian Republic and replace it with a corporatist state.

Kosice (Slovakia)
Town bombed on 26 June 1941 in a stage-managed incident to secure Hungary's entry into the war on the side of Germany. Three planes bombed Kosice, a town ceded to Hungary by the **Munich** Agreement, four days after Germany had attacked the Soviet Union. These planes were apparently Soviet but in reality they were German. This seeming act of aggression by Russia was sufficient to provoke a Hungarian declaration of war. On 4 April 1945, under the leadership of Edvard Benes, a National Front provisional government of Social Democrats, Socialists and Communists was established here as the liberation of Czechoslovakia rapidly gathered pace. **Prague** was liberated on 9 May.

Kosovo Plain (Serbia)
Region of southern Serbia, along the Albanian border. During the First World War the Serbian army had retreated to the Kosovo Plain by November 1915. Under attack from two sides, the Serbs withdrew across the mountains to Albania. Harsh terrain and wintry weather claimed thousands of Serbian lives. Given autonomous status in

1974, Kosovo suffered from ethnic tension between the Albanian and Slav populations, leading to open violence in the late 1980s. A state of emergency was declared in February 1990, the Kosovo government and parliament were dissolved and the region was formally annexed by Serbia in September 1990.

Kota Bahru (Malaysia)

Port on the South China Sea coast of northern Malaya. At dawn on 8 December 1941 a force of over 5,000 Japanese troops landed against stiff resistance from the 8th Indian Brigade. Once the beachhead was secured, the Japanese advanced inland to capture the airfield.

Kouang-Tchéou-Wan (China)

Occupied by France in 1898 for use as a naval station and coaling depot. In 1900 it was leased from China, and in the same year it was attached administratively to **Indo-China**.

Krasnoyarsk (Russia)

Site in Siberia of a crucial Soviet military installation. The radar station, the size of an Egyptian pyramid, was the centre of a dispute because it violated the American–Soviet Anti-Ballistic Missile Treaty.

Kreimhild Line (France)

German fortified position in western France during the First World War, completed in 1918.

Kreisau

Location of the estate of the German Count Helmuth von Moltke. The place gave its name to the Kreisau Circle, the group of German intellectuals, all firm Christians, who were bitterly opposed to Hitler. Although opposed on principle to violent action against the Nazi dictator, many were tried and executed after the July bomb plot on Hitler's life in 1944.

Kronstadt (Russia)

Naval base on Kotlin Island across the water from St Petersburg. Having opposed the provisional government since the February Revolution, the Kronstadt sailors supported the Bolsheviks in the October Revolution of 1917. Disenchantment with the Bolsheviks soon set in, fuelled by food shortages, strict economic measures and a lack of political freedoms. As strikes and food riots gripped Petrograd (**St Petersburg**), the sailors formed a Provisional Revolutionary Committee and openly demanded economic reforms, civil rights and new elections. The Soviet government declared the Kronstadt Mutiny a counter-revolutionary conspiracy and troops led by Mikhail Tukhachevsky stormed the mutineers' headquarters in the Kronstadt fortress on 17 March with heavy loss of life on both sides. Many of those involved were arrested and shot. The immediate effects of the Kronstadt Mutiny were to strengthen Bolshevik control.

Kuibyshev (Russia)

City on the Volga river, site in the Second World War of the relocation of parts of the Soviet government when Moscow itself was threatened by the German advance. The Central Committee of the Communist Party, all the diplomatic corps and many military agencies were moved there in October 1941.

Kumanovo (Macedonia)

Central city northeast of Skopje. The Turkish offensive into **Macedonia** during the First Balkan War was met by the Serbs on 24 October 1912. The three-day battle was a decisive victory for the Serbian army under King Peter I.

Kurdistan

Name of the homeland sought by 25 million Kurds living in Turkey, Iraq, Syria and Iran. The Kurds were denied a homeland in the post-First World War reordering of the Middle East and have since been fighting for independence. In the wake of the UN coalition's defeat of Iraq in the war over **Kuwait** in 1991 a Kurdish rebellion liberated the Kurdish area in northern Iraq and Western forces have since been protecting an autonomous area. The Iraqi Kurds, however, remain divided among themselves. Saddam Hussein took advantage of these divisions to ally himself with the Kurdish Democratic Party in 1996. Iraqi troops helped capture Arbil and provoke further confrontation with the USA. The Turkish Kurds are caught up in a widespread guerrilla war between the Kurdish Workers Party and the Turkish army.

Kure (Japan)

Second city of Hiroshima Province. From 1945 to 1951, the headquarters of the British Commonwealth Occupation Force in Japan.

Kuril Islands (Russia)

Archipelago of 56 islands stretching 750 miles from the northeastern shore of Hokkaido, Japan, to the southern tip of Kamchatka, Russia. Captured by the Soviet Union in the closing stages of the Second World War, the islands were ceded to the

Soviet Union under the **Yalta** Agreement of 1945, and the Japanese population forcibly repatriated. Japan still claims sovereignty over the four southern islands nearest to Hokkaido. Russia has so far resisted Japanese demands for their return and the issue remains a major source of dispute, Japan having refused economic aid to Russia ("no islands, no money") until the dispute is settled.

Kursk (Russia)

City in western Russia. Scene of the largest tank battle in history (5–15 July 1943). In early 1943 the advancing Red Army liberated Kursk and pushed forward into the German lines. The German counter-offensive, Operation Citadel, was planned as a pincer attack to regain the lost ground. Under Field Marshal Model the Germans, with 900,000 men and 2,700 tanks, confronted the Soviet forces of Marshal Zhukov, commanding 1,350,000 men and 3,300 tanks. Despite the pouring rain and muddy ground, the Germans initially had some success before retreating in the face of the Soviet counter-attack. This last major German offensive on the Eastern Front ended with German losses of 70,000 men, 1,500 tanks and 1,000 aircraft.

Kut-al-Amara (Iraq)

Town on the Tigris, in what is now Iraq, captured from the Turks by British and Indian troops in September 1915. General Townshend led an advance north to Baghdad but was defeated at **Ctesiphon** and fell back on Kut-al-Amara. The garrison then underwent a four month siege, falling to the Turks on 29 April 1916. 10,000 prisoners were taken and two-thirds of them died on the subsequent march across the desert. 23,000 of the relief force also died.

Kutch, Rann of (India)

Disputed territory in India, part of which is claimed by Pakistan. Pakistan and India fought a major tank battle in the region during the 1965 war.

Rann of Kutch

Kuwait

Independent sheikhdom in the Persian Gulf. The unprovoked invasion of Kuwait by Iraq in 1990 precipitated the Gulf War. See Appendix 2.

Kwai, River (Thailand)

River in central Thailand. During the Second World War Allied POWs were used by the Japanese as forced labour to build the "death railway" from Bangkok to Burma. The section over the River Kwai was immortalized by the Pierre Boule book "Bridge on the River Kwai" and the 1957 David Lean film of the same name. The bridge and a cemetery in nearby Kanchanaburi commemorate the thousands who died building the railway.

Kwajalein (Marshall Islands)

Second World War battle on this coral atoll in the west Pacific. With the Gilbert Islands recaptured, US Admiral Nimitz targeted the neighbouring Marshall Islands. On 1 February 1944 the 4th US Marine and 7th US Infantry divisions landed on Kwajalein atoll (Operation Flintlock). Three days of fierce fighting left all 8,000 Japanese defenders dead. Only 372 US troops were killed out of a landing force of 41,000.

Kwangju (South Korea)

Important southern city, the location of the Kwangju Massacre of May 1980. General Chun Doo-hwan, South Korea's military ruler, ordered his troops to suppress a pro-democracy demonstration. Official records say 224 people died, but reliable local sources place the death toll at 2,000. Chun Doo-hwan relinquished power in 1987 and was arrested in December 1995.

Ladysmith (South Africa)

City in northwest Natal near the border with the Orange Free State. Boer advances into Natal in October 1899 forced the British back to the railway junction of Ladysmith. Beginning on 2 November, the town was besieged and bombarded by the Boers under General Joubert. More than 3,000 defenders were killed in the four-month siege, but the garrison held out. On 28 February 1900, Ladysmith was finally relieved by British cavalry led by General Buller.

Laesong

See **Panmunjon**.

Lahore (Pakistan)

Leading city of the Punjab (previously in India) which gave its name to the Lahore Resolution, passed by the All-India Muslim League on 23 March 1940. The Lahore Resolution which specified the "basic principles" for a constitution once Britain quit India, and which stressed that those areas in which the Muslims were in a numerical majority should be grouped to constitute Independent States, effectively paved the way for the subsequent creation of Pakistan.

Lakehurst (United States)

Town in New Jersey which was the US terminus for transatlantic airship voyages. On 6 May 1937 the giant German airship *Hindenburg* exploded into a ball of flames as it started to land. Despite seven million cubic feet of burning hydrogen above them, 61 passengers and crew survived, but 36 died.

Lakitelet (Hungary)

Village which achieved fame as the birthplace of the conference which produced the Hungarian Democratic Forum, which went on to become the victor in the 1990 elections, the first free elections after the Communist era in Hungary.

Laknta (Chad)

Scene of battle on 22 April 1900 between French colonial forces and Rabah Zobeir, an Arab raider and slave trader. Rabah Zobeir was defeated and the French victory marked an important advance in putting an end to the slave trade.

Lancaster House (England)

Scene in London of talks on the independence of Zimbabwe (formerly Southern **Rhodesia**) which began on 10 September 1979. A treaty was signed at Lancaster House on 21 December and Zimbabwe became independent in 1980.

Lanet (Kenya)

Location of the army mutiny of 23 January 1964 which was suppressed with the help of British troops. A revolt took place the same day in **Jinja** in Uganda. Earlier in January there had been a coup in **Zanzibar** and an army revolt in Tanganyika.

Lang Son (Vietnam)

City and provincial capital in the north, the scene of armed conflict between China and Vietnam after rising tension between the two countries in 1979. Chinese forces launched an invasion of Vietnam on 17 February 1979 in retaliation for Vietnam's intervention in Cambodia. Following the fall of Lang Son on 3 March 1979 the Chinese government announced that it had accomplished its aims, and the withdrawal of its forces was completed by 16 March 1979.

Laon (France)

Fortress town northeast of Paris. German forces captured the town on 30 August 1914 and remained in occupation until late 1918. A French offensive across a broad front in August 1918 succeeded in slowly pushing back the German front line. Laon was eventually recaptured after heavy bombardment on 13 October 1918.

Lao People's Democratic Republic

See **Laos**.

Laos

Independent state in Southeast Asia (formerly part of French **Indo-China**). The scene of a protracted civil war from 1959 to 1975. The arrest of Prince Souphanouvong and other leaders of the Communist Pathet Lao on 28 July 1959 marked the end of attempts at coalition government and the beginning of a three-way conflict between Neutralists under Premier Prince Souvanna Phouma, Rightists under General Nosavan, and the Pathet Lao. International efforts to find a settlement led to a ceasefire on 3 May 1961 and recognition for the neutrality of Laos at a conference in Geneva on 23 July 1962, but fighting resumed in Laos, with growing involvement by North Vietnam, Thailand and the USA. The South Vietnamese army attacked Laos on 8 February 1971 to disrupt the **Ho Chi Minh Trail**. A new ceasefire agreement was reached on 21 February 1973, and a coalition government formed in 1974. Communist victories in Vietnam and Cambodia in April 1975 opened the door to a takeover by the Pathet Lao in Laos. The Pathet Lao declared the capital Vientiane liberated on 23 August 1975, and Laos was proclaimed the Lao People's Democratic Republic on 2 December 1975, with Prince Souphanouvong as President.

La Panne (Belgium)

Headquarters in the First World War of the Belgian Government.

Lapua (Finland)

Town which gave its name to the right-wing anti-Communist Lapua Movement. It arose in 1929 as a semi-Fascist movement calling for the suppression of the Finnish Communist Movement and its front organizations (which it achieved in October 1930). It was itself banned in 1932. The Lapua Movement exhibited all the excesses of other far-right European Fascist groups.

Lari (Kenya)

Scene of the Lari Massacre of 26 March 1953 during the Mau Mau rebellion in **Kenya**. In the massacre, the Mau Mau murdered over 100 Kikuyu tribesmen of the loyal chief Luka. Earlier, in 1952, they had assassinated Waruhiu, the senior chief.

Las Dos Erres (Guatemala)

Village located in the northern province of Pelen, the scene of a notorious 1982 massacre of local villagers. The massacre, by government troops or agents, took place during the administration of Gen Efrain Rios Montt.

Las Guásimas (Cuba)

Scene of battle in the Spanish–American War. In the US landing in Cuba (at Daiquiri on 22 June 1898), the Spanish offered no resistance but decided to hold Las Guásimas, a gap in the hills leading to **Santiago de Cuba**. The US forces drove the Spaniards back after a short battle.

Lashio

See **Burma Road**.

Lateran (Italy)

Palace in Rome, which gave its name to the Lateran Pacts of February 1929 between Mussolini's Fascist government and the Papacy. The pacts ended the long-standing Church–State conflict in Italy which had persisted since the *Risorgimento*.

Latrun (Israel)

Village lying to the west of **Jerusalem**, the scene of heavy and repeated combat during the 1948 Arab–Israeli War as Zionist forces attempted to secure the road to Jerusalem.

Latvia

Northeastern European country on the Baltic Sea, and one of the **Baltic States**. Latvia declared its independence from Russia on 18 November 1918. Two years of

135

fighting German and Soviet occupying forces finally secured complete independence. Latvia was incorporated into the Soviet Union in 1940, but invaded and occupied by Germany in 1941. This ended in 1944 with Soviet re-annexation. National unrest during the later 1980s led to multi-party elections and a new Popular Front government. A March 1991 referendum resulted in 73.7 per cent voting for independence, which was declared on 21 August 1991 and recognized by the Soviet Union on 10 September 1991.

Lausanne (Switzerland)

Resort which gave its name to the Treaty of Lausanne of 24 July 1923. Under this treaty Turkey surrendered its claims to territories of the **Ottoman Empire** occupied by non-Turks, effectively surrendering the Arab lands. The Turks retained Constantinople and eastern Thrace in Europe. Both sides of the Greek–Turkish border were demilitarized. Turkey took Smyrna from Greece but surrendered all the Aegean islands except **Imbros** and Tenedos which were returned to Turkey. The annexations of **Cyprus** by Britain and of the **Dodecanese** by Italy were also recognized.

Lebanon

Independent state in the Middle East. A former French-mandated territory, Lebanon's history has been dominated by internal conflicts:
1) civil war broke out in April 1958 between the pro-Western government of President Chamoun, dominated by Maronite Christians, and pro-Nasserite Muslims. Following the overthrow of the Iraqi monarchy in an army coup on 14 July 1958, President Chamoun appealed for aid, and on 15 July US troops landed in **Beirut**;
2) prolonged civil war (and invasion) between 1975 and 1991. Tensions between the Christian and Muslim communities in Lebanon were exacerbated by the influx of Palestinian guerrillas expelled from **Jordan** in 1971. A state of civil war existed after a massacre of Palestinians by Phalangist gunmen on 13 April 1975. Syrian forces were drawn into the conflict on 1 June 1976. A ceasefire was agreed to on 17 October 1976, backed by an Arab Deterrent Force consisting mainly of Syrian troops, but fighting soon resumed. Palestinian raids into Israel led to an Israeli incursion into Lebanon from 15 March to 13 June 1978. Israel launched a full-scale invasion of Lebanon on 6 June 1982 and forced a Palestinian evacuation from Beirut, beginning on 22 August 1982. Israel withdrew its forces from Lebanon during 1985. Fighting between the various factions continued unabated. Eventually, Syrian forces occupied West Beirut in strength on 22 February 1987 to separate the warring militias. A bloody new phase in the conflict began in March 1989 when the Maronite Christian general, Michel Aoun, launched a "war of liberation" against Syria. This lasted until 13 October 1990, when Aoun sought sanctuary in the French embassy in Beirut. The problem of attacks on Israel from Lebanon produced Israeli military retaliation in 1995–6.

Le Cateau (France)

First World War battle (26 August 1914) around this town in northeast France between Saint-Quentin and Mons. The BEF and French Army, retreating from Mons, were threatened by the wide sweep of the German 1st Army. In the greatest battle involving British troops since Waterloo, the left flank of the BEF resisted 11 hours of heavy German assaults. Outnumbered and outgunned, the British eventually retreated south to Saint-Quentin under the cover of darkness. Despite sustaining over 8,000 casualties, the British succeeded in delaying the German advance long enough to let the main body of the BEF escape.

Ledo Road

Allied supply route between Ledo in Assam, India, and Myitkyina in northern Burma. With the **Burma Road** cut at Lashio in April 1942, the Allies planned an alternative route. Construction began around Ledo in December 1942, but it was not until Myitkyina and the Hukawng Valley had fallen in August 1944 that any progress was made in Burma. It was finished on 27 January 1945.

Lemberg (Ukraine)

Capital of **Galicia** in the Austro-Hungarian Empire, now L'vov in the Ukraine. Captured by the Russians on 3 September 1914, it was retaken during an Austrian counter-attack on 22 June 1915. In 1917 the Kerensky provisional government in Russia came under considerable Allied pressure to launch a new offensive on the **Eastern Front**. Despite domestic pressure for peace, the Russian assault against Lemberg began on 1 July 1917. The Germans counter-attacked on 19 July and the demoralized Russian army retreated in disarray. Known as the Kerensky Offensive, it was the final significant Russian action of the First World War.

Lena (Russia)

Large river in Russia and centre of a major gold-producing area, it was the scene in April 1912 of the Lena goldfield massacre. The 5,000 strikers, seeking higher wages and improved working conditions in an inhospitable region, were fired on by troops. Some 200 were killed and scores more wounded. The massacre led to industrial militancy throughout Tsarist Russia. The *Duma* (Russian Parliament) subsequently initiated an investigation which produced a damning indictment of the management of the goldfield.

Leningrad (Russia)

City on the Baltic coast formerly Petrograd, now known again as **St Petersburg**. On 1 September 1941 German troops reached Leningrad and began bombarding the city. Rather than risk an all-out assault, the Germans laid siege, cutting Leningrad off from the rest of Russia. Within two months 300 people a day were dying from starvation, and Russian attempts to lift the siege proved futile. Once winter had set in an ice road across the frozen Lake Ladoga enabled some supplies to be trucked in. For 900 days Leningrad was effectively isolated, besieged and bombarded, and the population decimated by cold, hunger and disease. The siege was finally lifted on 27 January 1944 after claiming an estimated one million lives.

Lens (France)

First World War battle for this town near **Lille**. Captured by the Germans in October 1914, Lens was the focus of constant fighting throughout the war. In May 1917 British and Canadian troops, seeking to divert German troops from the **Ypres** front, attacked the town. The battle descended into house-to-house fighting as the Germans held their ground. Allied losses at Ypres determined that any further assaults on Lens were abandoned in August 1917. The town was eventually recaptured on 3 October 1918.

Leticia (Colombia)

Territory in South America disputed between Colombia and Peru. Awarded to Colombia in 1922, but the subject of renewed friction in 1932 when Peru entered the territory and removed Colombian officials, and sporadic fighting occurred. After Luis Sánchez Cerro was murdered in April 1933, Peru softened its stance. In 1934 an international commission returned the territory to Colombia.

Leuven

Flemish name for **Louvain** (Belgium).

Leyte (Philippines)

Island between **Luzon** and Mindanao. On 22 October 1944 it was the first of the Philippine Islands to be invaded by the USA, triggering the Battle of Leyte Gulf (23–26 October) which was the last, largest and most decisive naval encounter in the war in the Pacific. The Japanese strategy of using a decoy force to draw away the US 3rd Fleet led to four separate engagements around the island. The main attack was against the US invasion force under General MacArthur. Half the attacking forces were defeated in Surigao Strait in this last encounter between battleships in the Second World War, but the Japanese nearly succeeded in destroying the beach head. Failing to press home his advantage, Kurita withdrew too early, giving the US 3rd Fleet time to arrive. Leyte Gulf marked the end of the Japanese challenge to US naval supremacy in the Pacific.

Lhasa

Capital of Tibet. The objective of the British Younghusband Expedition. The successful completion of this expedition led to the imposition of the Treaty of Lhasa on

7 September 1904, paving the way for trade between India and **Tibet**. Tibet was forced to pay an indemnity, the British occupying Chumbi Valley until this was done. China acquiesced in the Treaty in 1906.

Liaoyang (China)

Town in central Liaoning Province in southern Manchuria, scene of the first major land battle of the Russo-Japanese War. The Japanese army advanced inland along the railway meeting Russian defences concentrated to the south of Mukden. Fighting started with the Japanese attack on 25 August 1904, but neither side could gain the upper hand. The Russian counter-offensive on 1 September stretched Oyama's forces but was held. The Russians retreated with both sides suffering high casualties, (23,500 Japanese, 16,500 Russians).

Liberia

Independent republic in West Africa. Founded in 1847 as a homeland for freed slaves, the country remained a backwater for much of the twentieth century. Its early political history was dominated by William Tubman, president from 1944 to 1971. Economic decline produced a revolution in 1980 led by Master-Sergeant Samuel Doe. He in turn was faced with a revolt. The insurrection against his government began on 24 December 1989, with military action by National Patriotic Front guerrillas, who had infiltrated from the Ivory Coast under the leadership of Charles Taylor. President Doe was killed on 11 September 1990, after being wounded and captured by a splinter group of rebels led by Prince Yormie Johnson. Despite the presence of a peacekeeping force, established under the auspices of the Economic Community of West African States, fighting continued between Prince Johnson's men, the National Patriotic Front and forces formerly loyal to President Doe. Despite a ceasefire agreement at the end of 1990, there was continued violence. This violence has continued intermittently into the mid-1990s.

Libya

Independent state in North Africa. Formerly part of the **Ottoman Empire**, then conquered by Italy, after 1945 it came under British influence. It became an independent kingdom under King Idris until its fall in 1969 in a coup led by Colonel Gaddafi. Gaddafi's radical regime was suspected of close involvement with extremist terrorism, prompting the Libya Raid. US F-111 bombers struck at military and political targets in Libya in retaliation for what the US government alleged was Libyan involvement in bombing a Berlin disco and killing a US serviceman. The raid on 14 April 1986 was popular in the US but many of the USA's Western allies opposed it. Prime Minister Margaret Thatcher's decision to allow US jets to operate from British bases aroused much criticism in Britain.

Lidice (Czech Republic)

Central Bohemian village, northwest of **Prague**. In retribution for the assassination of SS Deputy Leader Reinhard Heydrich, the Germans destroyed the village on 10 June 1942. All 172 men were shot, and the women shipped to **Ravensbrück** concentration camp. Many of the 90 children were sent to Gneisau concentration camp, though some were racially screened, renamed and raised as Germans. The village was burned and levelled, and remains a monument to Czech resistance. A new village was built nearby in 1947.

Lille (France)

Largest city in northern France with significant industrial capabilities. Declared an open city by the French government early in the First World War, it was bombarded and occupied by German forces on 12 October 1914. German troops remained until forced to retreat in October 1918.

Lima (Peru)

Capital city, the location of the Lima Declaration of the Pan-American Conference of December 1938. This stated that any threat to the peace, security or territory of any American republic would be a matter of concern to all republics. It was a successful attempt by President Roosevelt to rally opinion on the US continent against totalitarianism in Europe, although some South American signatories openly sympathised with Fascism rather than the liberal democracy of the USA.

Limehouse (England)

Formerly very poor working-class area of London's East End famous for:
1) the radical rhetoric of Liberal politician Lloyd George in a heated speech at the time of the 1909 People's Budget;
2) the Limehouse Declaration, the statement put out on 25 January 1981 by the "Gang of Four" (the founding fathers of the Social Democratic Party), proposing the formation of a Council for Social Democracy as a protest against the Labour Party's newly introduced method of selecting a leader, and more generally against the Party's shift to the Left. "We believe", the Declaration said, "that the need for a realignment of British politics must now be faced". One of the Gang, Dr David Owen, lived in Limehouse.

Limoges (France)

Town which gave birth to the word *limoger*, denoting the process by which inefficient French officers in the First World War were relieved of battlefield command, but not of rank, by being transferred to army headquarters in the quiet area around Limoges. A substantial number of officers suffered this treatment during 1914 and 1915.

Linggadjati (Indonesia)

Resort village, location (near Cheribon in north Java) of the March 1947 agreement between the Indonesian nationalists and the Dutch authorities in which the new republic conceded the principle of a federal Indonesia. The agreement (sometimes known as the Cheribon Agreement) was not implemented.

Lithuania

Republic on the eastern shore of the Baltic and one of the **Baltic States**. On 16 February 1918 Lithuania declared its independence from the Russian Empire, but had to fight both German and Soviet troops before its independence was secured under the Treaty of Moscow on 12 July 1920. Annexed by the Soviet Union in 1940, Lithuania was invaded and occupied by Germany 1941–4. Multi-party elections in 1990 led to a new declaration of independence on 11 March 1990 followed by clashes with Soviet forces and economic blockade by the Soviet Union. Independence was finally achieved on 10 September 1991.

Little Rock (United States)

State capital of Arkansas. In September 1957 the town hit the headlines when the Governor, Orval Faubus, called out the National Guard to try to prevent black children from entering segregated white schools. In response President Eisenhower drafted troops into Little Rock to enforce educational desegregation, under the terms of a 1954 Supreme Court decision that had declared racial separation unconstitutional. The incident marked a turning point in the history of segregation in schools and led to a gradual change in white attitudes in Arkansas.

Lobos (Argentina)

Small town in Buenos Aires province, the birthplace of Juan Perón (on 8 October 1895).

Locarno (Switzerland)

Town in the south, which in 1925 gave its name to a series of diplomatic agreements known as the Locarno Treaties or Locarno Pact. The signatories (Britain, Belgium, France, Germany and Italy) guaranteed the existing borders and boundaries of Germany, Belgium and France, as laid out in the Treaty of **Versailles**, and reaffirmed the demilitarization of the **Rhineland**. Initialled in Locarno on 16 October 1925, the treaties were formally signed on 1 December 1925 in London. Following Locarno, Germany was admitted into the League of Nations in September 1926. The Locarno treaties were broken when Hitler sent troops into the Rhineland in March 1936.

Lockerbie (Scotland)

Scene of one of the worst terrorist acts against a civilian airliner. A Pan Am Boeing

747, flying from London to New York, was blown up by a bomb while flying above Lockerbie on 21 December 1988. The explosion killed 259 passengers and crew and also eleven residents of the village. Almost certainly the perpetrators were Middle East terrorists, but no one has yet been put on trial for the outrage.

Lod Airport (Israel)

Near Tel Aviv, the scene in 1972 of repeated attacks by left-wing terrorists. On 8 May a Belgian Sabena Airlines plane en route from Vienna to Tel Aviv was hijacked by four Black September terrorists and diverted to Lod Airport. Israeli paratroopers disguised as mechanics entered the plane on 9 May, shot dead two hijackers and wounded a third. On 31 May, three Japanese Red Army terrorists attacked passengers at Lod Airport, killing 26 and wounding 76.

Łódź (Poland)

Central town, southwest of **Warsaw**. During the early stages of the First World War, the German assault on Warsaw and Russian offensive into **Silesia** both collapsed, leaving the two sides facing each other at Łódź. Strong defence by the Russians prevented the German capture of the town but left them in danger of being encircled. On 5 December 1914 the Russians withdrew from the town and straightened their front line to protect Warsaw. In the Second World War, following the German occupation in September 1939, Łódź was the site of the first main Jewish ghetto, created in April 1940.

Lofoten Islands (Norway)

Group of islands off the coast of Norway, the scene of one of the most celebrated commando raids of the Second World War. Led by Brigadier Lord Lovat the task of the commandos was to destroy the fish-oil processing station there, from which Germany was obtaining glycerine for the manufacture of explosives. Commandos sank 12 ships, destroyed 18 factories and burned some 800,000 gallons of petrol and oil. They also brought back an ENIGMA machine which proved vital to the ULTRA deciphering operation. See **Bletchley Park**.

Lomé (Togo)

Capital city which gave its name to the Lomé Conventions. The first, signed on 28 February 1975, was a trade agreement between the European Economic Community and (originally) 46 developing states, by which the latter were granted tariff-free entry for their products into EEC territory together with increased aid and investment. A second agreement (Lomé II) was signed on 31 October 1979 by 58 African, Caribbean and Pacific states with the EEC promising further aid. The Lomé agreements were further extended in the 1980s.

London (United Kingdom)

Capital city.

1) On 26 April 1915 Britain, Russia and France signed the secret Treaty of London with Italy. In return for entering the First World War on the Allied side, Italy was promised territorial gains from Austria-Hungary. The Treaty, exposed by Russia in 1918, was never honoured in full after the war.

2) In the Second World War London became the focus of the German bombing campaign against Britain, known as the Blitz. Beginning on the night of 7–8 September 1940, the bombing raids continued until December 1940, killing 12,700 Londoners and prompting the evacuation of children. Provincial cities such as **Coventry** and Portsmouth were also badly hit. London came under attack again in the summer of 1944 when Germany used the V1 and V2 rockets against the city.

Londonderry (Northern Ireland)

Town also known as Derry. Scene of Bloody Sunday on 30 January 1972 when British paratroops shot 13 unarmed Roman Catholic civilians on a peaceful civil rights demonstration. The army claimed it was responding to IRA fire. A Tribunal of Inquiry conducted by Lord Widgery exonerated British troops but the events intensified the bitterness felt by sections of the Catholic community against Britain and encouraged support for the IRA. On 21 January 1993 Prime Minister John Major conceded that none of those shot had been carrying weapons.

Long Tan (Vietnam)

Rubber plantation in Phuoc Try Province, South **Vietnam**. The scene of a bitter engagement on 18 August 1966 in the Vietnam War between a company of 100 Australian troops and a much larger force of 2,500 North Vietnamese. Long Tan became a symbol of Australian valour as the company held out against the Vietcong until a relief force finally broke through. There were much larger Australian engagements in South Vietnam, but Long Tan was "the legend of ANZAC upheld".

Loos (France)

First World War battle (25 September–15 October 1914) near this town in the northeast. The British 1st Army under General Douglas Haig launched an all-out offensive against the German positions, in tandem with a French attack to the east. Using poison gas for the first time, the British reached the German rear lines before a lack of reserves stopped the advance and the Germans successfully counter-attacked. No significant ground was gained by either side and the casualties were considerable. Final estimates were 60,000 British, 25,000 German dead.

Lop Nor (China)

Remote site in the barren empty desert country of Xinjiang Uygur Autonomous Region in China, used as the testing ground for the Chinese nuclear weapons programme.

Los Alamos (United States)

Research station in New Mexico. In the 1940s it was the centre for nuclear research, and where the first atom bomb was designed and developed under the direction of Robert Oppenheimer. The hydrogen bomb was subsequently developed at Los Alamos.

Los Angeles (United States)

Southern Californian metropolis, scene of violent rioting in early 1992. The disturbances were the culmination of the year-long Rodney King case. On 3 March 1991 an amateur video captured King being beaten by four white Los Angeles police officers. An all-white jury acquitted the officers, sparking off the riots. Underlying ethnic tensions boiled over into widespread looting and violence between 29 April and 4 May 1992. Over 50 people were killed and $1,000 million of damage was done to property. Two of the officers were eventually retried and convicted for violating King's civil rights.

Louvain (Belgium)

University town east of Brussels. In the First World War it was declared an open city and captured by the Germans in August 1914. On 25 August unidentified shots were heard in the town and the Germans took heavy retribution. Many civilians were shot as the population was forcibly removed to Germany as labourers. Much of the town was looted and burned, including the famous university library. Restored after the war, the library was destroyed again in the Second World War, and restored once more by multi-national contributions.

Lübeck (Germany)

City in north Germany. Much of the town was destroyed on 28 March 1942 by Allied aircraft in the first major demonstration of area bombing.

Lublin (Poland)

City in the east that gave its name to the Soviet-backed Polish Provisional Government during the Second World War (Lublin committee). Following the **Katyn** massacre in April 1943, relations between the Soviet Union and the Polish Government-in-exile in London deteriorated. In July 1944 the Soviet leader, Joseph Stalin established the Polish Committee of National Liberation at Lublin as the alternative legitimate government. The Western Allies insisted that the post-war government should include some London-based Poles. A new provisional government, comprising mainly Lublin committee members, was proclaimed in December 1944 and finally recognized by the West in July 1945. Also the site of **Majdanek** concentration camp.

Lubyanka (Russia)

The most infamous prison in the former Soviet Union during the Communist era. Located in Dzerzhinsky Square, Moscow, the building eventually became the headquarters of the Cheka, the secret police, established by the Bolsheviks in December 1917. The Cheka (later to become the KGB) interrogated and tortured thousands of its victims here, all of whom were political prisoners. The building, since the fall of Soviet Communism, still houses the secret police – now the Federal Counter-Intelligence Service.

Ludlow (United States)

Scene in Colorado of one of the most bitter episodes in any labour conflict. During a strike of coalminers against John D Rockefeller on 20 April 1914, National Guardsmen fired on the families of the strikers, setting fire to their tented camp and killing 17 women and children.

Lüleburgaz (Turkey)

First Balkan War battle near this town in Thrace, 86 miles northwest of Constantinople. With their offensive repulsed at **Kirk-Kilissa**, the Turks came under attack from the Bulgarian army. The fierce three-day battle (28–30 October 1912) was a disastrous defeat for the Turks, who withdrew to the fortified defences around Constantinople. The advancing Bulgarians failed to break through the lines and an armistice was agreed.

Luneberg Heath (Germany)

Location, southeast of Hamburg, of the German surrender in the West, on 8 May 1945.

Lu-Shun

See **Port Arthur** (China).

Luxembourg

West European country landlocked by France, Belgium and Germany. It achieved complete independence in 1848, and in 1867 its neutrality was guaranteed by all the European Powers. Despite this, Luxembourg was invaded by Germany during both World Wars, in August 1914 and again in May 1940. In the post-war era Luxembourg entered into the Benelux Economic Union with Belgium and The Netherlands, and was a founder member of the EEC. In 1966 EEC members negotiated an agreement known as the Luxembourg Accord which enables member states to veto any Council of Ministers' decision which threatens their national interests.

Luzon (Philippines)

Largest island in the archipelago.

1) Invaded by the Japanese on 10 December 1941 and most of the island was captured by January 1942. The last US troops surrendered in **Bataan** on 9 April. Following the invasion of **Leyte** island in December 1944, US forces were set to recapture Luzon. The US 6th Army stormed ashore in Lingayen Gulf on 6 January 1945. With further amphibious landings around Manila Bay the US troops advanced along three fronts. By 4 March **Manila**, Bataan and **Corregidor** were all back in US hands. Japanese resistance in the mountains continued until the end of the war when the last 50,000 troops surrendered. The Luzon campaign was the largest undertaken by US forces in the Pacific, with nearly 8,000 killed. Japanese losses totalled 192,000.

Luzon

2) When the Philippines became independent on 4 July 1946 the wartime Communist Anti-Japanese People's Liberation Army, or *Hukbalahaps*, waged a guerrilla campaign against the government of the republic. By 1950 the *Hukbalahaps*, with an army of 15,000 men and support of the peasantry, had established control over central Luzon. However, with US backing, a new Defence Secretary, Ramon Magsaysay, revitalized the Philippine armed forces. Counter-insurgency operations together with a programme of land reform and the resettlement of dissidents meant that by 1954 the revolt had petered out. The *Hukbalahap* leader, Luis Taruc, surrendered on 17 May 1954.

L'vov (Ukraine)

See **Lemberg**.

Lys River (Belgium)

First World War battle in Belgian Flanders. A concerted assault by the Germans against the weak British positions along the Lys River began on 9 April 1918. The German 6th and 4th Armies captured **Messines Ridge** overwhelming the British 1st and 2nd Armies. On 11 April the Germans advanced towards the ports of Calais, Boulogne and Dunkirk but were held by the outnumbered Allies. French reinforcements were rushed to the front and the German attacks were eventually repulsed. The battle ended on 29 April with the Germans having gained 10 miles at the expense of 350,000 casualties. Allied losses were 305,000, over 90 per cent of which were British.

Maalot (Israel)

Settlement in the north where Palestinian guerillas took hostage a school full of Israeli children in May 1974. In the Israeli army rescue attempt which followed 22 children died.

Maastricht (The Netherlands)

Town in the south, near the border with Germany and Belgium. Maastricht is now synonymous with the Treaty of Maastricht, signed on 10 December 1991, following a summit of European leaders which set out agreements reached on the Treaty of European Union. Leading a party deeply divided on Britain's relationship with Europe, Conservative Prime Minister John Major obtained opt-out clauses on a single currency and the Social Chapter on the grounds of the defence of British national interests. The Treaty was ratified by Parliament, despite a vigorous campaign for a referendum on the issue led in the House of Lords by John Major's predecessor, Margaret (now Baroness) Thatcher.

Macao

Former Portuguese colony in south China first occupied in 1557 and recognized as a dependency by China in 1887. In 1961 it became an Overseas Province of Portugal and in 1974 an autonomous Chinese territory under Portuguese constitutional law with an elected Legislative Assembly. In 1987 Portugal agreed to return the territory to China in 1999. Formerly best known for its casinos, it is now a developing industrial centre.

Macau

See **Macao**.

Macedonia

Land-locked republic in the **Balkans**. Historically part of the **Ottoman Empire**, Macedonia was divided between Serbia, Bulgaria and Greece under the Treaty of **Bucharest** in 1913. This partition remained in force until the Second World War when Macedonia was occupied by Bulgaria. The Treaty of Paris (1947) affirmed that the major part of the country had become the Republic of Macedonia within the federal **Yugoslavia**. Macedonia declared its independence from Yugoslavia on 18 September 1991, although tensions with Greece over its name prevented recognition by the international community. Macedonia gained UN membership in April 1993 by agreeing to be temporarily known as the Former Yugoslav Republic of Macedonia. In 1995 Greece finally dropped its opposition to the name and Macedonia was recognized.

McMahon Line

Boundary separating **Tibet** and Assam province, India. Negotiated at the **Simla** Conference (October 1913–July 1914), it was named after the chief British representative Sir Henry McMahon. The agreement was never signed by China, leading to later border disputes with India, culminating in the Sino-Indian War of October–November 1962. See **Himalayas**.

Madagascar

Large island off the southeast coast of Africa. A French colony since 1896, Madagascar became part of the Vichy French Empire following the fall of France in 1940. Allied fears that Japan would seize control led to a British commando raid on 5 May 1942. Having taken the strategic harbour of Diego Suarez, the British captured the rest of the island by 6 November. A Free French administration took over on 8 January 1943. Madagascan independence was proclaimed on 26 June 1960. Known as the Malagasy Republic from 1958 to 1975.

Madrid (Spain)

Capital of Spain.

1) A Republican stronghold, besieged throughout the Spanish Civil War. Early Nationalist victories meant that by 6 November 1936 four Nationalist columns were advancing on Madrid from four directions. General Mola boasted that Franco supporters within the city gave him a "fifth column", a phrase that has been used ever since. Despite repeated offensives and bombardment during the next nine months the Nationalists failed to break through. Both sides suffered heavy casualties. An 18-month lull in the fighting ended when the besieged Republicans turned on each

other, fighting a civil war of their own 6–12 March 1939. Renewed Nationalist assaults on 26 March precipitated the complete collapse of Republican defences as thousands surrendered. Nationalist forces entered Madrid on 31 March, sealing Franco's victory.

2) In October 1991 the USA and Soviet Union sponsored peace talks between Israel and the Arab front-line states in a bid to reach a settlement in the Middle East. The Madrid Peace Process involved both bilateral talks between Israel and its neighbours, Jordan, Syria, Lebanon and the Palestinians, as well as multilateral talks involving many members of the international community. The process resulted in little progress since the talks were held in the glare of publicity and none of the parties was willing to offer significant compromise. The deadlock was only broken when Israel and the PLO held secret talks in **Oslo** which resulted in the signing of a Declaration of Principles on 13 September 1993 between Palestinian leader Yasser Arafat and Yitzhak Rabin in Washington DC. This agreement, and subsequent clarifications negotiated in Cairo, paved the way for Palestinian autonomy under the Gaza-Jericho first deal. The peace process made further progress when Jordan and Israel signed a peace treaty on 18 October 1994. Talks between Israel, Syria and Lebanon continued with some signs of progress. Meanwhile, at the multilateral talks Morocco, Oman and Qatar proved willing to establish ties with Israel, and the Gulf States relaxed their economic boycott.

Mafeking (South Africa)

Town near the Transvaal–Bechuanaland border. On 13 October 1899 5000 Boer troops attacked the British garrison at Mafeking. With only 700 soldiers and 600 armed civilians Colonel Baden-Powell resisted the assault, forcing the Boers to lay siege to the town. The outnumbered British resisted for 217 days until the siege was lifted on 17 May 1900 by a column of British cavalry. The Boers suffered 1,000 casualties to 273 British. The "relief of Mafeking" became the most celebrated event of the Boer War in Britain.

Magersfontein (South Africa)

Boer War battle in Cape Province, near **Kimberley**. The Boer retreat from Modder River halted at Magersfontein, where the pursuing British attacked on 11 December 1899. Although numerically inferior, the Boers had strong defensive positions and withstood the British assault. Having lost more than 1,000 men, the British withdrew. This was the second British defeat of "Black Week" coming between **Stormberg** and **Colenso**.

Maginot Line (France)

Series of fortifications, built between 1929 and 1935, along the whole eastern frontier of France. Named after the French Minister of Defence, André Maginot, it was the world's strongest and most modern defence system, consisting of thousands of forts, underground towns, railways and power stations. The line was constructed as a means of countering a German attack. Owing to the Belgians' refusal to extend the line along their frontier with Germany, and French reluctance to appear to "abandon" Belgium and build the line along the France–Belgian border to the sea, the defensive strategy relied on the Germans' inability to penetrate the **Ardennes** forest. This hope was seen as misguided when the Germans were able to turn the French flank by an advance through Belgium, and the Maginot Line was still virtually intact when France surrendered on 22 July 1940.

Mai Cell (Ethiopia)
See **Maichew**.

Maichew (Ethiopia)
Key battle on 31 March 1936 of the Italian invasion of **Abyssinia**. The Emperor, Haile Selassie, had risked his forces attacking the Italian base at Maichew. The Italians, who knew of the impending attack, used air and artillery power to defeat Haile Selassie's forces. The victory at Maichew opened the way to Addis Ababa.

Maikop (Russia)
Oil-producing centre, the smallest major oil well of the Caucasus and the only one seized by the Germans in their drive on the area after 1941. The Nazis were driven out of the area in 1943.

Maisaloun (Syria)
In 1920 French forces invaded Syria seeking to oust the Arab government of King Faisal and assert their rights to mandatory power in the Levant. Faisal's forces under General Yussuf al-Azma were defeated at Maisaloun on 26 July 1920 and the French went on to occupy Syria.

Majdanek (Poland)
Concentration camp in **Lublin** built in 1941. Liberated by advancing Russian troops on 23 July 1944 it was unique as the only concentration camp to be liberated while still operational. It had become an extermination camp in 1942 and an estimated 1,380,000 Jews were killed here during the holocaust.

Makelle (Ethiopia)
Fortress attacked by the Italians during the invasion of **Abyssinia** which began in October 1935. The Italians captured the fortress on 8 November 1935.

Malabar (India)

The southern area of Malabar was the scene of the Moplah rebellion of 1921. The Moplahs, a Muslim community, began agitating against British rule. In August 1920 they declared an independent Khilafat kingdom under Raja Ali Musaliar. Their anger turned against Hindus and the worst communal violence in India prior to Partition ensued. The Indian Army required very substantial forces to quell the rebellion.

Malagasy Republic

See **Madagascar**.

Malaya

Now part of the independent Southeast Asian state of Malaysia. Formerly part of the British Empire, the Federation of Malaya was proclaimed on 1 February 1948. It immediately became the target of Communist insurgents, a period known as the Malayan Emergency. Communist guerrilla activity began, and a state of emergency was declared on 6 June 1948. In April 1950 General Sir Harold Briggs was appointed to co-ordinate anti-Communist operations. He inaugurated the Briggs Plan for settling Chinese squatters in new villages to cut them off from the insurgents. General Sir Gerald Templer became high commissioner and director of military operations on 15 January 1952, and a new offensive was launched on 7 February 1952. British authorities announced that the Communist Party's high command in Malaya had withdrawn to Sumatra on 8 February 1954. The emergency was officially ended on 31 July 1960.

Malines (Belgium)

Location, between 1921 and 1925, of the Malines Conversations between a group of leading Roman Catholic and Anglican theologians on areas of possible agreement. On the Catholic side, the leading figure was the Cardinal Archbishop of Malines, Désiré Joseph Mercier, and on the Anglican side Lord Halifax. Although there were some important areas of agreement (e.g. that the Body and Blood of Christ was received at the Eucharist) no lasting achievement resulted from the talks.

Malmédy (Belgium)

Town in Liège province, the location on 17 December 1944 of the Malmédy Massacre when German troops, advancing at the start of the Battle of the Bulge, shot 100 American prisoners. See also **Eupen-et-Malmédy**.

Malmstrom (United Sates)

US airforce base in west central Montana. War supplies were sent to the Soviet Union

151

from here after 1941 and crews were prepared for the Berlin Airlift. It was later home for the first Minuteman missiles in 1961.

Malta

Mediterranean island near Italy. Strategically positioned between Sicily and Tunisia, it was crucial in the fight for the Mediterranean during the Second World War. Heavily defended by the British, Malta was constantly attacked by German and Italian bombers. By May 1942 2,470 air raids had made Malta the most heavily bombed place on earth, and the island was awarded the George Cross for valour. With Malta's supplies reduced to almost nothing, an Allied convoy fought its way through from Gibraltar, arriving on 15 August 1942. Post-war tension with Britain resulted in independence in 1964 and the creation of a republic in 1974.

Maluku Islands
See **Moluccas**.

Malvinas
Spanish name for the **Falkland Islands**.

Mamaev Kurgan (Russia)
See **Mamai Hill**.

Mamai Hill (Russia)
Area within **Stalingrad**, scene of the bitterest fighting as the Germans attempted to conquer the city in 1942–3.

Manchukuo (China)
Name given to the Chinese province of **Manchuria** by the Japanese when they occupied it in 1931. They installed a puppet regime under the last Chinese Manchu emperor, Henry Pu Yi, which was overthrown by Chinese Communists and the Soviet Union in 1945.

Manchuria (China)
Northeastern region. Russian–Japanese rivalry for its control ended with Russia's defeat in the Russo-Japanese War of 1904–5. By 1930 it had effectively become a Japanese colony, a position that was consolidated when Japanese forces captured **Mukden** in October 1931, sparking off an international crisis. In February 1932 Japan

created the puppet state of **Manchukuo**, using it as a base for its invasion of China in 1937. In the closing stages of the Second World War Soviet troops invaded from Mongolia and Vladivostok, crushing Japanese resistance. Manchuria was reunited with China after the war.

Mandalay (Burma)

Town and river port in central Burma. Forever associated, as a result of the poems of Rudyard Kipling, with a romantic view of British imperialism ("Come you back you British soldiers, come you back to Mandalay"). It was captured by Japanese troops in May 1942, before being recaptured in March 1945 by Allied forces under General Slim.

Manerplaw (Burma)

Town near the Thai border which is the headquarters of the Karen rebels. In 1990 when the ruling State Law and Order Restoration Committee refused to recognize the victory of the anti-government pro-democracy forces in the 1990 general election, the opposition National Coalition Government of the Union of Burma was established at Manerplaw.

Manila (Philippines)

Capital city, scene of one of the worst atrocities committed by the Japanese during the Second World War. The month-long Rape of Manila in February 1945 left 100,000 people dead. Survivors recalled how Japanese troops lobbed grenades into air-raid shelters filled with refugees, herded civilians into buildings where they brutally tortured, killed and mutilated rape victims. The events of February 1945 were one of the main factors in President Truman's mind as he decided to use nuclear bombs to avoid the bloodbath of an invasion of Japan.

Mannerheim Line

Defensive measure across the Karelian isthmus. Named after Finnish military leader Carl Mannerheim, it was built in 1931-8 and designed to protect Finland from Soviet aggression. One million Soviet troops attacked in force on 30 November 1939 and were initially held at the Mannerheim Line. Continued bombardment and renewed assaults by the Soviet Union achieved a breakthrough, and a harsh peace was imposed on the Finns on 13 March 1940. In June 1941 Finland took advantage of the German assault on the Soviet Union and attacked the Russians. Despite early gains, the Finns were eventually overwhelmed and by September 1944 had to agree to a disadvantageous armistice. See also **Karelian Isthmus**.

Manzanar (United States)

Internment camp in California near the small town of Independence. Constructed in

1942, the camp held 10,000 Japanese-Americans interned during the Second World War after the attack on Pearl Harbor. In all, the US military authorities rounded up 110,000 people of Japanese descent (some two-thirds of them US citizens) living on the west coast of America and shipped them to ten internment camps. Plans to build a museum at Manzanar caused great controversy in 1996.

Maraçesti (Romania)

First World War battle for this strategic railway junction near the Ukraine–Romanian border. Crushing Austro-German victories during 1916 in **Galicia** and **Dobrudja** and the fall of Bucharest left the Romanian army in tatters. The remnants retreated with Russian reinforcements behind the River Sereth (Seret) into Moldavia. The Romanians, in their biggest battle of the war, then succeeded in repelling all the German assaults of August 1917.

Marco Polo Bridge (China)

Military incident near this crossing outside Beijing, when on 7 July 1937 Japanese troops, searching for a missing soldier, tried to enter the town of Wan-p'ing. The town's garrison blocked their entry, a shot was heard and firing started. Ceasefire negotiations failed as both sides refused to concede any ground. The conflict spread across central China and four years later this undeclared war became part of the Second World War in the Pacific.

Mareth Line (Tunisia)

At the end of its retreat across Libya General Rommel's Afrika Korps halted inside the Tunisian frontier and dug in along the Mareth Line, which had originally been constructed by the French to defend Tunisia from Libya. Rommel attacked General Montgomery's pursuing 8th Army in March 1943 but was driven back and lost 52 tanks, and subsequently returned to Germany. The Allies continued their attacks and by 26 March had broken through the line and took 7,000 German and Italian prisoners. On 7 April British forces met US troops advancing from the west and so prepared for the climax of the battle for North Africa.

Margival (France)

Small village in the north near Soissons, it was Hitler's headquarters in northern France during the Second World War. Chosen as the command centre for the planned invasion of England. Nazi strategy to counter the D-Day **Normandy** landings was planned here. There were fears in 1995 that the site might become a leisure centre attracting neo-Nazi fanatics.

Marianas Islands

Archipelago in the central western Pacific, 1,500 miles south of Japan. Occupied by

Japan during the First World War, the islands became a Japanese mandate under the League of Nations in 1919. Within bomber range of Japan, they were an important target for US forces during the Second World War. The three main islands of Guam, **Saipan** and Tinian were all recaptured 15 June–10 August 1944, but at great cost. Over 4,500 US troops died along with over 40,000 Japanese. The Northern Marianas became a US-administered UN Trusteeship after the war, becoming a self-governing commonwealth in 1978.

Mariel (Cuba)

Port which achieved fame as the embarkation point for thousands of disaffected Cubans seeking to flee Fidel Castro's Communist regime for Miami in Florida. During the Mariel affair, between April and June 1980, some 125,000 Cuban migrants boarded US-bound vessels. The exodus was officially permitted by the Cuban authorities after dissidents occupied the Peruvian embassy in Havana in April 1980. However, the USA protested that many of the Cuban migrants included criminals and drug addicts whose activities were blamed for destabilizing some southern US states. In December 1984 Cuba agreed to take back alleged criminals in exchange for Cuban political prisoners.

Marne (France)

First World War battles along this river in central eastern France. By early September 1914 the Germans had advanced to within 35 miles of Paris, forcing the British Expeditionary Force (BEF) and the French 5th Army to retreat. A French counter-attack on 4 September against the exposed German right flank precipitated a German withdrawal on 9 September. This defeat meant the end of Germany's Schlieffen Plan, designed to quickly defeat France, and the descent into trench warfare. The second battle (15 July–7 August 1918) was again a decisive German defeat. General Ludendorff's renewed threat to Paris was stopped by a Franco-American counter-offensive. The ensuing Allied advance culminated in the Armistice in November.

Martin (Slovakia)

Scene in the Second World War of the shooting by Soviet partisans of the German General Otto, military attaché for Bucharest, on 24 August 1944. The killing of the Nazi general caused Hitler to despatch huge SS and *Wehrmacht* reinforcements to Slovakia. This in turn led to the planned Slovak national uprising (*see* **Banska Bystrica**) being brought forward.

Maseru (Lesotho)

Capital of Lesotho (formerly Basutoland). The object of a major attack on 9 December 1982 by South African forces on alleged ANC targets in the city. Over 30 South

Africans and 12 Lesotho nationals were killed in the attack, carried out by 100 commandos of the South African Defence Force. The attack – the largest South African incursion into any country except Angola and Namibia – was a response to the increasing strength of the ANC inside South Africa itself.

Masurian Lakes

First World War battles in this marshy region of East Prussia, now in Poland. The Russian invasion of East Prussia in 1914 was planned as a pincer movement. With one arm decisively defeated at **Tannenberg** (26–30 August 1914), the second arm, the Russian 2nd Army under General Rennenkampf, held a defensive line from the Baltic Sea southwards to the Masurian Lakes. On 5 September 1914 General Ludendorff led the German 8th Army against the Russians. In danger of being outflanked, Rennenkampf retreated while counter-attacking the German centre to prevent encirclement. By 13 September the Russians were defeated, having lost 125,000 men. In the second battle (7–21 February 1915) the Germans, attempting to knock Russia out of the war, attacked from the east and north. After a fortnight of fighting in freezing conditions, three of the Russian corps had retreated, leaving 200,000 casualties and prisoners behind.

Matsu (Taiwan)

Small island in the East China Sea near **Taiwan**. In 1949 Nationalist Chinese forces, retreating to Taiwan from the Chinese mainland, occupied the neighbouring islands of **Quemoy** and Matsu. Bombardment of the islands by the Communist Chinese in September 1954 sparked off an international crisis. The US 7th fleet was redeployed, but a military conflict between the USA and China was averted after intense diplomatic negotiations.

Mauban (Philippines)

Important port on **Luzon** island. In the Second World War it was the site of the Japanese landing on 23 December 1941.

Maubeuge (France)

First World War siege of this strategic town near the Belgian border. Sited at the junction of five main railway lines and heavily fortified, the town was chosen in 1914 as the forward base for the British Expeditionary Force (BEF). The German siege began on 25 August 1914 and lasted until the town was captured thirteen days later. The French garrison of 35,000 surrendered to a force half its size.

Mauthausen (Austria)

Nazi concentration camp near this village on the River Danube, 12 miles east of Linz. Established in April 1938 as a satellite of **Dachau**, it became an independent camp in the spring of 1939. It was the centre for anti-Nazi prisoners, including 10,000 Spanish Republicans, Soviet prisoners of war and troublemakers from other camps. Inmates were starved, beaten, gassed and forced to work in local quarries. 122,000 prisoners died before liberation by US troops in May 1945.

Mazu Dao
See **Matsu**.

Mecca (Saudi Arabia)
One of two leading Muslim holy cities where the Prophet Muhammad lived and worked at the dawn of Islam, the other being Medina. They are both located in western Saudi Arabia and the Saudi Royal Family is proud of its role as protector of the two holy places. It is one of the duties of a devout Muslim to make the pilgrimage, *Haj*, to Mecca once in his life and every year thousands of *Hajis* visit the site. On the first day of the Muslim year 1400 (1979), a band of Muslim fanatics seized the Great Mosque in Mecca in protest at Saudi Arabian policies. It took two weeks to suppress them and the government was clearly alarmed at the spread of Islamic militancy.

Mecca/Medina

Mechelen (Belgium)
See **Malines**.

Medellin (Colombia)
City in the north synonymous in the 1980s with drug barons and drug trafficking. The drugs cartel, led by figures such as Pablo Escobar Gaviria, had its origins in the marijuana boom of the 1970s. But marijuana was rapidly replaced in the 1980s by cocaine derived from Bolivia and Peru. After endemic corruption and terror, and massive cocaine penetration of the American market, the late 1980s saw an all-out war on the Medellin drugs cartel. The cartel was partly broken and Escobar was killed in December 1993.

Medina (Saudi Arabia)
See **Mecca**.

Medjugorge (Croatia)
Site (in former Yugoslavia, near Citluk) of a reported vision by six children of the

157

Virgin Mary on 24 June 1981. The incident caused major embarrassment to the atheistic Communist regime, not least because the vision apparently espoused the cause of Croatian nationalism.

Meech Lake (Canada)

Series of constitutional amendments in 1987 known as the Meech Lake Accord by Canadian Premier Brian Mulroney and the Prime Ministers of the ten provinces in an attempt to make the 1982 constitution acceptable to the people of **Quebec**. The concessions made to Quebec separatists included recognition of French as the dominant language in Quebec, powers for Quebec to control immigration into the province and recognition that amendments to the constitution require the agreement of all ten provinces. The Accord caused acute political disagreement in 1990 in such provinces as New Brunswick, Manitoba and Newfoundland. On 22 June 1990 the Accord failed when Manitoba and Newfoundland did not approve it.

Meerut (India)

City 40 miles northeast of Delhi. Scene of the initial outbreak of the Indian Mutiny in May 1857, the town also gave its name from 1929 to 1933 to the Meerut Conspiracy, the trial of 32 Indian trade union leaders, most of them Communist. The Meerut Conspiracy case, brought by the Government of India, only temporarily disrupted the Indian Communist movement. New leaders came forward and the publicity generated by the case was counter-productive for the British.

Megiddo (Israel)

City 15 miles south of Haifa. The setting in the First World War for the beginning of General Allenby's offensive against the Turks. After the capture of **Jerusalem** in December 1917 General Allenby trained new reinforcements for renewed assaults on the Turkish line in Palestine. On 19 September 1918 Allenby attacked, having deceived the Turks into believing his thrust would come east of the Jordan River. The Turkish line collapsed around Megiddo and opened the way for the capture of Damascus on 2 October and Aleppo on 28 October. The British captured 75,000 prisoners for the loss of 5,600 men.

Melilla

See **Ceuta**.

Memel (Lithuania)

Port in East Prussia put under League of Nations' control by the Treaty of **Versailles** in 1919, but seized by **Lithuania** in 1923. In March 1939 it was seized by Germany.

Left as part of German East Prussia by the Nazi–Soviet Pact, it was absorbed into the Soviet Union after 1945 until Lithuania regained its independence. Now known as Klaipeda.

Memphis (United States)
City in Tennessee where on 4 April 1968 black civil rights leader Dr Martin Luther King Jr was assassinated by James Earl Ray. His death triggered race riots in major cities across the USA. Ray was arrested in London on 7 June.

Menin Gate (Belgium)
One of the main entrances to **Ypres**, a town devastated by the First World War. The Menin Gate was opened in July 1927 by Field Marshal Plumer as a memorial to the armies of the British Empire and especially to those of their dead whose graves are not known. The names of 55,000 men who fell in the Ypres salient are inscribed on its wall. The Last Post is sounded each evening at 20.00 hrs.

Mersa Matruh (Egypt)
Following the retreat from **Gazala**, the British 8th Army under General Auchinlek halted at the Egyptian base of Mersa Matruh. On 26 June 1942 General Rommel's Afrika Korps attacked and, although outnumbered, routed the British who lost 40 tanks and 6,000 prisoners. The 8th Army fell back to **el-Alamein**.

Mesopotamia
Region between the Tigris and Euphrates rivers in western Asia. In 1913 Britain had acquired the Persian Abadan oilfield and when the First World War began it sought to protect the oilfield and the route to India. British forces marched north from Basra but suffered the disaster of **Kut al-Amara** in 1916. Forces under General Maude, however, occupied Baghdad on 11 March 1917 and briefly occupied the **Baku** oilfield in May 1918, as well as taking Mosul. After the armistice of **Mudros** (30 October 1918) the British occupied all of Mesopotamia and briefly considered creating a single British dominion consisting of Palestine, Jordan, Iraq and Iran.

Messina (Sicily)
Town which hosted an international conference in June 1955 attended by Belgium, France, Italy, Luxembourg, The Netherlands and West Germany. The six countries agreed to create "a common European market" alongside the European Coal and Steel Community. The plan reached fruition in the Treaty of **Rome** in 1957.

Messines Ridge (Belgium)

First World War battle near **Ypres** in Flanders. The Germans occupied the ridge and the nearby village of Messines in November 1914. On 7 June 1917 a British offensive against the German positions on the ridge was launched using over 500 tons of explosives to breach the lines. The Allies captured the ridge, holding it until 12 April 1918.

Meuse (France)

First World War battle along this river in eastern France. The German advance into France in August 1914 was temporarily checked by the French 4th Army, forcing a German retreat back across the River Meuse.

Mexico

Independent state in Latin America famous for its revolution. It began as peasant uprisings in the north, led by Francisco Madero in the state of Chihuahua, and in the south led by Emiliano Zapata, in Moretos state. In 1911 President Diaz was forced to resign and Madero became President after an interim period. Initially disbanding his rebel armies, he used the federal army to defeat a rising in the north and to contain the more leftward leaning forces of Zapata, who broke out into open revolution at the end of 1911 demanding radical land reform. A counter-revolution in Mexico City in 1914 led to three years of confused civil war with numerous factions led by irregular leaders, such as Pancho Villa in the north, who formed an unstable alliance with Zapata in the south. In 1914 American troops occupied Veracruz in retaliation for the arrest of US sailors, contributing to the overthrow of the counter-revolutionary regime in Mexico. In July, the moderate Carranza assumed the Presidency and was recognized by the USA in 1915, but was forced to continue fighting the forces of Villa and Zapata. Villa's forces won an important battle at Torreon in 1914, but were defeated at **Celaya** in April 1915. Crossing the American border, Villa sacked **Columbus**, New Mexico, in March 1916 and was pursued by General Pershing into Mexico until requested to withdraw by Carranza. A Congress summoned to Mexico in 1917 established a new constitution, bringing most large-scale fighting to an end.

Midway Islands

The central sea clash of 4 June 1942 between the USA and Japan fought almost entirely by carrier-borne aircraft, with the USA losing one carrier to Japan's four, and which marked the turning point which halted the Japanese Pacific advance.

Milne Bay (New Guinea)

Cove on the eastern tip. A Japanese invasion force stormed ashore on 26 August 1942, but was repelled by Allied defences, forcing a withdrawal on 6 September. This was the first Japanese attack to be defeated by Allied troops.

Minamata (Japan)

Site of the worst environmental incident in Japanese post-war history, when more than 8,000 were victims of mass mercury poisoning in the 1950s. A chemical firm, Chisso, pumped tons of mercury sludge untreated into the sea while the government allowed the company to continue the pollution unchecked. The victims, who ate fish contaminated with mercury, were only offered final compensation 40 years afterwards (in 1995) on condition that they drop lawsuits against Chisso.

Mitla Pass (Egypt)

The opening phase of the Israeli invasion of **Sinai** comprised a parachute drop on 29–30 October 1956 on the Mitla Pass, the strategic road junction which controlled movement in the Sinai Peninsula. The eastern end of the Pass was successfully blocked to Egyptian reinforcements but subsequent Israeli attempts to enter the Pass were beaten off.

Mittelbau (Germany)

See **Nordhausen**.

Mogadishu (Somalia)

West German commandos stormed an airliner hijacked by the Baader-Meinhof gang at the airport in the Somalian capital of Mogadishu on 18 October 1977. 86 passengers were released, and three hijackers and one commando killed in the one-minute gun battle.

Mogilev (Russia)

Town located east of Minsk, southwest of Smolensk. Military headquarters of the Tsar in the First World War.

Möhne River (Germany)

Its enormous reservoir was one of the targets of the famous Dambusters Raid in the Second World War. The reservoir was successfully bombed and its waters released in a daring RAF raid on 16 May 1943.

Moldavia

Ancient principality and one of the Danubian Principalities which were amalgamated into the state of Romania in the nineteenth century, leaving part of the Moldavian population living in the Russian Empire. On 12 October 1924 the Soviet Union created the Moldavian Autonomous Soviet Socialist Republic with its boundary with Romania on the River Dniester. The former Moldavian Soviet Socialist Republic included the earlier Autonomous Republic and areas of Bessarabia ceded by Romania to the Soviet Union on 28 June 1940 with a largely Moldavian population. Since 1985 there had been open agitation for greater national autonomy on the part of the Moldavians within the Soviet Union, leading in August 1991 to a declaration of an independent Moldova.

Moldova
See **Moldavia**.

Moluccas (Indonesia)
Islands formerly part of the Dutch East Indies. The Moluccans have long agitated for independence. They first proclaimed their independence on 26 April 1950. In 1957 objections to Javanese domination of Indonesian affairs and suspicion of Dr Sukarno's left-wing policies led the military commanders in Borneo, Sumatra and Celebes to refuse to acknowledge the authority of the cabinet. A Revolutionary Government of the Indonesian Republic was proclaimed on 15 February 1958. The authorities took military action against the right-wing rebels, capturing their headquarters at Bukittingi on 5 May 1958, and their capital Menado on 26 June 1958. The rebel movement finally collapsed when an amnesty was offered on 31 July 1961 and the civilian leaders surrendered. Opposition from Darul Islam was also suppressed by 1962.

Monastir (Macedonia)
Town in southern Serbia near the Greek border, now known as Bitola in Macedonia. An important railway junction and military base, the town was captured by the Bulgarians in November 1915 as they advanced to the Albanian border. A combined Allied force of Russian, French and Serbian troops assaulted the Bulgarian defences and recaptured the town on 19 November 1916.

Mons (Belgium)
Town in southwest Belgium, which was the scene of the first battle between British and German troops in the First World War. On 23 August 1914 advancing German units clashed with the BEF, which had taken up defensive positions along the Mons canal. Despite superior firepower, the British were soon overwhelmed by the more numerous Germans. At midnight the British started to retreat southwards to the French border. This "Retreat from Mons" signalled the failure of the Allies to halt the German invasion of France. The battle is popularly remembered for the legend of a white angel on horseback appearing during the night to help the British to retreat without huge losses. Known as Bergen in Flemish.

Monte Cassino (Italy)
See **Cassino**.

Montenegro

Constituent republic of **Yugoslavia**. Having remained outside the **Ottoman Empire**, Montenegro gained much territory following victory in the two Balkan Wars (1912 and 1913). Occupied by **Austria** during the First World War, it became part of **Serbia** in 1918 after a plebiscite deposed King Nicholas I. German and Italian forces invaded in 1941 provoking stiff resistance led by the Communists. In 1946 Montenegro became one of the six republics in President Tito's federal Yugoslavia. Following the break-up of Yugoslavia a referendum in March 1992 resulted in Montenegro remaining with Serbia in the rump Yugoslav Federation.

Montevideo (Uruguay)

Capital whose important harbour was the setting in the Second World War for one of the most famous naval episodes of the war. On 13 December 1939 the German pocket battleship, the *Graf Spee*, had been trapped in the harbour by British cruisers. Rather than risk defeat, it was scuttled by her captain and crew. See Battle of the **River Plate**.

Montgomery (United States)

City in Alabama which played a landmark role in the US black civil rights campaign. In 1955 Rosa Parks was arrested for defying segregation on city buses in Montgomery. There followed a highly effective boycott of the city buses (Martin Luther King was one of the organizers) which eventually succeeded in ending segregation and achieving integrated transport.

Montoire-sur-le-Loire (France)

Town on the Loire near Vendôme. Location of the famous meeting (in a railway carriage) on 24 October 1940 between Marshal Pétain and Adolf Hitler. Pétain accepted the policy of collaboration with the Germans (although he refused to give up the French fleet to German control). The reputation of Pétain was irretrievably ruined by his public acceptance of collaboration.

Montreux (Switzerland)

Town which gave its name to the Montreux Convention of July 1936. Under the Convention, which revised the 1923 Treaty of **Lausanne**, fortifications were permitted along the **Dardanelles** and Bosporus. Turkey had claimed that the Italian dictator, Benito Mussolini, was preparing to attack Asia Minor from Italian bases in the **Dodecanese**.

Monza (Italy)

Town in which King Humbert I of Italy was assassinated on 29 July 1900.

Moosburg (Germany)

Bavarian town famous in the Second World War for its enormous prisoner-of-war camp. When US forces liberated the camp on 29 April 1945 over 100,000 prisoners were released.

Moresnet (Belgium)

Along with **Eupen-et-Malmédy**, this area was awarded to Belgium by the Treaty of **Versailles** in 1919.

Morocon (Honduras)

Town at the centre of the border conflict between Honduras and Nicaragua in 1957. On 18 April 1957 Nicaraguan troops crossed the Coco River and invaded Honduras to seize disputed border territory. Honduras recaptured the town of Morocon on 1 May. The Organization of American States (OAS) arranged a ceasefire and withdrawal of forces on 6 May 1957.

Moscow (Russia)

Capital of Russia, previously capital of the Soviet Union.

1) Food shortage and war discontent fuelled popular unrest in Moscow during the winter of 1916–17. Strikes and protests undermined the government in **Petrograd** and Moscow played a significant part in both revolutions of 1917. It became the capital of the new Bolshevik state in March 1918. As a Bolshevik stronghold it was the target of White Army attacks during the Civil War (1918–21). On 12 July 1920 the Treaty of Moscow ended Soviet involvement in **Lithuania** and established Lithuanian independence. A second Treaty of Moscow on 16 March 1921 fixed the Soviet frontier with Turkey and established diplomatic relations between the two countries.

2) In August 1936 a five-day show trial in Moscow led to the execution of 16 opposition Communists, including Grigori Zinoviev, former Head of Comintern. Further purges and trials occurred in 1937, with many generals and prominent Communists executed for treason.

3) During the Second World War the Germans had advanced to within 20 miles of Moscow by December 1941 but were defeated by fierce Russian resistance and the severe weather.

4) The liberalizing reforms of President Gorbachev in the 1980s led to an attempted coup by hard-line Communists and generals on 19 August 1991. Gorbachev, on holiday in the Crimea, was ousted and replaced by an emergency committee, prompting mass demonstrations against the coup. This popular resistance, led by Russian president Boris Yeltsin, precipitated the coup's collapse and Gorbachev was reinstated on 22 August. In the aftermath of the coup the Soviet Union disintegrated.

Mostar (Bosnia-Hercegovina)

Ancient town whose most famous attraction was the old bridge (*Stari Most*), a slender stone bridge built in 1566 to cross the Neretva river. This bridge, with its single span elegantly bridging the Neretva, was an architectural treasure and a symbol of the city. After sustaining repeated hits, the bridge was destroyed by Croat bombardment in November 1993.

Motherwell (Scotland)

Parliamentary constituency which was the first to return a Scottish National Party member to parliament in a by-election. The SNP won the seat on 12 April 1945 but the seat was lost in the subsequent 1945 general election. No further SNP candidate was victorious until **Hamilton** in 1967.

Mount Grammos (Greece)

Communist stronghold in the Greek Civil War. The Greek Communist Party made the decision to renew the armed struggle on 12 February 1946, and fighting began on Mount Olympus on 30 March 1946. The Communists' wartime National Popular Liberation Army (ELAS) was renamed the Democratic Army of **Greece** in December 1946. The Communist guerrillas, supported by Albania, Yugoslavia and Bulgaria, were initially successful. On 29 December 1947 their leader, Markos Vafiades, proclaimed a provisional republic in the mountains of northern Greece. But large quantities of aid sent from the USA after the proclamation of the Truman Doctrine on 12 March 1947 enabled government forces to take the offensive on 19 June 1948. Yugoslavia ceased to support the partisans after its expulsion from the Comintern on 28 June 1948. Mount Grammos, a rebel stronghold, was declared cleared by government troops on 28 August 1949. The Greek Communist broadcasting station announced the end of hostilities on 16 October 1949.

Mountjoy (Ireland)

Prison in Ireland, made famous by the execution there, on 1 November 1920, of a young Dublin medical student, Kevin Barry. His death brought a strong surge of support for Irish independence and the song written to commemorate his hanging took its place in the folklore of the Irish Republican Movement. The 18-year old Barry was executed for his part in an IRA arms raid in Church Street in which six British soldiers died.

Mozambique

Independent republic in southeast Africa. A former Portuguese colony in which a war of liberation was launched in 1964. The Marxist nationalist movement FRELIMO launched its first attacks on 25 September 1964, and gradually took control of large areas of the countryside. By 1974 Portugal was forced to maintain an army in Mozambique of 24,000 white and 20,000 locally enlisted troops. After the coup in Portugal on 25 April 1974, negotiations were opened with FRELIMO. Despite a violent revolt by white settlers in Lourenço Marques on 3 September 1974, a ceasefire agreement was signed on 7 September 1974 and Mozambique officially became independent on 25 June 1975. From 1976 on, **Rhodesia** fostered a guerrilla campaign by anti-FRELIMO dissidents in Mozambique, which was harbouring Robert Mugabe's ZANLA. After 1980 South Africa took over the support of the MNR as part of its policy of "destabilizing" its neighbours. The MNR concentrated on sabotage and guerrilla raids on communications, power lines and foreign-aided development projects. Mozambique and South Africa signed a non-aggression pact, the **Nkomati** Accord, on 16 March 1984, but MNR activity continued. The possibility of peace emerged in 1990, with talks between the government and MNR in **Rome** in July. A peace accord was signed on 7 August 1992 and a formal signature of peace ended the war in October 1992.

Mudros (Greece)

The Armistice of Mudros on 30 October 1918 ended the **Ottoman Empire**'s role in the First World War and envisaged the demobilization of the Ottoman army. The Allies used it as a pretext to occupy Constantinople (now Istanbul) and parts of Anatolia, precipitating the revolt of Mustafa Kemal (Atatürk).

Mukden (China)

1) The Japanese Kwangtung Army seized Mukden on 18–19 September 1931 after alleging that China had bombed a Japanese railroad. Japanese forces went on to capture all of **Manchukuo** (as Manchuria was renamed) installing a puppet ruler (Henry Pu Yi). Japanese occupation lasted until 1945.

2) Scene of a key battle, Mukden-Chinchow, fought from 27 to 30 October 1948, in the Chinese Civil War. It resulted in the almost complete destruction of the nationalist Manchurian army by the Communists. See Appendix 2.

Mullaghmore (Ireland)

Scene of assassination of Lord Mountbatten by IRA on 27 August 1979, the same day as the **Warrenpoint** massacre. Lord Mountbatten, his grandson Nicholas Knatchbull, the Dowager Lady Brabourne and a local boy, Paul Maxwell, were killed when the IRA blew up their fishing boat off the coast of County Sligo.

Munich (Germany)

City in Bavaria.

1) In November 1923 Hitler led the Nazi Party into an abortive attempt to seize power

in Bavaria (known as the Munich Putsch) as a prelude to overthrowing the national government. At a right-wing meeting in a Munich beer-hall on 8 November, Hitler proclaimed a march on Berlin to install General Ludendorff as leader. A march by 3,000 Nazis into the centre of Munich the next day turned violent and resulted in 19 deaths and many arrests. Ludendorff was released but Hitler was sentenced to five years in prison, although he served only nine months.

2) On 29 September 1938 an international agreement signed in Munich by Hitler, Mussolini, British Prime Minister Chamberlain and French Prime Minister Daladier settled the **Sudetenland** problem which had threatened to provoke a general European war. **Czechoslovakia** was compelled to transfer the Sudetenland to Germany, as well as smaller areas to Poland and Hungary. Chamberlain also unilaterally obtained Hitler's signature on a piece of paper which renounced war between Britain and Germany, proclaimed as "peace in our time". A high point of Chamberlain's appeasement policy, the Munich Agreement sacrificed Czechoslovakia to give Britain and France time to rearm.

3) On 6 February 1958 the plane carrying the Manchester United football team, known as the "Busby Babes" (after their manager Matt Busby) crashed on the snow-covered runway at Munich airport. Eight players were killed along with eight journalists and three club staff.

4) The 20th Olympic Games, held in Munich in 1972, were overshadowed by the attack on the Israeli team's quarters in the Olympic village. On 5 September Black September Palestinian terrorists killed two Israelis and took another nine hostage. A frantic rescue attempt at Munich airport left all nine athletes dead, as well as two German policemen and five terrorists.

Murmansk (Russia)

Port where, in June 1918, British, French and US troops, commanded by the British General Frederick Poole, landed to support the anti-Bolshevik forces in the Russian Civil War. Although these forces seized **Archangel** in August, they were withdrawn late in 1919 after intermittent fighting against communist forces. It was also the major supply base and port for the Anglo-American convoys during the Second World War. Now the largest city north of the Arctic Circle.

Mururoa

Pacific atoll which forms part of French Polynesia (see map on p. 168). The atoll is 3,750 miles from Australia and 2,625 miles from the nearest point in New Zealand. Since 1966, it has been a testing site for the French nuclear weapons programme. Under President Chirac France resumed nuclear testing at Mururoa in 1995 against a background of worldwide protests. Greenpeace activists attempted to disrupt the programme, many Pacific nations voiced their protests but the British government noticeably failed to condemn the French action.

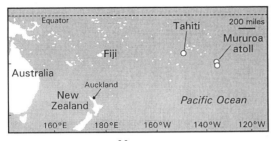

Mururoa

Muthannah (Iraq)

Town to the west of Baghdad, Iraq's largest chemical weapons plant during the 1980s, making mustard and nerve gases for use against Iran and Kurdish rebels. Along with Iraq's other non-conventional weapons it was dismantled by UN inspectors after Iraq's defeat in 1991 after the Gulf War.

Myanmar

See **Burma**.

Myitkyina (Burma)

Town on the Irrawaddy River near the Chinese border. Of great strategic significance for the control of Burma in the Second World War, and located on the **Ledo Road**, it was captured by the Japanese in 1942. It was liberated by Allied troops after a 78-day siege in August 1944.

My Lai (Vietnam)

Village, synonymous with low morale and over-reaction by US forces fighting in the Vietnam War. In November 1969 investigations commenced in the USA into reports that on 16 March 1968 US troops massacred all the inhabitants of the village. On 29 March 1971 Lieutenant William Calley was convicted of the murder of at least 22 Vietnamese and sentenced to life imprisonment (a sentence later substantially reduced). His immediate superior, Captain Ernest Medina, was acquitted. It was revealed at the trial that the action formed part of a punitive operation against areas suspected of aiding the Viet Cong. Grave doubts were raised in the USA about the role its armed forces were playing in **Vietnam**.

Nagaland (India)

Area in the northeast bordering Burma. On Indian independence in August 1947 the Nagas refused to become part of India and a Naga National Council declared independence. The area was nevertheless absorbed into India as part of Assam Province. There was violent guerrilla activity from 1955 until 1975, with a ceasefire from 1964 to 1972. Under the 1975 Shillong Accord Nagaland became a full state in the Indian Union but the area has remained tense.

Nagasaki (Japan)

City on Kyushu Island where the second atomic bomb (following **Hiroshima**) was dropped on 9 August 1945 as a demonstration to persuade Japan to surrender unconditionally. An estimated 40,000–70,000 were killed outright and an equal number injured. Over 50,000 have died since of injuries and illnesses connected with the bomb.

Nagorno Karabakh (Caucasus)

Disputed enclave which became a scene of conflict after 1988 on break-up of the Soviet Union. Nagorno Karabakh is a Christian Armenian enclave surrounded by Muslim **Azerbaijan**. The Karabakh forces secured a land corridor to **Armenia**. What began as guerrilla clashes in the late 1980s and early 1990s escalated briefly into full-scale war across the Caucasus, with modern weapons supplied by former Soviet troops.

Nagpur (India)

City where the extremist Hindu organization the Rashtriya Swayemsavak Sangh (RSS) was founded in 1925. Its aim was the creation of a Hindu nation and it trained volunteers in this task. It was banned in 1948 after involvement in the assassination of Mahatma Gandhi. It now co-operates with the main Hindu political movement, the BJP. See **Ayodhya**.

Namen (Belgium)

See **Namur**.

Namibia

Independent republic in southern Africa, formerly the German colony of **South West Africa**. Namibia was mandated to South Africa by the League of Nations on 17 December 1920. South Africa refused to recognize the South West Africa People's Organization (SWAPO), which was designated the "sole authentic representative of the Namibian people" by the UN in 1973. SWAPO launched a guerrilla campaign in October 1966, and this was stepped up in 1978 from bases in Angola and Zambia.

Following talks between South Africa, Angola, Cuba and the USA in 1988, implementation of a UN plan for Namibia's transition to independence began on 1 April 1989. Namibia became independent on 21 March 1990 after one of Africa's longest wars of liberation.

Namsos (Norway)

Port north of Trondheim. A combined Allied force landed on the night of 16–17 April 1940, and advanced south towards Trondheim. A second force landed at Aandalsnes to the south in an attempt to encircle Trondheim. Under constant aerial attack from the Germans and without reinforcements, the Allied forces were evacuated on 2 May 1940.

Namur (Belgium)

First World War battle around this city, southeast of Brussels. Surrounded by ten forts with trenches and minefields, Namur was the last major obstacle in the German advance on France. The German siege began on 20 August 1914, and the city was heavily bombarded for five days. All ten forts had fallen by 25 August and the city was forced to surrender.

Nanchang (China)

Capital city of Kiangsi province. The PLA was created here in 1927 after Communist forces rebelled against the Kuo-min Tang party. Nationalist headquarters 1933 to 1939 until it fell to Japanese forces.

Nanjing

See **Nanking**.

Nanking (China)

Major city and capital during the Nationalist period in power after 1928. It became infamous for the atrocities committed by the Japanese, known as the Rape of Nanking. When Japanese troops entered the city on 13 December 1938 an estimated 200,000 Chinese were killed. Many thousands of civilians were raped and tortured. Some estimates suggested one-third of all the houses in Nanking were burned. On 22 April 1949 the advancing Communist armies stormed and seized Nanking in the civil war.

Narita (Japan)

Controversial airport for Tokyo which the government decided to build in 1965 at Tomisato near Narita city. Its construction led to mass protests by students and local farmers on environmental grounds and its site was moved to nearby Sanrizuka. The protests mounted in strength and battles raged. The airport finally opened in 1978.

Narmada Dam (India)

The Narmada River in central India is believed by Hindus to spring from the body of the god Siva. A highly controversial scheme to dam the river provoked fierce opposition not only from Hindu fundamentalists but also from environmentalists in India and worldwide. Estimated to cost $5,500 million, the project would have displaced 300,000 people and badly affected the local environment. The Indian Government suspended the project in August 1993 after a mass rally by activists, and the cancellation of all loans by the World Bank, the main financer of the dam.

Naroch Lake (Belarus)

Scene of First World War battle. With the French under intense pressure at **Verdun** on the **Western Front**, Russia began a new assault in the East to divert the Germans. Beginning on 18 March 1916 the Russians gained some ground near the lake but were soon under heavy artillery fire. By 26 March an early thaw had reduced the ground to mud, and the Russians were cut down by German machine guns. Retreating to their original positions, the Russians had lost 100,000 men without any significant territorial gains.

Narvik (Norway)

Coastal town in the north, important as an ice-free port and centre for iron ore transportation. Early in the Second World War a surprise raid by the Germans seized the town on 9 April 1940. British troops landed nearby a few days later but were ill-equipped to deal with the wintry conditions. With French reinforcements, the Allies finally captured Narvik on 28 May. German advances elsewhere in Norway and the deteriorating situation in France compelled the Allies to withdraw, and by 6 June all Allied troops had been evacuated from the town.

Nasr City (Egypt)

Location near Cairo of the assassination of Egyptian President Anwar al-Sadat on 6 October 1981.

Nassau (Bahamas)

Capital and seaport. Agreement reached on 18 December 1962 between British Prime Minister Harold Macmillan and US President Kennedy after negotiations in Nassau that the US would supply Polaris missiles for use on Royal Navy submarines operating under NATO command. The agreement strengthened the Anglo-American relationship but led to the vetoing by President de Gaulle of Britain's application to join the EEC on the grounds that Britain was closer to the USA than to Europe.

Natzweiler (France)
Site in Alsace of the only Nazi concentration camp in the Second World War on French soil.

Naxalabi (India)
Village in the Himalayan foothills of Bengal which gave its name to the Naxalite Movement, a breakaway faction of the Communist Party of India. Founded in 1967 by Charu Majundar, the movement organized armed uprisings, strikes, riots and murders. It was violently crushed in 1977, and subsequently splintered into several groups.

Neka (Iran)
Site in the north of a nuclear research complex, believed by Western observers to be the place where Iran plans to build its Islamic bomb. Iran's nuclear weapons programme (the Great Secret Project) was begun in the 1980s. It is believed to be a major objective of the fundamentalist regime of the Iranian ayatollahs. Assistance and expertise has been sought from China, Pakistan and (more recently) Russia since the fall of Communism. Neka is in the remote Mazandaran province, close to the central Asian republic of Turkmenistan.

Nery (France)
First World War battle in this village near **Compiègne** in the northwest. Retreating British forces encamped in the village were attacked by German troops on 1 September 1914. For over two hours "L" Battery of the Royal Horse Artillery kept the Germans at bay. When reinforcements arrived, only one British gun remained. "L" Battery won three Victoria Crosses, with 45 officers and men killed or injured.

Netherlands East Indies
Former name of Indonesia during the period of Dutch colonial rule. Occupied by Japan during the Second World War, Indonesia became an independent state on 17 August 1945, beginning an ultimately successful four-year war of independence.

Neuilly (France)
Eighteenth century chateau northwest of **Paris**, giving its name to the peace treaty between Bulgaria and the Allies. Negotiated at the **Paris** Peace Conference, it was signed on 27 November 1919 and came into effect on 9 August 1920. Bulgaria was

forced to cede western Thrace to Greece, southern **Dobrudja** to Romania and other small areas to Yugoslavia. Its army was limited to 20,000 men and provisions were made for reparations to be negotiated, although 75 per cent of the reparations ordered were later remitted.

Neuve-Chapelle (France)

First World War battle centred on this village in French Flanders. Initially taken by the Germans in October 1914, the British launched an offensive to recapture it on 12 March 1915. A massive artillery bombardment against the village and the German lines preceded the infantry assault. The British 1st Army took the village and four German lines of trenches. 16,000 German reserve troops were rushed in and contained the British advance on 13 March. Without the necessary reinforcements, and lacking artillery superiority, the British attack faltered and the new lines became fixed.

Newbury (England)

Along with **Twyford Down**, one of the major protest sites against motorway construction in the 1990s. The campaign to stop the building of a £67 million, 8.5 mile by-pass to carry the A31 around Newbury developed during 1995. Construction of the by-pass began in 1996 but was delayed by some of the largest anti-road protests ever seen.

New Delhi (India)

Since 1911 the capital. Mahatma Gandhi was assassinated here on 30 January 1948 by a Hindu nationalist on his way to a prayer meeting. It was also the place of assassination of Indira Gandhi on 31 October 1984 by a member of her Sikh bodyguard.

New Guinea

Large island in the Pacific, north of Australia. In 1920 the eastern half of the island, previously divided between Britain and Germany, was mandated to Australia by the League of Nations. The western half remained part of the Dutch East Indies. Japanese forces invaded in July 1942 and advanced across the Owen Stanley mountains towards Port Moresby. The Australians, with US reinforcements, counter-attacked and contained the Japanese on the north coast. Savage fighting in hostile terrain continued for the rest of the Second World War, with many casualties on both sides. The last jungle units of the Japanese did not surrender until September 1945. The eastern half gained independence as Papua New Guinea. The western half, now called Irian Jaya, joined Indonesia.

New Hampshire (United States)

New England State and one of the original Thirteen Colonies. The primary elections held here, usually in late February or early March, are the first major tests of public opinion in a US Presidential election year. Campaigning in this small state enables Presidential hopefuls to gain media attention and voter recognition more easily. The outcome can be crucial to both rank outsiders and political heavyweights. In 1968 President Johnson beat Senator Eugene McCarthy by such a narrow margin that it prompted Senator Robert Kennedy to enter the race, and contributed to Johnson's decision to withdraw. For Jimmy Carter, victory here in 1976 gave him his first extensive national exposure. Success in New Hampshire is seen as crucial in establishing the momentum to win the Presidential nomination.

Niagara (United States)

Site of conference from May to June 1914 at which the sponsors, Argentina, Brazil, Chile and the USA, hoped to bring an end to the Mexican civil war. They suggested Victoriano Huerta should give up the presidency. The conference was not successful.

Nicaragua

Independent republic in Central America. Important in world affairs after 1978 for its bitter civil war and for the controversial nature of US involvement. Civil war was precipitated by the murder of President Somoza's leading opponent, newspaper editor Pedro Chamorro, on 10 January 1978. The rebels made steady advances, and Somoza finally fled the country on 17 July 1979. Civil war continued as the Sandinista government faced two military threats: the first, the Democratic Revolutionary Front, a group of rebels led by dissident Sandinist Eden Pastora, mounted raids from its base in Costa Rica; the second, the Nicaraguan Democratic Front or Contras, was a force of ex-National Guardsmen who operated from their exile in Honduras and who received extensive US aid until the US Congress halted funding on 15 June 1984. The Sandinista regime declared a state of emergency in May 1982, but disunity among its enemies enabled it to function despite the guerrilla threat. On 8 August 1987 leaders of the five Central American countries, including Nicaragua, met in Guatemala City to sign a peace accord calling for the democratization of Nicaragua and for Contra-Sandinista negotiations. A 60-day ceasefire was announced in Sapoa on 23 March 1988; subsequently the US Congress reinstated humanitarian aid to the Contras as a further incentive to peace. Violence in the run-up to the 1990 elections led President Ortega to end the ceasefire on 1 November 1989. The Sandinista government was defeated in the elections held in February 1990. The military chief of the Contras, Israel Galeano, with 100 of his soldiers, handed in their weapons to UN forces on 27 June 1990, formally marking the end of their guerrilla campaign.

Nijmegen (The Netherlands)

On the Waal River, ten miles south of Arnhem. The US 82nd Airborne Division dropped troops here in September 1944, but although they captured the town they were unable to rescue the Allied forces trapped at nearby **Arnhem**.

Nkomati

Small river on the border of South Africa and **Mozambique** which gave its name to the accord of March 1984. Under the accord, South Africa promised not to support the Mozambique rebel MNR in return for Mozambique's undertaking not to back the outlawed ANC's activities in South Africa. However, MNR activity continued. The possibility of peace emerged in 1990, with talks between the government and MNR in Rome in July. A peace accord was signed on 7 August 1992 and a formal signature of peace ended the war in October 1992.

Nomonhan (Mongolia)

Location in eastern Mongolia on the border of **Manchuria** of a clash between Russian and Japanese forces from May to September 1939. Further expansionism towards Mongolia suffered a sharp reverse when Japanese forces were defeated by the Red Army under General Zhukov.

Nordhausen (Germany)

Site of a subsidiary concentration camp of **Buchenwald**. The camp, originally called Dora but later renamed Mittlebau, was a slave-labour establishment engaged on top secret production of V1 and V2 rockets. Some 60,000 prisoners worked in the underground network of tunnels. Nearly 20,000 died here.

Normandy (France)

Location of 50-mile stretch of coastline in the north, the landing site of the D-Day invasion in the Second World War (see map on p. 176). Using a fleet of over 4,000 ships, the largest amphibious assault in history took place on 6 June 1944. Five landing beaches were designated – from west to east: **Utah** (US 4th), **Omaha** (US 1st and part of 29th), **Gold** (British 50th), **Juno** (Canadian 3rd) and **Sword** (British 3rd). Codenamed Operation Overlord, it was under the supreme command of General Eisenhower, with General Montgomery commanding the ground forces. Four beaches were captured easily, but fierce German resistance was met by the US troops at **Omaha**. Allied casualties were lighter than anticipated with 2,500 dead in a total of 11,000. By 12 June the beachheads were linked up to form the base for the liberation of France and the assault on Germany.

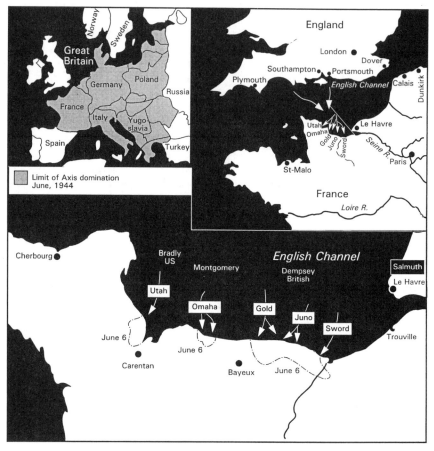

Normandy

North Cyprus

Independent Turkish-backed republic in the northern half of **Cyprus**. It is not recognized by the international community and owes its existence to the attempts by the Greek Cypriot EOKA organization to secure union (*enosis*) with mainland Greece.

Northern Ireland

Comprises the six counties Antrim, Armagh, Down, Fermanagh, Londonderry and Tyrone. With Cavan, Donegal and Monaghan, they originally formed the province of Ulster, but in 1923 these three were made part of the Dominion of Ireland, while the others remained part of the United Kingdom. In 1968 long-standing sectarian animosity between the Catholic and Protestant communities in Northern Ireland degenerated into violent conflict, sparked by the campaign for Catholic civil rights. British troops were deployed in **Londonderry** on 14 August 1969 and **Belfast** on 15 August at the request of the government of Northern Ireland. The first British soldier to be killed was shot by an IRA sniper in Belfast on 6 February 1971. Internment without trial was introduced on 6 August 1971, and direct rule from London was imposed on 30 March 1972. On Bloody Sunday (30 January 1972) British troops opened fire on a Catholic civil rights march, and thirteen people were killed. At the peak, in August 1972, there were 21,500 British soldiers in Northern Ireland, but this was reduced to 10,000 by the mid-1980s. Over 3,160 people had died in the conflict by the end of August 1994, when the IRA called a complete cessation of military operations. This was followed by a reciprocal offer from the Loyalists (13 October 1994). In 1996, however, IRA bombings in mainland Britain heralded the end of the ceasefire and the security situation deteriorated markedly.

Northern Rhodesia (now Zambia)
See **Rhodesia**.

Northern Territories
Japanese term for the four islands (Habomai, Shikotan, Etorofu and Kunashiri) off Japan's north coast which were incorporated into the former Soviet Union in 1945. They are now part of Russia's **Kuril Island** chain.

North-West Frontier
Border area of Afghanistan and India in the northwest of the **Punjab**, inhabited by Pathan tribes who were mostly followers of Islam. The **Khyber Pass** dominated the frontier and was of great strategic importance to the defence of India. Britain annexed the region in 1849 and made it a separate Indian province in 1901. It has been part of Pakistan since 1947.

Norway
North European country between Sweden and the North Sea. Although neutral at the start of the Second World War, Norway was invaded by Germany on 9 April 1940. Taken by surprise and betrayed by the pro-Nazi Vidkun Quisling's fifth-columnists, the Norwegian forces retreated. Allied attempts at counter-attacks in **Narvik** and **Namsos** were short-lived and by 9 June Norway had been conquered. King Haakon VII escaped to set up the Government-in-exile in London. A sizeable German garrison remained throughout the war, finally surrendering to Norwegian resistance forces on 8 May 1945.

Notting Hill (England)
Area in west London which was the scene of racial disturbances, primarily of attacks by white youths on West Indian immigrants, in August 1958. It was also the site of

Peter Rachman's slum property empire in the 1960s. The Notting Hill Carnival celebrates West Indian culture annually in August.

Nowa Huta (Poland)
Industrial complex near Krakow. The sprawling complex, with its vast steelworks, originally built in the 1940s on the site of a former village, is a symbol of the ecological disasters of Communist rule in eastern Europe. The former Lenin Steelworks has now been renamed the Sendzimir Works.

Ntarama (Rwanda)
Site of one of the worst atrocities of the 1994 civil war in **Rwanda** where over 1,000 men, women and children were massacred in the local church. It is now one of the massacre sites left as a witness to the horrors of the conflict.

Nuba (Sudan)
Mountains in central Sudan, scene in the 1990s of the attempted genocide of the Nuba peoples by the Muslim fundamentalist regime which seized power in Khartoum in 1989. The Nuba, a black African people, have resisted attempts to make Sudan an extremist Islamic state (some Nuba are Christians, but the majority are Muslim). The blockade of the Nuba mountains has hid the atrocities of this genocide from the outside world.

Nuba

Nunavut (Canada)
Self-governing Inuit-(Eskimo)-populated territory created out of the former North-West Territories. A referendum in November 1992 voted in favour of this scheme. The territory comprises 20 per cent of Canada's land area.

Nuremberg (Germany)
City (also known as Nürnberg) famous for:
1) the Nuremberg rallies of the 1930s. The mass rallies were orchestrated by Propaganda Minister Joseph Goebbels at Nazi Party Congresses in Nuremberg from 1933

to 1938 and were intended to rouse participants and impress observers with oratory and militaristic display;

2) the major raid by Allied bombers in the Second World War. On the night of 30–31 March 1944 no less than 94 British planes were shot down, out of an attacking force of 795 aircraft. It was the costliest raid of the war;

3) the Nuremberg Trials, held from 1945 to 1947, a joint US, British, French and Soviet International Military Tribunal, which tried 177 Germans and Austrians for crimes against peace and humanity and war crimes, 25 being hanged, 35 acquitted and the rest imprisoned. The main trial took place between November 1945 and September 1946 of 21 leading Nazis, 10 of whom were executed on 16 October 1946.

Nürnberg (Germany)
See **Nuremberg**.

Nyos, Lake (Cameroon)
Volcanic lake in northeast Cameroon from which toxic gas escaped on 26 August 1986 causing an ecological disaster. Nearly 2,000 people died in lakeside villages as the cloud of carbon dioxide and hydrogen sulphur erupted and a further 20,000 living further away were badly affected. It was one of Africa's worst such disasters.

Oakland (United States)

City in California.

1) Scene of a three-day general strike by 100,000 workers in support of store clerks in December 1946. The call for a general strike, which began on 3 December, came after police had escorted non-unionized truck drivers through the clerks' picket lines. Strikers brought the city to a complete halt, set up patrols to prevent looting, discouraged hoarding of necessities and monitored prices. The strike ended when the city authorities promised not to use police to break picket lines.

2) Location where the Black Panther Party, a paramilitary black power organization was established in October 1966 by Bobby Seale and Huey Newton.

Oak Ridge (United States)

City in eastern Tennessee, now part of metropolitan Knoxville. In August 1942 it was chosen as the base for the US wartime atomic energy research, codenamed the Manhattan Project. Refugee scientists from occupied Europe joined those from the USA, Britain and Canada to develop the atom bomb. By 1945 over 75,000 lived in the town, which was demilitarized in 1949. In 1955 the US Congress voted to permit land sales, and Oak Ridge was incorporated as a city in 1959.

Obninsk (Russia)

Site in the former Soviet Union, southwest of **Moscow**, where the first Soviet atomic power station was opened on 27 June 1954.

Ocean Island

See **Banaba**.

Oder-Neisse Line

Boundary along the rivers Oder and Neisse between Poland and Germany giving to Poland a fifth of Germany's 1938 territory and a sixth of its population, provisionally agreed by USA, UK and the Soviet Union at **Yalta** and **Potsdam**. Not officially recognized by West Germany until 18 November 1970 as part of Chancellor Willy Brandt's *Ostpolitik* reconciliation.

Ogaden (Ethiopia)

Disputed area contested by **Somalia** and Ethiopia. The turmoil in Ethiopia after the overthrow of Emperor Haile Selassie on 12 September 1974 led the Somali Republic to pursue its claim to the Ogaden by fostering a guerrilla movement in the area, the Western Somali Liberation Front. A Somali-backed offensive in 1977 gave the guerrillas control of the southern desert area, and an attack launched against Harar on

23 November 1977 narrowly failed. However, with Cuban and Soviet support, Ethiopia launched a counter-offensive on 7 February 1978 and recovered control of the Ogaden. On 9 March 1978 Somalia announced the withdrawal of its forces from the Ogaden.

Ogoniland (Nigeria)

Region inhabited by the Ogoni, a people in the oil-rich River State in southeastern Nigeria. In 1995 the protests of the Ogoni at the pollution and destruction of their land reached a world audience. Ken Saro-Wiwa, the founder and leader of the Movement for the Survival of the Ogoni People, was sentenced to death and executed by the Nigerian military regime, after a trial condemned as a parody of justice, for his alleged involvement in the murder of four Ogoni chiefs after rioting. The trials and sentences aroused worldwide anger. The Ogonis, who have demanded a share of oil revenues, are one of 20 main ethnic groups in the Niger Delta.

Ogoniland

Okinawa (Japan)

Pacific island occupied by Japan in the Second World War. Its recapture was the next US target after **Iwo Jima**. Like Iwo Jima, Okinawa would be used as a forward base to bomb Japan. After an intensive air and sea bombardment, the first landings on Okinawa took place unopposed on 1 April 1945. The operation was covered by a fast carrier group under Admiral Marc Mitscher and a British task force. These suffered heavily from attacks by hundreds of *kamikaze* suicide planes. As the US troops moved south on the island, they had to overcome a series of carefully prepared fortified lines, defended tenaciously by the Japanese. A counter-attack was defeated on 4 May,

Okinawa

and organized resistance ended about 22 June. The US army had suffered over 7,000 killed and 32,000 wounded, and the navy had also suffered about 10,000 casualties. At least 110,000 Japanese had been killed on Okinawa. Occupied by the USA until 1972, when it was returned to Japan.

Oklahoma City (United States)

Capital of the state of Oklahoma, the scene in April 1995 of the worst urban terrorist incident in US history. The car bomb attack on a federal government building left 168 dead and many scores missing in the rubble. A suspect, Timothy McVeigh, who had links with the Michigan Militia (a far-right anti-government group) was quickly arrested. The bomb (estimated at 1,200 lb) was of a similar size to the one which exploded at the World Trade Center in New York in February 1993.

Olympia Exhibition Centre (England)

In west London, the scene of mass rallies by Oswald Mosley's BUF supporters (Blackshirts) in the 1930s. However, the violence which occurred at these meetings when stewards ejected hecklers, often with considerable brutality, alienated much potential support from Mosley, particularly among sympathetic Conservatives and newspaper barons. See also **Cable Street**.

Omaha (France)

One of the **Normandy** beaches used on D-Day, 6 June 1944. Landing site for the US 5th Corps, it proved one of the most difficult beachheads to secure. Rough seas hampered the assault and the German 352 Division heavily bombarded the beach. By midnight on D-Day only one mile of ground had been won, with over 3,000 US casualties.

Oman

See **Dhofar**.

Omarska (Bosnia-Hercegovina)

Site of an alleged concentration camp. It was claimed Bosnian Serbs systematically tortured and murdered their prisoners as part of their ethnic cleansing policies. In May 1993 a War Crimes Tribunal was set up to investigate these allegations and the alleged war criminals faced trial in 1996.

Omdurman (Sudan)

City at the confluence of the Blue and White Nile rivers. By the end of August 1898 General Kitchener's advance up the Nile had reached the Mahdist capital of Omdurman. Facing a numerically superior force, Kitchener attacked on 2 September and quickly overwhelmed the Mahdists. Although short, the battle was immensely significant. Mahdist strength was broken, with 15,000 casualties, and the British re-established their control over the region, culminating in the creation of **Anglo-Egyptian Sudan** in January 1899. Omdurman also marked the emergence of the machine gun as the dominant fighting weapon.

Omsk (Russia)

City at the confluence of the Irtysh and Om rivers, important during the Russian Civil War as headquarters of the anti-Bolshevik White Government led by Admiral Alexander Kolchak.

Oradour-sur-Glane (France)
Village in the west, scene of one of the worst massacres of the Second World War. On 10 June 1944 German SS troops killed 642 men, women and children. Since the massacre, the burnt-out shell of Oradour has remained unaltered, a memorial to that event.

Oran (Algeria)
(Wahran in Arabic.) Second largest port with adjacent Mers-el-Kebir. The fall of France in June 1940 left a big question-mark over the fate of the large French fleet, part of which was stationed in Oran. British forces, pre-empting any German control of the fleet, arrived off Oran on 3 July 1940. An ultimatum was issued to the French – join the Allies, disarm the ships or scuttle the fleet. When the French refused, the British opened fire. In the 15-minute bombardment the ships *Bretagne*, *Provence* and *Dunkerque* were all destroyed or disabled. Only the battle cruiser *Strasbourg* escaped. Over 1,000 French sailors died. Oran remained in Vichy French hands until the Allied landings of Operation Torch on 8 November 1942. The French bombarded Gibraltar in retaliation and the action caused deep resentment towards Britain and General de Gaulle's Free French.

Ordzhonikidze (Georgia)
City in the Caucasus region of the former Soviet Union, now in Georgia, which marks the most easterly point reached during the German invasion of Russia. From this high point of August 1942 the Germans retreated in the face of the Soviet counter-attack.

Orgreave (England)
Scene of one of the crucial confrontations during the 1984–5 miner's strike. Thousands of Yorkshire miners attempted to force the closure of the British Steel coking plant near **Sheffield** in a series of clashes on 29 and 30 May, 1 and 18 June 1984. There were large numbers of arrests and injuries and complaints of police violence. Charges of riot and unlawful assembly against fourteen miners were dropped a year after their arrest.

Orpington (England)
Surburban northwest Kent scene of a remarkable Liberal by-election victory on 14 March 1962 in which Eric Lubbock (later Lord Avebury) transformed a Conservative majority of 14,760 into a 7,855 Liberal majority. Although the seat was held until 1970, the long-awaited Liberal revival failed to follow Lubbock's victory. The result led also to the coining of the phrase "Orpington man".

Osirak (Iraq)

Site of Iraq's nuclear reactor. It was bombed on 7 June 1981 by Israeli F-16 fighters in an attempt to stop Iraq from developing nuclear weapons.

Oslo (Norway)

Capital city of **Norway**. For the Oslo Accords, part of the Middle East peace process, see under **Madrid**.

Ostend (Belgium)

Port on the North Sea coast captured by the Germans on 14 October 1914. It was developed as a minor naval base during the First World War. In the spring of 1918 the British made two unsuccessful attempts to close the harbour entrance.

Otranto Barrage

Blockade created across the entrance to the Adriatic Sea during the First World War. Stretching from Otranto in southeast Italy to Corfu, it was made from floating nets and guarded by lightly-armed fishing boats. It was moderately successful at containing the Austrian fleet until a concerted attack in May 1917 damaged many of the patrol ships. The Barrage was abandoned by the Italians as being indefensible, leaving Allied shipping in the Mediterranean at the mercy of German–Austrian submarines.

Ottawa (Canada)

Capital and site of the Imperial Economic Conference of 1932. In a series of agreements between Britain and the major territories of the Empire a system of imperial preferences was instituted. All constituent parts of the Empire were to put home producers first, Empire producers second and foreign ones last. Britain imported agricultural produce from the Dominions without charging tariffs and exported manufactured goods back at preferential rates. The formation of GATT in 1947, resulting in trade liberalization, and Britain's closer ties with Europe soon made imperial preferences redundant.

Ottoman Empire

Replacing the Byzantine Empire in the fourteenth century, it ruled much of the eastern Mediterranean until its collapse in 1923. During the nineteenth century, most of its European territory was lost, culminating in the Balkan Wars of 1912–13 after which only Thrace remained. The 1908 revolution by the Committee of Union and Progress or "Young Turks" led to a liberalization of government and decline in the power of the Sultan, and prompted **Austria-Hungary** to annex **Bosnia-Hercegovina**. The Empire entered the First World War on 31 October 1914 on the side of the

Central Powers. Despite holding out at **Gallipoli**, the Turks had a bad war, being forced out of **Mesopotamia** and Palestine. On 30 October 1918, the Empire capitulated to the Allies. Under the Treaty of **Sèvres** (10 August 1920) all Arabian provinces became British or French mandates and much of eastern Turkey was lost to an independent **Armenia**. The ensuing civil war and Greek invasion led to the overthrow of Sultan Mehmed VI and declaration of a republic in October 1923. Peace was finally achieved under the Treaty of **Lausanne** (24 July 1923), with Turkey regaining the eastern provinces.

Ouchy (Switzerland)

Location of the peace treaty ending the Italo-Turkish War of 1911–12. The war had begun on 29 September 1911 when Italy declared war on Turkey with the aim of seizing the Ottoman Territories of Cyrenaica and Tripoli (modern Libya). By November Italy had defeated the Turks in North Africa. In May 1912 Italian troops occupied the **Dodecanese** islands in the Aegean. Turkey recognized these Italian conquests in the Treaty of Ouchy of 15 October 1912.

Ourcq River (France)

Scene of the beginning of the French counter-attack, northeast of Paris, on 6 September 1914 in the first Battle of the Marne.

Oxford University (England)

Famous in the 1930s for the celebrated debate in the student Oxford Union Debating Society on 9 February 1933, when a resolution was passed by 275 votes to 153 that "This House will in no circumstances fight for its King and Country". Taken by British and foreign opinion as a sign of the spread of pacifism and anti-war sentiment among the younger generation, the resolution attracted disproportionate attention in view of the unrepresentative nature of the debate and those participating. It was also not widely noticed that the phrase "King and Country" referred to the more blinkered patriotism associated with the First World War which was subject to attack in a wave of anti-war literature and memoirs from the end of the 1920s. The debate was widely interpreted abroad as marking a decline in Britain's willingness to fight, a point reinforced by the victory of an anti-rearmament candidate at a by-election in East Fulham in October 1934.

Paardeberg (South Africa)

Small town near Bloemfontein in Orange Free State. In a turning point of the Boer War, the British won a significant victory and seized the advantage. The relief of **Kimberley** on 15 February 1900 forced the Boers under General Cronje to retreat. On 18 February the British attacked at Paardeberg with a frontal assault on the Boers' fortified wagon train. The high casualty figures (320 killed, 940 wounded) prompted the British to change tactics and encircle the Boers. The siege lasted until 27 February when Cronje surrendered with 4,000 men, and the British advanced towards **Bloemfontein**.

Padania (Italy)

Name given by the Northern League, the separatist Italian political movement, to those provinces in the north of Italy which wanted to break away from the rest of Italy. In May 1996, Umberto Bossi, leader of the Northern League, used this name in his announcement to the self-styled "Parliament of the North" in Mantua. An independent Padania was declared by Bossi in September 1996 in a rally at Venice.

Pale (Bosnia)

Seat of government of the Bosnian Serb administration headed by Radovan Karadjic during the civil war in Bosnia after 1993.

Palestine

Disputed region in the eastern Mediterranean. After its defeat in the First World War, the **Ottoman Empire** lost much of its territory in the Middle East. Transjordan (see **Jordan**) became a British mandate in 1919, later being split into the separate mandates of Transjordan and Palestine. Following the Second World War, violence between Arabs and Jews escalated and Britain, unable to cope with the situation, turned the problem over to the UN General Assembly which recommended the creation of two states. The state of **Israel**, proclaimed on 14 May 1948, absorbed most of the allotted Arab areas in the subsequent conflict. Jordan annexed the **West Bank** in 1950, but it was reoccupied by Israel during the Six Day War in 1967 (see Appendix 2 for Arab–Israeli Wars). In October 1974 the Arab League recognized the Palestine Liberation Organization (PLO) as the sole representative for the Palestinians. Despite progress towards peace at **Camp David** in 1978, civil unrest in the Occupied Territories continued throughout the 1980s, culminating in the *intifada*, or popular uprising, in December 1987. The peace process finally bore fruit at **Madrid**, and limited self-rule was granted to **Gaza** and some areas of the West Bank. Yasser Arafat was elected first President of the Palestinian Authority in 1996.

Panama

Central American republic whose strategic position has led to frequent US military

187

intervention in its affairs, not least because of the vital **Panama Canal**. US forces occupied Panama in 1908, 1912, 1918 and 1941. President Noriega declared that a state of war existed between his country and the USA on 15 December 1989. An off-duty US marine, Lieutenant Robert Paz, was killed at a roadblock on 16 December. US forces began the invasion of Panama, code-named Operation Just Cause, on 20 December. Fighting ended on 31 December. President Noriega took refuge in the Vatican embassy in Panama City, but gave himself up to US forces on 3 January 1990.

Panama Canal

Waterway, 50.7 miles long, across the Panamanian isthmus linking the Pacific Ocean and the Caribbean. Begun in 1882, it was finally completed on 15 August 1914 at a cost of almost $400 million. A 1903 treaty had granted the USA control of the Canal Zone, but in 1977 this was renegotiated. The new Panama Canal Treaties established that Panama will gain complete control by 1 January 2000, although the Canal will remain neutral.

Panjshar Valley (Afghanistan)

Valley region, 60 miles northeast of the capital Kabul, the scene of intense Mujaheddin resistance following the Soviet invasion of 1979. Heavy Soviet bombing led to a massive civilian exodus to Kabul. See also **Afghanistan**.

Panmunjon (Korea)

Village next to the **Demilitarized Zone** between North and South Korea where armistice talks were moved following their opening at Laesong on 8 July 1951. Following early tension, agreement was reached at Panmunjon on the division of Korea on 27 July 1953.

Papua New Guinea

See **New Guinea**.

Paris (France)

Capital of France.

1) The Paris Peace Conference opened on 18 January 1919 and was attended by all 32 Allied and associated states. Its deliberations resulted in the Treaty of **Versailles** and the League of Nations, and it was formally wound up in January 1920. The inter-war Paris Pact (or Kellogg-Briand Pact) was a French-led attempt to tie the USA into European security. Signed on 27 August 1928, it developed into a multilateral agreement, with all signatories agreeing to settle disputes by peaceful means.

2) During the Second World War Paris fell to the Germans on 14 June 1940 and

remained occupied until liberation on 25 August 1944. The Paris Peace Treaties between the Allies and Italy, Romania, Hungary, Bulgaria and Finland were signed in February 1947.

3) In early May 1968 30,000 students clashed with police on the streets of Paris. The Latin Quarter was the scene of running street battles and over 1000 people were injured. By the end of May France was crippled as ten million workers went on strike and joined the protests. President de Gaulle dissolved the National Assembly and won a landslide victory at the general election in June. Although de Gaulle restored control his prestige was irreparably damaged.

4) US involvement in the Vietnam War was brought to an end under the Paris Peace Talks of 1973.

5) On 21 November 1990 the states of the Conference on Security and Co-operation in Europe (CSCE) adopted the Paris Charter, marking the formal end of the Cold War and division of Europe.

Parral (Mexico)
Place where Mexican revolutionary Pancho Villa was assassinated on 20 July 1923.

Passchendaele (Belgium)
First World War battle around this village in Belgian Flanders, also known as the 3rd Battle of **Ypres** (31 July–10 November 1917). Still persisting with accepted tactics, despite earlier failures and huge casualties, the British under General Haig unleashed a full frontal assault on German lines. The element of surprise was lost by the heavy initial bombardment, which also churned up the rain-sodden ground. The British infantry, bogged down in a sea of mud, could only inch forward under heavy fire and the first German mustard gas attacks of the war. A final offensive on 9 November secured both Passchendaele ridge and village. In gaining five miles of land the British lost 300,000 men (German casualties were 260,000), making Passchendaele synonymous with the futility of trench warfare. The Germans recaptured the lost ground in April 1918, losing it again to the Belgians in October 1918.

Pearl Harbor (Hawaii)
Major US naval base attacked by Japanese aircraft on 7 December 1941. The aircraft were transported on carriers as part of a larger fleet which left the Kuril Islands on 25 November, moving secretly for a surprise attack on the US fleet. No official declaration of war preceded the attack which took place while diplomatic negotiations were continuing between the two powers in Washington. There have been more recent suggestions that US intelligence, having broken Japanese diplomatic codes, was aware that the attack would take place. In less than two hours five US battleships, 14 smaller vessels and 120 aircraft were destroyed; 2,000 US sailors and 400 civilians were killed. The Japanese lost only 29 of their 353 aircraft. US aircraft carriers which

later proved invaluable in the battle of the Pacific were not in port when the attack occurred, and three damaged battleships were repaired. The US Congress declared war on Japan the following day. Japan's allies Germany and Italy declared war on the USA on 11 December. The attack failed in its main objective of gaining decisive sea superiority for Japan in the Pacific and the initial advantage won by the Japanese proved transitory.

Peenemunde (Germany)

Base on Usedom island on the Baltic coast. Developed in the 1930s as a rocket research station, it was used by the German military to test its pilotless bomb projects. These eventually became the V1 missile and V2 rocket. An RAF bombing raid on 17–18 August 1943 killed over 700 workers and scientists, and succeeded in delaying the rocket programmes. V1 and V2 offensives were not finally launched until mid-1944. Evacuated by the Germans in March 1945, several scientists were captured by the US troops and later developed the US space programme.

Pegasus Bridge Cafe (France)

Famous in the Second World War as the first French building to be liberated in the D-Day landings in **Normandy** in 1944. It was known in June 1944 as the Buvette de Tramway. It was liberated by men of the 6th Airborne Division whose targets were the bridges over the Orne River and the parallel canal.

Peking (China)

Capital (now known as Beijing).

1) In 1900 it was at the centre of the Boxer Rebellion. The "Boxers" was a popular term for members of the Society of Harmonious Fists, a secret organization opposed to European commercial interests in China at the turn of the twentieth century, which had the tacit approval of the Chinese authorities and the Dowager Empress. Its members attacked Christians and workers on European-controlled railways, prompting the European states to take steps to protect their nationals. British troops were fired upon at Taku. In an uprising on 19 June 1900, the European legations were besieged and the German minister assaulted. A six-nation expeditionary force including Japanese and US troops, landed at Tientsin on 14 July and stormed Peking on 14 August, forcing the Empress and Dowager Empress to flee. A peace agreement, the Boxer Protocol, was signed by China and 12 nations on 7 September 1901.

2) Peking fell to Mao Tse-tung's Communist troops on 22 January 1949 after the victory at **Huai-Hai**. He proclaimed the People's Republic of China from the Gate of Heavenly Peace on 1 October 1949. In June 1989 pro-democracy demonstrations in **Tiananmen Square** in Peking were brutally crushed by the government.

Peleliu-Angaur

Second World War campaign in the Palau islands east of the Philippines. US troops mounted a large amphibious assault on the island of Peleliu on 15 September 1944, followed by Angaur on the 17th. The latter proved less of an obstacle and was captured in three days. Japanese defences in Peleliu were stronger and more entrenched, and held out until 25 November. US casualty rates (40 per cent) were the worst for any amphibious landing in US history. More than 13,000 Japanese defenders died.

Pergau (Malaysia)

Remote area of forest in the north. Located close to the Thai border, it was the site chosen for a dam to be paid for with British overseas aid money (agreed in 1991). The dam (the largest aid project to be funded by the British government) evoked much controversy. It became a major scandal in 1994 because of alleged links between aid for the dam and the award of defence contracts.

Perm (Russia)

Site of former Soviet labour camp in the foothills of the Ural mountains. The former *gulag* housed the men the Soviet Union feared most. Since the fall of Communism and the collapse of the Soviet Union, the remains of the camp are being turned into a memorial to the estimated 14 million people who died in Soviet prison camps. In all, the camps of the *gulag* killed more people than all Hitler's concentration camps, mostly during Stalin's "Reign of Terror" from 1929 to 1953.

Peru

Republic in South America, scene of protracted civil war in the 1980s. The combatants were Peruvian armed forces and right-wing death squads versus guerrillas of the *Sendero Luminosa* (Shining Path), and the Tupac Amaru urban terrorist movement. The campaign against the government by this Maoist guerrilla movement began in May 1980, and continued throughout the decade. Despite the arrest of its leader, Shining Path violence still continues. An estimated 25,000 people have died in the conflict.

Petrograd

City on Baltic coast of Russia. Later known as **Leningrad** and **St Petersburg**.

Philadelphia (United States)

Town in the southern state of Mississippi. In 1964 three young civil rights activists were abducted and brutally murdered by the Ku Klux Klan. The atrocity sparked one of the most bitter episodes in the campaign against racism in the deep south. The killings had shocked the USA during what became known as the "Freedom Summer". The film "Mississippi Burning" was based on these events. After a marathon struggle in Washington, the Civil Rights Act was signed into law by President Lyndon Johnson on 2 July 1964. The Act outlawed segregation in public facilities and racial discrimination in employment and education. The Act also empowered federal agencies to sue businesses or organizations which failed to open up to all races.

Philippines

Archipelago between the Pacific Ocean and South China Sea. Ceded to the USA after the Spanish–American War of 1898, the islands were self-governing by 1940. Japanese forces attacked on 8 December 1941 driving back US and Philippine forces to the **Bataan Peninsula** and on to **Corregidor** island. General MacArthur escaped to Australia and the Allies surrendered on 6 May 1942. US reoccupation began on 20 October 1944, with the invasion of **Leyte**. The islands were liberated one by one over the next few months, with the capital **Manila** captured on 4 March 1945. Although MacArthur proclaimed the islands' liberation in July, the last pockets of Japanese resistance did not surrender until August 1945.

Philippine Sea

Second World War battle near Guam, east of the Philippines Islands. The US invasion of the **Marianas Islands** in June 1944 provoked the Japanese into a decisive naval confrontation. The US had marshalled 15 aircraft carriers and 956 planes to confront the nine Japanese carriers with 473 planes. During eight hours of fierce dogfighting on 19 June, the Japanese lost 330 aircraft in what became known as the Great Marianas Turkey Shoot. Two Japanese carriers were sunk, but the US suffered little damage, losing only 30 aircraft. The battle destroyed Japanese sea power and opened up the Philippines to invasion.

Piave River (Italy)

First World War battles along this river in the northeast. Defeat at **Caporetto** forced the Italians to retreat to the Piave River. The first Austrian attack across the river in November 1917 was successfully repulsed. A second battle started with an Austrian assault on 15 June 1918. A bridgehead was secured but could not be held, resulting in a disastrous withdrawal on 22 June, ending the final offensive attempted by the Austro-Hungarian Empire. The third battle is usually known as **Vittorio Veneto**.

Pilsen (Czech Republic)

Town in former Czechoslovakia now known as Plzen, which housed the principal armament factories that were used in the First World War for the Austro-Hungarian forces. The ordnance factories came under Nazi control when Germany occupied Czechoslovakia in 1938.

Pingfang (China)
Village in the puppet state of **Manchukuo** in north China where a secret research centre conducting experimentation on live human beings was operated by the Japanese army's Unit 731 from 1936 until August 1945. At least 3,000 Chinese, Russians, Mongols and Koreans were injected with viruses, exposed to poison gases, frozen or dissected alive. On Japan's surrender, attempts were made to destroy the centre. The USA released the 3,000 officers and men involved at the centre without trial or punishment in exchange for the research data.

Placentia Bay
Location off Newfoundland of the wartime meeting between President Roosevelt and Winston Churchill on 14 August 1941. It was at this meeting that the Atlantic Charter (the declaration of British and US war aims and general strategy) was signed.

Plains (United States)
Home town of former US President Jimmy Carter. Located in southwest Georgia, near Americus, the name became briefly one of the best-known of political place names during his presidency.

Plei Me (Vietnam)
Fort near the Cambodian border. On 19 October 1965 6,000 Viet Cong and North Vietnamese troops attacked the fort in one of the largest Communist offensives of the **Vietnam** War. The fort's garrison of 400 South Vietnamese Rangers and 12 US Special Forces officers was reinforced by 250 more Rangers helicoptered in the next day. Besieged and bombarded for over a week, the fort held out with the aid of drops from US transport planes. On 27 October the siege was lifted by units from the US 1st Cavalry Division (Airmobile), and the Communist forces retreated into Cambodia.

Plzen (Czech Republic)
See **Pilsen**.

Polish Corridor
Narrow strip of land linking Poland to the Baltic Sea and separating East **Prussia** from the rest of Germany. Created in 1919 to give Poland access to the sea, it formed part of the new Polish state. Despite German protestations, the Poles colonized the northern half and built a new port at Gdynia. After the successes of the **Rhineland** and **Czechoslovakia**, Hitler turned towards Poland. In March 1939 he laid claim to the Free City of **Danzig**. By August this claim had broadened to the whole Corridor. On 1 September Germany invaded Poland. British and French guarantees to Poland were invoked, and they both declared war on Germany on 3 September 1939. Incorporated into Germany during the Second World War, the Corridor reverted to Poland after it.

Pondicherry (India)

Formerly the main French trading base in India, it was the collective name for the French territories (Pondicherry, Karaikal, Mahe and Yanam) whose administration was taken over by India by treaty in 1954 and which were ceded by France in 1962.

Poona (India)

Scene of the famous fast of Gandhi in 1932 in protest at the Communal Award of 4 August 1932 given by the British Prime Minister Ramsay MacDonald. Under this Award separate representation was given not only to Muslims but also to the depressed classes (untouchables). Gandhi's "fast unto death" was ended by the Poona Pact of 24 September 1932. Under this the election of the representatives of the depressed classes would be through general constituencies in which all non-Muslims voted.

Poperinghe (Belgium)

Small town, the railhead in the First World War for the notorious **Ypres** salient and the closest habitable town to the front line.

Port Arthur (Australia)

Resort town in Tasmania, the scene of the worst massacre in Australian history when a lone gunman, Martin Bryant, killed 35 people in April 1996. The killings, coming so soon after the **Dunblane** killings in Scotland, prompted John Howard's newly-elected Liberal-National Party government to introduce draconian anti-gun laws on the use of automatic and semi-automatic firearms.

Port Arthur (China)

Ice-free port and naval base at the southern tip of Liaotong Peninsula in **Manchuria**. Under the Treaty of **Shimonoseki** (1895) the port was initially leased to Japan but returned to China after Western intervention. Russia occupied the whole peninsula in 1897, linking Port Arthur to the Trans-Siberian Railway. A relentless siege (5 May 1904–2 January 1905) by the Japanese succeeded in capturing the port and destroying the Russian fleet in the harbour. The Treaty of **Portsmouth** (1905), which ended the Russo-Japanese War, transferred the port to Japan. It was renamed Ryojun and remained in Japanese

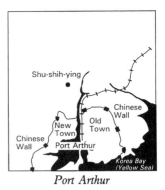

Port Arthur

hands until the end of the Second World War. Jointly controlled by China and the Soviet Union until the withdrawal of Soviet troops in 1955, it is now called Lu-Shun.

Port Huron (United States)

Seat of St Clair county in eastern Michigan. Site of the first convention of the Students for a Democratic Society (SDS), a radical left-wing movement founded in 1960. The Port Huron Statement, drawn up in June 1962, was a defining declaration of the principles of the USA's New Left. It denounced US foreign policy, nuclear weapons, capitalism and Soviet authoritarianism, while championing individual freedoms and participation in society.

Port Moresby

See **Kokoda Trail**.

Porton Down (England)

Site in Hampshire of the Centre for Applied Biological Research, originally the Germ and Chemical Warfare Research Base of the Ministry of Defence. It is the major British research centre for developments in germ and chemical warfare.

Portsmouth (United States)

Town in New Hampshire that gave its name to the treaty which ended the Russo-Japanese War of 1904–5. Signed on 5 September 1905, it detailed the outcome of Russia's defeat: surrendering the Russian lease on **Port Arthur**, ceding Southern Sakhalin to Japan, evacuating **Manchuria**, recognizing Japanese interests in Korea and paying war indemnities to Japan.

Portsmouth Harbour (England)

Famous naval base, scene of the still unresolved "Crabb affair" of 1956. Royal Navy frogman Commander Lionel "Buster" Crabb disappeared while searching the underside of the Soviet cruiser *Ordjonikidze* in May 1956. The cruiser had carried Soviet leaders Khrushchev and Bulganin on a visit to Britain. The British government denied any knowledge of Crabb's activities and the incident – and Crabb's fate – remained a mystery. Rumours suggested that he had defected, been drowned, or that he had been killed by British intelligence because of the possible political embarrassment that his action might cause.

Porvoo (Finland)

City whose cathedral gave its name to the 1995 Porvoo Declaration, an agreement uniting the Anglican Church in England with Protestant Churches in mainland Europe – effectively healing the 460-year-old rift between the Anglican church and the Lutheran churches of northern Europe. The agreement allows Lutherans in Scandinavia and the Baltic (and Anglicans in England) to regard themselves as

195

members of each other's churches, and to receive communion across the board. Each church mutually recognizes priests and bishops.

Posavina Corridor (Bosnia)
Strategic military link in the north where the lines of the Bosnian Serbs were at their weakest. It was a vital supply route for the Serbs of the **Krajina** after 1992.

Potsdam (Germany)
Site outside Berlin of the final wartime meeting of Allied leaders Stalin, Truman (replacing Roosevelt on his death) and Attlee (having defeated Churchill in a general election). The meeting from 17 July to 1 August 1945 was to formulate future Allied policies, to lay the basis for definitive peace settlements and to reach agreed policies on the treatment of Germany. The idea of partitioning Germany into a number of states was dropped and principles governing the treatment of the whole of Germany leading to disarmament, de-Nazification and demilitarization were agreed upon. The differing views of the Russians and the Western Powers on reparations were among the most intractable problems of the conference. It was agreed that the city of **Königsberg** (now Kaliningrad) was to be transferred to the Soviet Union and that the Polish–German frontier should be on the **Oder-Neisse Line**. The western interpretation of the **Yalta** Declaration on Liberated Europe could not be realized and the question of the Turkish Straits remained unsettled.

Po Valley (Italy)
Second World War battle along the longest river in Italy. On 9 April 1945 the Allies launched a massive offensive against the German forces in northern Italy. Within two weeks Bologna had fallen and the south bank of the Po had been reached. The Germans fell back across the river as the Allied advance intensified. Behind the German lines Italian partisans seized control of Milan and Venice, and executed the Fascist dictator Benito Mussolini on 28 April. As US troops entered Milan, the British rounded the top of the Adriatic and joined with Yugoslavian units. On 29 April 1945 the Germans, with nearly one million men, surrendered unconditionally.

Poznan (Poland)
City famous for the Workers' Uprising of 1956 against Communist rule. A revolt of workers seeking better conditions broke out in Poznan on 28 June 1956 and it was suppressed by the security forces. Casualties included 53 dead (nine of them soldiers) and 300 injured.

Prague (Czech Republic)
Capital city of the former **Czechoslovakia**, which gave its name to the "Prague Spring" of 1968, the liberalizing period of Communist rule under Alexander Dubcek

which provoked the Soviet-led invasion. Under Dubcek as Secretary of the Party, Ludvik Svoboda as President and Oldrich Gernik as Prime Minister, Czechoslovakia began the pursuit of a more liberal regime. Dubcek sought more contacts with the West, censorship was relaxed, and "socialism with a human face" replaced the rigours of the Antonin Novotny era, but he went too far. On the night of 20 August 1968, hundreds of thousands of Warsaw Pact troops invaded Czechoslovakia. The invasion was a testimony to Soviet military precision: troops and vehicles poured across the Czech border at 18 points, meeting no resistance. Not a single shot appears to have been fired by border guards. Equally massive was the airborne invasion: fleets of huge Soviet Antonov-12 four-engine turboprop transport aircraft airlifted thousands of troops and scores of light tanks into the main Czech airports. Although sporadic resistance occurred – mainly by teenagers in some cities – Czechoslovakia's liberal days were over. Some 70 people were killed and over a thousand wounded. No units of the Czech army were involved – its troops remained in their barracks.

Predappio (Italy)
Village on the road from Ravenna to Florence. As the birthplace of Benito Mussolini in 1883, it has a special place in Fascist history and has become a place of pilgrimage for old comrades and young Fascists who come each year on the anniversary of his birth and death.

Prince William Sound
Site off Alaska of the *Exxon Valdez* oil-spill disaster. The environmental calamity, just after midnight on 24 March 1989, devastated the region's wildlife and fisheries. It was the worst oil spillage (11 million gallons) in US history. After a lengthy court case, a jury decided that recklessness by the Exxon Corporation and the captain (Joseph Hazelwood) of the damaged *Exxon Valdez* tanker caused the disaster. Plaintiffs in the federal court case included more than 10,000 commercial fishermen, Alaskan Indians and property owners who claimed they suffered economic harm as a result of the ecological disaster.

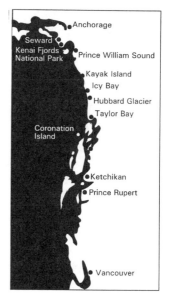

Prince William Sound

197

Pripet Marshes (Poland)

Inaccessible region significant in the Second World War. The Polish forces hoped to make a final stand in this area after the German invasion of September 1939 and the collapse of the main Polish defences. The advance of the Russian Red Army from the east destroyed this hope. The Pripet Marshes became a centre of underground resistance against the Nazis, not least for Polish Jews fighting extermination in the holocaust.

Prussia (Germany)

Dominant region of Germany covering most of the northern part of the country. After the First World War Prussian possessions such as **Danzig**, **Memel**, North Schleswig and Upper **Silesia** were lost, and Prussia itself split by the **Polish Corridor**. Following the Second World War northeast Prussia was annexed by the Soviet Union and the remainder divided between Poland and the Allied zones in Germany.

Przasnysz (Poland)

Town in the northeast 45 miles north of **Warsaw**. A strategic rail junction, the town was the focus of heavy fighting between Russian and German forces during the First World War. The main German assault came in February 1915 when a three-pronged assault failed to break through the Russian defences. The arrival of Russian reinforcements from the west forced a German retreat with the loss of over 10,000 prisoners. A renewed German assault later in 1915 succeeded in capturing the town.

Przemysl (Poland)

Town in the southeast near the present border with the Ukraine. Heavily fortified by the Austrians, Przemysl was the only town on the **Eastern Front** to endure a long siege during the First World War. Encircled by Russian forces on 24 September 1914, the town was besieged until March 1915. Austrian troops in **Galicia** attempted to relieve the fortress but failed to break through Russian lines. The garrison surrendered on 22 March 1915 with over 119,000 men taken prisoner. The fortress fell to advancing German troops in June 1915. During 1939–41, as a result of the Nazi–Soviet Non-Aggression Pact, Przemysl was divided by the German–Soviet border.

Puerto Rico

Caribbean island ceded to the USA by Spain in 1898. A Commonwealth with local self-government was established in 1952, and all Puerto Ricans are US citizens. A referendum in November 1993 resulted in 48 per cent voting to retain the current status, 46 per cent voting for full US Statehood and 4 per cent for independence.

Pugwash (Canada)

Village in Nova Scotia, the location of the first of a series of conferences of leading international scientists from the developed and developing countries to discuss the social responsibilities of science. Held regularly since July 1957. The first conference was held at the prompting of Bertrand Russell and Albert Einstein, and convened by the US philanthropist Cyrus Eaton.

Pukthunistan
Border territory which Afghanistan claimed (on Pakistan's independence from Britain in 1947) should be a separate state for the Pukhtuns (Pathans) living in the new Pakistan. Afghanistan opposed Pakistan's entry into the UN and the dispute was a source of friction in relations between the two states. In 1961 Afghanistan backed tribal unrest in Pakistan.

Punjab
Northwestern province of British India until 1947 when the eastern section became the Indian state of Punjab and the west a province of Pakistan. Despite the 1960 Indus Waters Treaty settling disputes over irrigation canals, the area was the scene of fighting between India and Pakistan in 1965 and 1971. In 1966 Indian Punjab was divided to create a Sikh majority state of Punjab and a Hindi-speaking state of Haryana. Militant Sikhs campaigned for an independent homeland of Khalistan and direct presidential rule was imposed in May 1987.

Purple Line
Location of the 1967 ceasefire line running along the top of the **Golan Heights**. The Syrian army attacked Israeli defences along this line on 6 October 1973 at the start of the 1973 War. Despite initial Syrian success, by 10 October the attackers had been driven back across the line.

Pusan (Korea)
City on the south coast of the Korean peninsula. The lightning attack by the North Koreans on 25 June 1950 sent the South Korean forces into full retreat. Even with US reinforcements arriving on 5 July, the retreat continued and the North Koreans threatened to capture the whole peninsula. A defensive perimeter was established around Pusan in the south, and all through August was under extreme pressure. Despite capturing bridgeheads across the Naktong River, the North Koreans failed to break through and the key city of Taegu held. By 10 September the North Koreans had reached their furthest line of advance. The **Inchon** landings six days later relieved the pressure by switching the battleground back to the north.

Pusan

Qana (Lebanon)

Site of a UN base southeast of the port of Tyre. On 18 April 1996 102 civilians, including mothers and children sheltering here, were killed when the UN compound was hit by Israeli artillery fire. Israel had launched attacks by aircraft and artillery on a range of targets in Lebanon after attacks by Iranian-backed *Hezbollah* guerrillas with Katyusha rockets on settlements in northern Israel. Israel claimed faulty maps had led to the casualties, but a UN report said that the shelling was unlikely to have been the result of error. The UN Secretary-General, Boutros Boutros-Ghali, was bitterly criticized by Israel and the USA for his handling of the affair.

Qibyá

Site of the massacre of 69 Palestinian villagers in 1953 when Israeli commandos led by Ariel Sharon attacked the village just inside the **West Bank** in retaliation for a Palestinian terrorist raid in Israel.

Qingdao (China)

See **Tsingtao**.

Quang Tri (Vietnam)

Battle in March–April 1972 in which a North Vietnamese division crossed the border into South Vietnam's Quang Tri province, capturing Quang Tri city and many prisoners. South Vietnamese forces recaptured the city in September.

Quebec (Canada)

French-speaking part of Canada, important for:

1) the Quebec Conferences of 1943–4. These were strategic planning meetings between President Roosevelt and Winston Churchill, the first (19–24 August 1943) addressed the **Normandy** landings and operations in Italy and Southeast Asia; the second (13–16 September 1944) considered the advance into, and post-war treatment of, Germany and the defeat of Japan;

2) *"Québec Libre"* Slogan of the *Parti Québécois*, the voice of separatism in Quebec province. French President Charles de Gaulle encouraged separatist hopes in a speech in favour of *"Québec libre"* in Montreal in July 1967. The *Parti Québécois* won substantial electoral support in provincial elections. In August 1977 a law was passed making French the only official language in the province. However, a referendum held on 20 May 1980 to decide whether the province should negotiate a looser form of political association with the rest of Canada proved a blow to the *Parti Québécois* and checked its drive towards independence. 84 per cent of the population of Quebec voted; almost 60 per cent were against secession. In the 1990s separatism remained a major issue. A referendum on the issue was only lost by the separatists by the narrowest of margins in 1995. See also **Meech Lake**.

Quebrada del Yuro (Bolivia)
Site where the remnant of Che Guevara's guerrilla band was attacked and he was killed 8–9 October 1967.

Quemoy (Taiwan)
Chinese Nationalist island six miles off the mainland. When the defeated Chinese Nationalist forces took refuge on Formosa (**Taiwan**) on 7 December 1949, they also retained strong garrisons on Quemoy, **Matsu** and the Tachen Islands, only a few miles offshore. Communist artillery carried out heavy bombardments of Quemoy. On 6 February 1955 the US 7th Fleet began the evacuation of 25,000 troops and 17,000 civilians from the Tachen Islands in the face of mounting Communist threats. Heavy shelling of Quemoy resumed on 23 August 1958, but threats of invasion were countered by a US military build-up. Sporadic shelling continued until 1962. Now known as Kinmen.

Querétaro (Mexico)
Assembly in this city on 5 February 1917 which drew up the revolutionary constitution in the Convention of Querétaro during the Mexican Civil War.

Qumran
Remote spot in Judaean Hills near the Dead Sea, the site of the discovery of the Dead Sea Scrolls by a wandering Bedu shepherd boy in 1947. Some 800 fragments of scrolls were discovered in 11 caves between 1947 and 1956. They include poetry, legal texts and the earliest known sections of the Bible and were probably written by the Essenes, a breakaway Jewish sect.

Rabat (Morocco)

Location of the 1974 Arab Summit which confirmed the PLO in its role as the only legitimate representative of the Palestinians. For the first time King Hussein of Jordan agreed that the Palestinians had a right to sovereignty in all of liberated Palestine, under PLO leadership.

Rabaul (Papua New Guinea)

Port on the northeast coast of New Britain in the Pacific. An early Japanese target in the Second World War, the small Australian force there was overpowered in January 1942. By mid-1943 it had been extensively developed and formed the core of Japan's system of bases. Instead of risking a head-on assault, the Allies decided to isolate and encircle this stronghold. Beginning in June 1943 the Allied counter-offensive slowly captured strategic points in New Britain and neighbouring islands. Japanese communications to Rabaul were severed and over 90,000 troops left stranded in the bases, eventually surrendering on 6 September 1945.

Rabta (Libya)

Site 40 miles south of Tripoli where in the late 1980s Western intelligence believed Colonel Gadaffi, the Libyan leader who has close international links with terrorist outrages, was building a chemical warfare plant. After much worldwide publicity the project was apparently shelved. Some reports said a new underground facility was being constructed near Tarhuna, 40 miles southeast of Tripoli.

Radfan (Yemen)

Area north of Aden (now Yemen), scene of clashes (between 1963 and 1967) of British armed forces and South Arabian federal army units versus NLF versus FLOSY (with Egyptian and North Yemeni support). After the creation of the South Arabian Federation in January 1963, British troops were involved in suppressing internal disorders in Aden and in fighting in the Radfan area north of Aden against rebel tribesmen supported by Egypt and North Yemen. At a constitutional conference in London in June 1964, agreement was reached for the independence of the Federation by 1968. Civil war developed between the two rival nationalist movements FLOSY and NLF. When Egyptian support for FLOSY ended after the Six Day War in 1967, the NLF, with the backing of the federal army, won control of the country. The withdrawal of British troops began on 15 August 1967 and was completed on 29 November.

Radom (Poland)

Town 70 miles south of Warsaw, site of a Russian victory in the First World War. Austrian troops, retreating after their defeat at **Ivangorod**, were broken up into smaller fighting units because of the densely-forested terrain outside Radom. The

Russians, more experienced in forest combat, defeated the Austrians. Radom itself finally fell on 28 October 1914.

Rafah

Town on the border of Egypt and the **Gaza Strip** attacked by Israel in the initial phase of its invasion of the **Sinai**. In a meticulously planned operation the Israeli forces captured the town and advanced west into the Sinai.

Ramadi (Iraq)

Following the capture of **Baghdad**, the British resumed their advances. Maude marched on the Turkish garrison at Ramadi, 60 miles west of Baghdad and overwhelmed the Turks on 28–29 September 1917 taking most of them prisoner.

Rangoon (Burma)

Capital of **Burma**, now known as Yangon in Myanmar. Captured by the Japanese on 8 March 1942, its recapture became the prime Allied objective in Burma. The capital was eventually retaken on 2 May 1945.

Rann of Kutch

See **Kutch, Rann of**.

Rapallo (Italy)

Coastal resort in Liguria in the northwest, which gave its name to two inter-war treaties. The first in November 1920 attempted to settle territorial disputes between Italy and the Kingdom of Serbs, Croats and Slovenes (later called **Yugoslavia**). Italy received the **Istrian Peninsula**, the Kingdom won Dalmatia, and **Fiume** (Rijeka) became a free city. The second treaty in April 1922 was between the Soviet Union and Germany. Both countries agreed to forgo any financial claims which either might bring against the other following the First World War. In contravention of the **Versailles** Peace Treaty, the Soviet authorities secretly allowed German troops to train in the Soviet Union. Also known for the Rapallo Conference (November 1917) which created a Supreme War Council, the first Allied attempt at achieving unity of command.

Raratonga

Largest of the Cook Islands in the Pacific. In 1985 the island was the host for the Treaty of Raratonga where the nations of the Pacific set out to create a nuclear-free zone. This has failed to prevent the French, for example, defying world opinion with atomic testing at **Mururoa**.

Rastenburg (Poland)

Headquarters of Hitler, where the assassination attempt led by Claus Count Schenk von Stauffenburg took place on 20 July 1944. Rastenburg was the site of the Wolf's Lair (*Wolfschanze*) the alternative capital of the Third Reich, a concrete city buried deep in the forests of eastern Poland. The famous July Plot against Hitler failed – five people were killed in the attempt, but Hitler narrowly escaped. His hair was set alight and his trousers shredded, but he escaped serious injury. The plotters were executed.

Rava-Russkaya (Ukraine)

Scene of Russian victory against the Austrians in the First World War. On 9 September 1914 this Russian success opened up a 40-mile gap in the Austrian line, paving the way for an advance into **Galicia**.

Ravensbrück (Germany)

Nazi concentration camp in Mecklenburg, opened in 1936. It housed women prisoners (including Allied female agents). An estimated 90,000 women died here before the camp was liberated by the advancing Red Army.

Rawalpindi (Pakistan)

City in Punjab. A treaty signed here in 1919 acknowledged the independence of the state of **Afghanistan**. Interim capital of Pakistan, 1959–69. A conspiracy was plotted in Rawalpindi by left-wing army officers to oust Prime Minister Liaquat Ali Khan (who was assassinated here on 16 October 1951). Zulfiqar Ali Khan was hanged here on 4 April 1979.

Reichswald

Second World War battle around this forest between the Maas and Waal rivers on the Dutch–German border. In February 1945 advancing Canadian and British troops were checked when the Germans opened the rivers' sluice gates and flooded the areas around the forest. Strong German defence and the hazardous terrain delayed the Allied Forces until 21 February when the forest was finally cleared.

Remagen (Germany)

The seizure of this small town's vital bridge (the Ludendorff Bridge) across the Rhine by the US 9th Armoured Division on 7 March 1945 paved the way for the Allied advance deep into the heart of Nazi Germany. The bridge was still standing when discovered by a US army patrol. Heavy tank traffic and German bombing caused it to collapse some days later but by then the Allies had crossed the Rhine in strength elsewhere.

Rethondes (France)
See **Compiègne**.

Reykjavik (Iceland)
Capital, scene on 11–12 October 1986 of the confused and inconclusive meeting between US President Reagan and Soviet First Secretary Gorbachev at which apparent initial agreement on strategic nuclear warhead numbers, mutual withdrawal of missiles from Europe and the eventual banning of all ballistic missiles foundered because of Soviet concerns about the US Strategic Defense Initiative (Star Wars).

Rhineland (Germany)
Large populous region of western Germany around the river Rhine. Under the Peace Treaty of **Versailles** in 1919, Germany kept control of the Rhineland as long as it remained demilitarized. The last occupying Allied troops left in June 1930. On 7 March 1936 Hitler, renouncing the Rhineland clauses of the Versailles and **Locarno** treaties, sent in German troops who were under orders to retreat if opposed. Neither France nor the League of Nations resisted the move or retaliated. Towards the end of the Second World War it was the focus of heavy fighting as the Allies approached Germany. A series of Allied attacks (8 February–24 March 1945) captured most of the west bank and the vital bridge at **Remagen**, paving the way for the final invasion. After the war the Rhineland was incorporated into West Germany.

Rhodesia
Large area of southern Africa, under British control since the days of Cecil Rhodes. Southern Rhodesia (now **Zimbabwe**) was a self-governing British colony after 1923, Northern Rhodesia a British protectorate after 1924. They were briefly joined in the **Central African Federation**. Northern Rhodesia became independent as Zambia in 1964. Southern Rhodesia, where white rule was entrenched, saw an increasingly bitter war against nationalist forces. Black nationalist guerrilla activity in Southern Rhodesia grew after the unilateral declaration of independence by Ian Smith's white minority regime on 11 November 1965. Two guerrilla forces were operating: ZIPRA, the military wing of Joshua Nkomo's Zimbabwe African People's Union, based in Zambia and recruiting from the Ndebele peoples; and ZANLA, the military wing of Robert Mugabe's Zimbabwe African National Union, based in Mozambique and recruiting from the Shona peoples. These two groupings united to form the Patriotic Front on 9 October 1976. A settlement for an end to the conflict based on a new constitution was reached at the conclusion of a conference at **Lancaster House**, London, on 15 December 1979. Zimbabwe became an independent republic on 18 April 1980.

Rif Mountains (Morocco)
Range stretching from northwest to southeast along the Mediterranean coastline. Although nominally part of the Spanish protectorate of Morocco, it was effectively

independent. The Rif Republic was declared by Abd el-Krim whose tribal forces inflicted a devastating defeat at **Anual** in 1921 on the Spanish garrison. The Rif Republic was finally defeated by combined French and Spanish armies in 1926.

Riga (Latvia)
Capital of the Baltic country of **Latvia**. In September 1917 Germany launched a massive offensive against Riga, capturing the city on 3 September. Kerensky's provisional government in Russia buckled under the pressure of another major defeat and the Bolsheviks seized power in the October Revolution. Latvian independence was proclaimed in Riga in November 1918. Germany reoccupied the city from June 1941 until liberation on 15 October 1944.

Rijeka
See **Fiume**.

Riom (France)
Town in Auvergne, north of Clermont-Ferrand. The **Vichy** Government established the Supreme Court of Justice here during the Second World War. In February 1942 several prominent French leaders were tried for their role in the defeat of France by Germany in 1940. The most notable defendants were former Prime Ministers Leon Blum, Edouard Daladier and Paul Reynaud who had formed the backbone of the pre-war government. After two months the Riom trials were suspended without verdicts and never reconvened.

River Plate
Scene of Second World War naval battle off the Atlantic coast of South America. After weeks of harassing Allied shipping, the German battleship *Graf Spee* was finally caught in the mouth of the River Plate on 13 December 1939. A British squadron (HMS *Exeter*, *Ajax* and *Achilles*) engaged the Germans in an 80-minute battle. The *Graf Spee* was badly damaged and sought refuge in neutral **Montevideo**, chased by the *Ajax* and *Achilles*. Only given 72 hours sanctuary by the Uruguayans and with British reinforcements imminent, the *Graf Spee* steamed out of the harbour and was blown up by her own crew.

Rivonia (South Africa)
Location near Johannesburg of the Rivonia Trial (October 1963–June 1964), the most famous political trial in modern South Africa. South African police discovered the headquarters of the military wing of the ANC at Liliesleaf Farm in Rivonia. The leaders of the ANC (eight in all, including Nelson Mandela, Walter Sisulu and Govan Mbeki)

and also two whites were subsequently charged with sabotage and conspiracy to cause violent revolution. The trial attracted massive worldwide media attention. All except one defendant were found guilty, most serving their sentences on **Robben Island**.

Rizal Reef

Disputed area in the South China Sea. A rich fishing ground, it is claimed by both Malaysia and the Philippines. In 1979 (and also in 1981) the dispute again erupted.

Rjukan (Norway)

Power station and "heavy water" plant in southern Norway, west of Oslo. In an attempt to prevent Germany using heavy water for developing atomic weapons, the plant was destroyed by SOE commandos on 28 February 1943. Rebuilt within five months, it was targeted again on 16 November 1943 by US Air Force bombers, but only the power station was damaged. Production of heavy water continued until a shipment bound for Germany was sunk by SOE operatives in January 1944.

Robben Island (South Africa)

Small island in Table Bay five miles from the mainland. Initially serving as an insane asylum and leper colony (1846–1931), it was designated a maximum security prison in the mid-1960s. Many political opponents of the apartheid regime were imprisoned here, most notably ANC leader Nelson Mandela. He was sentenced to life imprisonment on 14 June 1964 after being convicted of sabotage and conspiracy to overthrow the government. He was finally released on 11 February 1990 as part of the process of dismantling apartheid in South Africa. Stone quarried from the island is still used in Cape Town buildings.

Rome (Italy)

Capital of Italy. In the autumn of 1922, with Italy on the brink of civil war, King Victor Emmanuel III invited Fascist leader Benito Mussolini to form a government. On 30 October Mussolini arrived in Rome from Milan, followed by 24,000 Blackshirts from Naples – the so-called March on Rome. The Rome–Berlin Axis was formed on 1 November 1936, developing into the Rome–Berlin–Tokyo Axis in September 1940, and was to last until the Allied victory in 1945. The Treaties of Rome, signed on 25 March 1957 by Belgium, France, Italy, Luxembourg, The Netherlands and West Germany, established the EEC and EURATOM. The Economic Treaty created a "common market" with freedom of labour and capital movement, common trading policies and abolition of internal tariffs.

Rostock (Germany)

Town in the east which became notorious on 25 August 1992 for violent disorders directed against asylum-seeking foreign nationals. Neo-Nazi extremists set fire to a reception centre for asylum seekers. Some German residents clearly approved of this action and the local police were slow in stopping the violence. The episode was a dramatic indication of the strength of extremist right-wing support in Germany and of a renascent racism.

Rostov (Russia)

City near the mouth of the River Don in the south of the former Soviet Union. Operation Barbarossa succeeded in advancing German front lines deep into Russia by late 1941. In November the German 1st Panzergroup thrust towards Rostov and took the city on 20 November. A fierce Soviet counter-attack across the frozen Don recaptured the city on 29 November forcing a German withdrawal. This first military setback in the German invasion plans precipitated the resignation of Panzergroup leader von Runstedt. Rostov fell again to the Germans in July 1942, finally being liberated by advancing Soviet troops on 1 February 1943.

Roswell (United States)

Town in southeastern New Mexico, notorious for the "Roswell Incident" of 1947 when a UFO reportedly crashed in the surrounding desert. The area was immediately sealed off by the military and has remained closed ever since. The official silence on the events has fuelled rumours of aliens being captured and scientifically investigated.

Rotterdam (The Netherlands)

Second largest city and main port. Following the German invasion of the Low Countries on 10 May 1940, Rotterdam was heavily bombed. Over 900 died and most of the city centre and port area was destroyed. Few public buildings escaped, with the City Hall, the Stock Exchange and the Post Office reduced to rubble. The Dutch Government ordered its troops to stop fighting on 14 May in order to save other cities from the same fate.

Route 66 (United States)

2,448-mile long road linking Chicago with Los Angeles. Officially designated in 1926, it was the first cross-country road to be paved (1938). Although many parts of it have been replaced by Inter-State Highway I-40, it has remained part of US folklore as the USA's "Main Street" and inspired a TV series, a song and considerable memorabilia.

Ruanda-Urundi

See **Burundi** and **Rwanda**.

Ruby Ridge (United States)

Site in Idaho of the confrontation between white supremacist Randy Weaver and FBI agents in 1992. FBI agents besieged his home, and his wife, son and a US marshal were shot dead. Weaver won $3 million compensation from the US government. Echoes of this confrontation were seen in the stand-off in 1996 when FBI agents encircled the compound of the Freemen of Montana at "Justus Township", Jordan, Montana.

Rudnik Ridges (Serbia)

First World War battle along the Kolubra River near Belgrade. Following the stalemate in the Battle of the **Drina** (8–17 September 1914), Serb forces under General Putnik withdrew in the face of a renewed Austrian assault in November. By 2 December Belgrade had fallen and the Austrians had crossed the Kolubra River. The following day Putnik decided to counter-attack from his defensive positions on the Rudnik Ridges. With the Kolubra River in flood behind them, the Austrian defence started to collapse after five days of fierce fighting. The Serbs pushed forward and recaptured Belgrade on 15 December, but not without high casualties on both sides – 170,000 Serbs and 227,000 Austrians. Also known as the Battle of the Kolubra.

Rufiji River (Tanzania)

First World War battle near the longest river in **Tanganyika**, East Africa. After the Allied victory of 1915 in German **South West Africa**, the battleground moved to East Africa. In two years of sporadic fighting the Germans eluded the larger South African forces. The decisive battle occurred on 28 November 1917 when a combined Allied Force defeated the Germans near the Rufiji River. The German general, Lettow-Vorbeck, escaped with a few others and remained at large for another year until his surrender on 25 November 1918.

Ruhr (Germany)

Industrial heartland and most populous region situated in the Ruhr river valley. Under the peace terms of 1919 Germany was forced to pay reparations in kind, in the form of coal and coke, to France and Belgium. In January 1923, following German defaults on reparations, French and Belgian forces occupied the Ruhr, prompting German passive resistance. With the German economy paralysed, inflation rocketed and the Deutschmark collapsed. The dispute was finally settled by the Dawes Plan of 1924 and the occupying troops withdrew the following year. Hitler's rearmament programme led to the re-establishment of the region's heavy industry from 1933 onwards. Heavily bombed during the Second World War, 75 per cent of the area was destroyed. The Ruhr became part of the Federal Republic of Germany after the war.

Rumani (Egypt)

Turkish troops under German colonel Baron Friedrich Kress von Kressenstein intercepted a British column under General Murray on 4 August 1916 but in the ensuing battle the Turks were defeated and retreated with the loss of 6,000 men. The British lost 1,130 and they were free to continue their advance to al-Arish from where they could attack into Palestine.

Rwanda

Independent republic in central Africa, formerly part of the German colony of Ruanda-Urundi. It was then administered by Belgium, first as a League of Nations Mandate and then a UN Trust Territory. After disturbances in 1959, a referendum in 1961 showed a majority for the republican party, the Parmehutu. The Republic of Rwanda became independent on 1 July 1962. On 6 April 1994 the president of Rwanda, Juvenal Habyarimana, died with the Burundi president in a rocket attack on their aircraft. Following his death, rebel Rwandan Patriotic Front forces advanced on the capital Kigali from the north, forcing the self-proclaimed president Theodore Sindikubwado's government to move to Gitarama. Mass killings of Tutsis by the government militia and Hutu death squads began and by 7 May an estimated 200,000 Tutsis had died while thousands more had become refugees.

Saar (Germany)

Major industrial region with rich coal deposits on the French–German border. Under the **Versailles** Peace Treaty (1919) the territory was to be administered by the League of Nations with the coal mines going to France. Provision was made for a referendum after 15 years and it was duly held in February 1935. The result was an overwhelming vote for reunification with Germany, which subsequently took place. After the Second World War the Saar was occupied by French troops and incorporated economically into France. A second referendum in 1955 again voted for reunification with Germany, which was finally achieved in 1959.

Sabah (Malaysia)

Formerly British North Borneo. It was united with Labuan in 1946 to become a Crown Colony. In 1963, adopting the name Sabah, it became part of the Federation of Malaysia.

Sabarmati (India)

Site of Mahatma Gandhi's retreat (*ashram*). It was highly significant in 1930 when Gandhi led his followers on what became known as the Salt March from Sabarmati to Dandi, to defy the ban on the private manufacture of salt imposed by the British authorities. On 5 May 1930 Gandhi was arrested. The protests continued and in all 60,000 people were subsequently arrested and imprisoned.

Sabra and Shatila (Lebanon)

Two Palestinian refugee camps in West **Beirut**, the site of a massacre on 16 September 1982 by Lebanese Christian militiamen who killed hundreds of their inhabitants. Israel came under international criticism for permitting the massacre since it had encouraged the militiamen to enter the camps. An internal Israeli investigation led to the resignation of senior officials and officers.

Sachsenhausen (Germany)

Nazi concentration camp north of Berlin. Many well-known public figures were held here, including the former Chancellor of Austria, Dr Kurt von Schuschnigg and the religious leader Pastor Niemöller.

Safad (Israel)

Strategically important town in Galilee, captured by Zionist forces in a series of operations known as Yiftach in late April 1948.

Sagaing (Burma)

Town situated southwest of Mandalay on the Irrawaddy River. In 1988 it was the scene of a massacre of pro-democracy demonstrators by the military regime. Over 300 protesters were killed.

Saigon (Vietnam)

City which became the capital of South Vietnam after the country's partition in 1954. During the **Vietnam** War it served as the headquarters of US troops, and was badly damaged in the Tet Offensive in January 1968. Most of the US personnel were withdrawn following the **Paris** Peace Accords of 1973, although the South Vietnamese under President Thieu fought on. By April 1975 the North Vietnamese were close to the city, prompting Thieu to resign and escape. The last US troops were airlifted out along with as many Vietnamese as could be crammed in the helicopters. On 30 April the North Vietnamese entered the city, renaming it Ho Chi Minh City.

Saint-Germain-en-Laye (France)

Western suburb of **Paris**, which gave its name to the peace treaty between the Allies and Austria after the First World War. Negotiated at the Paris Peace Conference, it was signed on 10 September 1919 by the new Austrian Republic, which had replaced the old Austro-Hungarian Empire in November 1918. Under the treaty union with Germany was forbidden, the Austrian army was limited to 30,000 men and provisions were made for reparations payments. New frontiers were imposed with Austria losing most of its territory and becoming land-locked. The largest share (**Bosnia-Hercegovina**, Dalmatia and Slovenia) became part of the new Kingdom of Serbs, Croats and Slovenes, later called **Yugoslavia**. Bukovina, **Galicia** and South **Tyrol** went to Romania, Poland and Italy respectively.

St.-Lô (France)

Fortified town in **Normandy** which was an early objective in the Allied invasion of France in the Second World War. Six weeks after the D-Day landings on the Normandy beaches intense German defence had confined the Allies to a beachhead 20 miles deep. St.-Lô, a main communications centre and headquarters of the German 84th Corps, was the first goal of the Allied push into France. The town was captured from the Germans on 21 July 1944 by the US 1st Army under General Bradley. It then served as the Allied centre for Operation Cobra, the planned breakout from the hedgerow country of northern Normandy. Beginning on 28 July, this resulted in the Allies advancing deep into Brittany.

Saint-Mihiel (France)

Scene of First World War battle on the River Meuse near **Verdun** in western France. The initial German assault in September 1914 had created a salient around Saint-Mihiel. By September 1918 Allied victories on the **Marne** and at Amiens paved the way for a renewed offensive. German forces, already retreating from Saint-Mihiel, were surprised by a full Allied assault on 12 September. US and French troops attacked from three sides, isolating the main German force. Over the next 36 hours the Germans were expelled from the salient with over 15,000 troops taken prisoner.

Saint-Nazaire (France)

Seaport on the Atlantic coast with large dry-dock facilities. It was a key base for the German navy during the Second World War. In a daring attack on 28 March 1942, British commandos sailed the old destroyer *Campbeltown* against the dock gates, detonated the explosives on board and destroyed the gates. The objective of disabling the dock was achieved, but at a loss of 144 men dead or missing.

St Petersburg (Russia)

City on the Baltic coast known as Petrograd 1914–24 and **Leningrad** 1924–91. As the Tsarist capital of Russia, it was the focus of revolutionary activity. Strikes during 1904 culminated on 22 January 1905 in a peaceful march by unarmed strikers to the Winter Palace. Government troops opened fire on the crowds, killing over 500 marchers. This Bloody Sunday massacre fuelled the discontent leading to a general strike in October, until it was violently suppressed in December. Renamed Petrograd, the city was the scene of serious rioting in 1917, fuelled by war discontent and food shortages. The revolution resulted in Tsar Nicholas II's abdication on 16 March and the formation of Alexander Kerensky's Provisional Government. In a second coup on 7 November 1917 Red Guards stormed the Winter Palace and brought the Bolsheviks to power.

Saint-Quentin (France)

See **Guise**.

Saint-Valery-en-Caux (France)

Site in northern France of one of the great moments of heroism in the early days of the Second World War: the last stand of the gallant Scots 51st Division under General Fortune in June 1940 as the British Expeditionary Force was evacuated from Dunkirk. Up to a thousand soldiers died, and more than 8,000 were taken prisoner when they were trapped, along with the French Army Corps, by the advancing German forces under General Rommel. The decision by General Fortune to surrender has been the subject of continued and bitter controversy. It now appears he had little alternative after the air support which was vital to evacuation was withheld.

Saipan

Tiny Pacific island in the Japanese-held **Marianas Islands** invaded by the USA on 15 June as part of the counter-attack on Japan. It achieved notoriety because of the many islanders who committed suicide en masse after the US invasion. On 6 July the Japanese commander, General Saito ordered mass suicide, taking his own life together with his senior officers: an act followed by many civilians and the remaining members of the Imperial Army. Some killed themselves by gathering in groups around a grenade and pulling the pin. Others hurled themselves off Saipan's high cliffs. Thousands fled through the jungle and risked dying of thirst; flame-throwers were used to try to flush them out in a period of horrendous carnage.

Sakarya River (Turkey)

Battle of the Greek–Turkish War (1920–23) centred on this river in the northwest. Having captured Smyrna (Izmir) in May 1919, the Greek army had continued to move inland from the Aegean. The establishment of a nationalist provisional government under Mustafa Kemal (later Kemal Atatürk) prompted a further Greek offensive in June 1920. Approaching the new capital of Angora (Ankara) the Greeks met a last-ditch Turkish defence at the Sakarya River. In a crucial battle (August 24–September 16) the Turks defeated the Greeks, paving the way for a Turkish counter-offensive the following August and expulsion of Greek forces from Turkey by September 1922. The war ended with the Treaty of **Lausanne** (1923).

Sakht-Sar (Iran)

See **Kamsar**.

Sakiet (Tunisia)

Town, the scene of a major clash with France. On 8 February 1958 the French air force bombed the Tunisian town killing 79 people, in retaliation for Tunisian assistance to the Algerian rebels. Clashes took place as Tunisia demanded the evacuation of French bases. On 17 June 1958 the French agreed to withdraw from all bases except **Bizerte**.

Salang Highway (Afghanistan)

Vital strategic route north from Kabul, leading to the former Soviet Union. The important Salang Tunnel lies 62 miles north of Kabul and was opened in 1964.

Salerno (Italy)

Port on the Gulf of Salerno, south of Naples. In the early hours of 9 September 1943 the Allied forces stormed the beaches of the Gulf. Expecting weak resistance after the Italian armistice the previous day, they were unprepared for the stiff German defences. With fragile beachhead positions, the Allies only just held out until reinforcements from the British 1st Army arrived on 16 September. German troops withdrew and Naples was captured on 1 October.

Salo (Italy)
Location near Lake Garda of the short-lived "puppet" government established by the Italian Fascist dictator Benito Mussolini in October 1943. Mussolini had been rescued by German paratroopers from the custody of the Allies and the ensuing Salo Republic nominally controlled that part of Italy not already captured by the advancing Allies. In 1945, as Italy fell to the Allies, Mussolini attempted to flee but was captured and shot by Communist partisans.

Salonika (Greece)
Port in the north now known as Thessaloniki. Annexed by Greece in 1913, Salonika became the base for the Allied *Armée d'Orient* during the **Vardar River** battles of the First World War. By September 1918 over 350,000 Allied troops from Serbia, Greece, France, Britain, Italy and Russia were stationed in the city. Following the success of the final Vardar offensive, an armistice was signed in Salonika between Bulgaria and the Allies on 30 September. Allied casualties during the Salonika campaign were greater from malaria (481,000) than from fighting (18,000).

Saltley (England)
A coke depot in Birmingham, the successful closure of which by mass picketing in 1972 because of police fears of violence (the Battle of Saltley Gate) symbolized the victory of the National Union Mineworkers in their strike and established the Yorkshire miners' leader Arthur Scargill as a leading trade union figure.

Salum-Halfaya Pass (Libya)
See **Halfaya Pass**.

Samashki (Chechenia)
Village, 25 miles west of Grozny, capital of the self-declared republic of **Chechenia**. It was alleged in 1995 that a massacre of some 200–250 villagers occurred here as Russian Interior Ministry troops closed in on Bamut, the last rebel stronghold in the Chechen lowlands. The massacre immediately drew comparisons with the US massacre of Vietnamese at **My Lai** in 1968. It was alleged that in Samashki troops had torched villagers with flame-throwers and thrown grenades into cellars housing women and children.

San Carlos (Falkland Islands)
Site chosen by the British War Cabinet for the landing of British troops to recapture the islands from Argentina. The landing took place on 21 May 1982. On 25 May the British ships *Coventry* and *Atlantic Conveyor* were sunk. On 28 May, the battle of

Goose Green was won by the British. The battle of Port Stanley began on 11 June and on 14 June the Argentines surrendered. See Falkland Islands in Appendix 2.

San Francisco (United States)

Coastal California city, most of which was destroyed by a powerful earthquake in April 1906, leaving over 900 dead and thousands homeless. On 25 April 1945 San Francisco hosted a conference attended by delegates from the 50 Allied nations then fighting the Axis Powers. The conference drafted the UN Charter, signed on 26 June, which created the key collective security provisions and ruling bodies of the UN. A second international conference in 1951 negotiated the peace treaty between the Allies and Japan. Coming into effect in April 1952, it provided for reinstatement of Japanese sovereignty, Korean independence and the renunciation of Japanese claims to **Taiwan**, the Pescadores, southern Sakhalin and its Pacific Mandates. Disputes over the **Kuril Islands** prevented the Soviet Union from signing the treaty.

Saniquellie (Liberia)

Location of meeting on 19 July 1959 in the village of Saniquellie to agree the principles on creating a Community of Independent African States. The meeting, resulting in the Saniquellie Declaration, was attended by President Nkrumah of Ghana, President Touré of Guinea and President Tubman of Liberia.

Santa Cruz (Indonesia)

Scene of a massacre in cemetery in Dili, the capital of **East Timor**. The Indonesian authorities (who had seized control of this former Portuguese colony) committed a massacre of unarmed protesters in November 1991 which outraged world opinion.

Santa Cruz (Solomon Islands)

Second World War naval battle near these volcanic Pacific islands 345 miles east of **Guadalcanal**. As both sides attempted to reinforce their positions on Guadalcanal, they clashed off Santa Cruz on 26 October 1942. Simultaneous air strikes led to severe damage to both fleets. The USS *Hornet* was torpedoed and sank, while the USS *Enterprise* took a direct hit on the flight deck and retreated. The Japanese victory was tempered by the damage to the carrier *Shokaku* and the loss of over 100 experienced pilots.

Santander (Spain)

City on the Biscay coast. During the Spanish Civil War the north coast was a crucial battleground. With a victory in **Bilbao**, the Nationalists pushed westwards along the coast through the Cantabrian mountains. By 14 August 1937 they had reached

Santander and its 50,000 Republican defenders. Being ill-equipped and with little training, the Republican troops quickly retreated in the face of heavy bombing. On 25 August General Davila, the Nationalist commander, led his troops into the city as Republican leaders fled.

Santiago de Cuba (Cuba)
City in the east founded by the Spanish in 1514, and site of the Moncada Barracks. In the first armed confrontation of the insurrection of 1953, a small group of rebels led by Fidel Castro attacked the barracks. Government troops repulsed the assault, killing three rebels and capturing the rest. 68 were executed, although others including Castro were later released. Despite the mission's failure, the date (26 July) was used to name Castro's revolutionary cause – the 26 of July Movement. The city was finally captured by Castro forces on 2 January 1959.

Sapoa (Nicaragua)
Border town which gave its name to the Sapoa truce of March 1989 in the civil war in **Nicaragua** between the Sandinistas and the Contras.

Saragossa (Spain)
Civil War battle for this city in northern Spain on the **Ebro River**. On 24 August 1937 the Republicans attacked along a broad front from Catalonia into Aragon with the aim of capturing Saragossa. Nationalist defences held around the key towns of Huesca in the north and Tervel in the south. The Republicans suffered heavy casualties and by the end of the September the offensive had collapsed.

Sarajevo (Bosnia-Hercegovina)
Capital city.
1) Austria-Hungary's annexation of Bosnia in 1908 fuelled Bosnian nationalism and Serb opposition. On 28 June 1914 the heir to the Austro-Hungarian throne, Archduke Franz Ferdinand, and his wife were assassinated by Gavrilo Princip, a Bosnian nationalist. The murders sparked off the chain of events which led to the First World War.
2) In 1990 the disintegration of **Yugoslavia** led to a three-way civil war in Bosnia between the Croats, Muslims and Bosnian Serbs. Sarajevo was the focus of intense fighting and of UN attempts to lift the Serbian siege of the capital. By the spring of 1995 continued bombardments by the Bosnian Serbs had reduced much of the city to rubble. UN forces eventually secured the heights around the city, with the help of NATO air raids. Under the **Dayton (Ohio)** Peace Accord of December 1995, Sarajevo became an open united city and capital of the new federal Bosnia.

Sarawak (Malaysia)

State of Malaysia, on the island of Borneo. Ruled by the Brooke family, the "White Rajahs", after it was ceded in 1841 by the Sultan of Brunei. A British Crown Colony after 1946, it joined the Federation of Malaysia in 1963 (after a guerrilla war in 1962–3).

Sarawak

Sarikamis (Turkey)

First World War battle in the northeast near the present border with **Armenia**. 60,000 Russian troops advanced into Turkey from their base in Kars, meeting their Turkish opponents on 29 December 1914. In a fierce five-day battle in freezing conditions the 95,000 Turks were routed and retreated in disarray. Only 18,000 Turkish troops manage to escape.

Saverne (France)

See **Zabern**.

Savo Island (Solomon Islands)

Scene of naval victory by Japan on 9 August 1942 over a US naval force protecting landing on **Guadalcanal**.

Scapa Flow (Scotland)

Wide sheltered anchorage on the Orkney Islands. Its defences were greatly improved during the First World War when it served as the home base for the British Grand Fleet. After its surrender, the German Fleet was confined here in 1918. In protest at the terms of the **Versailles** Peace Treaty, the German crews scuttled and sank their own ships, 71 in total, on 22 June 1919. In the Second World War it was again a British Fleet base, where HMS *Royal Oak* was sunk by a U-boat in October 1939. After numerous air raids the fleet put to sea. The base closed in 1956.

Scapa

Schengen (Luxembourg)

Location which gave its name to the Schengen Accord signed by the Benelux countries (Belgium, Luxembourg and The Netherlands), Germany and France on 14 June 1985. Subsequently extended by the Schengen Convention of June 1990 (signed by Germany, France, Spain, Portugal and the three Benelux countries), the agreement abolished all border checks between the signatory states. It came into effect in March 1995 but "Schengenland" caused major administrative chaos. States outside Schengen feared that if, for example, Greece and Italy joined, control over illegal immigration would be seriously weakened.

Schleswig-Holstein (Germany)

Most northerly province along the border with Denmark. Annexed by Prussia in the 1860s, its future after the First World War was decided by plebiscites in 1920, which resulted in new borders on national lines. North Schleswig voted to return to Denmark, becoming South Jutland. After the Second World War the southern province was incorporated into Germany and became a state of the Federal Republic.

Schweinfurt (Germany)

City 60 miles east of Frankfurt, and centre of the German ball-bearing industry during the First World War. A key strategic target for the Allied bombing campaign, it was raided on 17 August 1943 with substantial losses in Allied aircraft. The US 8th Air Force attacked again on 14 October 1943 using B17 Flying Fortress bombers. Although the factory was badly damaged, US losses were disastrous. Out of 291 aircraft, 60 were destroyed and 138 damaged, resulting in further long-range attacks being postponed until adequate fighter cover was available.

Scottsboro (United States)

Town in Jackson County, northern Alabama. In April 1931 nine black men, the youngest being 12 years old, were convicted of raping two white girls on a train. None of the defendants had any legal counsel until the first day of the trial and all nine were sentenced to death or life imprisonment. The US Supreme Court overturned the ruling, but the defendants were retried and reconvicted. In a second ruling the Supreme Court again overturned the convictions. After further retrials, reconvictions and appeals, most of the men were finally released. The last survivor, Clarence Norris, was granted a full pardon in 1976. The case is seen as a landmark in US constitutional law and civil rights.

Scutari (Albania)

See **Shkodër**.

Sedan (France)

The French, under Marshal McMahon, were caught and overwhelmed by the German army at the fortress of Sedan with Napoleon III personally surrendering, on 2 September 1870, ending the authority of the Second Empire and leading to the proclamation of the French Third Republic. Revenge for the defeat at Sedan remained a prime objective with many French.

Sedd-el-Behr (Turkey)

Village on the **Gallipoli** peninsula. Heavily fortified and strategically situated on the northern side of the entrance to the **Dardanelles**, it was the scene of Allied landings during the Gallipoli campaign of the First World War.

Sellafield (England)

See **Windscale**.

Selle (France)

First World War battle (17–25 October 1918) along this river in the north and part of the last major Allied offensive on the Western Front. In September 1918 four Allied armies pushed forward from their lines capturing the key towns of Saint-Quentin and **Cambrai** and forcing the Germans to withdraw to the River Selle. The Allies resumed their advance on 17 October using waterproofed tanks to cross the Selle. This phase of the offensive ended on 25 October with the Germans retreating behind the River Scheldt, which subsequently fell to the Allies on 1 November. German troops were still retreating when the armistice came into effect on 11 November. Also known as the Battle of Cambrai–Saint-Quentin.

Selma (United States)

Seat of Dallas county in central Alabama. In 1965 it was the focus of the voter registration drive, a major part of the civil rights struggle. Martin Luther King had chosen it as a prime example of the disenfranchisement of blacks in the South despite the 1964 Civil Rights Act. Of the 13,115 eligible blacks in Selma only 335 were registered to vote. A peaceful protest began on 18 January 1965 but encountered fierce opposition from local whites. Protesters were tear-gassed and beaten by state police. Two demonstrators died, including a clergyman from Boston, prompting a mass march to Montgomery, the State capital. President Johnson was forced to mobilize the National Guard to protect the marchers from continued white opposition.

Semtin (Czech Republic)

Town that was the centre for the manufacture of the explosive Semtex. A versatile, odourless plastic explosive, its name was derived from the contraction of "Semtin" and "explosive" to give Semtex.

Senkaku Islands

Uninhabited group of islands in the East China Sea between Okinawa and Taiwan, which are claimed by Japan, China and Taiwan (they are known to the Chinese as the Diaoyutai archipelago). The waters around the islands are believed to contain rich oil and natural gas reserves. The dispute erupted in October 1990, when Japanese patrol boats prevented two Taiwanese vessels putting men ashore to claim sovereignty. Tension over the disputed islands came to the fore again in 1996 and China conducted military exercises in the area.

Serbia

Republic in southeastern Europe. Independent from Turkey since 1878, Serbia emerged victorious and larger after the two Balkan Wars of 1912–13. Tension with Austria-Hungary, particularly over **Bosnia-Hercegovina** (annexed by Austria in 1908), culminated in Archduke Franz Ferdinand's assassination in **Sarajevo** in 1914, precipitating the First World War. Serbia was defeated and occupied, but survived to enjoy the fruits of victory. Having annexed Bosnia-Hercegovina, Serbia joined the new Kingdom of Serbs, Croats and Slovenes in December 1918 (renamed **Yugoslavia** in 1929). Occupied by Germany during the Second World War, Yugoslavia was re-constituted as a federal republic in November 1945. Ethnic tensions within Yugoslavia led to Serbia annexing **Kosovo** province in September 1990, and Croatia and Slovenia declaring their independence on 25 June 1991. The ensuing civil war was fuelled by President Milosevic's plans for a Greater Serbia. The independence declarations by Bosnia-Hercegovina and **Macedonia** in 1992 left only a "rump" Yugoslavia of Serbia and **Montenegro** which was not recognized by the UN. The Western blockade and military setbacks in Croatia and Bosnia led Serbia to the negotiating table, and a peace deal was agreed in **Dayton (Ohio)** in November 1995.

Seria (Brunei)

Oil town occupied in December 1962 by rebels seeking to overthrow the sultan. The rebellion collapsed rapidly after intervention by British troops.

Sétif (Algeria)

Site of massacre of 6,000 Arabs in 1945 by French police and European settlers in retaliation for the killing of 103 Europeans. The massacre helped provoke the Algerian War of Independence which broke out in 1954.

Sevastopol (Ukraine)

Chief city of the Crimea which resisted capture in the German assault of 1941. It fell after the siege of 3 June 1942 (falling on 1 July 1942). It was liberated by Russian forces on 9 May 1944.

17th Parallel (Vietnam)

Dividing line at latitude 17° North between North and South **Vietnam** set by the terms of the **Geneva** Agreements in July 1954.

Seveso (Italy)

Town in the north between Milan and Como. On 10 July 1976 a violent explosion at the Icsema chemical plant released a cloud of the weed-killer TCDD containing dioxin, an impurity resulting from the production of TCDD. Dioxin produces severe skin rashes (chloracne) and is suspected of causing cancer and deformations in unborn children. Widespread evacuations were carried out as the number of chloracne cases rose and the contaminated area spread. The EEC Seveso Directive was issued in 1982 to guard against future similar disasters. In 1983 five executives of Icsema received sentences of up to five years in prison for contravening safety regulations.

Sèvres (France)

Town near Paris where:

1) the post-First World War peace treaty was imposed on the **Ottoman Empire** on 10 August 1920, which was never ratified by Turkey. Under its proposals, the old Turkish Empire's territorial losses included:

(a) **Cyprus** (to Britain);

(b) Rhodes, the **Dodecanese**, and Adalia (ceded to Italy);

(c) part of European Turkey (to Bulgaria);

(d) eastern Thrace (to Greece); Greek claims to Chios and other islands recognized; Greece allowed to occupy Smyrna for five years until a plebiscite held;

(e) **Hejaz** and Arabia (became independent);

(f) League of Nations Mandates over Syria (to France); Palestine, Iraq and Transjordan (to Britain).

In addition, the **Dardanelles** were placed under international control; Turkey was occupied by British, French and Italian troops and the Covenant of the League of Nations was written into the Treaty.

2) French Prime Minister Mollet and Israeli Prime Minister Ben Gurion met from 22 to 24 October 1956 to agree the invasion of Egypt to oust President Nasser. The agreement, to which Britain became party after the urging of Prime Minister Anthony Eden, called for Israel to invade the **Sinai**, then for France and Britain to issue an ultimatum for both Egypt and Israel to withdraw their forces from either side of the **Suez Canal**, failing which the British and French would intervene militarily.

Shaba Province (Zaïre)

Formerly **Katanga Province**, Shaba again became of importance when, on 8 March 1977, the province was invaded from Angola by some 2,000 insurgents claiming to be members of the Congolese National Liberation Front. President Mobutu appealed for African support on 2 April 1977. On 10 April French transport aircraft carried 1,500 Moroccan troops to Zaïre and they helped the Zaïre army to repel the invasion. On 11 May 1978 a second invasion from Angola by some 3,000 rebels took place. French and Belgian paratroopers were sent to Kolwezi to rescue European hostages on 19 May 1978 and the invaders were dispersed. Zaïre and Angola signed a non-aggression pact on 12 October 1979.

Shaho River (China)

Location of indecisive battle in **Manchuria** during the Russo-Japanese War. Following the stalemate of the battle of **Liaoyang** in August 1904, the Russians retreated northwards with Japanese forces in pursuit. 15 miles south of **Mukden** (Shenyang) the Russians halted and fighting broke out in October along a 40-mile front. Heavy rains reduced the battle to a deadlock and both sides dug in for the winter.

Shanghai (China)

Most populous city and largest port in China where the Communist party of China was founded in 1921. The city's capture by the Nationalist Army of Chiang Kai-shek on 21 March 1927 was the decisive factor in Chiang's victory over the northern warlords. In April 1927 the Communist party was violently suppressed during street fighting with Nationalist soldiers, an event known as the Shanghai Massacre. The city was attacked by Japanese troops on 13 August 1937 and finally captured on 8 November after three months of bitter fighting. Nationalist control resumed after the Second World War but the fall of Shanghai to Communist forces on 26 May 1949 sealed Chiang's defeat in the Civil War. A declaration in February 1972 (known as the Shanghai Communiqué) paved the way for the re-establishment of normal US relations with Communist China.

Shankill (Northern Ireland)

Heart of Ulster loyalism, consisting of a street of terraced houses running due west of the centre of Belfast.

Shantung (China)

Northeastern province of China. The granting, at the Treaty of **Versailles**, of the former German colonial outposts in this region to Japan led to massive opposition in China. Demonstrations over the "Shantung Question" gave birth to the May 4th Movement and spurred on Chinese nationalist and revolutionary zeal.

Sharpeville (South Africa)

Township where a massacre of black protesters took place on 21 March 1960 when a demonstration against the South African apartheid pass laws near Johannesburg caused the police to open fire, killing 67. The massacre provoked international condemnation, the withdrawal of some foreign capital, and brought South Africa close to civil war. In addition to the 67 deaths (many of women and children), 186 others were wounded. In all 1,700 people were detained. Both the ANC and the PAC were subsequently banned.

Sharqat (Iraq)

Battle, in October 1918 60 miles from Mosul, representing the culmination of the British campaign to occupy **Mesopotamia**. A British force under General Cobbe defeated a Turkish force under General Hakki, taking 18,300 men prisoners for the loss of 1,886 men. The defeat marked the end of the war in Mesopotamia and Britain occupied Mosul on 14 November.

Shashamane (Ethiopia)

Site of the Rastafarian settlement of between 40 and 50 Rastas and Afro-Americans, many from Jamaica. Originally prospering, and enjoying favoured status under the Emperor Haile Selassie, it found itself in a contradictory position when the revolution of 1974 overthrew the monarchy and led to a Marxist regime.

Shatila

See **Sabra** and **Shatila**.

Shatt al-Arab

River, formed by the conjunction of the Tigris and Euphrates rivers which runs into the northern Arabian–Persian Gulf. The waterway forms the border between Iran and Iraq but the two countries have long disputed the exact boundary. In 1975 Iraq signed a treaty under duress and in 1980 took the opportunity of the Iranian revolution to attack and regain control of the waterway. Iraq was, however, beaten back and during its war against the UN coalition in 1990–91, Iraq agreed to return to the provisions of the 1975 treaty which granted Iran sovereignty over half of the river.

Shenyang

See **Mukden**.

Shenzhen (China)

Village designated in 1980 as China's first Special Economic Zone by Deng Xiaoping. Scenes of chaos and rioting erupted in a stampede to buy shares at the newly-opened Stock Exchange there in August 1992. See also **Guangdong**.

Shillong

See **Nagaland**.

Shimonoseki (Japan)

City on the southwest tip of Honshu, which gave its name to the peace treaty ending the First Sino-Japanese War (1894–5). The nine-month war ended on 17 April 1895 with Japan victorious. China accepted Korean independence, recognized Japanese claims for reparations and ceded Formosa (**Taiwan**), the Pescadores islands and Liaotong Peninsula to Japan.

Shkodër (Albania)

(Scutari.) Town near the border with **Montenegro**. Early in the First Balkan War (October 1912–May 1913) Montenegro attacked across its border with the **Ottoman Empire** and besieged Shkodër. The siege lasted until 22 April 1913 when Montenegrin forces captured the city after a heavy assault. Under pressure from its Balkan League allies and the Great Powers, Montenegro ceded the city to newly-independent **Albania**.

Siachen

Disputed area in Kashmir, the scene of conflict between India and Pakistan. India seized the area in 1984. Siachen, a glacier region surrounded by 20,000 ft high mountains, is probably the world's highest battleground. The area, which has never been properly demarcated, is a major hurdle in attempts to normalize relations between India and Pakistan. Indian soldiers have resisted attacks by Pakistan to recapture the desolate and mountainous region, over which both claim sovereignty, and which borders on China.

Sibilla (Saudi Arabia)

At the battle of Sibilla in 1929 the founder of the modern state of Saudi Arabia, Abd al Aziz Ibn Sa'ud, took on and crushed the Wahhabi fighters (the *Ikhwan*), whom he had previously built up as Islamic fundamentalist warriors to spearhead his conquests in the Arabian Peninsula. The *Ikhwan* had, however, become too powerful and Ibn Sa'ud's victory ensured the dominance of the House of Sa'ud over the religious establishment.

Sicily (Italy)

Largest island in the Mediterranean. The invasion of Sicily marked the first stage of the Allied counter-offensive in Europe during the Second World War. Victory in North Africa had paved the way for Operation Husky, the amphibious assault on Sicily. On 10 July 1943 the British 8th Army under General Montgomery and the US

7th Army under General Patton stormed ashore. The US troops pushed rapidly inland from the southern coast to capture the capital, Palermo, by 22 July. British troops advanced up the east coast overcoming stiff German resistance on the slopes of Mount Etna. As both armies closed in on Messina, most of the Italian and German troops were evacuated across to the mainland. Messina finally fell on 17 August 1943, leaving Italy open to invasion.

Sidi Barrani (Egypt)
Battle on 9–12 December 1940 60 miles inside Egypt's western frontier which marked the beginning of the North African campaign in the Second World War. The Italian 10th Army under Marshal Graziani had encamped at Sidi Barrani but the British Western Desert Force under General O'Connor mounted a surprise attack which resulted in the rout of the 75,000-strong Italian force and the capture of 38,000 prisoners. The British lost 600 men and pressed on into Libya.

Sidi bel Abbès (Algeria)
The headquarters of the French Foreign Legion until Algerian independence.

Sidi Messaod
See **Anual**.

Sidi Rezegh (North Africa)
Attack on 18 November 1941 against the Afrika Korps and their Italian allies reached Sidi Rezegh, the key to besieged **Tobruk**.

Sidney Street (England)
Thoroughfare in Stepney in the East End of London. On 3 January 1911 three Latvian anarchists were besieged in No. 100 by armed police. The three were wanted in connection with the murder of three policemen during a jewellery shop raid in Houndsditch on 16 December 1910. Shots were exchanged, and army reinforcements called in by the Home Secretary, Winston Churchill, who took command at the scene. The house caught fire, claiming the lives of two of the anarchists. "Peter the Painter", the leader, escaped.

Sidra, Gulf of
Crisis which erupted when US Navy F-14 fighters shot down two Libyan Su-22 jets over the Gulf of Sidra about 62 miles from the Libyan coast on 19 August 1981. Libya claimed the Gulf as territorial waters but the USA insisted it was international waters and had been holding naval exercises in the Gulf in an attempt to test Libya's resolve.

Siegfried Line

Originally, the defences between Lens and Rheims on the German **Western Front** in September 1918; later, the defences built to emulate the **Maginot Line** which the Nazis believed invulnerable. Not as extensive as the Maginot Line, it was strong enough around Saarbrücken to resist French attacks at the beginning of the Second World War. US forces reached this German line of defence in the West on 1 February 1945; British and Canadian forces broke through it the same month, crossing the Rhine near Millingen in the northern sector (where the line was weaker) on 8–9 February.

Sierra Maestra (Cuba)

Former guerrilla stronghold of the rebels led by Fidel Castro. The first attempted uprising led by Castro in **Santiago** and Bayamo on 26 July 1953 was suppressed. He was imprisoned but granted an amnesty in May 1955. He led an unsuccessful landing in Oriente Province on 30 November 1955, but commenced a successful guerrilla campaign based in the Sierra Maestra. Castro launched a final offensive in October 1958 and General Batista fled the country on 1 January 1959.

Sihanouk Trail

See **Ho Chi Minh Trail**.

Silesia (Poland)

Strategic region of eastern Europe with important mineral and industrial resources. Until the First World War the province was divided between Prussia (later Germany) and Austria. Following the Allied victory, and a series of plebiscites, Upper Silesia went to Poland, Lower Silesia to Germany and Austrian Silesia to Czechoslovakia. Germany occupied the whole region during the Second World War, after which Silesia became part of Poland. Over ten million German nationals were expelled to become refugees in West Germany.

Silicon Valley (United States)

Popular name since the 1960s for an area south of San Francisco Bay in California. Running from Palo Alto in the north to San José in the south, it encompasses the Santa Clara valley and towns of Sunnyvale and Cupertino. Regarded as the birthplace of the microchip and computer, the headquarters of both Apple and Hewlett-Packard are here. Its unofficial capital is San José.

Simferopol (Ukraine)

Major city of the Crimea. In 1918 it was the capital of the Crimean nationalist government as the Tsarist Empire disintegrated. In 1920 it became capital of the White Government led by the anti-Bolshevik leader General Wrangel.

Simla (India)

In colonial times, the summer capital of British India located in the Himalayan foothills of the Punjab. Important in 1906 for the Simla Declaration, led by the Aga Khan, which set out Muslim demands that they should vote as a separate Muslim electorate and that their vote should be weighted in their favour to reflect their political importance. In 1972, the Simla Agreement was signed here. This treaty between India and Pakistan followed the end of the 1971 war which resulted in the independence of **Bangladesh**.

Simonstown (South Africa)

Important former British naval base 30 miles south of Cape Town. In April 1957 it was handed over to South Africa, becoming the headquarters of the South African Navy. Under the Simonstown Agreement, Britain retained the right to use the naval base at any time (even if Britain was at war and South Africa was not involved). South Africa agreed to buy warships and other naval vessels from Britain. The Labour Government in Britain after 1964 refused to supply arms to South Africa and the agreement was suspended.

Sinai

Peninsula which forms easternmost part of Egypt, mainly desert. Following the escalation of tensions in October 1956 between Egypt and Israel because of Egyptian-backed guerilla raids into Israel and Israeli counter-raids, President Nasser closed the **Tiran Strait** to Israeli shipping and formed a joint military command with Jordan and Syria. Claiming this was a *casus belli* Israel attacked into the Sinai on 29 October. By the time the UN imposed a ceasefire on 5 November Israel had occupied all of the Sinai. The Israeli invasion provided the necessary cover for the British and French to attack Nasser under the pretext of enforcing a disengagement of forces. For events in 1967, see Appendix 2 p. 308.

Singapore

Island at the southern tip of the Malay peninsula. Heavily fortified by the British, it was considered impregnable to attack from the sea. The Japanese, having conquered **Malaya**, launched their assault from the north across the Johore Strait. On the night of 7–8 February 1942 5,000 Japanese troops crossed the narrow waterway to establish strategic bridgeheads. The damaged causeway, dynamited by the retreating Allies, was repaired and Japanese reinforcements flooded across. With most of its defences pointed seaward, Singapore city could not resist for long, despite the presence of 80,000 British, Australian and Indian troops. Under heavy aerial bombardment, unable to successfully evacuate any personnel and with supplies diminishing the Allies surrendered on 15 February. Described by Churchill as "the worst disaster and largest capitulation in British history", this defeat exposed Australia and the Dutch East Indies to attack.

Sinüiju (Korea)

Scene of aerial battle, the largest conflict of jet aircraft yet fought. The conflict took place in April 1951 when a force of 80 Russian MIG 15s were met by 115 USAF fighters escorting 32 Super Fortress bombers. 46 Russian MIGs were destroyed or damaged.

Sitges (Spain)

The Sitges Agreement of 1957 took its name from this small resort near Barcelona when the leaders of the Liberal and Conservative parties of Colombia held talks which resulted in the end of the worst of the *violencia* engulfing their country. The agreement ushered in a period of oligarchic power-swapping in the *Frente Nacional*.

Six Counties

See **Northern Ireland**.

Skaggerak

Scene of First World War naval battle. See **Jutland**.

Slapton Sands (England)

Scene of 1944 Second World War disaster, kept secret at the time. A large-scale training exercise ahead of the D-Day landings was intercepted by a German E-boat with disastrous consequences. Several hundred US troops were killed. The authorities imposed a veil of secrecy over the calamity.

Slovakia

See **Czechoslovakia**.

Smolensk (Russia)

Important city 250 miles west of Moscow. During Operation Barbarossa (the 1941 German invasion of Russia), the city was encircled and the Soviet Union suffered a major defeat in the "Smolensk pocket". An estimated 310,000 men were killed or captured by the Germans between 16 July and 6 August 1941 and some 3,200 Russian tanks lost. The only advantage for Russia was that the German delay in taking Smolensk enabled the defences of Moscow to be strengthened.

Smolny Institute (Russia)

Building in Petrograd (**St Petersburg**), formerly a convent, which was the military and planning centre of the Bolshevik leaders during the Russian Revolution. It was the headquarters of the Military-Revolutionary Committee of the Petrograd Soviet. The second congress of the All-Russian Executive Committee met here after the October Revolution.

Sobibor (Poland)

Nazi concentration camp located northwest of **Lublin** near the **Pripet Marshes**. It is estimated 250,000 Jews were murdered here. The camp was closed in 1943 after a rebellion by inmates.

Soignies (Belgium)

Town 22 miles southwest of Brussels. It earned its place in military history as the location of the first skirmish between British and German troops in the First World War. Cavalry units on scouting duties clashed in woods south of Soignies in August 1914.

Sokal (Ukraine)

First World War battle near this town on the Austro-Russian border, now in the **Ukraine**. In one of the first engagements on the **Eastern Front** 300,000 Austrian troops advanced northwards from **Lemberg** (L'vov) in preparation for the invasion of Russia. Having mobilized more quickly, the Russians had two armies ready. Over 700,000 Russian troops attacked on 13 August 1914, defeating the Austrians and forcing them to retreat back to Lemberg.

Solingen (Germany)

Five Turkish women were killed in May 1993 in this steel town near Düsseldorf after arson attacks on a workers' hostel by neo-Nazis. The outrage was the worst example of racial violence since the Nazi era. It was followed by days of riots and protest marches. The four neo-Nazis responsible were given heavy prison sentences when convicted in October 1995.

Soloheadbeg (Ireland)

Town in County Tipperary where the first action of the 1919–21 Irish War of Independence against Britain was fought on 21 January 1919. Members of the 3rd Tipperary Brigade of the Irish Volunteers ambushed a force of the Royal Irish Constabulary, killing two constables.

Solomon Islands

Pacific archipelago northeast of Australia. The Japanese offensives of the Second World War reached the Solomon Islands on 13 March 1942. By July all the main islands had been captured. The Allies counter-attacked on 7 August with the invasion of **Guadalcanal** and Tulagi by the US 1st Marine Division. Stubborn Japanese resistance was not overcome easily, with the US troops facing repeated counter-offensives on land and continued attacks at sea. Guadalcanal was finally captured on 9 February 1943. Many months of fierce fighting followed as the Allies battled for each island in turn.

Solovki (Russia)

Northernmost monastery in the world, built on an archipelago in Russia's remote White Sea. It was one of the first Soviet death camps, later becoming infamous for housing senior figures in the Orthodox Church. About 50 of the 250 Orthodox bishops who perished in the Soviet era died here.

Somalia

Independent republic in the Horn of Africa. It came into being on 1 July 1960 as a result of the merger of the British Somaliland Protectorate (independent on 26 June 1960) and the Italian Trusteeship Territory of Somalia. In October 1969 the armed forces took over power and assassinated the President. In the 1980s, the country became synonymous with famine and anarchy after prolonged civil war which dated back to 1981 when the Somali National Movement began attacks in northern Somalia in an attempt to overthrow President Siad Barre. Fighting intensified when larger forces were deployed on 27 May 1988 to create bases in the north. The country's second city, Hargeisa, fell to the rebels on 31 May and it was subsequently retaken by government forces, but fighting continued. A second rebel group, the Somali Patriotic Movement, was formed in the south in 1989, and a third, the United Somalia Congress, in 1990. The three groups began co-operating against the government and in January 1991 **Mogadishu** fell to the rebels. Further rebel in-fighting then occurred. Following difficulties in food distribution, and large-scale famine, a US-led UN force landed in Somalia in December 1991. There were clashes with the local warlord, General Aidid. The last US peacekeepers left on 25 March 1994. See also **Ogaden**.

Somaliland

Northern area of **Somalia** in which the Somali National Movement declared independence in May 1991. The area is the same as the former British Somaliland Protectorate (which had become part of Somalia in 1960 on independence). The independence of Somaliland has not been recognized by the international community.

Somme (France)

First World War battle along this river in the northeast. In one of the greatest and most costly battles on the **Western Front**, the Allies attempted to break through

German trenchlines along a 20-mile front. The infantry assault began on 1 July 1916. On that day the British Army suffered its heaviest toll ever for one day's fighting – 60,000 casualties including 20,000 dead. After weeks of deadly attrition a renewed offensive by General Haig on 15 September used tanks for the first time in battle. When the battle ended on 18 November the Allies had gained only seven miles and suffered 625,000 casualties. German losses were similarly high.

Songhua Jiang (China)
See **Sungari River**.

Sonora (Mexico)
Second largest state in the northwest. As the home state of four Mexican presidents, and numerous key politicians, its influence gave birth to the term "Sonora clique". Its pre-eminence in Mexican politics was broken by President Lázaro Cárdenas del Rio.

Soummam (Algeria)
Location of a key congress of the Algerian nationalist movement in August 1956. Under the leadership of Abbane Ramdane, the Soummam Congress affirmed the primacy of the political arm of the FLN over the military and created the National Council of the Algerian Revolution and the Executive and Co-ordinating Committee.

Southall (England)
Suburb in west London with a high Asian minority population, the scene of a violent anti-National Front demonstration on 23 April 1979 in which a teacher, Blair Peach, died from a blow to his head from a truncheon. There were allegations that he was killed by a Metropolitan Police Special Patrol Group officer but demands for a public inquiry were rejected.

South Braintree (United States)
Town near Boston, Massachusetts. On 15 April 1920 a robbery at a shoe factory in South Braintree left two men dead. Two Italian anarchist immigrants, Nicola Sacco and Bartolomeo Vanzetti, were tried and convicted of the crime in July 1921. Publicity in the case, fuelled by protests across Europe and South Africa, focused on evidence that the men had been wrongly identified and the belief that they had been convicted because of their anarchist principles. An independent commission upheld the convictions, and the men were executed on 23 August 1927, prompting silent demonstrations in Boston and London, and violent protests in New York and Philadelphia.

Southern Rhodesia (now Zimbabwe)
See **Rhodesia**.

South Georgia
Island in the South Atlantic, a British Dependency captured by Argentine forces in 1982 at the time of the **Falklands** War. British troops recaptured the islands on 25 April 1982. See Falklands War, Appendix 2.

South Tyrol
See **Tyrol**.

South West Africa
In 1884 Germany declared the area a protectorate, and the boundaries were defined by the Heligoland Treaty of 1890. The territory was the scene of the Herero Revolt of 1907, crushed by the Germans with great brutality. In the First World War, Union of South African troops attacked and conquered the territory in 1915. Later a mandate was awarded to South Africa by the League of Nations. See also **Namibia**.

Soweto (South Africa)
South West Townships, a black area near Johannesburg, scene of 16 June 1976 student demonstrations against government attempts to impose the Afrikaans language in education. The protest developed into three days of riots, with 236 non-whites killed by police and two whites killed by rioters; on 6 July the government withdrew its proposal but the area remained a central flashpoint in anti-government agitation. Along with **Sharpeville**, Soweto remained one of the landmark events in the struggle against white supremacy.

Spain
Kingdom in the Iberian peninsula. Most important, in terms of international history, for the bitter civil war of the 1930s. In July 1936 Spanish generals, led by Franco, rose against the Republican government and plunged Spain into civil war. Despite international declarations against foreign involvement, Italy, Germany and Portugal aided the generals and Russia and France helped the Republicans. In addition International Brigades were formed by volunteers from many states to fight for the Republicans, and helped to defeat the Nationalists in the battle of **Guadalajara**, 1937. By early 1939 the Nationalists held most of Spain. **Madrid** fell on 28 March. See Appendix 2.

Spandau (Germany)
Suburb of Berlin, most famous for its prison which held Rudolf Hess after 1945. Hess, Hitler's former deputy, had flown to Scotland in 1941 on a bizarre peace

mission. Eventually Hess became the only prisoner in Spandau. In 1989 he apparently committed suicide by hanging himself.

Spanish Sahara
See **Western Sahara**.

Spion Kop (South Africa)
Boer War battle along the heights southwest of **Ladysmith**, Natal. In a second attempt to relieve besieged Ladysmith the British, under General Buller, crossed the Tugela River on 19 January 1900. The Boers were driven back for three days until the British captured the heights of Spion Kop. Unable to reinforce their positions with artillery because of the steep slopes, the British succumbed to a Boer counter-attack on 23 January. By the next day Buller conceded defeat and withdrew back across the Tugela, having lost 87 officers and 1,647 men.

Spratly Islands
Small archipelago in the South China Sea, believed to lie in the middle of a massive underdeveloped oil field. The islands also straddle the vital sea route along which Japan receives oil from the Middle East. They are disputed by China, the Philippines and Vietnam, as well as Malaysia, Brunei and Thailand. In April 1992, China extended its territorial waters to cover both the Spratly and Paracel Islands.

Springfield (United States)
White mobs attacked black areas in this Illinois city on 14–15 August 1908 following the accusation that a black man had raped a white woman. Eight black people were killed and over 2,000 fled the city. No whites were arrested for the deaths.

Sri Lanka
Independent republic in the Indian Ocean. Formerly known as Ceylon, and part of the British Indian Empire. Since 1977, an increasingly bloody civil war between the Sri Lankan armed forces and the Tamil separatists has engulfed the island. Tension between the Tamil minority and the Sinhalese majority in Sri Lanka led to rioting in the northern town of **Jaffna**, beginning on 14 August 1977, in which 125 people died. The situation grew more serious in the 1980s. Acts of terrorism by the Tamil Tigers provoked violence by the army against the Tamil community. A state of emergency was declared on 4 June 1981. Sri Lanka signed an accord with India on 29 July 1987, regarding a Tamil homeland, and a peace-keeping force was set up on Sri Lanka. Hostilities took place between the IPKF and Tamil separatists. The Tamils objected to the Indian presence, and began a guerrilla campaign against the government. India

withdrew its last troops on 24 March 1990. Civil strife has worsened in the 1990s as government troops responded to guerrilla attacks with an all-out offensive against Tamil strongholds in the Jaffna peninsula.

Sriperumbudur (India)
Location in south India in Tamil Nadu, 28 miles from Madras, of the assassination of Rajiv Gandhi on 21 May 1991 while he was campaigning in the general election. He was the victim of a young Tamil woman who had triggered explosives strapped to her back while presenting him with a bouquet. The Tamil Tigers fighting for independence in **Sri Lanka** were immediately accused of the outrage.

Ssupingchieh (China)
See **Szepingkai**.

Stalingrad (Russia)
City on the River Volga in the south. Known as Tsaritsyn under the Tsars, it became Volgograd in 1917, Stalingrad in 1925, and Volgograd again in 1961. An important industrial centre and port, it was a prime objective of the German drive into the Caucasus region during 1942. The German 6th Army under General von Paulus launched its first main assault on 19 August 1942, supported by the 4th Panzer Army. Soviet troops were pushed back into the city and the battle was reduced to house-to-house fighting. In one of the most intense battles of the war German troops inched their way forward through the rubble, with both sides suffering terrible casualties. On 19 November 1942 a massive Soviet counter-offensive succeeded in encircling and trapping 200,000 Germans in Stalingrad. German attempts to relieve them were defeated and the beleaguered von Paulus was left to fight winter, disease and the Soviet troops unaided. By 31 January 1943 Soviet advances had decimated the 6th Army and the remnants surrendered. Coinciding with the Allied victories in North Africa, defeat at Stalingrad proved that the German *Wehrmacht* was not invincible.

Stallupönen
Location of the first military action on the **Eastern Front** in the First World War. On 17 August 1914 a German corps attacked a Russian force preparing to advance into East **Prussia**.

Stanleyville (Zaïre)
Scene of a rebellion by dissident government troops after the independence of the Congo. Thousands of black and white civilians were massacred before the city was recaptured on 24 November 1964 by government troops and Belgian paratroopers. Now known as Kisangani. See **Belgian Congo**.

Stenger Line
See **Adolf Hitler Line**.

Stockholm (Sweden)
Capital in which Swedish Prime Minister Olaf Palme was assassinated as he walked home from the cinema on 28 February 1986. His wife was injured in the attack, and the assassin was never caught.

Stonewall Inn (United States)
Famous meeting place for the gay community in New York. The events of 26 June 1969, when police raided the Stonewall Inn, became part of the folklore of gay history. Serious street disturbances followed the raid, marking the first violent response by the homosexual community to police action and initiating a new, militant phase of gay activism, reflected in a plethora of new gay rights organizations. A branch of Stonewall, the gay pressure group, was formed in Britain in 1988.

Stormberg (South Africa)
Town in Cape Province near the border with the Orange Free State. In December 1899 British forces launched a major offensive against the Boers. The central front of this three-pronged assault concentrated on pushing the Boers back from their advance towards Queenstown. Badly directed and organized, the British column of 3,000 stumbled into heavy enemy fire on the night of 10 December. Retreating quickly with 89 men killed and 600 taken prisoner, British forces had suffered the first defeat of what became known as Black Week.

Stormont (Northern Ireland)
Suburb of Belfast giving its name to the building housing the Northern Ireland Parliament until the imposition in 1972 of direct rule from London. Stormont was the location of the Northern Ireland Assembly 1973–4, and is the present site of the Northern Ireland Office.

Stresa (Italy)
Town on Lake Maggiore in Piedmont which gave its name to the Stresa Front, the agreements made at the conference of 11–14 April 1935 attended by the leaders of Italy, Britain and France. They agreed a common front against Hitler's intention to rearm and reform the *Luftwaffe*, condemning Germany's actions and supporting the **Locarno** Treaties. Britain's separate agreement with Germany on naval matters in June 1935, France's negotiations with Russia to form a pact in May, and Italy's invasion of **Ethiopia** in October undermined the Front's impact.

Subic Bay (Philippines)
Major US naval base until 1992 when the USA transferred its facilities to other bases in Southeast Asia.

Suchow (China)
Location of decisive battle of the Civil War, fought from December 1948 to January 1949. Communist forces, advancing on Guangzou (Canton) inflicted an estimated 250,000 casualties on the defending Nationalist armies, effectively destroying the morale of Chiang Kai-shek's remaining forces.

Sudan
See **Anglo-Egyptian Sudan**.

Sudetenland (Czech Republic)
German-speaking area of northern Bohemia assigned to **Czechoslovakia** in 1919. Claimed by Hitler for the Reich, the Sudetenland became the centre of an international crisis in 1938 over Germany's attempt to revise the **Versailles** Treaty by force. The threat of general European war was temporarily averted by the **Munich Agreement**, in which Czechoslovakia was forced to cede the Sudetenland to Germany.

Suez Canal (Egypt)
The 106-mile long canal was opened in 1869, with Britain acquiring the largest share in 1875. British troops were stationed along it in 1882 and the Constantinople Convention of 1888 provided that the canal be "free and open" in "time of war as in time of peace". The British nonetheless closed it to enemy ships in 1914 and 1939. In 1948 the Egyptian authorities refused access to Israeli shipping. British troops left the **Canal Zone** in June 1956. Following Egypt's nationalization of the Suez Canal on 26 July 1956, Britain, France and Israel agreed secretly for Israel to attack Egypt through the **Sinai** while Britain and France occupied the Canal Zone on the pretext of separating the combatants. Israel attacked on 29 October, followed by Britain and France on 31 October. The move provoked intense international and domestic criticism. The USA applied economic pressure on Britain and the countries were forced to accept a ceasefire on 6 November and the deployment of a UN Emergency Force. The affair marked the beginning of the end of British influence in the Middle East and pushed President Nasser closer to the Soviet Union. The canal was again closed in 1967 and remained so until June 1975 when it was cleared.

Sumgait (Azerbaijan)
Located north of Baku, this oil-rich city was the scene in March 1988 of the first

239

ethnic massacre in the closing era of the Soviet Union. Some 32 Armenians were killed by an Azeri mob, beginning the subsequent ceaseless blood-letting between Azeris and Armenians.

Sungari River (China)

Civil War battle along the largest tributary of the Amur River in **Manchuria**. In January 1947 Communist forces under Mao Tse-tung attacked the Nationalists across the frozen Sungari, but were repelled after two weeks of fierce fighting. Two further assaults in February and March were also unsuccessful. In May the Communists launched their largest offensive in the war so far, pushing 270,000 troops across the river. Although the Nationalists eventually checked this advance, the initiative in Manchuria had been lost to the Communists. See Appendix 2.

Sunningdale (England)

The Sunningdale Agreement, on a Protestant–Catholic power-sharing assembly and the creation of a Council of Ireland, was agreed in 1973 following a Conference on Northern Ireland. Those Unionists opposed to power-sharing won widespread support in the February 1974 election. The old links between the Conservatives and Unionists at Westminster were broken. Sunningdale is the location of the Civil Service College in Surrey.

Suomussalmi (Finland)

Site of bitter fighting in the Russo-Finnish Winter War of 1939–40. Two Russian divisions suffered very heavy casualties at the hands of Finnish troops between 8 December 1939 and 11 January 1940.

Surabaya (Indonesia)

First capital when the war of independence began in 1945. The declaration of the independence of the republic of Indonesia (formerly **Dutch East Indies**) was proclaimed by the Nationalist leaders, Sukarno and Hatta, on 17 August 1945. British, Indian and Dutch troops began to arrive on 29 September 1945. British troops captured the rebel capital of Surabaya on 29 November 1945. The Dutch recognized Indonesia (comprising Java, Sumatra and Madura) on 13 November 1946. The withdrawal of British troops was completed on 30 November 1946.

Surat (India)

Coastal city in Gujarat, famous for the Surat Conference of the Indian National Congress held there in 1907. This witnessed bitter clashes between the moderate and militant wings. The meeting broke up in disorder but the more moderate element eventually prevailed.

Susak
See under **Fiume**.

Suvalki (Poland)
Town occupied by Germany in 1914, it became Polish in 1921 but was annexed again by Germany in 1939 following the Nazi–Soviet Pact.

Suvla Bay (Turkey)
First World War battle in this bay on the western shore of the **Gallipoli** Peninsula. In an attempt to strengthen the Allied position in Gallipoli 25,000 troops landed at Suvla Bay, north of **Anzac Cove**, on 6 August 1915. The landings met with little serious Turkish opposition, but the opportunity to capitalize on the situation was not immediately taken. Turkish reinforcements quickly arrived and the British attacks were repulsed. The ensuing stalemate continued until Allied troops were evacuated on 20 December.

Suwalki (Poland)
See **Suvalki**.

Sverdlovsk (Russia)
See **Yekaterinburg**.

Sword Beach (France)
Most easterly of the **Normandy** landing beaches attacked during D-Day, 6 June 1944. The British 3rd Infantry Division stormed ashore, supported by the British 6th Airborne Division, and advanced inland. Fierce opposition from the German 21st Panzer Division prevented the Allies from reaching their immediate objective of **Caen**.

Szepingkai (China)
Civil War battle for an important railway junction 70 miles north of **Mukden, Manchuria**. The capture of Mukden by the Nationalist Army on 16 March 1946 prompted the Communists to occupy Szepingkai. 70,000 Nationalist troops marched northwards and attacked the Communists on 16 April. In the first major battle of the Civil War the Nationalists defeated the numerically superior Communists' forces during five weeks fighting and captured Szepingkai on 20 May.

Taba (Egypt)

Red Sea resort returned to Egypt by Israel as part of the Middle East Peace Process, it was itself the location of the 24 September 1995 Peace Accord between Israel and the Palestinians. Under the Accord (which was bitterly opposed by *Hamas* and other militant Palestinian groups), Israel agreed that the Palestinians of the **West Bank** would be granted Home Rule. A staged troop withdrawal by Israel would begin, and a new Palestinian Council with legislative and executive powers would be created. The first pull-out of Israeli forces would take place from **Jenin**, Nablus, Tulkarm, Qalqilya, Ramallah, and Bethlehem. However, 140,000 Jewish settlers would remain with Israeli protection.

Tachen Islands

See **Quemoy**.

Tacna (Peru)

Province disputed by Peru and Chile. Occupied by Chile during the war of the Pacific (1879–83). The long diplomatic wrangle was settled in 1929 when it was awarded to Peru.

Taff Vale (Wales)

Valley in the south which became famous in the history of industrial relations. In July 1901 the House of Lords granted the Taff Vale Railway Company an injunction against the Amalgamated Society of Railway Servants for damages caused by picketing in an official strike, enabling the company to win £23,000 compensation. The result, seen as an attack on the right to strike, encouraged increased union support for the Labour Representation Committee, the forerunner to the Labour Party, and prompted a Liberal Government to give unions immunity from similar actions by the 1906 Trades Disputes Act.

Taif (Saudi Arabia)

Location of agreement in October 1989 on new constitutional arrangements for **Lebanon** made by 70 surviving members of the last Lebanese parliament elected in 1972. The Taif Accord was sponsored by Saudi Arabia, Morocco and Algeria and paved the way for an end to the civil war with the country under Syrian overlordship. The reforms eroded Christian Maronite dominance in government with the President becoming subject to a cabinet made up equally of Christians and Muslims and the parliament equally divided.

Taiwan

Island off the coast of China, formerly known as Formosa. Ceded to Japan under the Treaty of **Shimonoseki** (1895), it remained part of the Japanese Empire until the end of the Second World War. In December 1949 Nationalist forces under Chiang Kai-shek withdrew to Taiwan after being defeated by the Communists on the Chinese mainland. Still claiming sovereignty over the mainland, the Republic of China (Taiwan) was recognized by the USA as the government of China. China's UN seats were occupied by Taiwan until being replaced by the People's Republic in October 1971. Relations between the two Chinas were normalized in May 1991 when Taiwan finally recognized the People's Republic of China.

Talana Hill (South Africa)
Site near Dundee of a British defeat in the Boer advance on **Ladysmith**, 20 October 1899.

Tallinin Line
See **Dewline**.

Tambov (Russia)
Province south of Moscow, the scene of the Antonov Uprising of 1920–21, one of a series of large-scale peasant risings in areas such as the Volga Basin, Siberia and the northern Caucasus. An army made up of peasants, deserters and others displaced by the Russian Revolution attacked Bolshevik requisition squads and party headquarters. The rising was eventually put down during 1921 by troops under the command of the Bolshevik generals Antonov-Ovseyenko and Tukachevsky with great severity.

Tammany (United States)
Headquarters of the Democratic Party in New York City and a political term used to signify "machine" control of the political process and the corruption that goes with it. It came to exert a very powerful influence over New York politics, particularly after 1860 when William Marcy Tweed made it the city's dominant organization. Tammany rule therefore became synonymous with large-scale corruption and most Tammany "bosses" became very wealthy. Its control extended beyond the city to embrace New York state government and until 1932 it had an important and sometimes decisive role in Democratic politics.

Tampico (Mexico)
Major port city, location of the Tampico Incident of 1914 when the crew of the USS *Dolphin* were arrested. After the Mexican leader Victoriano Huerta refused to honour the US flag, US warships were despatched to the Gulf of Mexico by President Woodrow Wilson even though the sailors had already been released.

Tanganyika

Former German colony in East Africa, the first location of the Maji Maji revolt of 1905. The territory became a British Mandate after the First World War, achieving independence in 1961. In 1964 it united with **Zanzibar** to become the United Republic of Tanzania.

Tangier (Morocco)

Declared an international zone by the 1906 treaty of **Algeciras** and in 1923, at a time of unrest in the French and Spanish protectorates in Morocco, it became a free port. It was occupied by Spain from 1940 to 1945 but united with Morocco on independence in 1956. In 1962 it again became a free port, though still an integral part of the kingdom of Morocco.

Tangshan (China)

Coal-mining city 93 miles east of Beijing (Peking), scene in 1976 of the most devastating earthquake in Asia since the Second World War. Measuring 7.8 on the Richter Scale, the earthquake killed an estimated 500,000 people.

Tannenberg (Poland)

First World War battle (26–30 August 1914) near this village in East **Prussia**, now Grunwald in Poland. Russia's major opening offensive on the **Eastern Front** was a two-pronged attack into East Prussia, with the Russian 1st Army under Rennekampf advancing from the north and the 2nd Army under Samsonov attacking from the south. Poor co-ordination between the two armies gave the Germans time to regroup and concentrate their counter-attack to the south whilst Rennekampf was still marshalling his troops. On 26 August General Hindenburg surprised Samsonov by outflanking and encircling the 2nd Army near Tannenberg. Surrounded on three sides by the German 8th Army, and with the Masurian marshes effectively blocking any retreat, the Russians were heavily mauled by the German assault. In one of the biggest defeats in military history only 60,000 Russians escaped through the marshes, leaving 92,000 as prisoners and over 30,000 dead. Hindenburg then turned north to attack Rennekampf (the battle of **Masurian Lakes**), who had failed to help the beleaguered 2nd Army. This catastrophic defeat shattered Russian morale to such an extent that it never really recovered during the rest of the war.

Tannu Tuva

Remote formerly semi-independent republic on the borders of the Soviet Union and Mongolia, it was annexed by the Soviet Union in 1944.

Tanzania

See **Tanganyika**.

Taranto (Italy)

Naval base in the south, raided on 11 December 1940 by British torpedo bombers. In a highly successful operation, severe damage was inflicted on the Italian fleet (three battleships were damaged by torpedos) which subsequently withdrew to safer bases.

Tarawa (Kiribati)

Second World War engagement on this atoll in the Gilbert Islands (now part of Kiribati) 2,800 miles northeast of Australia. On 20 November 1943 the US counter-offensive in the central Pacific began with amphibious landings on Tarawa and nearby Makin atoll. Despite heavy aerial bombardment from the US Air Force, the assault was badly organized with most of the landing craft beaching on the reefs. Marines had to wade ashore under heavy gunfire. A fierce three-day assault on the Japanese defences followed, with high casualties on both sides. Only 100 of the 4,700 Japanese troops survived, with US losses totalling 1,000 dead and 2,000 wounded.

Targuist (Morocco)

Headquarters of the nationalist leader Abd el-Krim during his revolt (the Rif War) against Spanish rule. In 1926, a Franco-Spanish military agreement was reached to co-ordinate suppression of the Rif War. Franco-Spanish forces reduced Rif fortifications and took Targuist. Abd el-Krim surrendered to the French and was exiled to Réunion.

Tarnopol (Ukraine)

First World War battle around this town in Polish **Galicia**, now Ternopol in the Ukraine. In July 1917 mass desertions from the 11th Russian Army severely weakened the Russian positions, and as more men left, a 25-mile gap in the front opened up. An Austro-German offensive began on 19 July and burst through the gap. Tarnopol was captured by the Germans on 22 July and the whole Russian front started to collapse.

Tartu (Estonia)

Town, also known as Dorpat, location of the peace treaty signed on 14 October 1920 between Finland and the Soviet Union, recognizing the independence and sovereignty of Finland. The treaty determined the frontier between the two states: Finland agreed that Eastern **Karelia** and the two frontier provinces of Repola and Parajärvi should belong to the Soviet Union, with West Karelia assigned to Finland; Russia agreed that the ice-free port of Petsamo on the Barents Seas should belong to Finland; finally, certain Finnish islands in the Gulf of Finland were neutralized. The treaty was re-affirmed in 1932 and 1934 when non-aggression agreements were signed and a Conciliation Commission established for the settlement of disputes. The non-aggression agreements were due to expire in 1945, but were interrupted by the 1939 Russo-Finnish conflict, the Winter War.

Tashkent (Uzbekistan)
A declaration of truce took place between India and Pakistan after a conference convened at Tashkent in the Soviet Union (3–10 January 1966). Alexei Kosygin, Chairman of the Council of Ministers of the Soviet Union, acted as mediator between Lal Bahadur Shastri, Prime Minister of India and Ayub Khan, President of Pakistan, in a settlement which ended the war on the **Kashmir** border and restored Indian–Pakistani relations.

Tattenham Corner (England)
Part of the Epsom (Surrey) racecourse. The famous left-hand corner was the location of the fatal incident in 1913 when a suffragette, Emily Davison, threw herself in front of the King's horse. She was trampled to death in the most dramatic demonstration of the suffragette era.

Teapot Dome (United States)
Area of Wyoming containing navy oil reserves at the centre of one of the biggest scandals in US history. The name became synonymous in US political vocabulary for government corruption. In 1921 President Harding transferred supervision of naval oil reserve lands from the navy to the Secretary of the Interior, Albert Fall, who secretly granted exclusive rights to the reserves at Teapot Dome to Mammoth Oil Co. This was followed by his secret leasing of portions of Elk Hills reserves in California to the Pan American Petroleum Co., who "loaned" Fall $100,000. When the scandal broke, Fall was convicted of bribery and conspiracy, fined $100,000 and became the first Cabinet member to be imprisoned. Although never implicated, Harding died before the full extent of the scandal became known.

Tehran (Iran)
Location of war-time meeting in Iran (then Persia) (28 November–1 December 1943) between Winston Churchill, President Franklin Roosevelt and Marshal Stalin (with the combined Chiefs of Staff, Anthony Eden and Harry Hopkins attending) to plan military strategy in Europe and the Far East. It was agreed that "Overlord", the Anglo-American invasion of northern France, would take place on 1 May 1944. Stalin promised that Russia would join in the war against Japan in the Far East after victory over Germany had been achieved. The future of Poland and Germany was also discussed.

Tel Aviv (Israel)

Location of the assassination of the Israeli Prime Minister, Yitzhak Rabin on 4 November 1995. Rabin was assassinated after leaving a huge pro-peace rally by a young Jewish extremist, Yigal Amir, a 27-year old Israeli law student at Bar-Ilam University. The assassination of Rabin, the hero of the 1967 War, long-serving elder statesman and winner of the Nobel Peace Prize, stunned the whole of Israel and threatened to derail the tortuous Middle East peace process.

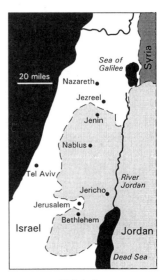

Tel Aviv

Telengāna (India)

In northern Hyderabad, scene in 1946 of one of the most formidable of modern peasant insurrections. The uprising, against the pro-British ruler (*nizam*) of Hyderabad, engulfed 3,000 villages spread over 16,000 square miles. Despite the despatch of central government troops in September 1948, the movement was not suppressed until 1951. Outside of China, it was one of the largest Communist-led uprisings in Asia.

Temple Mount

Complex in **Jerusalem's** Old City, also known as Harem al-Sharif, which incorporates the Western Wall of the Jewish Temple where devout Jews go to mourn the destruction of the Temple in ancient times. The Wall abuts the holy Muslim site of the Harem al-Sharif with the Dome of the Rock and the Al-Aqsa mosques. The site was located in East Jerusalem from 1948 until 1967 when Israeli troops captured all of Jerusalem from Jordan. It has been the scene of clashes as Jewish extremists have sought to provoke confrontations and Palestinians during the *Intifada* have sometimes harassed Jews praying. Control over the Muslim holy sites is disputed between the Palestinians, the Jordanians and Saudi Arabia. Renewed conflict erupted in September 1996 when Israel opened a tunnel near the Temple Mount. Opening the tunnel close to Islam's third holiest site, sparked clashes with Israeli soldiers that left 63 Palestinians, 14 Israelis and an Egyptian dead in four days.

Tenedos
See **Lausanne**.

Tenerife
One of the Canary Islands off the northwest coast of Africa. On 27 March 1977 two jumbo jets crashed on the ground at Tenerife airport. In the worst disaster in aviation history, 574 people were killed when the KLM 747 collided with the Pan Am jet.

Terai (Nepal)
Bordering the Indian states of West Bengal, Bihar and Uttar Pradesh, an area of flat plains, the inhabitants are mainly of Indian origin. In recent years anti-government dissidents opposed to the Nepal authorities have been active here.

Terezin (Czech Republic)
Located 50 miles north of Prague, the Nazis turned this former garrison into a transit camp for Czech Jews in 1941. Between 1941 and 1945 some 140,000 Jews passed through en route to the death camps of **Auschwitz**. Only 20,000 survived the holocaust. Terezin became famous (despite the horrors of the time) as a centre of flourishing music which helped the victims of Nazi barbarity to survive mentally. The conductor Rafael Schächte was among the inmates. The Nazis eventually made propaganda use of the music.

Ternopol (Ukraine)
See **Tarnopol**.

Thessaloniki (Greece)
See **Salonika**.

38th Parallel (Korea)
Latitude 38° north, dividing North Korea from South Korea, a demarcation line established at the 1945 **Yalta** Conference as a preliminary to unification and the holding of democratic elections. The north's invasion of the south and the subsequent Korean War from 1950 to 1953 ended hopes of immediate peaceful unity. See Appendix 2.

Tho Chu (Vietnam)
Disputed island, claimed by both Cambodia and Vietnam. Under Vietnamese control, but Khmer Rouge guerrillas continue to press for its return.

Three Gorges Dam (China)

Huge 394-mile long reservoir on the **Yangtze River**. A controversial project which will displace 1.3 million people from 300 towns and villages and effectively drown hundreds of years of dynastic heritage. The scale of the project is massive. When completed, the flow of the Yangtze will have been changed by a 1.5 mile long, 578 feet high dam generating one-ninth of China's annual consumption of electricity. In the city of Wanxian, 800,000 people will have to be relocated. Ocean-going vessels will be able to reach Chungking, China's largest city. There is great controversy among environmentalists about the project.

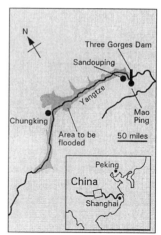

Three Gorges Dam

Three Mile Island (United States)

Nuclear power station near Harrisburg, Pennsylvania. An accident in the pressurised water reactor on 28 March 1979 brought the nuclear core within one hour of complete meltdown. Human error and defective equipment had left part of the core without essential cooling water. Although some exposed fuel melted, the swift introduction of more water prevented disaster. The reactor building was badly contaminated, although only very low-level radiation was released into the environment. 190,000 people were evacuated from nearby towns.

Tiananmen Square (China)

Largest public square in the world, in central Beijing (**Peking**). Thousands of demonstrators protested in the square in early May 1989, calling for more democracy, an end to corruption and the resignation of the Communist leadership. On 13 May over 3,000 students in the square went on hunger strike. Martial law was declared in Beijing on 20 May. As the protesters' support grew, the hard-line government sent in troops on the night of 3–4 June. An estimated 5,000 people were massacred as troops opened fire on the unarmed demonstrators to restore Communist control.

Tibet

Also known as Xizang Zizhiqu. Autonomous region under British control following the collapse of the Chinese Empire in 1911, Tibet retained its autonomy until 1950–51 when Communist Chinese troops re-occupied the country. They invaded across the eastern frontier of Tibet on 7 October 1950. An agreement was signed on 23 May 1951 giving China control of Tibet's affairs, and Chinese troops entered **Lhasa** in September 1951. The Dalai Lama remained as a figurehead ruler, but there was widespread guerrilla activity against the Chinese forces of occupation. The last serious resistance came in 1959. On 10 March 1959 an uprising took place in Lhasa, but it was suppressed by Chinese tanks, and on 30 March the Dalai Lama fled to asylum in India. Tibet was administered as a province of China until 1965 when it became an autonomous region of the People's Republic. A further revolt in 1987 met with heavy repression.

Tikrit (Iraq)
Small town of 20,000–30,000 people on the Tigris north of Baghdad, birthplace of President Saddam Hussein and for long his powerbase. Its enormous influence made it a second capital – in the 1990s the town supplied four leading members of the Revolutionary Command Council. Apart from Saddam Hussein, Tikrit provided the Vice-President, foreign and defence ministers, the commander of the Republican Guard and the mayor of Baghdad.

Timisoara (Romania)
City which became the cradle of the revolt against the Ceausescu dictatorship. On 17 December 1989 Romanian security forces fired on protesters in the city, and fighting spread to Bucharest and other major cities. The army changed sides on 22 December, supporting the popular uprising against the Ceausescu regime. Ceausescu and his wife were executed by firing squad on 25 December, having been found guilty of genocide by a military court.

Timor (Indonesia)
In the colonial period this East Indies island was originally divided between Portugal (eastern half) and The Netherlands (western half). Occupied by Japan in the Second World War, Dutch Timor became part of Indonesia in 1949. For events in Portuguese Timor, see **East Timor**.

Tiran, Straits of
Narrow seaway providing Israel and Jordan with access to the Red Sea. It was blockaded to Israeli shipping by Egypt in 1956 and 1967, provoking crises both times.

Tobruk (Libya)
Scene of German siege of British and Commonwealth troops during the Second World War. General Wavell's army captured Tobruk in January 1941 along with some 25,000 Italian prisoners. On the arrival of General Rommel's Afrika Korps Wavell withdrew leaving a largely Australian garrison to endure an eight-month siege. In November 1941 the garrison broke out after being reinforced from the sea. The town

was besieged again from June 1942 and its South African and Australian garrison capitulated on 20 June. 23,000 men were taken prisoner but the town was retaken by General Montgomery on 13 November 1942.

Tokyo (Japan)

Capital city, much of which was destroyed and many thousands of people killed in a severe earthquake in September 1923. During the Second World War US fire-bombing raids devastated most of the city centre. Beginning on 9 March 1945, the attacks continued until 14 August 1945, killing over 100,000. The Japanese surrender was signed on 2 September 1945 aboard the USS *Missouri*, anchored in Tokyo Bay. From May 1946 until November 1947 27 Japanese leaders were tried in Tokyo for war crimes. Although Emperor Hirohito was never tried, former Prime Minister Tojo was one of seven sentenced to death. In 1995 nerve gas attacks on the Tokyo underground, allegedly by the Aum Shinryuku sect, left 12 dead and many injured.

Tonkin, Gulf of

Waters off **Vietnam**. Scene of confrontation which marked a crucial phase in the growing US involvement in the Vietnam War. The "Americanization" of the war by President Lyndon Johnson took place in successive stages between August 1964 and June 1965. On 2 August 1964 the destroyer USS *Maddox* of the 7th Fleet was attacked by three North Vietnamese patrol-torpedo boats in the Gulf of Tonkin. There was a second attack on the *Maddox* and the *Turner Joy* by six patrol-torpedo boats on 4 August. In retaliation US planes flew 64 sorties over North Vietnam on 5 August, attacking naval bases and oil installations. On 7 August the US Congress approved the Gulf of Tonkin Resolution, allowing the President to take all necessary measures to repel any armed attack against the forces of the USA and to prevent further aggression. Retaliatory raids on North Vietnamese naval installations and oil refineries were mounted. President Johnson used the resolution as authority to escalate US involvement in Vietnam. The President in effect held a blanket authorization to expand the US military commitment in Southeast Asia.

Tonypandy (Wales)

Town in the Rhondda Valley, scene of violent clashes during a miners' strike in November 1910. The belief that a number of miners were killed when Home Secretary Winston Churchill ordered troops to confront the strikers soured his relations with the labour movement for many years. Churchill had, in fact, prevented troops requested by the Chief Constable of Glamorgan on 10 November from being deployed. They remained in reserve while unarmed police successfully restrained the demonstrating miners.

Torgau (Germany)

Bridge over the River Elbe where Soviet armies advancing west and US troops advancing east met on 25 April 1945 at the end of the Second World War.

Torreon

See under **Mexico**.

Torrington (England)

Former parliamentary constituency in rural Devon, famous in March 1958 for a by-election victory for the Liberal candidate, Mark Bonham-Carter, over the Conservatives. This was the first Liberal by-election victory since 1929 and heralded the more significant revival that was to come at **Orpington**.

Toulon (France)

Seaport and naval base on the Mediterranean coast. The Allied offensive in North Africa of November 1942 prompted the occupation of **Vichy** France by German troops. Most of the Vichy French fleet was anchored in Toulon harbour, and on 19 November Hitler ordered its capture. Despite orders to flee to **Dakar**, the fleet stayed. The dockyard was attacked on 27 November and the fleet commander, Admiral Labarde, ordered the scuttling of all ships. Only five submarines escaped.

Tourane (Vietnam)

French name for **Da Nang**.

Toxteth (England)

Inner city area of Liverpool, scene of violent rioting in July 1981. Rioting also occurred in April 1981 in **Brixton**, as well as at **Southall** and the Moss Side area of Manchester. The riots were the first occasion the police used CS gas and marked a step towards future police methods of riot control.

Trafalgar Square (England)

Scene of violent demonstration against the widely unpopular poll tax (or community charge) on 31 March 1990, the culmination of prolonged nationwide protests. Over 130 were injured, including 57 police, and 341 were arrested in fighting and looting which spread throughout the centre of London. Prime Minister Margaret Thatcher – who was deeply committed to the poll tax – was replaced as Conservative leader in the autumn; plans to replace the poll tax were announced a year after the riot.

Transjordan
See **Jordan**.

Transkei
See **Bophutsatswana**.

Transylvania (Romania)
Disputed mountainous western province of Romania. Prior to the First World War, it had been the most easterly part of the Austro-Hungarian Empire (although a large proportion of its inhabitants spoke Romanian). Under the Treaty of **Trianon** it was confirmed as part of Romania. In 1940, Carol II of Romania was forced to return much of the region (including the valuable mines) to Hungary. The Russians advanced into the area in 1944 but it was eventually returned in 1947 to Romania. The Magyar minority received guarantees of linguistic freedom under the Romanian constitution and a Magyar University was established at Cluj in 1952. However, the autonomous status of Magyar districts was later discontinued and there was a greater drive to standardize Romanian life. One of the catalysts for the Romanian uprising of December 1989 which overthrew Ceausescu was the persecution of the Hungarian minority and their clergy in Transylvania, sparking off demonstrations in **Timisoara** among both ethnic Hungarians and the Romanian majority against despotic rule.

Treblinka (Poland)
Located 50 miles northwest of Warsaw, it was one of the most important German extermination camps. Rebuilt in 1941 with gas chambers it was used to put 800,000 Jews to death before a mass escape by the inmates in April 1943. Many Nazi ss guards were killed in the revolt and the camp eventually closed in November 1943.

Treetops Hotel (Kenya)
Remote bush hotel in Kenya, built in the branches of a fig tree. Princess Elizabeth was staying here with the Duke of Edinburgh when news of George VI's death broke on 6 February 1952. She flew back to Britain on 8 February as Queen.

Trentino-Alto Adige
See **Tyrol**.

Trianon (France)
Palace near **Versailles**, the setting for the peace treaty of the Allies with Hungary, concluded on 4 June 1920. Hungary was reduced to a rump state and forced to pay reparations to the victorious Allies.

Trieste (Italy)

City at the northern tip of the Adriatic Sea, the main port of the Austro-Hungarian Empire. Trieste was given to Italy after the First World War as part of the deal struck with the Allies in April 1915. Occupied by Germany 1943–5, it was awarded to Yugoslavia in 1945. As a result of Italy's protests the Free Territory of Trieste was created by the UN Security Council in 1947, dividing the area between the two countries. This compromise proved unworkable and the ensuing deadlock continued until 1954 when negotiations in London resolved the impasse. Italy received the city and port of Trieste (91 square miles) while Yugoslavia gained the surrounding parts of the **Istrian Peninsula** (202 square miles). The agreement was formalized and all claims settled in an October 1975 treaty.

Trucial States

Name given to the seven emirates of the lower Persian Gulf from the early 1820s until they became the United Arab Emirates in 1972: Abu Dhabi, Ajman, Dubai, Fujaira, Sharja, Ras al-Khaima and Umm al-Qaiwan. The name came from the "truce" – an annual assurance from local leaders that they would not indulge in piracy – gained by the British political agent at Sharja in 1823.

Tsaritsyn

See **Stalingrad**.

Tsarskoe Selo (Russia)

Imperial palace of the Tsars of Russia located 15 miles outside St Petersburg.

Tsingtao (China)

Seaport on the Yellow Sea coast. Created a German colony in 1898, it became a free port a year later. Following the Japanese declaration of war on Germany in 1914 the city was besieged on 2 September 1914 by 23,000 Japanese troops. A concerted assault on 6 November led to the city's surrender the following day. Japanese control was not relinquished until the **Washington** Conference of 1922, when Japan returned Tsingtao to China only to re-occupy it during the Second World War. Now called Qingdao, the city produces one of the most popular beers in China.

Tsuni (China)

City in north Kweichow province where in 1935 Mao Tse-tung established his predominance and authority in the party at the conference of the Central Political Bureau of the Chinese Communist Party.

Tsushima

Group of islands and strait of water between Japan and Korea. In the most significant naval engagement since Trafalgar the Russian fleet was largely destroyed by the faster and stronger Japanese ships. Tsar Nicholas II had dispatched the Baltic Fleet to the Far East in an attempt to end the Japanese domination of the Russo-Japanese War. On 27 May 1905 the Russians were intercepted in the Tsushima Strait and lost five ships by nightfall. The remaining Russian ships attempted to reach Vladivostok but were cut down by Japanese torpedoes. The Japanese victory was so complete that it left the Russian government suing for peace and facing domestic revolution.

Tulsa (United States)

Seat of Tulsa County, Oklahoma, scene of one of the bloodiest race riots in US history in 1921 when 79 people died.

Turaba (Saudi Arabia)

Location of battle in 1919 in which Saudi forces defeated Hijazi troops under the Hashemite Sheikh Abdullah. The battle marked the start of a struggle for supremacy in Arabia between Hashemite forces and the Saudis.

Tyrol

Alpine region divided between Austria and Italy. Although the whole region had been part of the Austro-Hungarian Empire since 1815 the southern half was Italian-speaking and coveted by Italian nationalists. After the First World War the Allies awarded South Tyrol to Italy and mass migration of the German minority followed. After the Second World War Austrian hopes of a reunification of the Tyrol were dashed, and although the terms of an Austro-Italian agreement provided Bozen (Bolzano) province with autonomous powers, these were largely cancelled by the incorporation of the area into the Italian province of Trentino-Alto Adige, created by the Italian constitution of 1948, in which Italians outnumbered German speakers by two to one.

Ucurena (Bolivia)

Location of land reform declaration of Ucurena in 1953, the highpoint of the Bolivian revolution. The *Decreto Supremo* was witnessed by over 200,000 peasants.

Uganda

Former British colony granted independence on 9 October 1962, becoming a republic on 8 September 1967. The President, Milton Obote, was overthrown on 24 January 1971 by the troops led by General Idi Amin who took over as President. His subsequent regime became synonymous with brutality, terror and barbarism. In 1972 Amin expelled all Asians who had not accepted Ugandan citizenship. He was strongly condemned for his action by Tanzania and Zambia and in 1974 Amin alleged that these countries were planning an invasion. In November all but five British diplomats were expelled and relations between Britain and Uganda further deteriorated. Following the events at **Entebbe** Britain broke off all diplomatic relations. Amin's increasingly tyrannical rule provoked an invasion from Tanzania. He fled the country in 1979, living in exile in Saudi Arabia.

Ukraine

Eastern European republic on the north shore of the Black Sea. Under Russian rule since the eighteenth century, Ukraine declared its independence in June 1917. Two years of civil war followed, and in 1922 West Ukraine was transferred to Polish control while East Ukraine became a constituent republic of the Soviet Union. Already devastated by famine and Stalinist purges, Ukraine was ravaged by the Second World War. After the war Ukraine regained the Western provinces and Crimea, along with other territory from Czechoslovakia and Romania. In 1986 a nuclear accident at **Chernobyl** seriously affected the surrounding environment. On 24 September 1991 Ukraine again declared its independence. In a referendum held on 1 December, 90 per cent of the population voted for independence, and Ukraine was recognized by Canada, USA and the EU.

Ulster

Region of Ireland which was divided in 1921 between the Irish Free State and the United Kingdom. Three counties (Cavan, Donegal and Monaghan) became part of the Irish Free State, while six (Antrim, Armagh, Down, Fermanagh, Londonderry and Tyrone) became **Northern Ireland** within the UK. The term Ulster is now generally used to signify these six counties.

Uluru

See **Ayers Rock**.

United Arab Republic

Name of the short-lived political union of Egypt and Syria, proclaimed in 1958. Following a military coup in Syria in 1961, the union collapsed (although Egypt retained the name United Arab Republic until 1971).

Upper Silesia

See **Silesia**.

Ust-Kamenogorsk (Kazakhstan)

Industrial city, scene of an environmental near-disaster in September 1990 when a cloud of beryllium appeared over the city after an explosion. This threatened over 100,000 inhabitants and could have become a "chemical **Chernobyl**". The event went relatively unreported in the West.

Utah Beach (France)

Most westerly of the **Normandy** landing beaches attacked during D-Day, 6 June 1944. The US VII Corps stormed ashore against weak defences, captured La Madeleine and linked up with airborne forces six miles inland.

Vaal Krantz (South Africa)

Boer War battle for this village southwest of **Ladysmith**, Natal. Following his defeat at **Spion Kop** General Buller launched a third attempt to relieve besieged Ladysmith. On 5 February 1900 he led 20,000 British troops across the Tugela River and captured Vaal Krantz. For two days the British resisted repeated counter-attacks by the Boers but could make little more progress themselves and Buller withdrew back across the Tugela on 7 February. This was the last major defeat for the British in the war.

Valley of the Fallen (Valle de los Caidos) (Spain)

Huge, fulsome memorial, sited north of El Escorial near the village of Guadarrama, to the fallen of the Spanish Civil War. It is effectively a Fascist memorial to Franco, and to the Falangist leader José Antonio Primo de Rivera, both of whom are buried here. Political prisoners of the defeated left-wing forces were used to build this monument.

Van Tuong Peninsula (Vietnam)

Central location of build-up of Viet Cong which prompted Operation Starlight, the first large-scale combat engagement for US troops since the Korean War. 5,000 US marines blocked the peninsula's exits and moved in on 30 August 1965. Hemmed in against the sea, the Viet Cong could not resist for long. By the afternoon of 31 August US troops had reached the sea and more than 700 Viet Cong had been killed.

Vardar River

Scene of First World War battles along this Balkan river flowing southeast to **Salonika** (Thessaloniki). Bulgaria's entry into the war in September 1915 led to an Allied offensive up the Vardar valley on 12 October. The defeat of **Serbia** on 3 December precipitated a complete Allied retreat back to Salonika on 12 December. A second Allied offensive in August 1916 gained little ground and the front stabilized. The final battle began on 14 September 1918 with a combined Allied assault along the whole front. Bulgarian defences collapsed in the face of the Allied advance, Skopje was captured and Bulgaria surrendered on 30 September.

Vatican

Tiny independent state ruled by the Pope. Located within the city of Rome, its independence was guaranteed by the **Lateran** Treaty of February 1929 between Pope Pius XI's Secretary of State, Cardinal Gaspari, and Mussolini's Fascist administration. The Vatican is all that now remains of the once-extensive territories in Italy ruled by the Papacy (the Papal States). The Vatican gave its name to the two great ecumenical councils of the modern Roman Catholic Church:

Vatican I. First Ecumenical Council for 300 years, summoned by Pope Pius IX in 1869 which produced the doctrine of Papal infallibility.

Vatican II. Second Ecumenical Council summoned by Pope John XXIII in January 1959 to consider increased collaboration with other churches and renewal of the faith. The council lasted a year and published 16 decrees pointing towards a closer relationship with non-Catholic churches, the use of the vernacular rather than Latin in the liturgy and a greater humanism in Catholic doctrine. Many people expected that the tone of the council presaged a relaxation of the church's position on birth control, but the 1968 Encyclical, *Humanae Vitae*, condemned its use.

Venda
See **Bophuthatswana**.

Venlo (The Netherlands)
Town on the border with Germany, scene of the Venlo Incident of 1939. Two British intelligence officers, lured across the border into Germany on the pretext of linking up with anti-Nazis, were kidnapped in November 1939 by German SS men in disguise. Under torture they were forced to reveal important intelligence secrets.

Vercors (France)
Mountainous inaccessible region, southwest of Grenoble, which became famous in the Second World War for the attempted Vercors Rising. After the D-Day landings in June 1944 French Resistance forces, numbering some 3,500, grouped here. The Germans discovered the plan and despatched troops to clear the area. The French partisans suffered heavy losses.

Verdun (France)
Scene of one of the most terrible battles of the First World War, fought from 21 February to 16 December 1916 on the **Western Front**. In a huge offensive, German forces suffered 450,000 casualties in an attempt to break through on a 15-mile front to capture French fortifications and shatter their morale. The German plan, devised by General von Falkenhayn, was to throw the whole weight of the German offensive against the heavily fortified French fortress of Verdun. Fort Douaumont and Fort de Vaux fell. Marshal Pétain was charged with the defence along with Generals Nivelle and Mangin, feeding fresh divisions into the salient, eventually rotating three-quarters of their infantry battalions in the battle. Successive German offensives in March and April cost the attackers huge casualties, but pressure was eased on the French by the Brusilov offensive in the east and the opening of the Somme offensive in the west. The German offensive closed on 11 July and on 29 August Falkenhayn was replaced by General Hindenburg and General Ludendorff who went onto the defensive to meet attacks from Nivelle in the autumn. Losses in dead and wounded reached almost a million on both sides, the French suffering the heavier casualties.

By holding their position and recapturing ground lost, the French scored a tactical victory which was the epic French triumph-in-arms of the war, making the reputation of Pétain and Nivelle. The losses, however, deeply affected the French army, revealed in the mutinies of the following year. It was the longest and bloodiest battle of the First World War.

Vereeniging (South Africa)

City near Johannesburg which gave its name to the treaty ending the Boer War. Paul Kruger met other Boer commanders at Vereeniging in May 1902 and they voted to accept the British terms for surrender. The treaty itself was signed by the Boer leaders in Pretoria on 31 May 1902. The Orange Free State and South African Republic were placed under British colonial rule, with the promise of future self-government, a general amnesty was declared and £3 million provided for reconstruction. The question of native voting rights was postponed until after self-government had been achieved.

Verriers Ridge (France)

Scene of a disastrous battle involving Canadian troops during the 1944 **Normandy** campaign. On 25 July the Montreal Highland Regiment, the Black Watch, attacked a strongly defended German position near **Caen** and of the 325 who went into action, only 15 returned. Their commanders experimented with "artificial moonlight" by bouncing floodlights off the clouds, but succeeded only in making their men easy targets by silhouetting them.

Versailles (France)

Location of treaty signed on 28 June 1919 by Germany and the victorious powers of the First World War. It was the fruit of the **Paris** peace conference of 1919–20 and established the League of Nations. The treaty, forced on Germany by the "Big Four", was signed only under protest. It was criticized for its harshness in Germany and the USA (where Congress refused to ratify it) and criticized for its supposed leniency in France and Britain. Its terms included:

a) the surrender of German colonies to the League of Nations as Mandates;

b) the surrender of German-held territory to Belgium, Lithuania and Poland;

c) the surrender of **Alsace-Lorraine** to France and of **Danzig** to the League as a Free city;

d) French control of the **Saar**; occupation by the Allies of the **Rhineland** for 15 years;

e) payment of reparations;

f) prohibition of Austro-German union;

g) limitation of the Germany army to 100,000 men;

h) suspension of conscription;

i) limitation of the Germany navy to vessels under 10,000 tons.

The army was to have no tanks, heavy artillery or poison gas and there was to be no German airforce or submarines. Germany had to accept a clause admitting her guilt for the war and another providing for the trial of the Kaiser and other military leaders. In practice, there were no trials of war leaders and ways were found of circumventing the clauses that restricted German military forces. The Nazis, who derived great propaganda from the treaty and the "November Criminals", refused to continue paying reparations when they came to power in 1933.

Vichy (France)

Provincial spa town where the interim autocratic French government was established between July 1940 and July 1944. The Vichy regime was anti-republican, and collaborated extensively with the Germans who occupied the areas it controlled in November 1942. After the liberation of France in 1944, Marshal Pétain and the Vichy ministers established a headquarters in Germany.

Victoria Falls

On the border of Zambia and Zimbabwe, location of talks in August 1975 aimed at resolving the Rhodesian problem. See **Rhodesia**.

Vienna (Austria)

Former capital city of the Austro-Hungarian Empire. Capital of the Austrian republic. Known as "Red Vienna" from 1920–34. In 1934 there was street fighting between socialists and government troops. Chancellor Dollfuss was murdered here by the Nazis. In 1938 Hitler entered Vienna and proclaimed *Anschluss* (union with the German *Reich*).

Vietnam

Independent republic in Southeast Asia, originally a French territory. It was occupied by the Japanese during the Second World War.
1) In the northern part of the country, Ho Chi Minh formed the Viet Minh, a guerrilla army seeking independence. See the Indo-China War (1946–54) in Appendix 2.
2) Following the division of Vietnam at the **Geneva** Conference in 1954, Ngo Dinh Diem became president of South Vietnam and secured US support. His government became increasingly authoritarian and repressive, and unrest grew. See the Vietnam War (1959–75) in Appendix 2.

Vilna (Lithuania)

Much-disputed ancient capital of **Lithuania** (also known as Vilnius or Wilno). Control of this city was a bitter cause of dispute between Poland and Lithuania in the period between the two World Wars. A part of Tsarist Russia prior to 1917, it became the focus for the new Lithuanian state after the Bolshevik Revolution. It was seized by Polish forces in October 1920 and incorporated into Poland in 1922. Following the German and Soviet invasion of Poland in September 1939, Vilna was returned to Lithuania. It became part of the Soviet Union when the Baltic States were absorbed after 1945.

Vilnius
See **Vilna**.

Vimy Ridge (France)
One of the most famous engagements involving Canadian troops in the First World War. Vimy Ridge was captured by Canadian forces in April 1917 during the battle of **Arras**. The cost, in terms of casualties, was enormous, with 11,285 Canadian fatalities.

Vis (Croatia)
Island in the Adriatic opposite Split. In the Second World War, when German forces forced Tito to flee from **Yugoslavia**, this was the main base and headquarters of the partisans after autumn 1943 prior to the liberation of Belgrade in October 1944.

Visegrad (Hungary)
Town in which the organization known as the Visegrad Triangle was formed in February 1991. The original members were Czechoslovakia, Hungary and Poland. When Czechoslovakia split into the Czech Republic and Slovakia, the grouping became known as the Visegrad Four. The Visegrad Four was formed to persuade the West of the merits of large-scale investment and put their case for early membership of the EU and other Western European groupings.

Vittorio Veneto (Italy)
First World War battle (24 October–3 November 1918) near this town in the northeast. It was the final confrontation between the Allies and the Austro-Hungarian Empire. A comprehensive victory for the Allies, it caused an Austrian collapse across the whole Italian front. Also known as the third battle of **Piave River**.

Voeren
Flemish name for **Fourons**.

Volgograd

See **Stalingrad**.

Vorkuta (Russia)

One of the huge labour camps in the Pechora basin in the Stalinist years of terror. Along with **Kolyma**, these two camps symbolized the political repression and nightmare of the Gulag Era. It was closed by Nikita Khrushchev.

Vukovar (Croatia)

Town in **Eastern Slavonia** on the river Danube, made infamous in the Serbo-Croat conflict of 1991 as a first example of "ethnic cleansing". The conflict over Vukovar left an estimated 15,000 dead and some half a million refugees as the town fell to Serb forces. Under the **Dayton (Ohio)** Accord, it is to return to Croatia.

Vyborg (Russia)

Port located 70 miles northwest of St Petersburg. It gave its name to the Vyborg Manifesto of 1906, when 180 deputies met to protest at the dissolution of the first parliament (*duma*) by Tsar Nicholas I in July 1906. Vyborg was in Finland from 1918 to 1945.

Waco (United States)

Location in Texas of compound of the Branch Davidian sect. It gained worldwide publicity after four US federal agents were killed on 28 February 1993, attempting to search the compound for illegal guns and to arrest the cult leader, David Koresh. A 51-day siege by hundreds of officers ended on 19 April when tear gas was pumped into the compound. Shortly afterwards flames engulfed the compound, leaving 72 cult members (including 17 children) dead. A government report later criticized the handling of the siege by the authorities.

Wahran (Algeria)

See **Oran**.

Wake Island

Central Pacific island about 2,300 miles west of Hawaii. Home to a US Air Force base, it was attacked by Japanese forces on 8 December 1941. 500 US Marines resisted for two weeks until finally surrendering on 23 December 1941. The island remained in Japanese hands until the end of the war.

Wall Street (United States)

Street in lower Manhattan, New York City, and heart of the US financial district. Named after a defensive wall erected by Dutch settlers, it has become synonymous with the American financial sector. Both the New York Stock Exchange and the Federal Reserve Bank are housed here. The collapse of the American stock market on 24 October 1929, known as "the Wall Street Crash", precipitated a worldwide depression throughout the 1930s.

Wallonia (Belgium)

French-speaking southern region of Belgium where linguistic and cultural separation from the rest of Belgium has led to major disputes (see **Fourons**) and to a growing demand for devolution since 1970. Parliament approved devolved power for the regions of Wallonia, Flanders (the Flemish-speaking area) and Brussels in July 1993.

Wal Wal (Ethiopia)

Oasis in Ogaden region on the border with Italian Somaliland. Italy provoked an incident here on 5 December 1934. In a clash between Italian and Ethiopian troops, some 100 Ethiopians were killed and 30 Italian colonial troops. Italy demanded reparation for the incident, while the Ethiopian government requested an international investigation. It was an Italian ploy prior to their full-scale invasion of Ethiopia. Italy duly invaded Ethiopia without a declaration of war on 3 October 1935.

Walworth Road (England)

Thoroughfare in south London where the Labour Party has had its headquarters since 1980, when it moved from Smith Square. The headquarters was named John Smith House in memory of the party's leader from 1992 until his sudden death in 1994.

Wannsee (Germany)

Villa in the **Berlin** suburb of Grossen-Wannsee. On 20 January 1942 fifteen leading Nazi officials met at a secret conference to decide on the final solution to the Jewish question (*Endlösung der Judenfrage*). Attended by Richard Heydrich, Chief of Reich Security, and Adolf Eichmann, the conference discussed how to organize the deportation and destruction of Jews across Europe. Any forced displacement of Jews had to appear to be only "resettlement" to prevent panic and rebellion. All Jews were to be taken to labour camps in Eastern Europe, where harsh work and living conditions would kill off many through natural diminution. Any survivors would be executed. Although extermination and murder were never explicitly mentioned, the aim was clear. Of the two men most responsible for instrumenting the "final solution", Heydrich was assassinated in Prague later that year and Eichmann was executed for war crimes in May 1962 in Israel.

Wapping (England)

East London former docklands site of the editorial offices and printing works of Rupert Murdoch's News International, publishers of *The Times* and the *Sun*. News International's sudden move there from Fleet Street destroyed the power of the print unions and allowed the rapid introduction of new technology into newspaper production. Wapping was the scene of heavy picketing and of a particularly violent mass demonstration in January 1987 which resulted in complaints about indiscriminate police violence.

Warrenpoint (Northern Ireland)

County Down holiday resort where 18 British soldiers were killed by the Provisional IRA in a double bombing on 27 August 1979.

Warrington (England)

Cheshire town where the Provisional IRA exploded two bombs on 29 March 1993, killing two boys aged three and twelve, and arousing widespread anger.

Warsaw (Poland)

Capital city. On 28 September 1914 German troops advanced on Warsaw, at that time under Russian rule. The Germans were blocked along the River Vistula and forced to retreat. Two further assaults in December 1914 and January 1915 were also defeated. Warsaw was finally captured on 5 August 1915. Germany invaded Poland again in September 1939, with Warsaw falling on 27 September. In 1940 the Germans created the Warsaw Ghetto, a crowded segregated area for the city's 433,000 Jews, most of whom were then deported to extermination camps. On 19 April 1943 the SS, attempting to clear out the remaining Jews, were attacked by Jewish partisans. Fighting ended on 16 May with the demolition of the synagogue. As the Soviets approached Warsaw in 1944, the Polish Home Army rose up against the Germans on 1 August. The Red Army halted its advance, leaving the Poles to fight on alone. All appeals for help were ignored and reinforcements disarmed. The Poles could not resist unaided and surrendered 2 October 1944. Warsaw was liberated on 17 January 1945. In response to West Germany joining NATO, the USSR established the Warsaw Pact in 1955. The Eastern European Mutual Assistance Treaty, signed in Warsaw on 14 May 1955, created a military alliance that lasted until the collapse of Communism. It was formally dissolved in July 1991.

Washington DC (United States)

Capital and site of an international conference of Pacific powers in 1921–2. A Four Power Pact, signed on 13 December 1921 by the USA, Japan, Britain and France, provided for the signatories to consult each other on Pacific issues. The Five Power Naval Limitation Treaty, signed on 6 February 1922 by the above four countries plus Italy, aimed to control any military build-up in the Pacific. Restrictions were placed on each country's capital ships, in a ratio of 10:10:6:3:3 for USA:Britain: Japan:France:Italy respectively. A Nine Power Pact, signed by the above plus The Netherlands, Portugal, Belgium and China, confirmed Chinese sovereignty and trading rights.

Watergate (United States)

Complex which houses the Democratic Party national headquarters in Washington DC, which was broken into on 17 June 1972. Five men were arrested and two of their accomplices were tried and convicted. James McCord, one of the convicted burglars, charged that there had been a cover-up of the burglary. In the wake of the McCord accusation, and the investigative reporting of Carl Bernstein and Bob Woodward of the *Washington Post*, a special Senate committee chaired by Senator Sam Ervin held nationally televised hearings into the Watergate affair in the spring and summer of 1973. Former White House Counsel John Dean charged that the Watergate break-in was approved by Former Attorney General John Mitchell and that White House aides Bob Haldeman and John Ehrlichman were involved in the cover-up. In May 1973, then Attorney General Elliot Richardson appointed Archibald Cox as a special prosecutor to investigate the entire Watergate Affair. Cox began to uncover evidence of improper conduct in the Nixon re-election committee, and illegal wire-tapping by the Administration. In July 1973, it became known that presidential conversations in the White

House had been taped since 1971. In October 1973, when Cox tried to obtain these tapes from the President, Nixon fired him. This touched off calls for Nixon's impeachment from the press and from some in government. The House Judiciary Committee began an impeachment inquiry, which ended in the adoption of three articles of impeachment against Nixon in July 1974. On 5 August 1974, Nixon released the transcripts of three of the recorded conversations that Special Prosecutor Leon Jaworski (whom Nixon had appointed to replace Cox) had sought from him. Nixon admitted that he had known about the Watergate cover-up shortly after the burglary had occurred and that he had tried to stop the FBI's inquiry into the break-in. On 9 August 1974 Nixon resigned and Vice President Gerald Ford was sworn in as president. The next month, Ford pardoned Nixon for any crimes he might have committed as president; however, Mitchell, Haldeman, Ehrlichman and Dean were among those who were convicted for their part in the Watergate scandal.

Watts District (United States)

Week of riots in this predominantly black and Hispanic district of southwest Los Angeles began on 11 August 1965. Thirty-four died and over 1,000 were injured in protests against economic deprivation, social injustice and military conscription for the Vietnam War. The events allegedly created a white backlash against progress that blacks were attempting to make through the civil rights movement.

Wedding (Germany)

Suburb of **Berlin**. Predominantly Communist in the 1920s, it became synonymous with the struggle against the Nazis. With the appointment of Joseph Goebbels as *gauleiter* of Nazi party organization in Berlin, and his reorganization of the SA to take on the Communists in the streets, bloody brawls became a commonplace after 1927. Serious unrest occurred in May 1929 when Communist workers clashed with armed police. Some 33 civilians, many innocent bystanders, were killed. The backlash against the violence aided the Nazis.

Wei Hai-wei (China)

Yellow Sea port on the Shantung Peninsula in the northeast. In the final months of the Sino-Japanese War Japanese forces attacked the Chinese fleet anchored in Wei Hai-wei harbour. Over five days (4–9 February 1895) five Chinese ships were sunk by Japanese torpedo boats and land batteries. On 12 February the Chinese fleet surrendered and its commander, Admiral Ting, committed suicide. The Japanese capture of Wei Hai-wei forced China to accede to the surrender terms of the Treaty of **Shimonoseki**.

Weimar (Germany)

Town where the German National Constituent Assembly met in February 1919. It gave its name to the German Republic of 1918–33. The town was chosen to allay fears of the Allied powers and the other German states about Prussian domination in Berlin, and also to escape from the associations attached to the former capital city. The economic problems which beset the Weimar Republic and the concomitant unemployment facilitated the rise of Hitler, and in March 1933 he suspended the Weimar Constitution of July 1919 to make way for the Third Reich.

Wembley Stadium (England)

Football stadium in west London. On 13 July 1985, in response to the famine in Ethiopia, two rock concerts were organized to raise money. The British one was held in Wembley Stadium, with the US counterpart at the JFK Stadium in Philadelphia. "Live Aid" was watched by an estimated global audience of 1.5 billion in 160 countries, and raised over £50 million in the UK alone.

Wenceslas Square (Czech Republic)

Main square in the Czech capital of **Prague**, the scene of mass peaceful protests by tens of thousands of demonstrators on 21 November 1989. The Communist government resigned in disgrace after this mass demonstration of popular feeling.

West Bank

Area on the west bank of the River Jordan which was annexed by **Jordan** in the wake of the 1948 Arab–Israeli War. In 1967 Israel occupied the territory and settled it, seeing it as a defensive barrier against Arab attacks. Israeli governments also regarded it as part of the biblical Jewish homeland and labelled the area Judea and Samaria. The Palestinians regard it as their homeland and have been fighting for its return. Under the Oslo Accord which emerged from the **Madrid** Peace Process, Israel would hand over power in the West Bank to an elected Palestinian National Authority. Disputes, however, continued over the

West Bank

extent of Israeli withdrawal, the removal of settlers and the future status of the West Bank. The worst fighting since 1967 took place in September 1996 over the opening of a tunnel in Jerusalem near the **Temple Mount**.

Western Desert (Egypt)

Area west of the Nile leading up to the Libyan border which was the scene of much of the fighting between Britain and the Axis during the Second World War.

Western Front

Battleground of the First World War between Germany and the Allies. Stretching from the Belgian coast through northeast France to the Swiss border, the front was dominated by trench warfare and high casualty figures.

Western Sahara

Former Spanish colony in northwest Africa. The territory was claimed by both Morocco and Mauritania, while there was also an independence movement, the Polisario, formed in 1973 and supported by Algeria. On 6 November 1975 King Hassan of Morocco sent 350,000 unarmed Moroccans in a Green March into the Western Sahara. They were recalled after three days, but agreement was reached in Madrid on 14 November 1975 for a Spanish withdrawal and joint administration of the territory after 28 February 1976 by Morocco and Mauritania. Their armed forces came into conflict with the Polisario, which proclaimed the Saharan Arab Democratic Republic. On 5 August 1979 Mauritania came to terms with Polisario, but Morocco moved to occupy the whole of the Western Sahara. Libya recognized the Polisario in April 1980. In 1984 Morocco built a 1,600-mile defensive wall from the Moroccan town of Zag to Dakhla on the Atlantic coast, protecting the economically important north of the territory and creating an effective stalemate. A ceasefire was agreed to in September 1991 after 16 years of civil war.

Whiddy Island (Ireland)

An 150,000 tonnes French oil tanker exploded at the Gulf oil terminal on this island in Bantry Bay, County Cork, on 8 January 1979, following a fire on board. Forty-three crew members and seven shore workers were killed. An inquiry blamed the oil companies involved for the disaster.

Wilhelmshaven (Germany)

Naval base, one of the locations, on 28 October 1918, of the mutiny of the German High Seas Fleet at the end of the First World War. See **Kiel**.

Wilhelmstrasse (Germany)

Thoroughfare in **Berlin** and the location of major government buildings such as the Reich Chancellery. It was the symbol of German foreign policy from 1871 to the end of the Third Reich in 1945.

Wilmington (United States)

During a campaign to prevent black citizens exercising their right to vote, a white mob attacked the black community in Wilmington, Carolina, in November 1898, killing over 30 people and burning down the offices of a black newspaper.

Wilno
See **Vilna**.

Windscale (England)
Site of nuclear power plant in Cumbria, the scene of Britain's worst nuclear disaster when the plutonium-producer caught fire on 7 October 1957. After this accident, with public relations in mind, its name was changed to Sellafield. However, doubts about environmental and health factors have persisted, despite continued development of nuclear power at the site (most controversially the THORP reactor).

Woensdrecht (The Netherlands)
Air base 70 miles southwest of Amsterdam, which was the scene of major anti-nuclear protests in 1986 while it was being converted into a site for the deployment of US Cruise missiles. Over four million people signed the *volkspetitonnment*, an anti-Cruise petition. The planned deployment was scrapped in 1988.

Woomera (Australia)
Town in South Australia. Location of the Long Range Weapons Establishment, it was a joint British–Australian rocket testing centre for many years after 1947.

Wounded Knee (United States)
Scene of the massacre in South Dakota of at least 200 Hunkpapa Sioux, mostly women and children, by a unit of the US 7th Cavalry shortly after Christmas 1890. The events at Wounded Knee Creek now symbolize the end of the Plains Indians' resistance to US expansion.

Xapuri (Brazil)

Site in the rain-forest of the Amazon, location of the campaign by the indigenous leader Chico Mendes against the exploitation and brutal repression of the local peoples. His vicious murder made the name briefly world-famous.

Xizang Zizhiqu

See **Tibet**.

Xuan Loc (Vietnam)

Location 37 miles east of **Saigon** of one of the final defeats of the South Vietnamese forces in the Vietnam War. The South Vietnamese failure in 1974 opened the way for North Vietnamese troops to encircle Saigon completely.

Yalta (Crimea)

The most crucial "Big Three" meeting of the Second World War was held at Yalta, 4–11 February 1945. Agreements reached between Winston Churchill, President Franklin Roosevelt and Marshal Stalin virtually determined the reconstruction of the post-war world. France was admitted as an equal partner of the Allied Control Commission for Germany but the practical details of Allied control were not worked out in Protocols III, IV, V and VI. The future of Poland, one of the most contentious issues of the conference, was referred to in the ambiguously-worded Declaration on Poland in Protocol VII, where no agreement was made as to the reconstruction of the Polish government. Being anxious to secure a firm Russian undertaking to join in the war against Japan, Roosevelt acceded to Salin's condition that Russia should resume her old rights in China, lost as a result of the Russo-Japanese War of 1904–5, and a secret tripartite agreement was signed to this effect on 11 February 1945. Agreement was reached on the creation of a World Organization of the UN and the voting formula for the Security Council. It was agreed to call a conference in **San Francisco** in April 1945, to draw up a charter for the UN.

Yalu River

Waterway forming the border between China and Korea. With the Russians block-aded in **Port Arthur**, the Japanese launched a land offensive from Korea. On 1 May 1904 Japanese troops reached the Yalu River and, meeting little Russian resistance, crossed at Gishu (Wiju). The main Russian force was encountered the next day at Kiu Lien Cheng and completely defeated. This dramatic Japanese victory was the first occasion in modern times that a European army had been defeated in battle by an Asiatic force using Western technology and strategies.

Yan'an (China)

Formerly Yen-an, the headquarters, in Shanxi province, of the Chinese Communist Party since the Long March of 1934–5. It was here that their basic revolutionary policies and style were developed (the Yan'an Spirit). It remained the Communist headquarters throughout the entire Japanese war until falling to the Nationalists in 1947. It was recaptured by the Communists under Peng Dehuai in 1948.

Yangon (Myanmar)
See **Rangoon** (**Burma**).

Yangtze River (China)

One of the great rivers of China, the site of the Yangtze Incident of 20 April to 31 July 1949. The British frigate *Amethyst* was shelled on the Yangtze River, a hitherto international waterway claimed exclusively by Chinese Communists. Seventeen crew members were killed. A failed rescue attempt led to further casualties. *Amethyst* remained moored on the river until successfully breaking out on 30–31 July. The incident deeply soured relations between Britain and China.

Yarralumla (Australia)
Official residence of the Governor General of Australia, in Canberra. It achieved notoriety as the location of the sacking of Prime Minister Kerr in 1975.

Yasukuni Shrine (Japan)
Memorial to the Japanese war dead of the Second World War. Visits to the shrine by government leaders, right-wingers and nationalists have let to protests within Japan as well as in such Asian countries as China. It is widely seen outside Japan as a symbol of Japanese militarism.

Yawata (Japan)
Industrial city, the target on 15 June 1944 for the first air strike by US B-29 bombers.

Yekaterinburg (Russia)

Became Sverdlovsk in 1924. Located in the eastern foothills of the central Ural mountains, it was here that Nicholas II, the last Tsar of Russia and his family were executed in 1918 by the Bolsheviks. Reverted to its former name after the fall of communism.

Yellowstone (United States)
In the environmental movement Yellowstone occupies a unique place as the first National Park to be created anywhere in the world. Established in 1872, the Yellowstone is partly in Idaho, partly in Montana, but mostly in Wyoming.

Yen-an (China)
See **Yan'an**.

Yogyakarta (Indonesia)
Former sultanate in Central Java. Centre of revolt against Dutch rule from 1825 to 1830 and a leading centre of the nationalist fight for independence 1945 to 1949.

Youyighuan Friendship Pass
Popular name for the crossing point on the Chinese–Vietnamese border. Now, a less than appropriate name given the recent hostilities between the two countries.

Ypres (Belgium)
Town, the scene of protracted fighting and four specific battles in the First World War. From 12 October to 11 November 1914 German forces failed to capture the town, being repelled again in an offensive opened by using poison gas from 22 April to 24 May 1915. From 31 July to 6 November 1917 the British mounted a bloody but fruitless attack, suffering 300,000 casualties. In September 1918 British troops advanced in the area as part of the final push against the retreating German armies. See also **Passchendaele**.

Yser (Belgium)
First World War battle along this river in the west. A combined French–Belgian force successfully defended the front line along the Yser between Nieuwpoort (Nieuport) on the coast and Diksmuide (Dixmude). Between 15 and 31 October 1914 repeated German assaults were rebuffed, until German artillery reinforcements threatened to overpower the Allies. The sluicegates at Nieuwpoort were opened, flooding the German positions, which were below sea level, and drowning hundreds. Although Diksmuide was later captured from the Allies, the front line stabilized for the rest of the war.

Yugoslavia
1) State created as a result of the break-up of the Austro-Hungarian Empire, uniting the Balkan Slavonic peoples in a South Slav State (Yugoslavia). Following the con-quest of **Serbia** by the Central Powers, an agreement known as the Corfu Pact was drawn up on 20 July 1917 between the Serbian government-in-exile on the island of Corfu, ied by Nikola Pasic, and the leader of the Yugoslav Committee, representing the Slavs in Austro-Hungary, Ante Trumbic. It proclaimed that all the South Slavs would unite to form a single Yugoslav kingdom under the royal house of Serbia. The state known initially as The Kingdom of Serbs, Croats and Slovenes was proclaimed

on 1 December 1918. The Kingdom formally adopted the name Yugoslavia on 3 October 1929.

2) During the Second World War two rival governments emerged, a royalist government-in-exile in London and Josip Tito's self-proclaimed Communist national Committee of Yugoslavia, established in November 1943 at the Jajce Congress. A joint post-war government was set up on 29 November 1945. According to the constitution passed on 31 January 1946 the Federal Republic was to be composed of six republics: Serbia, Croatia, Slovenia, **Bosnia-Hercegovina**, **Macedonia** and **Montenegro**. In April 1963 the country's formal name was altered to the Socialist Federal Republic of Yugoslavia.

3) Serious internal tensions broke out in Yugoslavia following the death of Tito in 1980. The result has been the various conflicts involving Croatia, Bosnia-Hercegovina and Serbia. See also **Dayton (Ohio)**.

Zabern (France)

Town in **Alsace-Lorraine,** now known as Saverne, scene of the 1913 Zabern Incident. A protest demonstration resulted in the detention of 28 local people by the German commander of a regiment stationed nearby. The army commander had acted unconstitutionally (as there had been no breakdown of law and order). However, the commander was acquitted at the ensuing court-martial, thus providing further evidence of the growing power of the military in Germany prior to 1914.

Zaïre

Country which faced political crisis following Belgium's sudden announcement of independence in 1960. Fighting began during elections in May and erupted once more on independence on 30 June. Troops in the para-military *Force Publique* mutinied against their Belgian officers and attacked Europeans, forcing many from the country. The mineral-rich province of **Katanga** seceded from the Congo Republic under Moise Tshombe, with Belgian and white mercenary backing. The Congo Republic appealed for UN support and a UN peace-keeping force was deployed. Colonel Mobutu seized power in a military coup, ousting the radical premier Patrice Lumumba, who was murdered in 1961. Instability continued and a series of independent governments were formed in Katanga, Stanleyville and Kasia. In November 1965 Mobutu led a second army coup and proclaimed himself president. See also **Belgian Congo.**

Zanzibar (Tanzania)

Island in the Indian Ocean, now part of Tanzania. Formerly it was a sultanate and a British protectorate after 1890 administered by a British Agent. Prior to British rule it was the centre of the Arab slave trade on the east coast of Africa. Zanzibar became independent in December 1963. In January 1964 the sultanate was abolished by a revolution and the People's Republic of Zanzibar established. Zanzibar joined with **Tanganyika** to form a united republic which was named Tanzania; it retained its own executive and legislature. The First Vice-President of the united republic is the head of the executive in Zanzibar under the title of President of Zanzibar.

Zbruch River (Russia)

Prior to the First World War, the river which formed the frontier of Austria-Hungary and Russia. From 1921 to 1939 it marked the border between Poland and the Soviet Union.

Zeebrugge (Belgium)

Port on the North Sea.

1) On the night of 22–23 April 1918 British forces under Admiral Keyes launched a surprise attack on the German harbour facilities. Three blockships were sunk in the harbour channel and the viaduct to the breakwater destroyed. Zeebrugge was effectively useless to the Germans for the rest of the First World War.

2) Site of the *Herald of Free Enterprise* disaster of 6 March 1987. This British roll-on-roll-off ferry overturned after leaving the harbour with its bow doors open. The disaster (in which 193 died) opened up a major debate on maritime safety and led to a significant tightening of safety measures on passenger ferries.

Zefat (Israel)

See **Safad**.

Zimbabwe

See **Rhodesia**.

Zunyi (China)

See **Tsuni**.

Appendix 1:
The changing nations of the twentieth century

Abyssinia Name by which Ethiopia was formerly known.

Algeria Known as French Algeria until 1962.

Angola Known as Portuguese Angola until 1975.

Armenia Independent republic since September 1991. Formerly part of the Soviet Union. Briefly independent, 1919–20.

Austria Rump state, created in 1918 from German-speaking part of former Austro-Hungarian Empire.

Austro-Hungarian Empire The former Habsburg Empire which disintegrated at the end of the First World War.

Azerbaijan Independent republic since August 1991. Formerly part of the Soviet Union.

Bangladesh Prior to 1947 was part of British Indian Empire; 1947–71 known as East Pakistan.

Basutoland Known as Lesotho since 1966.

Belarus Independent republic since August 1991. Formerly known as Byelorussia and part of the Soviet Union.

Belgian Congo Known as Zaïre after 1971.

Belize Known as British Honduras until 1973, became independent in 1981.

Benin Until 1960 part of French West Africa, then Dahomey (until 1975).

Bhutan Formerly semi-autonomous kingdom linked to British Indian Empire.

Bosnia-Hercegovina Formerly part of Yugoslavia, Bosnia-Hercegovina declared independence in October 1991. Independence recognized by EU and USA April 1992.

Botswana Known as British Bechuanaland until 1966.

British Bechuanaland Known as Botswana since 1966.

British Guiana Now known as Guyana.

British Honduras Known as Belize after 1973.

Brunei Former British protectorate in British Borneo.

Burkina Faso Formerly French Upper Volta, then Upper Volta (until 1984).

Burundi Formerly part of German East Africa (to 1919), thereafter part of Belgian-controlled Ruanda-Urundi. Urundi became Burundi in 1962.

Cambodia Name by which Kampuchea was formerly known.

Cameroon Formerly French and British Cameroon. French Cameroon became independent in 1960, and in 1961 part of British Cameroon acceded to the independent, former French Cameroon to form a two-state Federal Republic, the United Republic of Cameroon in 1972 and the Republic of Cameroon in 1984.

Cape Verde Known as Portuguese Cape Verde until 1975.

Central African Republic Formerly part of French Equatorial Africa.

Ceylon Known as Sri Lanka since 1972.

Chad Formerly part of French Equatorial Africa.

Congo Formerly part of French Equatorial Africa.

Croatia Part of the Austro-Hungarian Empire (until 1918) and then part of Yugoslavia. Proclaimed independence from Yugoslavia in June 1991.

Cyrenaica Former Italian colony, now part of modern Libya.

Czechoslovakia Formerly part of Austro-Hungarian Empire (pre-1918).

Czech Republic Independent Republic since 1 January 1993. Formerly (with Slovakia) part of Czechoslovakia.

Dahomey Known as Benin since 1975.

Djibouti Known as French Somaliland until 1967, then French territory of Afars and Issas.

Dutch East Indies Also known as Netherlands East Indies, called Indonesia since independence in 1945.

Dutch Guiana Former name of Surinam.

Egypt British Protectorate until 1922.

Eire Previous name, 1937–49, of the Republic of Ireland.

Ellice Islands Previously part of the Gilbert and Ellice Islands, now Tuvalu.

Equatorial Guinea Formerly Spanish Territory of the Gulf of Guinea.

Eritrea Prior to 1941, an Italian colony, then until 1952 a British protectorate. From 1952 part of Ethiopia and an independent republic since 24 May 1993.

Estonia Formerly part of the Russian Empire. An independent state, 1918–40. Annexed by the Soviet Union (1940) it declared independence 1989 (recognized by the Soviet Union in September 1991).

Euzkadi The short-lived independent Basque Republic in Spain, proclaimed in 1936.

Finland Part of the Russian Empire until 1917 as an autonomous Grand Duchy.

Formosa Former name for Taiwan.

Gabon Formerly part of French Equatorial Africa.

Gambia Formerly British Gambia, now part of Confederation of Senegambia (with Senegal).

Georgia Formerly part of the Soviet Union. An independent Republic since May 1991.

German Democratic Republic (East Germany) formerly part of the united German state, divided as a result of the Second World War, but excluding part of former German state lost to the present state of Poland.

German Federal Republic Formerly part of the united German state divided as a result of the Second World War. West Germany from 1949 until reunification.

Ghana Formerly British Gold Coast, including British Togoland, formerly German Togoland (to 1922).

Gilbert Islands Previously part of the British colony of the Gilbert and Ellice Islands, now Kiribati.

Greenland Formerly a province of Denmark (to 1979).

Grenada Formerly part of British Windward Islands.

Guinea Formerly French Guinea.

Guinea-Bissau Formerly Portuguese Guinea.

Guyana Formerly British Guiana.

Hungary Part of the dual monarchy of Austria-Hungary and the Austro-Hungarian Empire until 1918.

India Formerly part of the British Indian Empire, then comprising present-day Pakistan and Bangladesh.

Indonesia Formerly Dutch East Indies.

Iran Known as Persia until 1935.

Iraq Formerly a province of the Ottoman Empire (Mesopotamia) made a British mandate in 1920. Independent since 1958.

Ireland, Republic of Formerly the Irish Free State, a dominion of Great Britain (1921–37), previously part of the United Kingdom. Also known as Eire (1937–49).

Israel Created in 1948 out of Palestine, a British Mandated Territory from 1920, previously part of the Ottoman Empire.

Ivory Coast Formerly French Ivory Coast.

Jamaica British colony until 1962.

Jordan Formerly Transjordan (to 1949), part of the united Palestine Mandate of Britain (1920–46), previously part of the Ottoman Empire.

Kampuchea Formerly Cambodia (to 1975), previously part of French Indo-China.

Kazakhstan Formerly part of the Soviet Union. An independent Central Asian Republic since December 1991 (the last of the former Soviet Republics to declare its independence).

Kenya Formerly British colony (to 1963), known as British East Africa to 1920.

Kiribati Formerly known as the Gilbert Islands, an independent Republic since 1979.

Kuwait Protected status under Britain until it became an independent state in 1961.

Kyrgysztan Formerly known as Kirghizia. Formerly part of the Soviet Union, it declared independence after the failed Moscow coup of August 1991.

Laos Formerly part of French Indo-China.

Latvia Formerly part of the Russian Empire. Independent from November 1918 until annexed by the Soviet Union in 1940. Independence was proclaimed on 4 May 1990.

Lebanon French Mandated Territory 1920–43, previously part of the Ottoman Empire.

Lesotho British Protectorate of Basutoland until 1966.

Libya Formerly Tripoli (Italian colony 1911–45).

Lithuania Formerly part of the Russian Empire. Independent from February 1918 until annexed by the Soviet Union in 1940. Independence was proclaimed on 11 March 1990.

Malawi Formerly part of the Federation of Rhodesia and Nyasaland (1953–64), previously British Protectorate of Nyasaland.

Malaysia Formerly the Federation of Malaya (to 1963), previously known as the Straits Settlements and the Federated Malay States.

Mali Formerly (with Senegal) the Federation of Mali (1959–60); previously part of French West Africa.

Mauritania French colony of Mauritania until 1960.

Mesopotamia Province of the Ottoman Empire, now called Iraq.

Moldova An independent republic since August 1991. Formerly part of the Soviet Union.

Mongolia Prior to 1924 known as Outer Mongolia.

Montenegro An independent Balkan State when freed from Ottoman rule. Became part of Yugoslavia after 1918.

Morocco Formerly French Morocco (to 1956) and Spanish Morocco which became part of independent Morocco in 1969.

Mozambique Known as Portuguese Mozambique until 1975.

Myanmar Formerly Burma (until 1989). Burma was part of British India before Independence in 1948.

Namibia Formerly South West Africa (to 1990), prior to 1920 German South-West Africa.

New Britain Former Germany colony (Bismarck Archipelago), subsequently mandated to Australia, now part of Papua New Guinea.

New Hebrides Now known as Vanuatu.

New Ireland Previously a German colony (Bismarck Archipelago) then an Australian-mandated territory, now part of Papua New Guinea.

Niger Formerly French West Africa.

Northern Rhodesia Known as Zambia after 1964.

North Korea Formerly part of Japanese-controlled Korea (1910–45); created separate state in 1948.

Nyasaland Now known as Malawi (since 1964).

Pakistan Prior to 1947 part of British Indian Empire.

Palestine British-mandated territory 1920–48, now mainly in Israel.

Papua New Guinea Australian mandated territory from 1920–45, thereafter Australian-governed to 1975. Prior to 1920 the area comprised German New Guinea and Australian-run Papua.

Persia Former name for Iran (to 1935).

Philippines US colony from 1898 until independence in 1946.

Poland An ancient kingdom, but prior to 1918 Poland's territory formed part of the German, Austro-Hungarian and Russian Empires. In 1945 its boundaries were substantially altered.

Ruanda-Urundi Previously part of German East Africa (to 1919) then mandated to Belgium. Split into the independent states of Rwanda and Burundi in 1962.

Rwanda Part of German East Africa to 1919, then mandated to Belgium as part of Ruanda-Urundi and following the Second World War part of UN trust territory of Ruanda-Urundi under Belgian administration. In 1962 Rwanda became the separate state of Rwanda. Urundi became Burundi.

Saudi Arabia Proclaimed the kingdom of Saudi Arabia in 1932, previously comprising kingdom of Hejaz and Arabia.

Senegal Formerly part of French West Africa. In 1959 joined with French Sudan, present day Mali, in the Federation of Mali, but from 1960 independent. In 1982 formed Confederation of Senegambia with Gambia.

Serbia An independent Balkan State after 1878 (when independence from the Ottoman Empire was gained). Part of Yugoslavia after 1918. Now (with Montenegro) part of the rump state of Yugoslavia.

Siam Former name for Thailand.

Sierra Leone British Sierra Leone until 1961.

Singapore British Crown Colony, then part of Malaysia (1963–5).

Slovakia Independent Republic since 1 January 1993, formerly part of Czechoslovakia. Briefly a Nazi puppet state in the Second World War.

Slovenia Formerly part of the Austro-Hungarian Empire. After 1918 part of Yugoslavia. Independence was declared on 25 June 1991.

Somalia Formerly British and Italian Somaliland, united as an independent state in 1960.

Southern Rhodesia Known as Zimbabwe after 1979.

South Korea Formerly part of Japanese-controlled Korea (1910–45); created separate state in 1948.

South West Africa Formerly German South-West Africa (to 1920) now known as Namibia since 1990.

Soviet Union Alternative name for the USSR until its collapse in 1991.

Sri Lanka British colony of Ceylon to independence in 1948; in 1972 changed name to Sri Lanka.

Sudan Known as Anglo-Egyptian Sudan until independence in 1956.

Surinam Known as Dutch Guiana prior to 1954 when it became an autonomous part of the Netherlands. Independent from 1975.

Syria Prior to 1918 part of Ottoman Empire, then placed under French League of Nations Mandate until independence in 1946.

Taiwan Ceded to Japan in 1895, the island of Formosa returned to China in 1945, but from 1949 became base for nationalist Chinese State under Chiang Kai-shek.

Tajikistan Formerly part of the Soviet Union, it declared its independence in 1991.

Tanganyika Previously part of German East Africa (to 1918), then under British control until independence in 1961. Joined with Zanzibar in 1964 to form Tanzania.

Tanzania Formerly German East Africa (to 1918), then League of Nations Mandated Territory of Tanganyika under British control. Following independence in 1961, it joined with Zanzibar (independent in 1963) in 1964 to form Tanzania.

Thailand Known as Siam until 1939.

Togo Known as German Togoland until 1918 when mandated under British and French control, then UN Trust territory. In 1957 British Togoland joined with the Gold Coast and became part of independent Ghana. French Togoland became independent in 1960.

Transjordan Former British mandate (1920–46), now known as Jordan.

Trinidad and Tobago   British colony until 1962.

Tripoli   Italian colony 1911–45, now part of modern Libya.

Tunisia   French Protectorate until independence in 1956.

Turkey   Formerly the central part of the Ottoman Empire which included much of the Middle East and Arabia. The Turkish Republic was founded in 1923, comprising most of the modern area of Turkey.

Turkmenistan   Formerly a Central Asian Republic within the Soviet Union. Independence was declared on 27 October 1991.

Tuvalu   Formerly known as the Ellice Islands (part of the British colony of the Gilbert and Ellice Islands). An independent State within the Commonwealth since 1 October 1978.

Uganda   British Protectorate until independence in 1962.

Ukraine   Formerly part of the Soviet Union. Independence declared after failed Moscow coup of August 1991.

Union of Soviet Socialist Republics (USSR)   Formerly the Russian Empire (to 1917). Dissolved in 1991 on collapse of Communism.

United Arab Emirates   Known as the Trucial States prior to 1971.

Upper Volta   Former name (1960–84) for Burkina Faso.

Uzbekistan   Formerly a Central Asian Republic within the Soviet Union. Independence was declared on 1 September 1991.

Vanuatu   Formerly the Anglo-French Condominium of the New Hebrides. An independent Republic since 30 July 1980.

Vatican   The sovereign city state, ruled by the Pope, and recognized by Italy in 1929.

Vietnam   Part of French Indo-China to 1954 when separated into North and South Vietnam, reunited as a single state in 1975.

Western Sahara   Formerly known as Spanish Morocco (to 1956) when divided between Mauritania and Morocco; in 1979 Mauritania relinquished its claim but it remains disputed between Morocco and an independence movement, the Polisario Front.

Yemen Arab Republic   Part of the Ottoman Empire until 1918, when it passed to local tribal control, becoming the Yemen Arab Republic in 1962.

Yemen, People's Democratic Republic   Formerly under British control, including part of Aden as the Protectorate of Aden; independent from 1967. United with Yemen Arab Republic in 1990.

Yugoslavia   Before 1918 the independent kingdom of Serbia and parts of the Austro-Hungarian Empire and Bulgaria. In 1918 Yugoslavia created as Kingdom of Serbs, Croats and Slovenes.

Zaïre   Known as the Belgian Congo until independence in 1959; name changed to Zaïre in 1971.

Zambia   Formerly known as Northern Rhodesia and a British Protectorate; in 1953 combined with Southern Rhodesia and Nyasaland in a Federation, dissolved in 1963, becoming independent Republic of Zambia in 1964.

Zanzibar   Former British Protectorate, became an independent state on 10 December 1963. On 26 April 1964, it united with Tanganyika to form the United Republic of Tanzania.

Zimbabwe   Formerly known as Southern Rhodesia; in 1953 combined with Northern Rhodesia and Nyasaland in a Federation; dissolved in 1963, becoming British colony of Rhodesia. It declared independence in 1965 as Rhodesia, but following the war and agreement of 1979 became known as Zimbabwe.

Appendix 2: Major wars

Boer War 1899–1902

The strained relations between the British Empire and the independent Boer republics of Transvaal and Orange Free State reached crisis point over the political rights of foreigners (*Uitlanders*) in Transvaal. In October 1899 a Boer ultimatum to Britain to withdraw border reinforcements was ignored, and the Boers launched offensives into Natal and Cape Colony. Ladysmith, Kimberley and Mafeking were all besieged, and three successive defeats at Stormberg, Magersfontein and Colenso during "Black Week" (10–15 December 1899) forced the British on to the defensive. British attempts to relieve Ladysmith ended in defeat at Spion Kop and Vaal Krantz. The arrival of Lord Roberts and Lord Kitchener galvanized the British to victory at Paardeberg in February 1900 and relief of all three besieged towns. The Boer capitals of Bloemfomtein and Pretoria were captured by June, ending all formal conflict. Boer resistance continued for 18 months with guerrilla attacks on British positions. Kitchener responded by burning Boer farms and incarcerating Boer women and children in concentration camps, where over 20,000 died. Boer leaders eventually capitulated at Vereeniging on 31 May 1902, ending the biggest and most expensive war for Britain between Waterloo and the First World War.

Related entries

Kimberley (October 1899–February 1900); **Ladysmith** (October 1899–February 1900); **Mafeking** (October 1899–May 1900); **Talana Hill** (October 1899); **Stormberg** (December 1899); **Magersfontein** (December 1899); **Colenso** (December 1899); **Spion Kop** (January 1900); **Vaal Krantz** (February 1900); **Paardeberg** (February 1900); **Bloemfontein** (February–May 1900); **Vereeniging** (May 1902).

Russo-Japanese War 1904–5

Increasing tension over Russian expansion in the Far East prompted a surprise Japanese attack on Port Arthur on 8 February 1904, leading to a nine-month siege. Despite the recent completion of the Trans-Siberian Railway, Russia was severely hindered by the huge distances involved. Bad leadership and domestic discontent did little to improve the situation. The Russian Far East Fleet was smashed in July 1904 and Port Arthur was captured in January 1905. Defeat on land at Mukden in March and annihilation at sea in the Battle of Tsushima in May crushed the Russians and prompted an internal revolution. With Japan close to bankruptcy and Russia in turmoil, both sides accepted President Roosevelt's mediation. A peace conference in New Hampshire led to the Treaty of Portsmouth on 5 September 1905. Japan won Port Arthur and southern Sakhalin, as well as recognition of her influence in Korea.

Related entries
Chong-jin (April 1904); **Yalu River** (May 1904); **Port Arthur** (China) (May 1904–January 1905); **Liaoyang** (August 1904); **Dogger Bank** (October 1904); **Shaho River** (October 1904); **Tsushima** (May 1905); **Portsmouth** (New Hampshire) (September 1905).

Italo-Turkish War 1911–12
On 29 September 1911 Italy declared war on the Ottoman Empire, seizing Cyrenaica and Tripoli (modern Libya) to which they had long advanced claims. By November they had defeated the Turks in North Africa and in May 1912 occupied the Dodecanese islands in the Aegean. Italian finances suffered severely in the war, but Turkey recognized their gains by the Treaty of Ouchy in October.

Related entries
Ouchy; **Dodecanese**.

Balkan Wars 1912–13
In 1912 Bulgaria, Greece, Montenegro and Serbia formed the Balkan League, and its anti-Turkish stance led to conflict with the Ottoman Empire over Macedonia. The First Balkan War started in October 1912 with the League attacking from three directions. The Turks never fully recovered from the simultaneous defeats at Kirk-Kilissa and Kumanovo and a further six months of fighting left the League victorious. Under the Treaty of London (May 1913) Turkey lost almost all of her European territory and Albanian independence was secured. But squabbling over the division of Macedonia quickly led to the Second Balkan War between Bulgaria and her former allies. Bulgaria attacked Serbia and Greece, but was quickly checked. Romania and Turkey both moved against Bulgaria in July, and by August 1913 the war was over. Bulgaria lost all of her gains from the first war and Turkey recaptured part of Thrace.

Related entries
Kirk-Kilissa (October 1912); **Kumanovo** (October 1912); **Lüleburgaz** (October 1912); **Catalca** (November 1912); **Shköder** (April 1913); **Bucharest** (August 1913). **Ottoman Empire**; **Serbia**; **Montenegro**; **Albania**; **Macedonia**; **Bucharest**; **London**.

First World War 1914–18
On 28 July 1914 **Austria-Hungary** declared war on **Serbia**, whom she blamed for the assassination of the Austrian heir to the throne a month earlier. Austria was supported

by her ally Germany, but they were faced by the "Entente" powers, Russia, France and Britain. In late 1914 the Germans failed to capture Paris despite the boldness of their invasion plan (the Schlieffen Plan), and the war settled into the deadlock of trench warfare on the **Western Front**. In the East the Germans defeated the Russian invasion of East Prussia at **Tannenberg** and the **Masurian Lakes**. In 1915 the Entente tried to break the deadlock on the Western Front by expeditions to the **Dardanelles** and **Salonika** in southeast Europe, and by inducing Italy to attack Austria, but to no avail. In 1916 both sides launched grand offensives on the Western Front, the Germans against **Verdun** and the Allies on the **Somme**, but despite enormous casualties the deadlock continued. At sea the British and Germans fought the drawn battle of **Jutland**. In 1917 both sides were given hope, the Germans by the Russian Revolution (which eventually removed Russia from the war) and the Allies by the United States' entry into the war. The next year proved decisive. The Germans launched a last great offensive (the Spring Offensive) in 1918 but this was halted and US support tipped the scales the Allied way. Germany agreed to an armistice in November. Her allies, Austria and Turkey, had already given up the fight, the Austrians defeated at **Vittorio Veneto** in Italy and the Turks defeated by the British in **Palestine** and **Mesopotamia**. Although the major engagements were fought in Europe, British and Arab forces fought major campaigns against the Turks in Arabia and Palestine and Mesopotamia. In Africa, the German colonies of **South West Africa** and **Tanganyika** were also the scene of fighting. In the Far East Japanese forces seized the German base of **Kiaochow**.

Chronology of events
1914

28	June	Francis Ferdinand assassinated in **Sarajevo**.
28	July	Austria-Hungary declares war on **Serbia**.
1	August	Germany declares war on Russia.
2	August	Germany invades Luxembourg; British fleet mobilized.
3	August	Germany declares war on France.
4	August	Germany invades Belgium; Britain and Belgium declare war on Germany.
5	August	Turkey closes **Dardanelles**.
5–12	August	Germans seize **Liège**.
6	August	Austria declares war on Russia.
7	August	British troops arrive in France.
10	August	Austrians invade Russian Poland.
10–20	August	Austrian advance on Serbia halted.
12	August	Britain and France declare war on Austria-Hungary.
14–24	August	French suffer defeats in Lorraine, the Ardennes and on the Sambre; British retreat from **Mons**.
17–20	August	Russians invade **East Prussia** and **Galicia**.
21–24	August	Battle of Charleroi.
22	August	Hindenburg becomes German Commander in East Prussia.

26–28	August	Germans cross the **Meuse**.
26–29	August	Russians defeated at **Tannenberg**.
5–9	September	Battle of the **Marne**.
5–11	September	Austrians defeated in the Battle of **Rava-Russkaya**.
8–16	September	Serbs halt second Austrian invasion at Battle of the **Drina**.
10–14	September	Russians forced to retreat from East Prussia following First Battle of the **Masurian Lakes**.
14	September	Falkenhayn replaces Moltke as German Commander-in-Chief.
14–18	September	Allied offensive fails at first Battle of the **Aisne**.
27	September	Russians invade Hungary.
28	September–	Austro-German offensive in east checked, leading to withdrawal
1	November	from Poland.
	September–	"Race for the Sea": series of outflanking manoeuvres towards
	October	the Channel fails.
9	October	Germans take **Antwerp**.
12	October–	First Battle of **Ypres**: Germans fail to reach Channel ports;
11	November	Allied counter-attack fails.
16	October	"Race for the Sea" concluded by Battle of the **Yser**.
1	November	Hindenburg becomes German Commander-in-Chief on **Eastern Front**.
2	November	Russians renew advance on East Prussia.
5	November–	Serbs repel third Austrian invasion.
15	December	
11–24	November	Russians retreat after Battle of **Lódź**.
14	November	Turkey proclaims Holy War.
2	December	Austrians take Belgrade.

1915

8–15	January	French attack halted by Germans at Battle of Soissons.
24	January	Battle of **Dogger Bank**.
7–21	February	Germans encircle Russian Tenth Army at Second Battle of the **Masurian Lakes**; Austrian attack in Carpathians collapses.
11	February	British air-raid on **Ostend** and **Zeebrugge**.
18	February	Germany commences submarine warfare against merchant vessels.
19	February–	British Navy fails to force the **Dardanelles** Straits.
18	March	
10–13	March	British advance checked at Battle of **Neuve-Chapelle**.
14–15	March	Battle of Saint-Eloi.
31	March	Zeppelin raids on southern English counties begin.
22	April–	Second Battle of **Ypres**: Germans employ poison-gas for the first
25	May	time.
25	April	Allied forces land on **Gallipoli** Peninsula.
2–4	May	Russian line between Gorlice and Tarnow broken by German–Austrian offensive, forcing Russians to retreat.

4 May	Italy leaves the Triple Alliance.
7 May	*Lusitania* sunk.
9 May– 18 June	Second Battle of Artois.
15–25 May	Battle of Festubert.
23 May	Italy enters war on Allied side and declares war on Germany and Austria.
1 June	German air raid on London.
20 June– 14 July	German offensive in the Argonne fails.
16–18 July	Russians defeated in Battle of Krasnotav.
4–5 August	Germans enter **Warsaw**.
6–21 August	Allied attacks in **Dardanelles** fail.
18 September	Germany limits submarine attacks in view of American hostility.
25 September– 6 November	Allied offensives at **Loos** and in Champagne.
28 September	British enter **Kut-al-Amara** after defeating Turks.
5 October	Allied forces land in **Salonika**.
7 October	Serbian army collapses in face of joint German–Austrian–Bulgarian offensive, and is evacuated to Corfu.
3 December	Joffre becomes French Commander-in-Chief.
7 December	Turkish forces lay siege to British at **Kut-al-Amara**.
19 December	Haig replaces French as British Commander-in-Chief.
20 December	Allied forces evacuated from **Anzac** "Cove" and **Suvla Bay** in Dardanelles (completed 9 January 1916).

1916

21 February– 18 December	Battle of **Verdun** results in 550,000 French and 450,000 German casualties.
15 March	Admiral von Tirpitz resigns.
29 April	British surrender at **Kut-al-Amara**.
15 May– 17 June	Austrians defeat Italians at **Asiago** but withdraw to strengthen Eastern Front.
24 May	Britain introduces conscription.
31 May– 1 June	Battle of **Jutland**.
4 June– 20 September	Massive Russian offensive in **Galicia**.
5 June	Arab revolt against Turkish rule begins.
6 June	HMS *Hampshire* sunk: Lord Kitchener drowns.
21 June	Turks begin offensive against Persia.
1 July– 18 November	Allied offensive at Battle of the **Somme**.
26 August	Italy declares war on Germany.

27 August	Romania enters war and commences invasion of Transylvania.
29 August	Hindenburg becomes German Chief of General Staff.
10 September–19 November	Allied forces launch offensive in **Salonika**.
15 September	British use tanks for first time during Battle of the **Somme**.
24 October–18 December	French launch successful counter-attacks at **Verdun**.
3 December	Nivelle succeeds Joffre as French Commander-in-Chief.
6 December	Bucharest captured; Russians and Romanians forced to retreat.
7 December	Lloyd George forms Coalition government in Britain.
12 December	Central Powers make peace offer.
13 December	British begin offensive in **Mesopotamia**.
30 December	Allies reject peace offer made by Central Powers.

1917

31 January	Germans announce resumption of unrestricted submarine warfare.
23 February–5 April	Expecting an Allied offensive, Germans withdraw to Hindenburg Line.
25 February	British recapture **Kut-al-Amara**.
11 March	British enter Baghdad.
12 March	Revolution in Russia leads to abdication of Tsar Nicholas II.
16–19 March	Germans take stand along **Siegfried Line**.
26–27 March	British fail to capture **Gaza**.
4 April	British launch offensive in Artois.
6 April	USA declares war on Germany.
9 April	French begin offensive in Champagne.
9 April–3 May	Canadians take **Vimy Ridge** during Battle of **Arras**.
16 April–9 May	French offensive fails at second Battle of the **Aisne**.
17–19 April	British attack fails in second Battle of **Gaza**.
7–8 June	British capture **Messines Ridge**.
15 June	Pétain becomes French Commander-in-Chief.
20 June	Outbreak of mutinies in French Army.
25 June	US troops land in France.
31 July–6 November	Third Battle of Ypres results in eventual capture of **Passchendaele**.
20 September	British resume offensive near **Ypres**.
24 October–12 November	Italians forced to retreat after Battle of **Caporetto**.
31 October–7 November	Turks forced to withdraw following third Battle of **Gaza**.
4 November	British forces reach Italian Front.
6 November	British take **Passchendaele**.

7 November	Bolshevik Revolution in Russia.
17 November	Clemenceau becomes French Prime Minister.
20 November– 3 December	First mass use of tanks at Battle of **Cambrai**.
2 December	Fighting ceases on Russian Front.
3 December	Austro-German campaign in Italy suspended.
7 December	USA declares war on Austria-Hungary.
9 December	Romania signs armistice; Allenby enters **Jerusalem**.

1918

8 January	President Wilson issues his Fourteen Points for ending the conflict.
18 February	Fighting resumes between Russia and Germany.
3 March	Bolsheviks accept German peace terms at **Brest-Litovsk**.
21 March– 4 April	Germans launch offensive on the **Somme**.
9–29 April	Germans launch offensive on the **Lys**.
14 April	Foch becomes supreme commander of Allied forces in France.
22–23 April	British raid on Zeebrugge.
7 May	Romania concludes Treaty of **Bucharest** with Central Powers.
27 May– 6 June	Germans launch offensive on the **Aisne**.
6 June– 1 July	Battle of Belleau Wood.
15–24 June	Italians repulse Austrian attack across the **Piave**.
13 July	Final Turkish offensive in Palestine.
15–17 July	Germans launch final (Champagne-Marne) offensive.
18 July– 6 August	Allied forces launch **Aisne-Marne** offensive.
21 July	US troops capture **Chateau-Thierry**.
3 September	German armies commence retreat to **Hindenburg Line**.
14 September	Allied armies begin offensive against Bulgarians.
19 September	Turkish army defeated in Battle of **Megiddo**.
25 September	Bulgaria requests armistice.
26 September	Foch launches final offensive, breaching Hindenburg Line on 27 September.
29 September	Bulgaria concludes armistice.
1 October	French forces take Saint-Quentin; British forces enter **Damascus**.
3 October	Prince Max of Baden becomes German Chancellor.
9–10 October	British take **Cambrai** and Le Cateau.
14 October	USA demands cessation of submarine warfare.
17 October	British reach Ostend.

20 October	Submarine warfare abandoned by Germany.
24 October–4 November	Italians defeat Austrians at **Vittorio Veneto**.
31 October	Armistice with Turkey comes into force.
3 November	Austria agrees to Allied peace terms; Mutiny in German High Seas fleet.
4 November	Armistice concluded on Italian Front; Germans withdraw to Antwerp–Meuse line.
9 November	Revolution in Berlin leads to proclamation of Republic.
10 November	William II flees to Holland; Emperor Charles of Austria abdicates.
11 November	Armistice concluded on Western Front.
21 November	German High Seas fleet surrenders to British.

Related entries

Western Front

Guise (August 1914); **Laon** (August 1914–October 1918); **Louvain** (August 1914); **Maubeuge** (August 1914); **Namur** (August 1914); **Soignies** (August 1914); **Nery** (September 1914); **Ourcq River** (September 1914); **Armentières** (October 1914); **Lille** (October 1914); **London** (April 1915); **Lens** (May 1917); **Flanders** (September–November 1918); **Saint-Mihiel** (September 1918); **Kiel** (October 1918); **Selle** (October 1918).

Kreimhild Line; **La Panne**; **Limoges**; **Menin Gate**; **Poperinghe**; **Versailles**; **Western Front**.

Eastern and other Fronts

Gnilla Lipa River (August 1914); **Heligoland Bight** (August 1914); **Sokal** (August 1914); **Stallupönen** (August 1914); **Ivangorod** (September 1914–August 1915); **Lemberg** (September 1914–July 1917); **Przemysl** (September 1914–March 1915); **Rudnik Ridges** (September 1914); **Radom** (October 1914); **Coronel** (November 1914); **Sharqat** (November 1914); **Hartlepool** (December 1914); **Sarakamis** (December 1914); **Bolimov** (January 1915); **Przasnysz** (February 1915); **Dunajetz** (April 1915); **Gaba Tepe** (April 1915); **Isonzo** (May 1915–October 1917); **Vardar River** (October–December 1915, September 1918); **Ctesiphon** (November 1915); **Katshanik** (November 1915); **Naroch Lake** (March 1916); **Baghche** (April 1916); **Gorizia** (August 1916–October 1917); **Rumani** (August 1916); **Monastir** (November 1916); **Tarnopol** (July 1917); **Maraçesti** (August 1917); **Ramadi** (September 1917); **Riga** (September 1917); **Beersheba** (October 1917); **Rufiji River** (November 1917); **Jericho** (February 1918); **Baku** (July–September 1918); **Mudros** (October 1918); **Wilhelmshave** (October 1918).

Cameroon; **Eastern Front**; **Mogilev**; **Murmansk**; **Otranto Barrage**; **Pilsen**; **Scapa Flow**; **Sedd-el-Behr**; **Austria-Hungary**; **Ottoman Empire**.

Afghan War 1919

In May 1919 Amir Amanullah declared a holy war (*jihad*) against Britain, crossed the border and occupied Bägh. While Jalalabad and Kabul were bombarded by the RAF, a British expedition drove the Afghans out of Bägh and forced the Khyber Pass into Afghanistan. An armistice was agreed on 31 May and the Treaty of Rawalpindi was signed on 8 August.

Related entries
Bägh; **Khyber Pass**; **Afghanistan**; **Rawalpindi**.

Greek–Turkish War 1920–23

By the Treaty of Sèvres, 1920, the Allies handed territory in Asia Minor to Greek control, but the Turks refused to accept this change, and General Mustapha Kemal resisted the Greek occupation. In 1922 he drove the Greeks from their last stronghold at Smyrna, secured control of the area around Constantinople and overthrew the Ottoman Sultan. In 1923 the Allies renegotiated the peace treaty with Turkey at Lausanne.

Related entries
Sakarua River; **Sèvres**; **Lausanne**.

Rif War 1921–6

Abd el-Krim led a revolt against Spanish colonial forces, defeating Spanish armies at Das Abara and Anual, in the latter killing 10,000 Spanish troops. In 1922 Abd el-Krim set up a "Rif Republic" and in 1924 defeated another Spanish army at Sidi Messaod. An invasion of French Morocco was halted and a Franco-Spanish army under the command of Marshal Pétain defeated the Rif forces under Abd el-Krim, ending the Rif Republic.

Related entries
Targuist; **Anual**; **Rif Mountains**.

Spanish Civil War 1936–9

In July 1936 Spanish generals, led by Franco, rose against the Republican government and plunged Spain into civil war. Despite international declarations against foreign involvement, Italy, Germany and Portugal aided the generals, and Russia and France helped the Republicans. In addition, International Brigades were formed by volunteers from many countries to fight for the Republicans, and helped to defeat the nationalists in the battle of Guadalajara, 1937. But by early 1939 the Nationalists held most of Spain. They finally captured Madrid on 28 March.

Related entries
Badajoz (August 1936); **Burgos** (October 1936); **Madrid** (November 1936–March 1939); **Corunna Road** (December 1936–January 1937); **Brihuega** (March 1937); **Guadalajara** (March 1937); **Bilbao** (March–June 1937); **Guernica** (April 1937);

Barcelona (May 1937); **Euzkadi** (June 1937); **Brunete** (July 1937); **Santander** (August 1937); **Saragossa** (August 1937); **Ebro River** (July–November 1938).
Valley of the Fallen.

Sino-Japanese War 1937–45

In July 1937 the Japanese seized upon the pretext of fighting between Chinese and Japanese troops at the Marco Polo Bridge in Beijing to launch an all-out invasion of China, which the Japanese dubbed the China Incident. The Japanese seized Shanghai after fierce fighting and took Nanjing and Guangzhou (Canton). The Chinese government was forced to abandon most of the Chinese coast and set up its capital in Chongqing (Chungking). Japanese forces were unable to conquer the whole of China, being resisted both by Nationalist Chinese troops under Chiang Kai-shek and increasingly by the Communist forces under Mao Tse-tung. Over half of all Japanese forces were still involved in China when war with the USA and Britain broke out in 1941. The USA gave assistance to the Chinese forces by airlifts from India. Communist forces waged a mainly guerrilla war in north China, while the Nationalists stood on the defensive in the southwest. Clashes between the Nationalist and Communist forces in the run-up to Japanese surrender in August 1945 prefigured the struggle for control of China which brought civil war and eventual Communist triumph.

Related entries
Marco Polo Bridge; **Shanghai**.

Russo-Finnish War 1939–40, 1941–4

War broke out on 30 November 1939 over Russian claims to Karelia, but Finnish resistance under Mannerheim led to several Russian defeats before Finland was forced to make peace and to cede territory in Karelia and the northern border area with Russia. In June 1941 the Finns joined the Germans in war against Russia, fighting mainly on the Karelian front north of Leningrad. Finland made peace with Russia in 1944, when the defeat of Germany seemed inevitable.

Related entries
Hangö; **Karelian Isthmus**; **Tartu**; **Mannerheim Line**.

Second World War

German forces invaded Poland on 1 September 1939, which led to declarations of war by Britain and France on 3 September. The Germans invaded the Low Countries on 10 May 1940, and France was compelled to sign an armistice on 22 June. The British army was evacuated from Dunkirk, while in the "Battle of Britain" the German *Luftwaffe* failed to defeat the RAF and establish air superiority which would have made an attempted invasion of Britain possible. Italy declared war on 10 June 1940, and Britain attacked Italian forces in North Africa. For over a year Britain and her Empire stood alone against the Axis powers. In 1941, however, the war was vastly extended, Japan joining the Axis and Russia, China and America joining Britain. The

Japanese rapidly overran many of the European colonies in Southeast Asia, but Hitler's invasion of Russia (June 1941) eventually proved a decisive mistake. In 1942 the Germans were defeated in North Africa and Russia, in 1943 the Allies invaded Italy, and in 1944 Britain and America opened the "Second Front" in France. The Allies linked up with the Russians on the Elbe on 28 April 1945 and the Germans accepted unconditional surrender terms on 7 May. In the Far East, major Japanese forces remained committed to the indecisive war in China, but American forces in the "island-hopping" campaign in the Pacific, and British forces via Burma, inflicted defeats on the Japanese forces. A huge bombing and submarine offensive had brought Japan near to defeat when atomic bombs were dropped on Hiroshima and Nagasaki in early August 1945. Japan surrendered on 14 August 1945.

Chronology of events in Europe and Africa 1939–45

1939

1	September	Germany invades Poland and annexes **Danzig**.
3	September	Britain and France declare war on Germany.
7	September	Germans overrun western Poland.
17	September	Soviet Union invades eastern Poland.
28	September	Fall of **Warsaw**.
30	September	Germany and Soviet Union settle partition of Poland; last of BEF arrives in France.
6	October	Peace moves by Hitler rejected by Britain and France; opening of **Auschwitz** concentration camp.
8	October	Western Poland incorporated into the Reich.
30	November	Soviet Union invades Finland.
13	December	Battle of the **River Plate**.

1940

12	March	Finland signs peace treaty with Soviet Union ceding territory on the **Karelian Isthmus** and in northeastern Finland.
9	April	Germany invades **Norway** and **Denmark**.
16	April	British forces land in Norway at **Namsos**.
2	May	Evacuation of British forces from Norway.
10	May	Resignation of Chamberlain as British Prime Minister, replaced by Winston Churchill.
14	May	Dutch army surrenders after bombing of **Rotterdam**.
28	May	Belgium capitulates.
29	May–3 June	Over 300,000 British and Allied troops evacuated from **Dunkirk**.
	June–September	Battle of **Britain**.
10	June	Italy declares war on Britain and France.
14	June	Germans enter Paris; French government moves to Bordeaux.

16	June	France declines offer of union with Britain; Marshal Pétain replaces Paul Reynaud as head of French administration.
17–23	June	Russians occupy **Baltic States**.
22	June	France concludes armistice with Germany.
24	June	France signs armistice with Italy.
27	June	Russia invades Romania.
3	July	Britain sinks French fleet at **Oran**.
23	August	Beginning of "Blitz" on Britain; "Battle of **London**".
12	October	Hitler cancels Operation Sealion for the invasion of Britain.
28	October	Italy invades Greece; Britain offers help.
11	November	Major elements of Italian fleet sunk at **Taranto**, Sicily.
9–15	December	Italian forces defeated at **Sidi Barrani** in North Africa.

1941

6	January	President Roosevelt sends Lend-Lease Bill to Congress.
6	February	German troops under Rommel sent to assist Italians in North Africa.
11	March	Lend-Lease Bill passes Congress.
6	April	German ultimatum to Greece and Yugoslavia; Britain diverts troops from North Africa to Greece.
7	April	Rommel launches offensive in North Africa.
11	April	Blitz on **Coventry**.
17	April	Yugoslavia signs capitulation after Italian and German attack.
22–28	April	British forces evacuated from Greece.
10	May	Rudolf Hess flies to Scotland and is imprisoned.
27	May	*Bismarck* sunk by Royal Navy.
20–31	May	Germans capture **Crete**.
22	June	Germans launch invasion of Russia (Operation Barbarossa); Finnish forces attack on **Karelian Isthmus**.
16	July	Germans take **Smolensk**.
11	August	Churchill and Roosevelt sign the Atlantic Charter.
8	September	Germans lay siege to **Leningrad**.
19	September	Germans take **Kiev**.
30	September–2 October	Germans begin drive on **Moscow**.
16	October	Russian government leaves **Moscow** but Stalin stays.
15	November	German offensive takes advance elements within 20 miles of Moscow.
20–28	November	German forces take **Rostov** but retreat.
5	December	Germans go onto defensive on Moscow front as Russians launch counter-offensive.
8	December	Britain and the USA declare war on Japan (see p. 304).
11	December	Germany and Italy declare war on USA.

1942

2	January	Britain, USA, Soviet Union and 23 other nations sign Washington Pact not to make separate peace treaties with their enemies.
20	January	**Wannsee** Conference decides "Final Solution".
28	March	RAF destroys much of **Lübeck**, first major demonstration of area bombing.
12–17	May	Russian offensive on **Kharkov** front defeated.
26	May	Signing of Anglo-Soviet treaty for closer co-operation.
29	May	Soviet Union and USA extend lend-lease agreement.
30	May	First British 1,000-bomber raid on **Cologne**.
6	June	Germans wipe out village of **Lidice**.
10	June	German offensive in the **Ukraine**.
21	June	Fall of Tobruk after Rommel's advance in North Africa; Eighth Army retreats to **el-Alamein**.
25	June	Dwight Eisenhower appointed Commander-in-Chief of US forces in Europe.
2	July	Fall of **Sevastopol**.
28	July	Germans take Rostov and northern Caucasus in drive to take **Baku** oilfields.
14	August	Raid on **Dieppe** by British and Canadians ends in failure.
5	September	Germans enter **Stalingrad**.
11–12	November	**Vichy** France occupied.
19–20	November	Russians began counter-attack at **Stalingrad**.
27	November	French navy scuttled in **Toulon**.
29	December	Final failure of effort by German forces to relieve **Stalingrad**.

1943

2	January	German withdrawal from Caucasus begins.
14–24	January	Churchill and Roosevelt at **Casablanca** Conference.
2	February	Last German forces surrender at **Stalingrad**.
8	February	Russian offensive takes **Kursk**.
14	February	Russians capture **Rostov**.
16	February	Russians take **Kharkov**.
15	March	Russians forced out of **Kharkov**.
20	April	Massacre of Jews in **Warsaw** ghetto.
26	April	Discovery of the **Katyn** massacre.
17	May	RAF bombs **Ruhr** dams, causing widespread destruction.
5	July	Germans launch an offensive on **Kursk** salient, (Operation Citadel).
10	July	Allied landings in **Sicily**.
12	July	Russian counter-offensive causes Germans to halt **Kursk** offensive.
26	July	Mussolini forced to resign; King Victor Emmanuel asks Marshal Badoglio to form a government; secret armistice signed with Allies.

23	August	Russians take **Kharkov**.
3	September	Allied landings in Italy; Italy surrenders unconditionally.
25	September	Russians take **Smolensk**.
13	October	Italy declares war on the Soviet Union.
6	November	Russians take **Kiev**.
28	November–	Churchill, Roosevelt and Stalin meet at **Tehran**.
1	December	

1944

22	January	Allied landing at **Anzio**.
27	January	Relief of **Leningrad**.
18	March	Fall of **Monte Cassino** to Allied forces.
2	April	Russians enter Romania.
2	June	Fall of Rome to USA.
6	June	"D-Day" landings in **Normandy**.
13	June	V1 "Flying Bomb" campaign opened on Britain.
1	July	Monetary and financial conference at **Bretton Woods**, New Hampshire.
9	July	Fall of **Caen** to Allied troops.
20	July	Failure of "July Plot" to assassinate Hitler.
26	July	Soviet Union recognizes the **Lublin** Committee of Polish Liberation in Moscow as the legitimate authority for Liberated Poland.
1	August	Rising of Home Army in **Warsaw**; American armies begin breakout from **Normandy**.
11	August	Allied landings in Southern France.
13–20	August	German forces destroyed in **Falaise** Pocket in France.
25	August	De Gaulle and Allied troops enter **Paris**.
30	August	Russians enter **Bucharest**.
4	September	Ceasefire between Soviet Union and Finland; Armistice signed on 19 September.
5	September	Brussels liberated by Allied troops.
8	September	V2 rockets begin landing in Britain.
17	September	Arnhem airborne landings.
3	October	Final suppression of **Warsaw** Rising by German forces.
14	October	British troops liberate Athens.
20	October	Belgrade liberated by Russians and Yugoslav partisans.
16	December	Germans begin **Ardennes** offensive, (Battle of the Bulge).

1945

3	January	Allied counter-attack begins in **Ardennes**.
17	January	Russians take **Warsaw**.
4–11	February	**Yalta** Conference.
13	February	Fall of Budapest to Russians; bombing of **Dresden**.
23	March	US armies cross Rhine at **Remagen**.

28	March	End of V2-rocket offensive against Britain.
20	April	Russians reach Berlin.
26	April	Russian and US forces link up at **Torgau.**
28	April	Mussolini killed by partisans.
30	April	Hitler commits suicide in Berlin; Dönitz is appointed successor.
1	May	German army in Italy surrenders.
2	May	Berlin surrenders to Russians.
7	May	General Jodl makes unconditional surrender of all German forces to Eisenhower.
8	May	Victory in Europe (VE Day).
9	May	Russians take Prague.
5	June	Allied Control Commission assumes control in Germany, which is divided into four occupation zones.
17	July–	**Potsdam** Conference.
1	August	

Related entries

Gleiwicz (August 1939); **Polish Corridor** (September 1939); **Mannerheim Line** (November 1939); **Suomussalmi** (December 1939–January 1940); **Narvik** (April 1940); **Eben Emael** (May 1940); **Channel Islands** (June 1940–May 1945); **Compiègne** (June 1940); **Saint Valery-en-Caux** (June 1940); **Dakar** (July 1940); **Maginot Line** (July 1940); **Montoire-sur-le-Loire** (October 1940); **Cape Spartivento** (November 1940); **Bardia** (January 1941–November 1942); **Amsterdam** (February 1941); **Beda Fomm** (February 1941); **Benghazi** (February 1941–November 1942); **Keren** (February–March 1941); **Cape Matapan** (March 1941); **Aliakmon Line** (April 1941); **Amba Alagi** (May 1941); **Heraklion** (May 1941); **Bialystok** (June 1941); **Halfaya Pass** (June 1941); **Kosice** (June 1941); **Salum** (June 1941); **Babi Yar** (September 1941); **Kuibyshev** (October 1941); **Mozhaisk** (October 1941); **Gondar** (November 1941); **Sidi Rezegh** (November 1941); **Demyansk** (January 1942); **Brunéval** (February 1942); **Saint-Nazaire** (March 1942); **Gazala** (May–June 1942); **Madagascar** (May 1942); **Malta** (May–August 1942); **Mersa Matruh** (June 1942); **Alam al-Halfa** (August 1942); **Ordzhonikidze** (August 1942); **Barents Sea** (December 1942); **Kasserine Pass** (February 1943); **Rjukan** (February 1943); **Mareth Line** (March 1943); **Möhne** (May 1943); **Hamburg** (July 1943); **Schweinfurt** (August 1943); **Salerno** (September 1943); **Cairo** (November 1943); **Nuremberg** (March 1944); **Adolf Hitler Line** (May 1944); **Antwerp** (May 1944); **Caesar Line** (May 1944); **Arromanches-les-Bains** (June 1944); **Cherbourg** (June 1944); **Gold Beach** (June 1944); **Juno Beach** (June 1944); **Omaha Beach** (June 1944); **Pegasus Bridge Café** (June 1944); **Sword Beach** (June 1944); **Utah Beach** (June 1944); **Vercors** (June 1944); **Verriers Ridge** (June 1944); **Rastenberg** (July 1944); **Saint Lô** (July 1944); **Alençon** (August 1944); **Banska Bystrica** (August–October 1944); **Gothic Line** (August 1944); **Martin** (August 1944); **Nijmegen** (September 1944); **Aachen** (October 1944); **Breskens** (October 1944); **Dukla Pass** (October 1944); **Colmar** (November

1944); **Bastogne** (December 1944); **Malmédy** (December 1944); **Reichswald** (February 1945); **Caserta** (April 1945); **Königsberg** (April 1945); **Po Valley** (April 1945); **Karlshorst** (May 1945).

Concentration Camps: **Auschwitz; Belsen; Belzec; Birkenau; Buchenwald; Chelmno; Dachau; Drancy; Fort Breedonk; Majdanek; Mauthausen; Natzweiler; Nordhausen; Ravensbrück; Sachsenhausen; Sobibor; Terezin; Treblinka.**

Miscellaneous: **Ardeatine Caves; Atlantic; Atlantic Wall; Colditz; Corsica; Hal Far; Kreisau; Lofoten; Malmstrom; Mamai Hill; Margival; Moosburg; Peenemunde; Placentia Bay; Pripet Marshes; Riom; Salo; Slapton Sands; Vis; Western Desert.**

Chronology of events in Asia and the Pacific 1941–5
1941
7	December	Japan bombs **Pearl Harbor** in Hawaii.
8	December	Japanese invasion of Thailand, Malaya and **Hong Kong**; Britain and USA declare war on Japan.
9	December	Japan invades the Gilbert Islands.
10	December	HMS *Prince of Wales* and HMS *Repulse* sunk off Malaya.
22	December	Japanese invasion of the **Philippines**.
25	December	**Hong Kong** surrenders.

1942
2	January	Japanese capture **Manila**.
11	January	**Dutch East Indies** invaded.
20	January	Japanese forces invade **Burma** from Thailand.
23	January	**Rabaul** and the **Solomon Islands** captured.
31	January	Last British troops withdrawn from Malaya.
15	February	Singapore surrenders; 130,000 troops captured.
27–28	February	Battle of **Java Sea**.
1	March	Batavia (Jakarta) falls to the Japanese.
8	March	Allied forces in Java surrender; **Rangoon**, Burma captured.
9	April	US forces on **Bataan** surrender.
29	April	Japanese capture **Lashio** cutting the Burma Road.
1	May	Fall of **Mandalay**.
4–8	May	Battle of **Coral Sea**.
6	May	Allied forces on **Corregidor** surrender.
20	May	Last British forces leave **Burma**.
2–5	June	Battle of **Midway**.
21–22	July	Japanese troops land on the northern coast of Papua **New Guinea**.
7	August	US marines land on **Guadalcanal**.
8	August	**Henderson Field** airbase captured by the Americans.
8–9	August	Battle of **Savo Island**.
11–12	October	Battle of **Cape Esperance**.
26	October	Battle of **Santa Cruz**.

1943

7	February	Remaining Japanese troops evacuated from **Guadalcanal**.
	April	Admiral Yamamoto killed when his aircraft is shot down.
29–30	June	US amphibious landings in New Guinea.
	August	Mountbatten becomes Supreme Allied Commander in **Burma**.
1	November	US marines invade Bougainville in the **Solomons**.
20	November	US forces land on **Tarawa** in the Gilbert Islands.
24	December	British advance into Northern Burma.
26	December	US landings in New Britain.

1944

1	February	US troops land on **Kwajalein** in the Marshall Islands.
7–8	March	Japanese offensive into India (the March on Delhi) begins.
4	April	**Kohima** besieged by the Japanese.
5	April	**Imphal** besieged.
3	June	Siege of **Kohima** lifted by the British.
15	June	US troops invade **Saipan** in the Mariana Islands.
19–20	June	Battle of **Philippine Sea**.
22	June	**Imphal** relieved by British troops.
9	July	US forces recapture **Saipan**.
21	July	US troops land on **Guam**.
4	August	Japanese retreat from **Myitkyina** in northern Burma.
15	September	US marines attack Peleliu island in the Palau group.
20	October	US forces land on **Leyte** in the **Philippine Islands**.
23–26	October	Battle of **Leyte** Gulf.

1945

9	January	US forces invade **Luzon** in the **Philippines**.
3	February	US forces recapture **Manila**.
19	February	US marines land on **Iwo Jima**.
21	February	British forces cross Irrawaddy River in Burma.
25	February	Large-scale incendiary raids on **Tokyo** begin.
7	March	US troops recapture Lashio, reopening the **Burma Road**.
9	March	Night raid on **Tokyo**.
19	March	Japanese evacuate Mandalay.
26	March	**Iwo Jima** surrenders.
1	April	US forces land on **Okinawa**.
3	May	British troops retake **Rangoon**.
22	June	**Okinawa** campaign completed.
12–15	July	Japan seeks Soviet mediation to end the war.
4	August	Last Japanese forces in **Burma** captured.
6	August	Atomic bomb dropped on **Hiroshima**.
8	August	Soviet Union declares war on Japan.
9	August	Atomic bomb dropped on **Nagasaki**.

9–12	August	Soviet troops invade **Manchuria** and Korea.
14	August	Japan surrenders (VJ Day).
2	September	Japanese surrender signed on board USS *Missouri*.

Related entries
Kota Bahru (December 1941); **Mauban** (December 1941); **Abucay** (January 1942); **Darwin** (February 1942); **Kokoda Trail** (August 1942); **Milne Bay** (August–September 1942); **Ledo Road** (December 1942–January 1945); **Aleutian Islands** (May 1943); **Cape St George** (November 1943); **Yawata** (June 1944).

    Changi; **Chungking**; **Yasukuni Shrine**.

Chinese Civil War 1946–9
Civil war between the Nationalist government under Chiang Kai-shek and the Communist forces resumed after the defeat of Japan in August 1945. Through the mediation of General Marshall, a truce was arranged on 14 January 1946. It broke down and US supplies to the Nationalists were halted on 29 July 1946. A Nationalist offensive in Shaanxi took the Communist capital, Yan'an, on 19 March 1947, but it was retaken in April 1948. As Communist forces advanced, Peking fell on 22 January 1949, Nanjing on 22 April 1949 and Shanghai on 27 May 1949. Mao Tse-tung proclaimed the People's Republic of China on 1 October 1949. The Nationalists withdrew to Taiwan on 7 December 1949.

Related entries
Szepingkai (March 1946); **Sungari River** (January–May 1947); **Kaifeng** (June 1948); **Huai-Hai** (November 1948); **Suchow** (December 1948–January 1949).

    Peking; **Shanghai**; **Taiwan**; **Yan'an**.

Indo-China War 1946–54
Following the surrender of Japan, Ho Chi Minh proclaimed the Democratic Republic of Vietnam at Hanoi on 2 September 1945. French and British forces regained control in Saigon, and after negotiations, French troops entered Hanoi on 16 March 1946. After French naval forces shelled the Vietnamese quarter of Hai Phong on 23 November 1946, an abortive Viet Minh uprising took place in Hanoi on 19 December 1946. Guerrilla warfare grew into full-scale conflict between the French and the Viet Minh forces under General Giap. On 20 November 1953 the French established a forward base at Dien Bien Phu to lure the Viet Minh into a set-piece battle, but the garrison of 15,000 men was overwhelmed on 7 May 1954. An agreement for a cease-fire and the division of the country at latitude 17°N was signed at the Geneva Conference on 27 July 1954.

Related entries
Hai Phong; **Dien Bien Phu**; **17th Parallel**; **Vietnam**; **Geneva**.

Arab–Israeli War 1948–9

Israel was invaded by the armies of its Arab neighbours on the day the British Mandate ended, 15 May 1948. After initial Arab gains, Israel counter-attacked successfully, enlarging its national territory. Only the British-trained Arab Legion of Jordan offered effective opposition. Separate armistices were agreed with Egypt (23 February 1949), Jordan (3 April 1949) and Syria (20 July 1949).

Related entries
Jericho; **Jordan**; **Latrun**; **West Bank**.

Korean War 1950–53

North Korean troops invaded the South on 25 June 1950. The UN decided to intervene following an emergency session of the Security Council, which was being boycotted by the Soviet Union. The first US troops landed at Pusan airport on 1 July 1950. General MacArthur mounted an amphibious landing at Inchon on 15 September 1950, and Seoul was recaptured on 26 September. The advance of the UN forces into North Korea on 1 October 1950 led to the entry of China into the war on 25 November 1950. Seoul fell to the Chinese on 4 January 1951, but was retaken by UN forces on 14 March 1951. General MacArthur was relieved of his command on 11 April 1951 after expressing his desire to expand the war into China. Truce talks began on 10 July 1951, and an armistice was finally signed at Panmunjon on 27 July 1953.

Related entries
Pusan (June–September 1950); **Inchon** (July 1950); **Imjin River** (April 1951); **Sinuiju** (April 1951).
Demilitarized Zone; **38th Parallel**; **Panmunjon**.

Vietnam War 1959–75

The Communists in South Vietnam (the Viet Cong) built up their strength and launched their first attack on the South Vietnamese armed forces on 8 July 1959 near Bien Hoa, killing two advisers. A state of emergency was proclaimed in the south on 19 October 1961. After attacks on the USS *Maddox* and *Turner Joy*, the US Congress passed the Gulf of Tonkin resolution on 7 August 1964, giving President Johnson wide military powers in South Vietnam. The sustained bombing of North Vietnam by US aircraft (Operation Rolling Thunder) began on 7 February 1965. The first US combat troops landed at Da Nang on 8 March 1965 and engaged the Viet Cong on 15 June. On 30 January 1968, Communist forces launched their Tet Offensive with heavy attacks on Saigon, Hue and 30 provincial capitals. On 31 March 1968 President Johnson announced the end of the bombing of the north, and on 13 May 1968 peace discussions began in Paris. On 25 January 1969 these discussions were transformed into a formal conference. US and South Vietnamese troops invaded Cambodia in 1970, and the South Vietnamese made an incursion into Laos in 1971. A new Communist offensive against the south began on 30 March 1972, and this led to a resumption of US bombing of the north on 6 April. The last US ground combat units were withdrawn on 11 August 1972. US bombing was halted on 15 January 1973, and a peace agreement was signed in Paris on 27 January. Two years later, a North Vietnamese offensive, which began on 6 January, overran the South, and Saigon was occupied on 30 April 1975.

Related entries

Hai Phong (November 1946); **Dien Bien Phu** (November 1953–May 1954); **Bien Hoa** (July 1959); **Gulf of Tonkin** (August 1964); **Da Nang** (March 1965); **Van Tuong** (August 1965); **Plei Me** (October 1965); **Chu Pong** (November 1965); **Ia Drang** (November 1965); **A Shau** (March 1966); **Khe Sanh** (January–April 1968); **My Lai** (March 1968); **An Loc** (April–July 1972); **Quang Tri** (April 1972); **Cam Ranh Bay** (April 1975); **Saigon** (April 1975).

Cambodia; **Geneva**; **Ho Chi Minh Trail**; **Laos**; **Paris**; **17th Parallel**; **Vietnam**; **Xuan Loc**.

Sino-Indian War 1962

After a series of incidents in the disputed border areas, Chinese forces attacked on 20 October 1962 and drove the Indian forces back on the northeast frontier and in the Ladakh region. India declared a state of emergency on 26 October 1962, and launched an unsuccessful counter-offensive on 14 November 1962. On 21 November, the Chinese announced that they would cease fire all along the border and withdraw 12½ miles behind the line of actual control that existed on 7 November 1959. No further fighting took place and the ceasefire held firm.

Related entries
McMahon Line; **Himalayas**.

The Six Day War 1967

Israel decided on a pre-emptive strike following Egypt's request for the withdrawal of the UN peace-keeping force from Sinai on 16 May, the closure of the Gulf of Aqaba to Israeli shipping on 22 May, and the signature of an Egyptian–Jordanian defence pact on 30 May. On 5 June 1967 Israel launched devastating air attacks on Egyptian air bases. Israeli forces then invaded Sinai and reached the Suez Canal on 7 June. By nightfall on 7 June Jordan had been defeated and Jerusalem and the West Bank were in Israeli hands. On 9 June Israeli troops attacked Syria and occupied the Golan Heights. A ceasefire was agreed on 10 June 1967.

Related entries
Gaza Strip; **Jericho**; **Jerusalem**; **Jordan**; **Radfan**; **Tel Aviv**; **Gulf of Aqaba**; **Suez Canal**; **Golan Heights**.

Yom Kippur War 1973

On 6 October 1973, the day of a Jewish religious holiday, Egyptian forces crossed the Suez Canal, overwhelming Israel's Bar-Lev defence line in a well-planned surprise attack. Syrian forces attacked the Golan Heights, but initial gains were surrendered by 12 October. In a daring counter-stroke on 15 October 1973, Israeli forces crossed to the west bank of the Suez Canal and encircled the Egyptian Third Army. A ceasefire became effective on 24 October 1973.

Related entries
Purple Line; Bar-Lev Line; Golan Heights.

Iran–Iraq War 1980–88
Hoping to exploit the instability of Iran after the fall of the Shah, Iraq abrogated the Algiers pact of 1975, by which it had been forced to accept joint control of the Shatt al-Arab waterway, and invaded Iran on 12 September 1980. Khorramshahr fell on 13 October, 1980, but the Iranian government did not collapse and its armed forces began to counter-attack successfully. Each side bombed the other's oil installations and attacked international shipping in the Gulf. Iran rejected Iraq's ceasefire overtures as the military stalemate deepened. On 9 January 1987 Iran launched a major offensive – codenamed Karbala-5 – with the aim of capturing Basra. The Iranians advanced some distance towards their objective, while suffering heavy casualties. In 1987 and 1988 Iraq made major advances and a ceasefire was organized in August 1988. The war is estimated to have cost almost a million casualties, with some of the heaviest land-fighting since the Second World War.

Related entries
Shatt al-Arab; Khorramshahr; Basra.

Falklands War 1982
On 2 April 1982 the Argentine dictatorship, under General Galtieri, launched a successful invasion of the islands, forcing its garrison of 18 Royal Marines to surrender. Argentine forces also seized the island of South Georgia. On 5 April a British Task Force set sail to recapture the islands and on 7 April an exclusion zone of 200 miles was declared around the island. On 25 April South Georgia was recaptured and on 1 May air attacks began on the Argentine garrison on the Falklands. The next day the Argentine cruiser *Belgrano* was sunk by a British submarine and on 4 May HMS *Sheffield* was hit by an Exocet missile. On 21 May British troops went ashore at San Carlos. Two British frigates, the *Ardent* and *Antelope*, were sunk and others damaged by air attack, but British troops took Darwin and Goose Green by the end of May and on 11–14 June an attack on Port Stanley led to the surrender of the Argentine forces.

Related entries
South Georgia; Goose Green; San Carlos; Falkland Islands.

Gulf War 1990
On 2 August Iraq invaded Kuwait. UN Resolution 660, condemning the invasion and calling for immediate and unconditional withdrawal, was passed the same day. The

USA ordered naval forces to the Gulf on 3 August and sent troops to Saudi Arabia on 7 August (Operation Desert Shield). UN Resolution 661, imposing economic sanctions on Iraq, was passed on 6 August. On 8 August Iraq announced the annexation of Kuwait. On 29 November UN Resolution 678 sanctioned the use of force if Iraq had not withdrawn by 15 January 1991. Britain joined the Allied armies (led by the USA), contributing land, sea and air forces. The Allied offensive against Iraq (Operation Desert Storm) began shortly before midnight on 16 January. The Allied ground offensive began on 24 February. Kuwait City was entered by the Allies on 26 February. With Kuwait liberated and the Iraqi army defeated, US President Bush ordered a ceasefire, which came into effect on 28 February. During the conflict, Allied forces lost 166 killed, 207 wounded and 106 missing or captured. Iraqi losses were estimated by some to be 200,000.

Related entries
Kuwait; Dhahran.